GOD'S AMBASSADORS

PULPIT & PEW

Jackson W. Carroll, series editor

Pulpit & Pew is a major research project whose purpose is to describe as comprehensively as possible the state of Protestant and Catholic pastoral leadership in the U.S. What are the trends, and what issues do clergy face? The project also aims to contribute to an understanding of excellent pastoral leadership and how it can be called forth and supported. Undertaken by Duke University Divinity School, the project is supported by a grant from Lilly Endowment, Inc. For further information, see *www.pulpitandpew.duke.edu.*

GOD'S AMBASSADORS

A History of the Christian Clergy in America

E. Brooks Holifield

WILLIAM B. EERDMANS PUBLISHING COMPANY
GRAND RAPIDS, MICHIGAN / CAMBRIDGE, U.K.

Published 2007 by
Wm. B. Eerdmans Publishing Co.
2140 Oak Industrial Drive NE, Grand Rapids, Michigan 49505 /
P.O. Box 163, Cambridge CB3 9PU U.K.
www.eerdmans.com
Printed in the United States of America

12 11 10 09 08 07   7 6 5 4 3 2 1

Library of Congress Cataloging-in-Publication Data

Holifield, E. Brooks.
God's ambassadors: a history of the Christian clergy in America /
E. Brooks Holifield.
p.   cm.
ISBN 978-0-8028-0381-8 (pbk.: alk. paper)
1. Clergy — United States — History.   I. Title.

BR517.H53   2007
262′.10973 — dc22

2007020987

To Sebastian, Sophia,
& Maxwell

Contents

Preface

I incurred multiple debts while writing this book, and three institutions deserve special mention as the sponsors who made its completion possible.

First, the book is a product of the Pulpit and Pew Project, a comprehensive sociological, theological, and historical investigation of the clergy in America sponsored by the Lilly Endowment and administered by Jack Carroll, John James, Becky McMillan, and Kenneth Carder at Duke University. I am indebted to the seminars and other gatherings that occurred under the auspices of the project.

Second, I did some of the writing while serving as a senior fellow in the Center for the Study of Law and Religion at Emory University, and my work received support through a grant from The Pew Charitable Trusts. In our seminar on "The Child in Law, Religion, and Society," our maestro, John Witte, made me newly aware of the important ways in which care for the child has been a consistent theme in ministry in America. My conclusions about these matters, as of others in the book, I must hasten to add, are my own and do not necessarily reflect the views either of the Center or of The Pew Charitable Trusts.

And finally, I am profoundly indebted to the Luce Foundation and to the Association of Theological Schools, which awarded me a Henry Luce III Fellowship that allowed me to have a sabbatical year to complete the book.

For incisive critiques of the manuscript, I am grateful to Scott Appleby, Mark Chaves, David D. Hall, Stephen Stein, and Grant Wacker. I learned much from conversations with Jonathan Strom, Rod Hunter, Stacia Brown, and Lee Smith at Emory; Ted Smith at Vanderbilt; Katarina Schuth at the University of St. Thomas; and the Rev. Robert J. Silva of the National Federation of Priests'

Councils. I had helpful exchanges with Ryan Holifield and Erin McClure. And I am grateful to the faculty of the Candler School of Theology at Emory University and colleagues in the historical studies program of Emory's Graduate Division of Religion for discussion that both clarified and corrected. I wish I could have had the wit — and the space — to incorporate every suggestion and take account of every criticism. For help with research, I thank especially Tom Simpson, Andrew Stern, and Elizabeth Cox. The Pitts Library of the Candler School of Theology at Emory University has been unfailingly helpful, and I am grateful to Dean Russell Richey at Candler and to Emory University for granting sabbatical time for research and writing. For never-ending discussions of words and their uses, I want to thank — once again — Vicky.

Introduction

Over the long course of American history, from the seventeenth century to the twenty-first, few occupational groups have been more prominent in the national culture than the Christian clergy. For the first 150 years of the colonial period, they had significant authority both in the local cultures of the villages and towns and in the broader realms of authorship, education, and institutional leadership. By the early eighteenth century, they were issuing laments and warnings about the decline of their influence, but their anxieties proved to be premature. Though now they occupy merely one niche in the manifold array of professional groups, the clergy still speak with authority to millions of Americans, and they oversee congregations encompassing 60 percent of the population. Yet despite some excellent specialized studies, we have no synthetic historical account of the Christian clergy in America.

The word "clergy" has never escaped a certain ambiguity. Its familiar meaning for Christians — the designation of ordained ministers — had its origins in the biblical account of the casting of "lots" *(kleroi)* to select an apostle to replace the apostate Judas (Acts 1:26) and in a reference in 1 Peter 5:3 to the pastoral spheres *(kleroi)* allotted to the "elders" of the community. By the second century, the word "clergy" referred to the bishops who oversaw local congregations and the elders who assisted them — leaders set apart by a ritual imposition of hands — though it could also embrace a hierarchy of lesser ministries, from grave diggers and doorkeepers to acolytes and sub-deacons. But by the end of the third century it designated only the ministers — bishops, elders, and deacons — who underwent ordination, and that definition structures this book. This is not a history of Christian ministry, but a history of the men and women ordained by

1

their churches to provide a distinctive leadership. Nonetheless, ordination in the fluid American setting has had countless permutations of meaning — and some groups have had non-ordained equivalents to ordained clergy — so my use of the term "clergy" will suffer from occasional imprecision. The clerical estate in America has always been a little rough around the edges.[1]

The history of any profession must be, at least in part, a story about authority, or the legitimate use of power. In the sociological traditions that stem from Max Weber, it has long been common to distinguish, in matters religious, at least three forms of authority. Clergy in America, as elsewhere, have appealed first to a "charisma of office," a claim that an official estate bears a distinctive gift of spiritual power. This is best represented in the Catholic and Eastern Orthodox conception of the priesthood as a channel for the transmission of divine grace by virtue of a ritual of ordination. The office itself bears a special status and confers extraordinary powers.

Clergy have also grounded authority in a "charisma of person," the granting of a divine gift to an individual man or woman. Personal charisma finds its best example in the Protestant minister who asserts a right to represent Christ solely because of a claim to have received a divine "call." Or this form of charismatic authority can be exemplified in the minister whose quality of life, insight, and religious depth elicit from a community both trust and an acknowledgment of rightful leadership.

Finally, priests and ministers have appealed to a "rational authority" derived from their knowledge and skill in promoting the aims of the church. Ever since the late sixteenth century this has been associated with a special education that sets the minister apart from the laity. By the early nineteenth century, many ministers argued that precisely such education ensured that the ministry would remain a respected "profession."[2]

The history of the American ministry unfolds as a complex series of episodes in which these three modes of authority — and more — were in play. Even in colonial America, Protestants debated about the relative weight of ordination, the divine call, and clerical education. In the nineteenth century, some Protestants insisted that ministry was solely a calling, never a profession, while Catholics accentuated the office and the ordination that elevated priests into it. Attempts to balance the three views of authority — or to position one against the others — have continued into the twenty-first century. One nationwide

1. George H. Williams, "The Ministry of the Ante-Nicene Church," in *The Ministry in Historical Perspectives,* ed. H. Richard Niebuhr and Daniel D. Williams (New York: Harper and Row, 1956), pp. 28-59.

2. Max Weber, *Sociological Writings,* ed. Wolf Heydebrand (New York: Continuum, 1994), pp. 31-46.

survey in 2001 found that 56 percent of the clergy believed that their ordination validated their office, and 44 percent stressed the importance of a special education, but almost 90 percent believed that their authority rested on a divine call and on competent leadership that engendered trust and respect. Some felt that the call alone was sufficient.[3]

A historian's approach to the question also suggests that assessments of clerical authority must include more than the application of ideal types. Almost every paragraph in this book is about authority — the authority of custom and tradition, of scriptures and theologies, of forceful personalities, of rational persuasion, of economic status, of emotional appeal — and challenges to that authority. Authority has rested not only on ordination, a divine call, and education but also, as Weber anticipated, on intangibles that slip through any web of abstraction. In face-to-face encounters, the informal authority of the minister has varied with cultural assumptions about good manners, proper dress, physical appearance, and fluency of speech as well as preconceptions about gender, age, race, and class. When one clergyman asked a parishioner, "Exactly why can't you accept me as your minister?" the reply came back: "You could never be my minister. I can't stand the way you dress."[4]

This book presents, in narrative form, three arguments about the history of the American clergy. First, it tries to show that clerical authority has assumed multiple forms, that it underwent continual evolution, and that its changing forms always registered the force of social location. Authority looked — and felt — different in a colonial mission, an urban eighteenth-century congregation, a nineteenth-century revival meeting, and a twentieth-century inner-city church. Equally important, the authority of priests and ministers changed in accord with the structural differentiation of the professions. The expansion in the number of professions since the nineteenth century has meant that most priests and ministers, most of the time, exercise their influence alongside other professionals, who both support them and compete with them.

Many argue that the history of the American clergy is a story about the decline of authority in the face of irresistible secularization. They point out that a society that once looked to the clergy as the experts who deciphered the mysteries of the world now look to other experts. They claim that fewer people now live beneath a "sacred canopy" and that more construct their worlds without

---

3. Jackson W. Carroll, *God's Potters: Pastoral Leadership and the Shaping of Congregations* (Grand Rapids: Eerdmans, 2006), p. 154. See also the theological discussion in L. Gregory Jones and Kevin R. Armstrong, *Resurrecting Excellence: Shaping Faithful Christian Ministry* (Grand Rapids: Eerdmans, 2006), pp. 79-110.

4. Weber, *Sociological Writings*, p. 32; Carroll, *God's Potters*, pp. 151-54. My colleague Bill Mallard gave me this snippet of a conversation reported to him by a young minister.

clerical assistance. Institutions that once yielded to the admonitions of priests and preachers now generate their own autonomous norms and ambitions. Vast business corporations have broken free of religious constraints; the logic of the market ignores theological wisdom; the nation-state operates within secular norms even though its rulers might seek private solace or political advantage by turning to sympathetic clerics.

The narrative of decline captures some truths about the fate of the American clergy in the past four hundred years. Priests and ministers no longer have the control over education, the voice in government, or the moral monopoly that they appeared to exercise in seventeenth-century Puritan New England. They no longer formulate legal enactments, discipline the merchants, dominate the printing presses, or regulate the universities as they did then. Newspapers no longer print their Sunday sermons, as they often did as recently as the late nineteenth century. The laity no longer depend on their advice about mundane matters in precisely the same way that Catholic immigrant laborers and their families in the 1890s sometimes depended on the priest for cultural knowledge, financial counsel, and access to jobs. On many matters, clergy appear to have ceded jurisdiction to physicians and psychiatrists, social workers and sociologists, scientists and the gurus of technology. The dwindling numbers of Catholic priests after 1960 and the membership losses in mainline Protestantism have intensified the sense that clergy do not have the authority they once did.[5]

Nevertheless, the second argument in this book is that the narrative of decline altogether fails to do justice to the complexity of clerical history. In the first place, the clergy never had an unchallenged influence in American life, even in seventeenth-century New England. Laments about decline romanticize the past (sometimes to manipulate the present). In the second place, the clergy continue to speak with some real authority in more than 300,000 local congregations. A focus on those congregations suggests a need to distinguish between central and subsidiary spheres of authority. In a variety of subsidiary spheres in which the clergy once had a strong voice — elite higher education and high literary culture, for example — other voices now prevail. In selected practices more integrally linked to the central sphere of clerical authority — such as counseling the troubled — other professions have attained public acceptance and prestige. But in what has always been the central sphere — congregational leadership — the clergy have as much authority now as they did in the seventeenth century.

5. Peter Berger, *The Sacred Canopy: Elements of a Sociological Theory of Religion* (Garden City, N.Y.: Doubleday, 1969), pp. 105-25; Andrew Abbott, *The System of Professions: An Essay on the Division of Expert Labor* (Chicago: University of Chicago Press, 1988), pp. 186-95, 308-14.

Most priests and ministers oversee, as they have for four centuries, congregations in which people worship, learn skills, make music, nurture children, discuss meanings, and contribute time and money for charitable causes. The deepest influence of the clergy has always occurred through both ritualized and face-to-face relationships within these small communities, in which more Americans have gathered weekly than in any other form of voluntary organization in the nation's history. Within particular denominations the authority of the clergy as congregational leaders has waxed and waned, but overall the story of congregational leadership reveals a pattern of unbroken continuity.

Of course, clergy have never had unlimited authority within those congregations. Their effectiveness has always depended on the responses of congregants. This was as true in the seventeenth century as it is in the twenty-first, and it means that the particular forms of clerical authority have shifted with the changing social location, the degree of education, the cultural choices, and the religious proclivities of the laity. Even in churches that assign pastors to congregations without their consent, the cleric retains pastoral authority only by earning the respect of parishioners. The authority of priests and ministers has been communal in ways that distinguish the clergy from any other profession.

In striking contrast to the tale of decline is the worry that the clergy — or at least one segment of them — have attained altogether too much authority in the culture. The concern is that a "network of preachers," many of whom are wedded to a theocratic view of government, have forged an alliance with the most conservative forces in American politics and pursued an intolerant, bellicose, and ultra-nationalist political agenda that generates public support for unilateral military action, contempt for other religions, and a coercive uniformity in American life. Those who voice this concern recognize the diversity among the clergy, but they fear that biblical literalism and an apocalyptic theology cobbled together from disparate passages of scripture have led one powerful group of clerics to promote policies that diminish support for a wise foreign policy, undermine a proper appreciation of science in American schools, and impose their values on every American. These critics warn of a "powerful clerical closeness to everyday community governance and political authority" that promotes a dangerous political agenda.[6]

The critique, however, can hardly be extended to embrace the vast majority of American priests and ministers. Most of them avoid political causes and cultural crusades, and in matters of politics and culture they are as ideologically diverse as Americans in general. In the past, other ministers have allied

---

6. Kevin Phillips, *American Theocracy: The Peril and Promise of Radical Religion, Oil, and Borrowed Money in the 21st Century* (New York: Viking, 2006), pp. 187, 214, 252, 259.

themselves with political trends — progressive, conservative, and reactionary
— and seemed for a moment to ride the wave of social change, but the trends
have always shifted, and the confidence of one era can fade quickly into the
melancholy resignation of the next. It is fully consonant with the American
tradition for clergy to express their convictions in the public square; it has also
been part of the American experience, as James Madison noticed in the eighteenth century, that competing views have generated checks and balances
when any particular faction overreaches.

The third prominent argument implicit in the narrative of this book is that
the American churches and clergy have collectively decided — by virtue of their
practices and their theologies — that the ministry is only partially a profession.
The modern professions like to think of themselves as vocational groups set
apart by a specialized higher education, dedicated to service on behalf of clients, governed by an ethical code, and motivated by ideals of public welfare
rather than exclusively by the aim of profit. Many among the clergy have long
seen their calling as a profession in that modern sense. The push for clerical
education that began in the sixteenth century established the ideal of the cleric
as a person distinguished and authorized by higher learning. In America, more
than in any European nation, however, that ideal came under attack, especially
after the American Revolution, and a "populist" disregard for — and suspicion
of — specialized clerical education has continued to permeate numerous denominations. In addition, many of the educated clergy themselves have questioned the adequacy of the "professional model," and debates about it have periodically recurred.

Alongside the three main arguments, the book proposes a theological
judgment, cast in a historical form. The clergy have always argued that the
source of the authority sustaining their vocation is ultimately the Christ whose
person and message they represent, as ambassadors bound in fidelity to a sovereign. They have understood this claim in diverse ways, and they have made only
infrequent efforts to explore its implications in explicit theologies of ministry.
Cultural and social changes, church traditions, and local customs have shaped
their ministry more than sustained theological reflection on the vocation. But
at the level of implicit assumptions, visible mainly in fragments of debate and
disagreement, an operative theology made a difference.

Floating beneath the surface of many of the debates over pastoral practice
was a paradox at the heart of Christianity. The Christian gospel has always affirmed both God's transcendence and God's immanence. God is the transcendent One who can never be identified with any form or structure in nature or
history, but God is immanent within those forms and structures. The paradox
found expression in traditional definitions of Christ as both fully divine and

fully human, fully other than humanity and fully one with humanity. It reappeared in the Pauline description of Christians as "those who deal with the world as though they had no dealings with it" (1 Cor. 7:31). The Christian tradition has reveled in paradoxes.

The original Christian gospel affirmed a kingdom of God that transcended all earthly kingdoms, and it displayed skepticism about human institutions and standards. It proclaimed, for instance, a Savior who defied the Roman governor who crucified him and whose apostles resisted the authorities in Jerusalem by insisting that they would "obey God rather than men" (Acts 5:29). While the New Testament affirmed, by implication, such institutions as family, marriage, and commerce, it refused to accord them absolute value. Jesus chided inquirers who wanted to attend to family matters — bury a father or bid their loved ones farewell — before they followed him, and he rebuked followers who placed their families before the demands of the gospel. Paul told early Christians that it was best for them not to marry. Rather than blessing material accumulation, moreover, Jesus told one wealthy listener to sell all he had and give it to the poor. Rather than encouraging his followers to accept worldly ideals of power and natural impulses of self-preservation, he told them to turn the other cheek when they were attacked and surrender their cloak when a robber demanded their coat. He taught them that they gained life by losing it and that the least among them would be the first. And Paul insisted that Christ erased even the distinctions between Jew and Greek, male and female, slave and free. God's transcendence entailed a vast gap between the divine kingdom and all earthly institutions.

Yet the Christian gospel was also world-affirming. It viewed the created order as good and validated its forms and structures. It accepted, for instance, the governance of secular authorities. Jesus told his followers to render to Caesar the things that were Caesar's, and Paul sought and received the protection of the Roman governors. The New Testament also affirmed such human institutions as marriage and commerce, depicting Jesus as attending feasts and weddings and as telling parables that assumed the acceptability of economic investment and profit. Paul told early Christians awaiting the end times to remain in their worldly callings until Jesus returned. The church flourished in later centuries by adapting itself to numerous cultures, incorporating their ideals, and supporting them with its doctrine and its treasure. God's immanence entailed the participation of earthly institutions in the divine *telos*.

The Christian clergy in America — like other clergy and churches throughout history — inherited, therefore, a gospel that was at the same time world denying and world affirming, and this meant that they embodied — and embody — an irreducibly paradoxical relation to American culture. On the one hand, they proclaim a message that stands as an affront to some of the revered convictions of American culture — convictions about wealth, family, power, military force, and the assumption that success can be measured, whether it is dollars or members who are counted. The gospel of God's transcendence suggests that every human enterprise stands under judgment. On the other hand, clergy — and the churches they lead — have been fully immersed in the culture, sharing its standards of citizenship, education, and success. The gospel of God's immanence in the world suggests, after all, that human cultures are worthy enterprises.

In short, ministry and priesthood have represented — to borrow an expression from Reinhold Niebuhr — an "impossible possibility." The tension at the center of Christianity called for priests and ministers to work within the culture and yet to offend it repeatedly. They were to adapt themselves to its forms while proclaiming that the Spirit makes all things new and renders every form merely provisional. They were to attract large crowds but not measure their success by such worldly standards. They were to allow themselves normal human goods and pleasures — and the financial means to attain them — and yet represent the norm of self-sacrificial love. They were to adapt themselves to cultural and technological innovation and yet remain aware of the potential for exploitation and self-promotion in every adaptation.

While some ministers advocated the building of great church edifices as symbols of God's presence in the world, others claimed that such magnificence was an idolatrous capitulation to worldly standards. While some called for higher levels of clerical education and the pursuit of professional standards, other ministers accused them of substituting human learning for the power of the Spirit and the wisdom of the world for "the foolishness of God" (1 Cor. 1:25). On both sides of the debates, clergy were struggling with the tension created by a gospel that affirmed both divine immanence and divine transcendence.

Theologians and historians have found various ways to describe the tension. Some have distinguished between the world-affirming church and the world-denying sect. Others have drawn distinctions between form and dynamics in the history of the church, or continuity and novelty, or structure and spirit in Christian thought and practice. The classic typology of H. Richard Niebuhr — which described a Christ of culture, a Christ against culture, a Christ above culture, Christ and culture in paradox, and a Christ-transforming culture — suggested the conceptual complexity that such a tension could engender. In everyday practice, clergy and congregations have rarely fit neatly into such typologies. They have been more likely to embody the tension, affirming one dimension of culture as an expression of divine immanence while denying another by virtue of assumptions about divine transcendence. Most American clergy have lived with the tension every day simply because it is so deeply engrained in the Christian faith.[7]

The tension between immanence and transcendence helps to explain — though only partially — the tendency of priests and ministers in almost every period of American history to view their office as a calling in crisis. This book returns frequently to clerical worries about ineffectiveness, vocational weakness, declining cultural status, powerlessness, and failings of one kind or another. Self-doubt appears to have been the vocation's constant companion. Social and historical trends and transitions explain much of the self-critical mood, but the sense of crisis also reflects the difficulty of living within the paradox, affirming the culture and its ideals while recognizing that, from the vantage of the gospel, success can be failure and failure can be success. Ministers are not immune to smugness, but the ministry is not a profession designed for self-satisfaction.

It has always been possible to relax the tension by baptizing the culture or by withdrawing from it into a separated sphere of sanctity. Some have affirmed immanence in a way that locates God unambiguously within the structures of national power, a market economy, and social movements and institutions. Others have affirmed transcendence in a way that renders suspect every involvement with the surrounding culture. But for most ministers and priests the tension remains, manifest repeatedly in the ordinary compromises and decisions of day-to-day ministry.

The historian's temptation is to rummage through history labeling one set of clergy as the baptizers of culture and another set as its prophetic critics. I have tried to resist the temptation. In real life, all priests and ministers both affirm and deny; they legitimate cultural forms and subvert them; they follow now one side and then another of the paradox. The Christian ministry will always be in crisis. Sociologists and historians can explain part of the crisis, but the rest is inherent in the very soul of the Christian tradition.

7. H. Richard Niebuhr, *Christ and Culture* (New York: Harper and Row, 1951), pp. 39-45.

CHAPTER 1

The Heritage

The Christian clergy stand in a tradition extending through more than two thousand years of history, and the ancient past forms a horizon that continually defines the contours of the profession. No other vocation has accorded greater weight to precedent and tradition, and the norms of clerical leadership often require vows of fidelity to ideals and practices honored by centuries of communal custom. The antecedents of the clerical vocation extend back into the institutions of ancient Israel, the ministry of Jesus, and the primitive Christian communities of first-century Mediterranean cultures. Many of its enduring expectations arose in early stages of the church's history, and its innovations — which have been frequent and far-reaching — have always raised the question of fidelity to origins in a revered past.

The clergy in America reflect the multitude of options that emerged during that long history. Because Americans decided in the eighteenth century to separate the church from the state, the American churches produced a confusing mosaic of norms and images for the ministry. After the Revolution it would have been impossible to establish a uniform national standard of clerical practice and competence or to attain the degree of standardization that marks most other professions. Each denomination — and often each local congregation — could establish its own standards, and the multiplicity of religious denominations prevented any consensus. Each Christian group claimed fidelity to the Christian past; they set forth a bewildering array of competing interpretations of what fidelity required and even of what constituted the relevant past. But the ministry is a profession that can be understood only with reference to a lexicon of words and a set of forms and practices that come from the church's long history.

The Authority of History

The original formative episode was the ministry of Jesus, who has been for the church not only the divine-human redeemer but also the prophetic and priestly figure whose example and mandates have formed clerical self-understanding. The writers of the New Testament amplified ancient Israelite understandings when they described Jesus as prophet and priest, and the example of the Jewish rabbinate in the first and second centuries informed Christian conceptions of ministry from the outset, but Christians read the Jewish scriptures in the light of their understandings of Jesus. The Christian clergy have repeatedly appealed to Jesus as a model, a source of mandates, and a ground of authority.

Just as he preached, taught, and healed, so also preaching, teaching, and healing became functions of Christian ministry. He told his hearers that he was among them as "one who serves," and he instructed his followers to feed the hungry, clothe the naked, welcome the stranger, and visit the sick and imprisoned. His example and his mandates helped to define the church's understanding of its ordained clergy. Because he told his closest followers to "make disciples of all nations, baptizing them in the name of the Father and of the Son and of the Holy Spirit," they saw themselves as under orders to evangelize and baptize. Because he instructed his disciples to eat and drink "in remembrance" of him, Christian ministers distributed bread and wine in a Eucharistic ritual. Because he told Peter and then the other disciples that "whatever you bind on earth shall be bound in heaven, and whatever you loose on earth shall be loosed in heaven," the vast majority of clergy in the history of the church felt obliged and authorized to call for penance and to forgive sins.[1]

Jesus told his disciples that they would have authority in the kingdom of heaven, so some clergy later argued that they, and not the laity, should govern the church. According to the Gospel of Matthew, Jesus designated one of his apostles, Peter, as the rock on which he would build his church, promising that Peter would hold "the keys of the kingdom of heaven." For the Roman Catholic Church, the promise to Peter became the warrant for the special authority of the bishop of Rome, since Peter was believed to have been the first occupant of what would become the Roman papal office. Christian writers also began by the second century to claim that bishops stood in a lineal succession from Peter and the other apostles, and that this unbroken succession conveyed authority from generation to generation.[2]

---

1. John 10:14, Luke 22:27, Matt. 25:42-45; Matt. 28:19-20, Luke 22:19, Matt. 16:19, Matt. 18:18.

2. Matt. 19:28, Luke 6:13, Matt. 28:20, Matt. 16:18; Benedict Sestini, "Introduction" (1816), *The Messenger of the Sacred Heart of Jesus* (April 1886), in Charles Curran, S.J., ed., *American Jesuit Spirituality: The Maryland Tradition, 1634-1900* (New York: Paulist Press, 1988), p. 273.

Americans found additional precedents in the New Testament's descriptions of charismatic communal leadership in the early church. The letters of the Apostle Paul, which preceded even the writing of the Gospels, described a perplexing array of leadership functions. In writing to Christians in Corinth, Paul named apostles, prophets, teachers, miracle workers, healers, administrators, and speakers in tongues. In other letters, he referred to bishops, deacons, deaconesses, prophets, and widows. He did not always clearly distinguish the functions. Later interpreters could not be sure whether he was saying that true churches should have "offices" of these descriptions or was merely taking note of functional responsibilities in various congregations.[3]

Other books and epistles in the New Testament added "evangelists" and "pastors" to the list, or they mentioned the leadership of "elders" (presbyters). A letter to Timothy assumed that the elders ruled the congregations and that they joined in a ceremony — the laying on of hands — linked to the gift of prophetic utterance. A letter to Titus appeared to equate the elder with the bishop *(episkopos).* By the time Luke wrote the book of Acts, he reported that the apostles, including Paul, appointed elders in every congregation they visited, and Luke seemed also to equate the elders with bishops.[4]

For American clergy, trying centuries later to model themselves after the examples of the New Testament, this chorus of hints and allusions provided a reservoir of arguments for conflicting understandings of the pastoral office. Some groups believed that the Bible authorized bishops as supervisors of elders, but others equated bishops with elders. Some contended that the church authority of the pastor came from the congregation, but others believed that it came from ordination by other clergy. Some thought that the New Testament warranted the ordination of women in imitation of the women prophets and deaconesses. Others restricted the ordained ministry to males because some of the epistles said that women should remain silent, or, in the case of Roman Catholics, because Jesus did not include women among his twelve disciples and (according to Pope Paul VI) because women could not image the male Jesus as men could. Some argued that a true church needed pastors, teachers, elders, and deacons, but others selected bishops, priests, and deacons as the essential offices. The fluid practices and definitions of the early church permanently affected — and complicated — the attempt to define ministry in America.

The denominations that insisted on bishops, elders, and deacons pointed to developments in the second and third century as the early church moved toward more uniform patterns. By the mid-third century, the church in most

3. 1 Cor. 12:28, Phil. 1:1, 1 Cor. 11:5, Rom. 16:1, 1 Tim. 5:3.
4. Eph. 4:11, 1 Tim. 4:14, Tit. 1:5-7, 1 Pet. 1:1, Acts 14:23, 20:17, 28.

regions elevated the bishop as the overseer of a congregation, the chief elder among the other elders. Only bishops could baptize, exercise judicial functions, and perform the rite of ordination. The church eventually developed the notion that the monarchical bishop, as the successor to the apostles ("apostolic succession"), was the only Christian minister who inherited their full apostolic powers, and that he authorized the ministry of his priests by granting them a share in these powers, known as "faculties."

The eldership expanded in the third century as the local bishop assumed distant oversight of new congregations, initially in the same city, and sent elders to perform the liturgical offices in his place, since only bishops and elders could preside at the Eucharist. Deacons occupied a third rank, though they retained ascendancy over sub-deacons, acolytes, exorcists, lectors, widows, and door-keepers, who held no official position in the class of the *kleroi,* or clergy proper. By the fourth century, the church in some regions assigned the deacon a special responsibility for service *(diakonia)* to the sick and the poor. The church in the West ordained only males, but the Eastern church ordained women over forty years of age as deaconesses. In several of the largest American denominations, the three offices have continued, though diversely defined.[5]

Most clergy in America have begun their ministry with a ritual whose origins can be traced to the earliest churches, which commissioned leaders with an imposition of hands that signified and bestowed a special gift or charisma. By the time of Tertullian (c. 160-c. 220) and Cyprian (d. 258), the church referred to these rituals as "ordinations." In the fourth century, a regional council decreed that ordination, like baptism, blotted out sin, and theologians during that period argued that the rite made the priest "holy and worthy of honor." By the fifth century, Augustine of Hippo said that it conveyed an "indelible character" that empowered the priest to perform a valid baptism despite personal failings. Seven centuries later, Peter Lombard (c. 1100-1160) spelled out the theological implications: ordination was a sacrament, and it conveyed "a spiritual power and office" that elevated clergy above the laity. In the sixteenth century, Protestants rejected this understanding, but Catholics and the Orthodox retained it. The American clergy found themselves in frequent conflict about it.[6]

5. George H. Williams, "The Ministry of the Ante-Nicene Church," in *The Ministry in Historical Perspectives,* ed. H. Richard Niebuhr and Daniel D. Williams (New York: Harper and Row, 1956), pp. 27-59, 45-51; George H. Williams, "The Ministry in the Later Patristic Period," in *The Ministry in Historical Perspectives,* pp. 64-66; Adolf Harnack, *The Mission and Expansion of Christianity in the First Three Centuries,* trans. James Moffatt (1st ed., 1908; New York: Harper and Brothers, 1961), pp. 122, 161.

6. Acts 6:6, 13:3, 1 Tim. 4:14, 2 Tim. 1:6, Tertullian, *Prescription Against Heretics, Early Latin Theology, The Library of Christian Classics,* ed. S. L. Greenslade (Philadelphia: Westminster

Accompanying these changes was an increasing tendency to depict the essential function of ministry as sacerdotal, or priestly. This meant that the commission of bishops and elders was to officiate at an altar on which Christ's sacrifice was perpetually reenacted. Some Christian writings identified the church rather than the clergy as the "royal priesthood," but bishops and elders were the ones who officiated at the Eucharist, and this magnified the sense of their priestly role. Christian writers began, by the time of Clement of Rome (fl. 96), to identify the celebrants with the Old Testament priests who presided at sacrificial altars.[7]

In the *Apostolic Tradition* of Hippolytus, which probably mirrored the practice of the church in Rome around the year 200, the bishop was a "high priest" and the bread and wine were an "oblation," or offering, to God. Within fifty years, Cyprian, Bishop of Carthage, could argue that the Eucharist was "a true and full sacrifice" to God and that the celebrant was truly a priest offering a sacrificial gift. Theologians later expanded this description into a full-blown doctrine that the priest, acting for Christ, repeatedly offered Christ's body and blood to God as a sacrifice so that Christians could appropriate the benefits of his death. This conception of priesthood as a sacrificial office retained its force among Catholic and Eastern Orthodox clergy, and in America it formed lines of division between them and most Protestants in understanding the ministerial office.[8]

The mass was the ritual in which this sacrifice occurred. It received its name in the third century because the priest ended the service with the Latin phrase *"Ita missa est"* ("You are dismissed"), and it formed the setting for the administration of the Eucharist (or Holy Communion), the church's chief sacrament. But the church also came to think of certain other rituals as sacraments — visible signs or forms, according to the definition of Augustine, that signified and conveyed the grace of God — and to say that normally they required a priest or the bishop. After the publication of Lombard's *Sentences,* the exercise of the priesthood came to be associated, above all, with the administration of seven sacraments. By baptizing infants, confirming the baptized, celebrating the Eucharist, administering penance, anointing the sick and dying, ordaining

---

Press, 1956), p. 62; Cyprian, "Letter 69," in *Early Latin Theology,* p. 152; Gregory Dix and Henry Chadwick, eds., *The Treatise on the Apostolic Tradition of St. Hippolytus of Rome* (London: Alban Press, 1968), pp. 3, 13, 16; Carl A. Volz, *Pastoral Life and Practice in the Early Church* (Minneapolis: Fortress Press, 1990), pp. 37, 40; Kenan B. Osborne, O.F.M., *Priesthood: A History of the Ordained Ministry in the Roman Catholic Church* (New York: Paulist Press, 1988), p. 206.

7. 1 Pet. 2:9; Osborne, *Priesthood,* p. 96.

8. Hippolytus, "Preface," in *The Treatise on the Apostolic Tradition,* pp. 5, 9; Bernhard Lohse, *A Short History of Christian Doctrine,* trans. F. Ernest Stoeffler (Philadelphia: Fortress Press, 1966), p. 135.

new priests, and presiding at marriages, the bishop or the priest employed outward and visible signs as means to communicate inward and spiritual grace.[9]

The priest's sacramental power found further muted expression in the custom of priestly consecrations and benedictions. The Carolingian church after 800 multiplied the priestly blessings, which came to include rituals for the blessing of churches, altars, bells, burial grounds, marriage partners, fields, sheep and cattle, weapons, travelers, pilgrims, and countless other objects viewed as necessary for well-being. To ward off evil, the priests also had the power to exorcise demonic spirits. Only bishops could consecrate churches and the chrism (holy oil) used in sacramental rituals, but ordinary priests entered into the daily lives of their parishioners with numerous benedictions deemed effective partly because of the priest's mediatory status.[10]

The Catholic clergy in America have always thought of themselves as either "regular" or "secular" priests, and this distinction also originated in the distant past. In the late third century, a company of Christians in Egypt journeyed to the desert to pray — and, once there, they stayed. These desert fathers and mothers were not clerics. In fact, bishops and clerical councils detested these "monks," who withdrew from sacraments, homilies, and episcopal oversight to live alone in caves and hovels, and fourth-century councils forbade clerics to join them. But ascetic imitators filled the deserts and forests, not only in Egypt but elsewhere, and some of them clustered in communities that submitted themselves to a common *regula,* or rule. By the mid-fourth century, these monastic communities were furnishing bishops for the churches.[11]

Sometime after 529, Benedict of Nursia in the monastery at Monte Cassino prepared the *Regula Monachorum* — the monastic rule — that would regulate communities throughout Europe. He did not design it for priests. He allowed priests to join his order, but many saw the monastic and priestly callings as incompatible. Monks and nuns were to live a cloistered life, seeking a higher perfection through prayer, liturgy, and penance. They were different from priests, who had sacramental duties among the laity. But priests entered the monasteries and monks sought ordination, and by the tenth century, priests under monastic vows outnumbered the lay monks. In turn, monasticism altered the priesthood.[12]

9. Osborne, *Priesthood,* pp. 200-18.

10. Gerd Tellenbach, *The Church in Western Europe from the Tenth to the Early Twelfth Century* (Cambridge: Cambridge University Press, 1993), p. 95.

11. Herbert B. Workman, *The Evolution of the Monastic Ideal* (1st ed., 1913; Boston: Beacon Press, 1962), pp. 16, 177.

12. Jean Leclerq, "The Priesthood for Monks," *Monastic Studies* 3 (1965): 58-69; R. W. Southern, *Western Society and the Church in the Middle Ages* (Harmondsworth: Penguin, 1970), pp. 224-26.

The monastic vision produced three types of organization that would permanently inform the practice of ministry, especially in the Roman Catholic Church. The first was the Benedictine ideal of the communal cloistered life, in which monks (many of whom were priests) dedicated themselves to contemplation and the repetition of the liturgy. The second was the eleventh-century canonical orders. Unlike the cloistered monks, the "regular" canons served a local congregation, organizing themselves according to a simple rule derived from Augustine that praised the sharing of possessions, communal prayer, and obedience to a leader. Augustine's rule appealed to priests attached to cathedrals and to others who organized "collegiate" churches with several clergy who vowed to accept it. The third form of organization appeared among the thirteenth-century mendicant (begging) friars who took vows to live in poverty and imitate Christ while serving as nomadic preachers. The Franciscans, for instance, were at first laypeople, but many became clerics, moving from place to place on a universal mission of preaching. The Dominicans were clerical from the outset and intent, above all, on combating error through study, preaching, and teaching. Other mendicant groups followed their lead. These three forms of order led Catholics to distinguish between "regular" or "religious" clergy, who took vows of poverty, chastity, and obedience and followed a rule, and "secular" or "diocesan" clergy, who took vows of chastity and obedience (but not poverty) and ministered under the authority not of the superior of an order but of a diocesan bishop.[13]

Monastic piety stood behind the practice of private confession to a priest who was empowered to require penance (from *poena:* punishment) and pronounce forgiveness. In the sixth century, Celtic monks produced penitential books that connected sins to their appropriate remedies. Employed first inside and then outside the monastery, these "penitentials" at first required arduous penitential acts as a condition of absolution by the priest, but priests eventually began to pronounce the absolution at the same time the confession was made, even though the acts of penance remained to be done. In 1215, the Fourth Lateran Council, describing penance as a medicine and priests as physicians of the soul, required every Christian to confess and receive absolution at least once a year. By the end of the fourteenth century, after Dominicans had refined the penitentials, confession and absolution formed the center of Christian pastoral

13. Douglas J. McMillan and Kathryn Smith Fladenmuller, eds., *Regular Life: Monastic, Canonical, and Mendicant Rules* (Kalamazoo: Medieval Institute, 1997), pp. 1-14, 39-44; C. H. Lawrence, *Medieval Monasticism: Forms of Religious Life in Western Europe in the Middle Ages* (London: Longman, 1984), pp. 68, 212; John P. Marschall, "Diocesan and Regular Clergy: The History of a Relationship, 1789-1969," in *The Catholic Priest in the United States: Historical Investigations* (Collegeville: Saint John's University Press, 1971), p. 405.

care. Most Protestants rejected the practice as implying that priests had to mediate the forgiveness of sins, but some Lutherans and Anglicans retained it.[14]

A further inheritance from the monastic heritage — the tradition of women religious — also influenced the ministry of the Catholic priest in America. By the sixth century, the Western church was eliminating the order of the deaconess, and although it endured longer in the East, it disappeared by the eleventh century. From the outset of monasticism, however, women entered the cloistered life. Augustine wrote both a masculine and a feminine version of his simple rule. The women's orders encountered opposition, but by the end of the thirteenth century monasteries for women in some regions outnumbered those for men. They observed the same liturgical offices as the monks. Most convents required a contemplative and cloistered life, but by the later Middle Ages, the sisters also fed the poor, nursed the sick, reared orphans, offered hospitality to pilgrims and travelers, and founded hospitals, almshouses, and schools. In America, the communities of sisters became, for more than three centuries, the steady allies of the priesthood.[15]

A final episode from the medieval past that determined the shape of ministry in America was the great schism between East and West that resulted in separate Catholic and Orthodox traditions. The schism occurred for many reasons. The political division of the Roman Empire in the third century laid its foundations. Ninth-century disputes stirred tensions about Trinitarian theology, a married clergy, the rules of fasting, and the celebration of the Eucharist. Assertions of papal authority in the ninth and again in the eleventh century led in 1054 to mutual excommunications between the Roman Pope and the Patriarch of Constantinople. When Western crusaders sacked Constantinople in 1204, the breach seemed irreparable. The Orthodox movement expanded through Greece and all of Eastern Europe and into Asia, setting up what would become self-governing national churches. Led by patriarchs, archbishops, bishops, priests, and deacons, these Eastern Orthodox churches filtered into America mainly in the nineteenth century, establishing congregations in which the clergy represented not only access to the sacred but also links to national cultures.[16]

14. Thomas O. Laughlin, "Penitentials and Pastoral Care," in *A History of Pastoral Care,* ed. G. R. Evans (London: Cassell, 2000), pp. 93-111; William J. Dohar, "Since the Pestilence Time: Pastoral Care in the Later Middle Ages," in *History of Pastoral Care,* p. 184.

15. McMillan and Fladenmuller, eds., *Regular Life,* pp. 39-49; Penelope D. Johnson, *Equal in Monastic Profession: Women in Medieval France* (Chicago: University of Chicago Press, 1991), pp. 49-57.

16. Timothy Ware, *The Orthodox Church* (Baltimore: Penguin Books, 1963), pp. 51-81, 297-300.

The Era of Reform

The two great reform movements of the sixteenth century — the Catholic Reform and the Protestant Reformation — set in motion the forces that would eventually reshape the work of priests and ministers. The Catholic reform of the pastoral office and the Protestant insistence on the priesthood of all believers and on the pastor as preacher gave rise to such diverse understandings of the clerical office that it became impossible for Christians to agree about the status or the function of the ordained ministry.

The Catholic Reform extended far beyond the sphere of the clerical, but sixteenth-century reformers shared a conviction that "serious diseases" had afflicted the priesthood. When Pope Paul III appointed a reform commission in 1536 under the leadership of Cardinal Gasparo Contarini, it complained that the church had ordained too many unskilled, ignorant, and immoral men, producing both scandal and "contempt for the ecclesiastical order." Too many bishops and priests accepted the salaries but failed to reside in their diocese or parish, leaving the cure of souls to lesser-paid "hirelings." Highly placed clerics bought and sold church offices with an eye to profit, and others held a plurality of positions, receiving the financial reward but doing no pastoral work in them. Cardinals often held several bishoprics distant from their place of residence. And some priests received permission to live with concubines. The commission's most frequent complaint was about absence of attention to pastoral work.[17]

The renewed passion for the pastoral work of priests in the sixteenth century led to a series of new religious orders — from the Theatines to the Capuchins to the Jesuits — devoted to preaching, service, education, and the cure of souls. The Jesuits, for example, launched in 1540 a mission of service in the world. They initiated preaching missions and encouraged catechetical instruction, established schools to train future priests, ministered in hospitals and prisons, and sponsored missionary tours outside Europe. They probably originated the term "mission" as a designation of an evangelistic effort abroad. They popularized the "retreat," a period of withdrawal for "spiritual direction" with lay Christians. They became experts in "casuistry," the theoretical knowledge that guided the case-by-case evaluation of the gravity of a sinful act, as well as the application of penances to be performed in reparation for the act. Along with the canons and other smaller orders, they gave the regular clergy a pastoral vocation.[18]

17. Gasparo Contarini, et al., *Consilium de emendanda ecclesia, Catholic Reform: From Cardinal Ximenes to the Council of Trent 1495-1563*, ed. John C. Olin (New York: Fordham University Press, 1990), pp. 68-79.

18. John O'Malley, "The Ministry to Outsiders: The Jesuits," in *History of Pastoral Care*, pp. 255-60; David Knowles, *From Pachomius to Ignatius: A Study in the Constitutional History of the*

The impulse to elevate pastoral work dominated the reform decrees of the Council of Trent (1545-1563). In effect defining the parish as the chief institution of the bishop's diocese, the Council decreed that pastors were to "reside personally in their church or diocese, and there to fulfill the duties of their office." They were to preach regularly and attain the education that would enable them to preach well. Each parish priest had to catechize children and youth every Sunday and feast day. The Council issued a new standardized missal — containing the liturgy of the mass — and it condemned non-resident bishops. The bishops now had a special responsibility for selecting and ordaining parish priests.[19]

At the same time, the Council reasserted the sacramental understanding of priesthood. In reaction to Protestant criticisms, Trent insisted that ordination was a sacrament and that it imprinted an indelible character and conveyed "the power to consecrate and offer the true body and blood of the Lord, and to forgive or retain sins." It emphasized the priest's power to offer the Eucharistic sacrifice, noting that "sacrifice and priesthood" were "joined together by God's foundation." It defended a hierarchy of orders, declaring that bishops stood at the apex, "higher than priests," and that their conferring of ordination required no "consent or calling of the people or of secular authority." It continued to distinguish the minor orders (porter, lector, exorcist, and acolyte) from the major orders (sub-deacon, deacon, and priest), and expected the "tonsured" cleric — a term referring to a shaving of the head that symbolized entry into the clerical state — to advance through all seven stages of ordination, moving further and further, as it were, away from the lay state. Trent insisted that an ordained priest could never again become a layperson, and it denied any claim that priests and the laity were "equally endowed with the same spiritual power." It also defended clerical celibacy, meaning no marriage and no sex.[20]

For centuries, the clergy had symbolized their distinctiveness by wearing special garments, and Trent forbade any deviation. It required that all clerics, regular and secular, "wear the proper clerical dress"; priests who wore lay apparel in public were subject to the deprivation of their offices. The Tridentine

Religious Orders (Oxford: Clarendon Press, 1966), pp. 61-68; Robert Bireley, *The Refashioning of Catholicism, 1450-1700* (Washington, D.C.: Catholic University of America Press, 1999), pp. 20-135. (I am grateful to Scott Appleby for clarifying several technical details in this chapter.)

19. Norman P. Tanner, ed., *Decrees of the Ecumenical Councils*, 2 vols. (London and Washington, D.C.: Sheed and Ward and Georgetown University Press, 1990), vol. 2, pp. 744-51, 763, 772; Bireley, *Refashioning of Catholicism*, pp. 49-57, 102, 104, 107.

20. Tanner, ed., *Decrees of the Ecumenical Councils*, vol. 2, pp. 716, 742; H. S. Schroeder, O. P., ed., *Canons and Decrees of the Council of Trent* (St. Louis: Herder, 1941), pp. 161, 163, 172-73, 182.

insistence on priestly honor reappeared for the next century in the self-descriptions of Catholic priests. In German sermons, the preachers described the priesthood as possessing almost unlimited spiritual power. Both Trent and the German preachers were intent on defining the priestly order in a way that defended church tradition and countered alternative proposals from the followers of Martin Luther.[21]

One consequence of Martin Luther's revolt in 1517 was a proliferation of new views about Christian ministry. Reformers influenced by Luther's example divided into alliances that produced four different understandings of ministry, each reflecting a different attitude about the relation between the clergy and the laity. The procession from the Catholic to the Lutheran, Anglican, Reformed, and Anabaptist conceptions of ministry shows the force of the Protestant Reformation as a laicizing movement that called into question the distinction between laity and clergy.

No Reformation writings had more influence on the doctrine of ministry than Luther's three treatises in 1520 calling for reform. In his *Open Letter to the Christian Nobility of the German Nation,* he announced that all Christians were priests. His doctrine of the priesthood of all believers countered belief that the ordained priesthood served as a special agency of mediation between God and humanity, and he added that the New Testament overruled compulsory celibacy for the clergy.[22]

In *The Babylonian Captivity of the Church,* Luther denied that ordination was a sacrament or that it conferred an indelible character that set the priesthood apart from other baptized Christians. He called for an end to monastic vows and religious orders, arguing that scripture justified no distinction between regular and secular clergy. He undercut the idea of priesthood by denying that the mass was a sacrifice by a priest. He questioned the sacramental character of penance, and while he still encouraged private confession, he denied that the priest had any special authority to pronounce absolution. His argument that scripture provided clear evidence for only two sacraments — baptism and the "sacrament of the bread" (or Eucharist) — challenged the notion that the main office of the clergy was sacramental. And in *The Freedom of a Christian,* he laid out his argument that "faith alone," apart from good works, "justifies, frees, and saves" — a doctrine that

21. Tanner, ed., *Decrees of the Ecumenical Councils,* vol. 2, pp. 743, 744; Renate Dürr, "Images of the Priesthood: An Analysis of Catholic Sermons from the Late Seventeenth Century," *Central European History* 33 (2000): 100-101, 104.

22. Martin Luther, *An Open Letter to the Christian Nobility of the German Nation Concerning the Reform of the Christian Estate, Three Treatises* (Philadelphia: Fortress Press, 1960), pp. 14, 16, 64.

further subverted the sacramental practices on which older understandings of priesthood rested.[23]

At the center of Luther's vision of ministry was the preacher: "The duty of a priest is to preach, and if he does not preach, he is as much a priest as a picture of a man is a man. . . . It is the ministry of the Word that makes the priest and the bishop." Since salvation came through grace by faith alone, and since the proclaimed Word of scripture awakened faith, "the office of preaching" overshadowed every other clerical duty. Ordination was merely the rite by which the church called its preachers to "the ministry of the Word." For over a century, a host of patrons, from city councils to monasteries, had multiplied preaching endowments, especially in the cities, and the fifteenth century witnessed a renaissance of preaching, but no one had ventured to say, as Luther said, that "whoever does not preach the Word" was "no priest at all."[24]

Luther dissolved many of the boundaries between the clergy and the laity. He argued that the ordained minister was simply a Christian chosen by the congregation to fulfill a function and that the congregation could dismiss the preacher who refused to preach the gospel. No rite of ordination was essential. The whole congregation, not the priest or the bishop, held the "keys of the kingdom" — the authority to forgive sins — and Luther invited the laity to confess to each other, assuring them that Christ had "given to every one of his believers the power to absolve even open sins." His encouragement of the clergy to marry drew them more closely into lay society, as did his insistence that in temporal matters they should be as much subject to the civil law as any other citizen. He also criticized the requirement for a special manner of dress that distinguished clergy from laypeople. When Luther preached, he wore a plain dark scholar's gown, adding only a white surplice for communion.[25]

Yet he was not willing to dissolve the boundaries completely, and both he and his movement gradually accentuated clerical authority. Luther was flexible about nomenclature — he employed the terms *minister, deacon, bishop, steward, presbyter* (elder), *preacher,* and *pastor* as interchangeable — but he accepted the need for a special office. He recognized the value of an ordination rite, and around 1535 he wrote a ritual with which ordained elders perpetuated the office by laying their hands on the heads of new "preachers and pastors." In some regions, Lutherans continued to consecrate bishops. In Sweden and Finland, they

23. Martin Luther, *The Babylonian Captivity of the Church, Three Treatises,* pp. 202, 214, 242, 244, 258; Martin Luther, *The Freedom of a Christian, Three Treatises,* p. 282.

24. Luther, *Freedom of a Christian,* pp. 245, 247.

25. Martin Luther, *Concerning the Ministry,* in *Luther's Works,* 55 vols., *Church and Ministry II,* ed. Conrad Bergendoff (Philadelphia: Fortress Press, 1958), vol. 40, pp. 37-38; Luther, *Babylonian Captivity,* p. 214; Luther, *Open Letter to the Christian Nobility,* pp. 18-19.

determined that only bishops could ordain ministers, and they claimed that Lutheran bishops stood in the episcopal succession.[26]

The idea of lay absolution, moreover, never took hold. By 1529, Luther instructed "the simple folk" to confess their sins to "the Priest," beseeching him to "declare forgiveness," though he interpreted this to mean that the minister merely announced God's prior forgiveness. In 1530, the Lutheran Augsburg Confession explained that the normal requirement for communion was confession to the pastor and his announcement of absolution. And Lutherans retained a distinctive clerical dress for liturgical occasions — including not only the long white surplice but also, in some regions, the more colorful chasuble, as an outward symbol of the ministerial office.[27]

A similar ambivalence marked the reformation in the Church of England. In 1550, the Anglican Bishop Thomas Cranmer published a ritual for the ordination of the clergy in a church still divided over its relationship to Roman tradition. Cranmer's rite, modeled on both Catholic and reformed models, conferred authority "to preach the Word of God, and to minister the Holy Sacraments" in a congregation. It omitted any suggestion that ordination conveyed a priestly power of consecrating the body and blood of Christ or offering a sacrifice. It also omitted any mention of the minor orders, and although it recognized bishops, priests, and deacons, it authorized for each order primarily a pastoral office. It removed any hint that the ordination rite was itself a sacramental act that conferred the office.[28]

Cranmer did not want to abandon Catholic tradition altogether. His ritual still assumed that ordination was to "the order of the priesthood," and it still assured the ordinand that "whose sins thou dost forgive, they are forgiven, and whose sins thou dost retain, they are retained." Cranmer kept a separate order of bishops, asserted that they stood in a succession that extended "from the

26. Luther, *Concerning the Ministry,* pp. 35, 40; "Ordination of Ministers of the Word," in *Works of Martin Luther* (Philadelphia: A. J. Holman, 1932), vol. 6, p. 238; Ernest C. Messenger, *The Reformation, the Mass, and the Priesthood,* 2 vols. (London: Longmans, Green, 1936), vol. 1, p. 156; Norman Sykes, *Old Priest and New Presbyter: Episcopacy and Presbyterianism since the Reformation* (Cambridge: Cambridge University Press, 1956), p. 39.

27. Martin Luther, *A Short Method of Confessing to the Priest, for the Use of Simple Folk,* in *Works of Martin Luther,* vol. 6, p. 215; Susan C. Karant-Nunn, *The Reformation of Ritual: An Interpretation of Early Modern Germany* (London: Routledge, 1997), pp. 124, 132; "The Augsburg Confession," *The Creeds of Christendom,* 3 vols., ed. Philip Schaff (1st ed., 1877; Grand Rapids: Baker Book House, 1966), vol. 3, p. 40; Jonathan Strom, *Orthodoxy and Reform: The Clergy in Seventeenth Century Rostock* (Tübingen: Mohr Siebeck, 1999), p. 66.

28. Messenger, *Reformation, Mass, and Priesthood,* pp. 479-80; Paul F. Bradshaw, *The Anglican Ordinal: Its History and Development from the Reformation to the Present* (London: SPCK, 1971), p. 32.

Apostles' times," and apparently thought that the power to ordain belonged only to bishops. He thought that bishops also had the authority individually to exercise the power of the keys, including the power of excommunication, a provision that angered some reformers. And he further angered reformers by specifying that the clergy wear special vestments.[29]

The reform altered clerical status in England. The government dissolved the chantries in which priests had received fees and endowments to celebrate the mass, often in solitude, for the benefit of individual laity, and it destroyed the monastic orders, eliminating the distinction between regular and secular clergy. It permitted the clergy to marry. Many English clerics adopted a Reformation theology that subverted notions of priestly mediation, and a Protestant English Prayer Book discouraged belief that the priest reenacted Christ's sacrifice. The Book of Common Prayer also narrowed the gap between the clergy and the laity by employing English rather than Latin as the language of the liturgy.[30]

Yet the Church of England, under the urging of the crown and the parliament, also retained pre-reformation conceptions of ministry. Against Puritan reformers hoping to emulate the church order of Swiss reformers, Bishop John Whitgift argued in 1572 that it was "the general consent of all the learned fathers, that it pertaineth to the office of a bishop to order and elect ministers of the word," and Anglicans continued to permit only bishops to ordain. By the 1590s, some Anglican theologians argued that the succession of bishops linked the Church of England to the church of the apostles. While Anglicans retained only the three orders, they held on to offices reminiscent of the medieval church, from archbishops and archdeacons to rural and cathedral deans. Following royal directives, moreover, the church made the clergy wear traditional liturgical vestments and an outdoor dress that symbolized their difference from the laity. And conservative clergy, faithful to Catholic tradition, remained active in rural areas and regions distant from centers of authority.[31]

Neither Anglicans nor Lutherans broke away as decisively from medieval traditions of ministry as the Reformed theologians of the Swiss cities. Ulrich Zwingli

29. Messenger, *Reformation, Mass, and Priesthood*, pp. 476, 485; Bradshaw, *Anglican Ordinal*, pp. 42-43; James L. Ainslie, *The Doctrines of Ministerial Order in the Reformed Churches of the 16th and 17th Centuries* (Edinburgh: T. and T. Clark, 1940), p. 73.

30. Bradshaw, *Anglican Ordinal*, pp. 13-34.

31. John Whitgift, *The Defence of the Answer to the Admonition*, in *Works of John Whitgift*, 3 vols., ed. John Ayre (Cambridge: Cambridge University Press, 1851), vol. 1, p. 437; Sykes, *Old Priest and New Presbyter*, pp. 61-64; Patrick Collinson, *The Religion of Protestants: The Church in English Society 1559-1625* (Oxford: The Clarendon Press, 1982), pp. 16, 32; Ronald Hutton, "The Local Impact of the Tudor Reformation," in *The English Reformation Revised*, ed. Christopher Haigh (Cambridge: Cambridge University Press, 1987), pp. 114-38.

in Zurich and John Calvin in Geneva shared most of Luther's theological positions, supported his rejection of older notions of priesthood, and joined him in elevating the office of preaching. In place of the daily masses, the church in Geneva under Calvin decided in 1541 to provide sixteen sermons a week, arranged so that Genevans could attend several. The Reformed churches also discarded traditional ceremonies, church adornments, liturgical vestments, auricular confession, and notions of apostolic succession that endured in the Church of England and some Lutheran regions. Their innovations shaped the understanding of ministry among Swiss, French, Dutch, and Hungarian Protestants, many of the churches of southern Germany, Scottish Presbyterians, the Puritan faction within the Church of England, and the Presbyterian, Congregational, Dutch Reformed, German Reformed, and Baptist churches of colonial America.[32]

Far more than Luther, the Swiss reformers read the New Testament as a source of detailed guidance on the functions of the minister. Calvin found in "the apostolic rule and the practice of the primitive Church" a mandate for four "ordinary" offices of ministry. Only one constituted a distinct clerical class: the minister or pastor (also known as "bishop" or "presbyter") was responsible for preaching and administering the sacraments, and he catechized children and adults, officiated at weddings and funerals, and visited members, the sick, and the imprisoned, in addition to helping with church discipline. The second office, that of teacher (or "doctor"), ensured correct interpretation of scripture. The teacher often taught in the Genevan Academy, though any minister could hold the teaching office. Laity filled the two remaining offices: the ruling elders worked with the minister to maintain discipline in the congregation and community, and the deacons cared for the poor and the sick. Few Reformed churches had the resources to institute the model, but Calvin established it in Geneva, and it remained an ideal. Seventeenth-century Reformed theologians argued that "God doth describe perfectly unto us out of His Worde that forme of government which is lawful, and the officers that are to execute the same: from which it is not lawful for any Christian Church to swarve." They thought that Calvin had come as close as anyone to describing that form of government.[33]

Reformed theologians further narrowed the divide between clergy and laity. In addition to defining lay ministerial offices, they eliminated the medieval

---

32. John Calvin, "Draft Ecclesiastical Ordinances," in *Calvin: Theological Treatises,* ed. J. K. S. Reid (Philadelphia: Westminster Press, 1954), p. 62.

33. John Calvin, *Institutes of the Christian Religion,* 2 vols., ed. John T. McNeill (Philadelphia: Westminster Press, 1960), vol. 2, pp. 1056-61; John Calvin, *The Necessity of Reforming the Church,* in *Calvin: Theological Treatises,* p. 206; Ainslie, *Doctrines of Ministerial Order,* pp. 23, 56-57; William G. Naphy, "The Renovation of the Ministry in Calvin's Geneva," in *The Reformation of the Parishes,* ed. Andrew Pettegree (Manchester: Manchester University Press, 1993), p. 113.

bishopric, and they constructed an ascending series of judicatories — from lo-cal sessions to regional presbyteries to provincial synods and national assem-blies — in which ministers and laity together governed the church. They also eliminated the requirement for private auricular confession to the pastor. While both Zwingli and Calvin permitted such a confession, and Calvin even allowed for a pastoral pronouncement of absolution, both emphasized that God alone could forgive sin, and the Reformed churches soon adopted Calvin's suggestion that the laity could confess to each other or participate in the general confes-sion that was part of public worship.[34]

Reformed churches found yet other ways to draw the laity into the work of ministry. They gave the power of discipline — the correction, excommunica-tion, and restoration of members — to ministers and laity working together. Two-thirds of Calvin's Consistory, the group that oversaw church discipline in Geneva, consisted of laymen. No longer viewing ordination as a sacramental act, Reformed churches sometimes allowed lay elders to join pastors in ordain-ing new clergy. Some called for the election of ministers by the laity, and though this proposal made little headway, the congregation usually enjoyed the right of assent to the presbytery's appointment of a new minister. And Reformed com-munities discarded all the symbolic vestments. Their ministers normally wore ordinary dress or black scholars' gowns in the pulpit.[35]

The Reformed churches did not, however, want to reduce the ministry to merely a lay office; they continued to distinguish the office of the ordained clergy. Only pastors could baptize or administer the Lord's Supper, and they alone had the authority to preach the Word. Reformed churches resisted lay exhorters who claimed that their spiritual gifts alone gave them a right to preach, and they established elaborate procedures of election, examination, and admission to the pastoral office. While they insisted on equality within the ministerial order — rejecting the hierarchy of bishops, priests, and deacons — they also elevated the preaching office to a special status, sought higher educa-tion for their pastors, and assumed that entry into the ministry signified a life-long vocation, from which desertion was a shameful act. The ministry was the agency, as Calvin wrote, through which God "dispenses and distributes his gifts to the church," and it embodied the power of the Spirit. It was to be held "in highest honor and esteem."[36]

To the continental Anabaptists it seemed that the Reformed clergy enjoyed

34. Ainslie, *Doctrines of Ministerial Order*, pp. 80-81; Calvin, *Institutes*, vol. 1, book 3, pp. 634-35.

35. Ainslie, *Doctrines of Ministerial Order*, pp. 37, 88, 151-52, 185-89; Calvin, "Draft Ecclesias-tical Ordinances," pp. 70-71.

36. Calvin, *Institutes*, vol. 2, book 4, p. 1055.

an altogether too exalted position. The fourth significant strand of Protestant reform, the Anabaptists included groups that sprang up in Germany in 1521 and Switzerland in 1525. Their core allegiance was to an understanding of the church as a separated community of the faithful, and their name (which meant "rebaptism") came from their insistence on adult baptism as the sign of entry into church membership. The movement reached no consensus about either belief or practice, but the largest group, which followed the leadership of Menno Simons in Holland and Friesland, formed a permanent community. Often vehemently anti-clerical, they viewed both other Protestant pastors and Catholic priests as traitors to the gospel, immoral and arrogant scoundrels who accepted salaries, governed false churches, and usurped the authority to preach.[37]

Insisting on the priesthood of all believers and the sole headship of Christ over the church, the earliest Anabaptists had no designated ministers. In mid-January 1525, the layman Conrad Grebel in Zurich baptized the former priest George Blaurock. A few days later, laymen in nearby Zollikon celebrated the Lord's Supper. These actions initiated a period in which lay Christians assumed duties elsewhere reserved for an ordained clergy. They preached, administered sacraments, confessed to one another, and wielded the power of the keys by exercising the discipline of excommunication and restoration in their congregations. Women as well as men preached on street corners and drew converts into the community. Despite savage repression, charismatic lay prophets and missionaries wandered the land and preached on the authority of their inward call. The first few months of the movement represented a logical culmination of the laicizing impulse latent in Luther's doctrine of the universal priesthood.[38]

As early as 1527, however, Anabaptists were electing pastors to "see to the care of the body of Christ," and some of them expected the congregation to support the pastor financially. By that time, some Anabaptists ordained "bishops" to officiate at baptism, communion, and ordinations; "ministers of the word" to preach and teach; and "deacons" to care for the poor and the church's material needs. In 1559, the Mennonite preacher Dirk Philips warned, in his pamphlet on *The Sending of Preachers or Teachers,* that it "was not everyone's thing to teach God's Word and to distribute the sacraments of Christ," and that normally no one was to assume the office of the minister without being chosen and ordained by the congregation. But even then, many congregations expected their pastors to earn a

37. Hans Jürgen Goertz, *The Anabaptists,* trans. Trevor Johnson (London: Routledge, 1996), pp. 77-87.

38. George Huntston Williams, *The Radical Reformation,* 3rd ed. (Kirksville: Sixteenth Century Journal Publishers, 1992), pp. 214, 218; Goertz, *The Anabaptists,* p. 115; Franklin H. Littell, *The Anabaptist View of the Church* (Boston: Beacon Press, 1958), p. 92.

living by manual labor, and they had no use for a learned ministry. They were suspicious of too much distance between the laity and their newly ordained clergy.[39]

Authorizing the Clergy

The logic of the Reformation — carried to an extreme — threatened to eliminate any distinction between clergy and laity. If all Christians were priests, why indeed was it necessary to have a separate clerical office? And how, granted such an office, were Protestants to understand its authority? For Catholics, the issue was different. How were they to maintain the momentum of clerical reform that Trent had set in motion and thus demonstrate to a divided Europe that the revitalized priesthood deserved the support and loyalty of European Christians? Both Protestants and Catholics turned their attention in the late sixteenth century to the problem of clerical authority.

The clergy had never been seen as a "profession" in the modern sense of an occupational group offering a service that required a special education. The term "profession" usually designated the avowal of poverty, chastity, and obedience that defined the "regular" Catholic clergy. Even though the Quaker George Fox could speak in the mid-seventeenth century of the "three great professions" of "physic, divinity (so called) and the law," it was not until the early eighteenth century, when the English essayist Joseph Addison wrote of "the three great professions of divinity, law, and physick," that the term began to attain the meanings it later held.[40]

The medieval clergy shared no common occupation. As one of the three estates of medieval society, they understood themselves, alongside the nobility and the commons, as a collectivity with a distinctive status, not an occupational group. The priestly order could include monks who resided within monastic enclosures, friars who wandered from place to place, teachers in schools and universities, lawyers in service to the church or the state, civil servants, diplomatic envoys, administrators, and others who never exercised the cure of souls in a parish. Many priests labored in chantries, or at chapels or side altars, in which they celebrated the mass for laity who gave endowments or paid fees.

---

39. Michael Sattler, "The Schleitheim Confession," in *Creeds of the Churches*, ed. John Leith, 3rd ed. (Atlanta: John Knox Press, 1982), p. 287; Eddie Mabry, *Balthasar Hubmaier's Doctrine of the Church* (Lanham: University Press of America, 1994), p. 88; Dirk Philips, *The Sending of Preachers or Teachers, The Enchiridion*, in *The Writings of Dirk Philips*, ed. Cornelius J. Dyck, William E. Keeney, and Alvin J. Beachy (Scottdale: Herald Press, 1992), pp. 218-19; Claus Peter Clasen, *Anabaptism: A Social History 1525-1618* (Ithaca: Cornell University Press, 1972), p. 80.

40. Rosemary O'Day, *The Professions in Early Modern England, 1450-1800* (Harlow: Pearson, 2000), pp. 3, 4.

Priests had no common educational preparation. Some village priests merely memorized the Latin words for the most familiar rituals. What defined the medieval priest was the authority to forgive sins and celebrate the mass, but many priests had functions unrelated to their sacramental power.[41]

Both the Catholic Reform and the Protestant Reformation moved away from the medieval past. Both movements aimed at a more educated clergy devoted to pastoral service within a community. Both attempted to attach to the pastoral office a high sense of moral responsibility, and both created institutions that nurtured a collective awareness of membership in a common calling. Catholics and Protestants joined in seeking greater internal control of recruitment and placement, and both groups attempted to reduce the power of lay patrons, whether nobles or princes.

The changes grew partly out of disappointed hopes about the momentum of reform. Despite the grand ideals of Trent and the confidence of the Protestant reformers, the ministry was hard to renew. As early as 1527, Luther was complaining, with reference to Protestant clergy, that "many pastors are practically unfit and incompetent to teach," and the visitations by Lutheran superintendents between 1527 and 1535 produced disillusioned reports of negligent and uninformed preachers. Calvin deposed nine ministers in Geneva, and of the remaining twenty-two, five resigned and two died. Reformers in Zurich complained about the preaching, and Zwingli's successor, Johann Heinrich Bullinger, confessed that it would take a long time for the rural clergy to meet the new expectations. Catholic reformers conceded that their vision also was hard to realize. The visitation records of bishops for decades after Trent reveal continuing pluralism and non-residence, nepotism, clerical misconduct, poor preaching, concubinage, and unseemly disputes with parishioners.[42]

Most early Protestant ministers had been Catholic priests, and the reformers were disappointed at how slowly they absorbed new ideas and practices. In Zurich, 75 percent of the preachers between 1523 and 1531 held a clerical post before the Reformation. Most Lutheran pastors in Saxony before 1550 had been priests, and others had been clerical schoolmasters, sextons, and choir directors. A survey of 176 Protestant preachers in Germany between 1520 and 1550 showed that three-

41. O'Day, *Professions in Early Modern England*, pp. 53-54; Tellenbach, *Church in Western Europe*, p. 341.

42. Susan C. Karant-Nunn, *Luther's Pastors: The Reformation in the Ernestine Countryside* (Philadelphia: The American Philosophical Society, 1979), pp. 8, 12 23, 24, 29; Naphy, "Renovation of the Ministry in Calvin's Geneva," p. 119; Andrew Pettegree, "The Clergy and the Reformation: From 'devilish priesthood' to new professional elite," in *Reformation of the Parishes*, p. 9; Bruce Gordon, "Preaching and the Reform of the Clergy in the Swiss Reformation," in *Reformation of the Parishes*, p. 80; Bireley, *Refashioning of Catholicism*, pp. 62-64, 101, 145-46.

fourths had been clerics earlier. Most Reformed clergy in Holland had been in Catholic orders. Almost all the English clergy in the city of York before 1560 had served in Catholic orders, and as late as 1577 Archbishop Edwin Sandys instituted investigations into their conservatism. It took time for this large company of ex-priests, many of whom were not literate, to adapt to Protestant ideals.[43]

When Catholic clergy withdrew — or accepted expulsion — from the parishes of Protestant regions, the result was a shortage of able preachers. Until the 1540s, England had more priests than parishes, but a decline in numbers that began in 1536 became so severe that by 1559 the Church of England felt constrained to ordain every applicant for a clerical post, a policy that it abandoned after two years. Dutch Reformed congregations, facing a shortage, offered admission to men of limited abilities and questionable doctrine, but then regretted the decision. As early as the 1530s, Lutherans in Ernestine Saxony were finding it hard to attract new clergy. And the shortages were not limited to Protestant regions. While some Catholic areas, especially in the cities, had more clerics than they could accommodate, shortages in others, like Austria and Bohemia, persisted until the eighteenth century.[44]

Part of the problem was that diocesan clergy received low pay and suffered from low status. The more fortunate higher clergy — from modestly paid parish priests to wealthy prelates — enjoyed the returns from a benefice (a right to receive revenues from a parish, a property, or an endowment). But large numbers of Catholic clergy held no benefice and had to hire themselves out to priests who held several, for whom they served as poorly paid curates (assistants). In England, as elsewhere, the non-beneficed clergy outnumbered priests with benefices. Most rural clergy farmed a plot of land, called a glebe. They received additional payment from mandatory tithes (usually paid in produce or in labor rather than cash) and for services like marriages, baptisms, burials, and private endowed masses. In the cities, the trend was toward monetary payments, but they tended not to increase with inflation.[45]

43. Gordon, "Preaching and the Reform of the Clergy," p. 68; R. W. Scribner, "Practice and Principle in the German Towns: Preachers and People," in *Reformation Principle and Practice,* ed. Peter Newman Brooks (London: Scolar Press, 1980), p. 99; Claire Gross, "Priests into Ministers: The Establishment of Protestant Practice in the City of York 1530-1630," in *Reformation Principle and Practice,* p. 221; Richard Fitzsimmons, "Building a Reformed Ministry in Holland, 1572-1585," in *Reformation of the Parishes,* p. 181.

44. Pettegree, "Clergy and the Reformation," p. 11; Fitzsimmons, "Building a Reformed Ministry in Holland," p. 177; Michael L. Zell, "Economic Problems of the Parochial Clergy in the Sixteenth Century," in *Princes and Paupers in the English Church 1500-1800,* ed. Rosemary O'Day and Felicity Heal (Totowa: Barnes and Noble, 1981), pp. 22, 31; Karant-Nunn, *Luther's Pastors,* p. 20; Bireley, *Refashioning of Catholicism,* p. 145.

45. R. Po-Chia Hsia, *The World of Catholic Renewal 1540-1770* (Cambridge: Cambridge

Protestant clergy also languished in poverty, especially after cities began to give them a yearly cash salary. They lost the income once generated by chantries, festival offerings, private masses, and fees. Luther complained that the reformed clergy were "poorer than their predecessors" and felt that they were "reduced to beggary." In the countryside, they sometimes lived in crumbling cottages and huts, owning no land and leaving no inheritance. Some Lutheran pastors in Brandenburg Ansbach-Kulmbach lived at a level of bare subsistence. Before 1560 in England many of the clergy were poor, with vast disparities between the upper and lower levels. Some even in urban areas farmed, taught school, took part-time jobs, or held more than one living. Pluralism continued among Protestants for reasons of economic necessity. Family responsibilities for Protestant clergy made financial want even more stressful.[46]

Patrons were to blame for some of the distress. Royal officials and wealthy private families — or even colleges and monasteries — purchased the rights to revenues from parishes and then paid the pastor after they took their cut. Patronage complicated reform, since it took placement out of the hands of the church and gave it to powerful families or court officials who might grant a benefice to political favorites, friends, or even the highest bidder, with little or no consideration for competence. The right to present a cleric to a benefice (known as an advowson) could be a valuable privilege, and patrons resisted any limits on their control of it. The Council of Trent had to recognize "the legitimate rights of patronage" even while warning that "ecclesiastical benefices cannot be reduced to servitude." The Council tried at least to empower bishops to make final decisions about appointments. Protestants made similar accommodations, seeing little option for change, for example, when the Lord Chancellor of England had the right to fill about 100 livings a year and the crown even more. In the late sixteenth century in England, a majority of the benefices were subject to patronage.[47]

No one solution could rectify the many perceived ills, but throughout Europe the one course of action that drew broad support from church officials

---

University Press, 1998), p. 115; Karant-Nunn, *Luther's Pastors*, pp. 33, 39-40; Claire Cross, "The Income of Provincial Urban Clergy," in *Princes and Paupers*, p. 69.

46. Karant-Nunn, *Luther's Pastors*, p. 43; C. Scott Dixon, "Rural Resistance, the Lutheran Pastor, and the Territorial Church in Brandenburg Ansbach-Kalmbach, 1528-1603," in *Reformation of the Parishes*, pp. 92-99; Zell, "Economic Problems," pp. 31-41; Cross, "Income of Provincial Urban Clergy," p. 77.

47. Rosemary O'Day, *The English Clergy: The Emergence and Consolidation of a Profession 1558-1642* (Leicester: Leicester University Press, 1979), p. 79; Tanner, ed., *Decrees of the Ecumenical Councils*, pp. 789-90; O'Day, *Professions in Early Modern England*, p. 67; Collinson, *Religion of Protestants*, p. 93.

and pious rulers alike was clerical education. Partly in response to the growing literacy of the European laity, and partly because of the new emphasis on preaching, both Catholics and Protestants placed their hopes for reform in an educated clergy. In 1563, the Council of Trent decreed that every diocese was to establish a seminary in which boys destined for a clerical office would receive instruction in "ecclesiastical studies," including scripture, canon law, the delivery of homilies, the performance of rites and ceremonies, the sacrament of penance, singing, church finance, grammar, "and other useful skills." Some of the bishops attempted to establish such schools, though it took over a century for the seminary movement to take hold. In the meantime, the Jesuits took up the slack. By 1626 they had founded 444 colleges and 100 seminaries. In 1552, with the founding of the German College — the first of several national colleges in Rome — the Vatican began also to support education for diocesan clergy, and eventually other orders, like the Lazarists under St. Vincent de Paul in France, experimented with new ways of forming an educated clergy. Catholics founded fifty new universities between 1550 and 1700, continuing a tradition of combining university training with apprenticeships to form the clerical elite.[48]

Clerical education assumed paramount importance among Protestants because their emphasis on preaching required a clergy able to interpret biblical texts. Having rejected the older view of ordination, they turned to education as a means of giving clergy an authoritative status. As late as 1548, complaints could be heard in Lutheran Germany about "tailors, cobblers, and the like" trying to fill Protestant pulpits, but between 1550 and 1700, Protestants in Europe founded thirty-three new universities, which took theological education for the clergy as a central aim. They made slow but steady progress. In 1540, only 28 percent of the Protestant clergy in Ansbach and Kulmbach in Germany attended a university, but by 1600 the number approached 80 percent. By the mid-seventeenth century, a graduate clergy was becoming the norm in Reformed Holland. In the 1580s, only 14 percent of the English clergy in Coventry and Litchfield were university graduates; by the 1630s, the ministry in England had become a predominantly graduate profession.[49]

The example of England illumines the extent to which Protestants combined university education with a variety of other institutions that nurtured

48. Tanner, ed., *Decrees of the Ecumenical Councils*, p. 751; Hsia, *World of Catholic Renewal*, p. 32; O'Malley, "Ministry to Outsiders," pp. 253-61; Bireley, *Refashioning of Catholicism*, pp. 135, 142; Joseph White, *The Diocesan Seminary in the United States: A History from the 1780s to the Present* (Notre Dame: University of Notre Dame, 1989), pp. 12-21.

49. Bireley, *Refashioning of Catholicism*, p. 135; Dixon, "Rural Resistance," pp. 88-89; Pettegree, "Clergy and the Reformation," p. 13; O'Day, *Professions in Early Modern England*, p. 73.

clerical formation and gave the clergy a sense of belonging to a group set apart. In response to complaints that university training offered little guidance for pastoral work, church officials drew the clergy into associations that improved their skills and nurtured a collective identity. At synods, convocations, lecture-ships, Bible studies, and prophesyings (in which different clergy preached ser-mons on the same text), English rectors and curates deepened the knowledge that distinguished them from laypersons. Catholics in Europe made similar use of synods and visitations to enhance priestly abilities.[50]

At the same time, the clergy produced a collection of edifying manuals that deepened the discourse about pastoral responsibilities. Depicting the ministry as necessary for salvation, they emphasized their roles as exemplary Christians, obligated to perform duties of charity, hospitality, learning, and piety. This out-pouring of books and sermons lifted up the duty of fidelity to the work of the parish. Among English Protestants, for example, a flow of pastoral manuals, such as Richard Bernard's *Faithfull Shepherd,* George Herbert's *Priest to the Temple,* and Richard Baxter's *Reformed Pastor,* promoted an ethic of pastoral duty. In a similar manner, the Council of Trent reminded priests that they were to know their parishioners, serve as examples, care for the poor, and show devo-tion to all their "pastoral duties." This required them, the Council emphasized, to "stay with and watch their flocks."[51]

Some have interpreted the emphasis on clerical duties — especially self-discipline and the moral discipline of parishioners — as part of the effort of the emerging nation-states to impose social discipline and authority on unruly subjects. And it is true that both Catholics and Protestants accepted close supervision and oversight by lay rulers, whether Protestant princes, Catholic emperors, or local magistrates. Certainly their desire to form a pious and moral laity coincided with the goals of governing authorities. But the clergy also as-sumed the right and duty to criticize rulers, an assumption leading to frequent conflict, and they saw themselves as mediators of the holy in ways that could distance them from the objectives of the state. They were interested in more than moral regulation, and their concern for clerical improvement was more than a desire to be effective civil bureaucrats.[52]

---

50. O'Day, *English Clergy,* pp. 70, 167; Collinson, *Religion of Protestants,* pp. 122, 129; Hsia, *World of Catholic Renewal,* p. 117.

51. Neal Ensle, "Patterns of Godly Life: The Ideal Parish Minister in Sixteenth- and Seventeenth-Century English Thought," *The Sixteenth Century Journal* 28 (1997): 3-28; Tanner, ed., *Decrees of the Ecumenical Councils,* p. 744; Collinson, *Religion of Protestants,* pp. 108-09.

52. Luise Schorn-Schütte, "The Christian Clergy in the Early Modern Holy Roman Em-pire: A Comparative Study," *Sixteenth Century Journal* 29 (1998): 729-30; R. Po-Chia Hsia, *Social Discipline in the Reformation: Central Europe 1550-1750* (London: Routledge, 1989), pp. 6-29;

The campaign for an educated and disciplined clergy faced hurdles. For a long period in England, for example, the ministry remained divided between an educated elite, consisting largely of university graduates, and a persisting cadre of unlearned clerics who embodied more clearly the standards of the local village than any uniform ideal of the godly pastor. The English Presbyterian Richard Baxter recalled that several of the parishes in rural Shropshire in the 1620s suffered patiently under drunken, ignorant, and scandalous clergy who never preached a sermon. The growing reliance on university education for all parish clergy could also distance the minister from the villagers and set off populist revolts in support of "plowman" and "mechanick" preachers, earnest lay exhorters who felt the inspiration of the Spirit. The reformer William Dell in England declared in the mid-seventeenth century that he would "rather hear a plain countryman speak in the church, that came from the plough, than the best orthodox minister."[53]

In seventeenth-century England, the civil wars of the 1640s produced a flurry of mechanic preachers who excoriated the parish clergy because of their educational pretensions. Baptists, Quakers, and "sectaries" on the margins of the English establishment declared that a call from God was the sole qualification for the exercise of the preaching office, and they dismissed the parish clergy as "hireling priests" who lacked the Spirit-filled power of a divine call. The Quakers George Fox and James Nayler asserted in 1653 that the true ministry was a gift of Jesus Christ and needed "no addition of human help and learning." They used the argument, familiar in populist circles, that Jesus "chose herdsmen, fishermen, and plowman" as his disciples and "fitted them immediately without the help of man." These groups carried forward an ancient anti-clerical and laicizing impulse that attained new force as a result of the Reformation and its doctrine of the priesthood of all believers. It would become a lasting feature of ministry in America.[54]

For the clergy of seventeenth-century Europe and England, the clerical office occupied the highest pinnacle of honor possible to mere mortals. Catholic priests spoke of themselves as holding "unlimited" power and might, a power that exceeded that of the angels, since God had never entrusted the key to heaven to an angel but only to a priest. An Anglican like George Herbert could

---

Luise Schorn-Schütte, "Priest, Preacher, Pastor: Research on Clerical Office in Early Modern Europe," *Central European History* 33 (2000): 1-39.

53. Collinson, *Religion of Protestants*, pp. 93-105; Barbara A. Johnson, *Reading Piers Plowman and the Pilgrim's Progress* (Carbondale: Southern Illinois University Press, 1992), pp. 76, 85, 96.

54. George Fox and James Nayler, *Soul's Errand to Damascus*, in *Early Quaker Writings 1650-1700*, ed. Hugh Barbour and Arthur O. Roberts (Grand Rapids: Eerdmans, 1973), p. 259.

speak of the minister as the "deputy" of Christ, standing "in God's stead to his Parish," authorized to "do that which Christ did," and able in the sacrament to "serve . . . up" with his hands the God who commanded the whole world. The English Calvinist reformer William Perkins spoke of the minister as the "Embassadour of the great Jehovah," the "very mouth of God," the "messenger of the Lord of Hosts," God's "angel." Perkins rejoiced that angels were called ministers and that ministers were called angels "as though they were almost all one." But ministers possessed an authority, he added, "which is so great, as never was given to any [other] creature, man or angel."[55]

These commendations grew out of an elevated sense of the ministerial office. The office itself conferred authority, but the new emphasis on education complemented this "official" authority. Both the advocates and the opponents of an educated clergy shifted attention from status to function: what clerics knew and what they did as preachers and pastors conferred authority. Rational and personal forms of authority now functioned more prominently alongside older medieval views of the authority of the office. In multiple ways, sixteenth-century reform introduced ideas and practices that exerted pressure on older conceptions of ministry, and on the outer margins of European culture the American clergy would have to adapt themselves to at least some of the consequences.

55. Renate Dürr, "Images of the Priesthood: An Analysis of Catholic Sermons from the Late Seventeenth Century," *Central European History* 33 (2000): 87-107; George Herbert, *The Country Parson,* in John N. Wall Jr., ed., *George Herbert* (New York: Paulist Press, 1981), pp. 55, 82; George Herbert, *The Temple,* in Wall Jr., ed., *George Herbert,* pp. 285-86; William Perkins, *The Workes of that Famous and Worthy Minister of Christ, in the Universitie of Cambridge, Mr. William Perkins,* 3 vols. (London: Legatt, Legge, and Welbie, 1612-13), vol. 2, pp. 159, 672; vol. 3, pp. 429, 438.

CHAPTER 2

A Bounded Authority

1493-1699

The American clergy shared with their European counterparts an exalted conception of their office. In New England, ministers described themselves as "messengers and ambassadors of God," instruments of saving grace "sent of God." Thomas Shepard in Cambridge explained that ministers stood "in the room of Christ" and that "their power" was "the power of Christ Jesus." God had set them apart and furnished them with "special abilities" so that they could serve as the means through which "the Spirit of Grace is principally and most abundantly dispensed." Without denying the freedom of God to save through other means, they considered "a powerfull Ministry" as "the ordinary means" that God had appointed to dispense salvation.[1]

To exalt the office was not to elevate the pride of the officeholder. Clerics acknowledged their own unworthiness. Shepard bemoaned his sinfulness, his lack of wisdom, and his inability. The Jesuit Christopher Morris in Maryland confessed his "sinnes and imperfections." The exaltation of the office made the weaknesses of its occupants all the more visible and painful. The layman

---

1. David D. Hall, *The Faithful Shepherd: A History of the New England Ministry in the Seventeenth Century* (Chapel Hill: University of North Carolina Press, 1972), p. 5; Richard Mather, *Church-Government and Church Covenant Discussed* (London: R. D. and G. D., 1643), p. 80; Thomas Shepard, *A Defence of the Nine Positions* (London: printer not given, 1645), p. 170; Thomas Shepard, *Subjection to Christ in all His Ordinances* (London: John Rothwell, 1652), p. 104; Shepard, *The Parable of the Ten Virgins Opened and Applied* (Rothwell, 1660), "To the Reader," n.p., pp. 96-97; Thomas Hooker, *The Unbelievers Preparing for Christ* (London: Andrew Crooke, 1638), p. 2. See David D. Hall's helpful introductory essay to the second printing of *The Faithful Shepherd* (Cambridge: Harvard University Press for Harvard Theological Studies, 2006), pp. xvii-xxxv.

Edward Johnson in New England viewed the Puritan clergy as men called by Christ to positions of authority in the churches, but he also recognized that they were "earthen vessels, men subject to like infirmities with our selves; sorry men, and carrying bout with them a body of sinne and death, men subject to erre."[2]

The office conferred authority, but the authority had boundaries. The errors and infirmities of the officeholders did not subvert the authority of the office, but contingencies of personality, judgment, and circumstance always affected the ways in which colonial laity accepted their ministers. Even in a society that honored ministerial authority, preachers and priests encountered, in the mundane transactions of towns and villages, not only the admiration but also the resistance and inertia of both ordinary and powerful people. When the minister Edmund Brown of Sudbury, Massachusetts, became embroiled in a dispute over land distribution in 1656, his opponents warned him not to "meddle." "Setting aside your office," said his chief competitor, "I regard you no more than another man." When Brown persisted, the opponents quit coming to church, and when he requested a council of ministers to resolve the dispute, the church would not consent. The clergy held an authoritative office, but their influence also rested on the quality of their relationships with men, women, and children who accorded them respect and honor but resisted anything they saw as presumption or excessive demand.[3]

Mission

The story of the clergy in America began with the Catholic mission to the people Europeans called Indians. After 1549, Spanish Dominicans, Jesuits, and Franciscans competed to construct mission stations, but only the success of the mission in St. Augustine after 1565 enabled the priests to expand their work more deeply into the eastern coastlands. In 1595, Spanish Franciscans organized five provinces along the coast, and within the next six decades they built thirty-eight mission stations that claimed the allegiance of some 26,000 Indians. Over

2. John Cotton, *The True Constitution of a Particular Visible Church, Proved by Scripture* (London: Satterthwaite, 1642), p. 2; Thomas Shepard, *Meditations and Spiritual Experiences of Mr. Thomas Shepard* (Edinburgh: Printing House, 1749), pp. 29, 33, 52; Robert Emmett Curran, S.J., ed., *American Jesuit Spirituality: The Maryland Tradition, 1643-1900* (New York: Paulist Press, 1988), p. 57; Edward Johnson, *Wonder-Working Providence of Sions Saviour in New England*, ed., William Frederick Poole (Andover: Warren F. Draper, 1867), p. 120.

3. Sumner Chilton Powell, *Puritan Village: The Formation of a New England Town* (1st ed., 1963; Garden City: Doubleday, 1965), pp. 161, 164.

a thousand miles away, Spanish conquests in 1598 began a thirty-year effort in New Mexico that produced twenty-five mission stations overseeing more than sixty Native American pueblos. Eventually, French Jesuits and Recollects were at work in the far north among the peoples who lived along the St. Laurent River. These early Catholic missionaries recognized — and sometimes asserted — that their endeavors served the ends of the European monarchs, but they understood themselves mainly as servants to "the master . . . of Heaven, of Earth, and of Hell."[4]

This dual service to two masters generated tensions. The priests had no reservations about legitimating European colonial aims. When the Jesuit Jean Allouez raised the cross before representatives of fourteen Indian nations in New France in 1671, he also erected the French Escutcheon and told the assembly that "the Great Captain of France, whom we call King," was the "Captain of the greatest Captains," without equal in the world. Missionaries reminded the monarchs that their missions could enhance royal "profits and advantages." Don Luís de Velasco, the Viceroy of New Spain, assured King Philip II that Dominican missionaries could "pacify" and "colonize" as well as evangelize. In the French and Spanish missions, the missionaries dwelt not only in the sanctuary but also in the marketplace of profit and calculation.[5]

Missionaries highlighted their usefulness to the monarchs because they depended on governmental support. The Franciscans in Florida, for example, received an annual subsidy from the royal treasury in Mexico City, designed to cover their subsistence and clothing as well as "ornaments, crosses, chalices, bells, and other things necessary for the service of the divine cult." The subsidies sometimes failed to materialize, or arrived two years late, and the missions survived only because the Indians contributed food as an offering to the church and a payment for priestly burials and weddings. But Indian contributions alone could not maintain the mission. Even though the missionaries lived for the most part in "holy poverty" and honored ascetic self-denial, they still needed the monarchs.[6]

---

4. R. G. Thwaites, ed., *Jesuit Relations and Allied Documents*, 73 vols. (Cleveland: Burrows Brothers, 1896-1901), vol. 15, p. 111; Maynard Geiger, *Biographical Dictionary of the Franciscans in Spanish Florida and Cuba* (Paterson: St. Anthony Guild Press, 1940), p. 125.

5. Thwaites, ed., *Jesuit Relations*, vol. 15, p. 111; George P. Hammond and Agapito Rey, eds., *Don Juan de Oñate: Colonizer of New Mexico*, 2 vols. (Albequerque: The University of New Mexico Press, 1953), vol. 1, p. 343; Herbert Eugene Bolton, ed., *Spanish Exploration in the Southwest* (New York: Charles Scribner's Sons, 1916), p. 131; John Tracy Ellis, ed., *Documents of American Catholic History* (Milwaukee: Bruce, 1956), p. 12; France B. Scholes, *Church and State in New Mexico 1610-1650* (Albuquerque: The University of New Mexico Press, 1937), pp. 11-22, 70-84.

6. Ellis, ed., *Documents*, p. 12; David Hurst Thomas, ed., *The Missions of Spanish Florida*

Yet even as they depended on royal money and relied on royal soldiers, the missionaries could be unrelenting critics of state-supported cruelty. They often struggled against the governing authorities, complaining that exploitation of the Indians stood in the way of conversion. Brother Juan de Escalona's impassioned letter of 1601 to the Spanish viceroy complaining of "the great outrages against the Indians" committed under Governor Don Juan de Oñate has served as a reminder of religious resistance to secular authorities. No other group among the French or Spanish in America so frequently defended the Indians against the governing regimes as the mission priests. When the governors thwarted the purpose of the mission, the priests complained.[7]

The priests saw their animating purpose as "the salvation of souls." By preaching, teaching, and exemplifying the faith, they would bring the natives into "the fold of the Catholic church." The Indians of the pueblo of Santo Domingo learned, when the Spanish came, that "if they were baptized and became good Christians, they would go to heaven to enjoy an eternal life of great bliss in the presence of God. If they did not become Christians, they would go to hell to suffer cruel and everlasting torment." Once within the fold, the converts could absorb the saving "knowledge of our Lord," cultivate the practices of divine worship, and begin to "live an orderly and decent Christian life."[8]

Converts learned the forms of devotion appropriate to the "altars where the body and blood of the Son of God may be offered." The priests sought to gather migratory Indians into villages because such close living made it possible to "preach and administer the sacraments to them with greater facility." The initial aim was baptism, often administered to large numbers, though Fray Alonso de Benavides, the first religious superior to the mission of New Mexico, observed that thousands of converts had to wait for baptism while they received instruction in the faith. Only bishops could offer the sacrament of confirmation, and the bishop of Santiago de Cuba Florida rarely visited, but the priests could grant absolution, dispense the last rites, and celebrate marriage, so the sacramental system remained largely intact. In some missions of New Mexico, the Pueblo Indians greeted the Franciscan friars along the road

(New York: Garland, 1991), p. 70; Robert Allen Matter, "Economic Basis of the Seventeenth-Century Florida Missions," *Florida Historical Quarterly* 52 (1973): 18-38; Lucy L. Wenhold and John R. Swanton, "A 17th Century Letter of Gabriel Diaz Vera Calderón, Bishop of Cuba," *Smithsonian Miscellaneous Collections* 95 (1936): 1-14.

7. Hammond and Rey, eds., *Don Juan de Oñate*, p. 1:694.

8. Thomas, ed. *Missions of Spanish Florida*, p. 69; Frederick W. Hodge and Theodore H. Lewis, eds., *Spanish Explorers in the Southern United States 1528-1543* (New York: Charles Scribner's Sons, 1907), p. 190; Hammond and Rey, eds., *Don Juan de Oñate*, pp. 60, 65, 339.

by calling out: "Praised be our Lord Jesus Christ! Praised be the most holy Sacrament!"[9]

The missionaries dwelt within a world of wonders. Both they and their Indian converts felt that they were surrounded by invisible powers about which the clergy had a distinctive knowledge. They were experts in the mysteries of the invisible world, and they claimed access to forces that brought healing and flourishing. The accounts of the missions overflow with miracle stories. Benavides said that the friars of New Mexico were able to convert the Pira and Tompira people because God favored them with "great miracles." Miraculous events often followed conversions, miracles delivered the fathers from danger, prayer brought rain in times of drought, lightning struck enemies of the friars, and the cross produced countless healings.[10]

Within this cosmos of wonders, the missions settled into a routine of prayer, sacramental celebration, pastoral labor, and administrative oversight. In the New Mexico missions, the priests and lay brothers rose at dawn each day as a Christian Indian rang the bell for Prime, one of the obligatory "hours" of prayer and devotion. After overseeing the chanting of the Indian singers in the choir and celebrating the morning mass, the priests provided instruction (on matters both religious and mundane) for two hours before saying the high mass and administering sacraments. At mealtime, they provided food for everyone, and after lunch they oversaw the schools, where boys learned to read, write, pray, and assist the priests, or they rehearsed the choirs and taught the Indians to play musical instruments, or they performed marriage ceremonies or traveled to neighboring pueblos for mass and confession.

Feast days, which were numerous, meant additional masses, sometimes with solemn processions and special services of baptism. The priests devoted a good part of one day every week to baptisms in the mission church. And they paused seven times each day and night to recite the prayers and scriptures of the *Breviarum Romanum* at the eight canonical hours of the day, often in harmony with the chanting of the singers in the choir. "Never do the matins at midnight fail," wrote Benavides, "and the other hours, and high mass at its time." Each day resembled every other.[11]

9. Hammond and Rey, eds., *Don Juan de Oñate*, p. 77, 135; Frederick Webb Hodge, George P. Hammond, and Agapito Rey, eds., *Fray Alonso de Benavides' Revised Memorial of 1634* (Albuquerque: The University of New Mexico Press, 1945), p. 132; Ellis, ed., *Documents*, p. 19; Mrs. Edward E. Ayer, ed., *The Memorial of Fray Alonso de Benavides 1630* (Chicago: privately printed, 1916), p. 34.

10. Hodge, et al., eds., *Benavides*, 53, 58, 72-73, 133, 195; Gaspar Pérez de Villagrá, *History of New Mexico* (1st ed., 1610; Los Angeles: Quivira Society, 1933), pp. 128, 147.

11. Ayer, ed., *Memorial*, p. 67; Hodge, et al., eds., *Benavides*, p. 61.

The priests did not limit themselves to sacred work. They oversaw grain and cattle farming and the weaving of wool, and they conducted training schools in the trades. They adjudicated disputes among the Indians, directed the work of sextons, cooks, bell ringers, and gardeners, distributed food and clothing to the poor, and supervised the building of churches and other structures. "All the wheels of this clock," Benavides wrote, "must be kept in good order by the friar, without neglecting any detail, otherwise all would be totally lost."[12]

Many performed these duties in isolation from other missionaries or as members of remote small groups. Benavides reported in 1634 that mission villages in New Mexico usually had "only one religious each," responsible for ministering to four or more neighboring pueblos. The work could be accomplished only because a small group of Indians who were "devoted to the service of the church" lived with the friar in the convent and maintained the daily round of sacred activities. In the decade following 1623, Benavides had only fifty-five friars in his whole province. More than half a century later, only about 120 Franciscan friars labored in New Mexico, while ninety worked in eleven convent houses in Florida.[13]

The missionaries enjoyed successes but encountered implacable resistance. They felt frustration when converts incorporated Christian beliefs into traditional views of powers and spirits. Indian shamans and medicine men opposed the missionaries and ridiculed their gospel. Violent revolts punctuated the missionary era, and the priests sometimes suffered the brunt of attacks from people who attributed droughts, sickness, and disasters to the abandonment of ancestral ways. In 1597, the natives of Guale Island, off the coast of Georgia, rebelled against the Spanish because the Franciscan friars had obstructed their "dances, banquets, feasts, celebrations, fires, and wars" and caused them to "lose the ancient valor and dexterity inherited from our ancestors." They killed every Franciscan they could find. In 1680, the Pueblos of New Mexico rebelled against the suppression of their ritual sites and burned "all the images and temples, rosaries and crosses" of the mission. Most of the mission outposts eventually disappeared.[14]

---

12. Hodge, et al., eds., *Benavides*, p. 102; Ayer, ed., *Memorial*, p. 21; Herbert Bolton, "The Mission as a Frontier Institution in the Spanish-American Colonies," *American Historical Review* 23 (1918): 45.

13. Hodge, et al., eds., *Benavides*, pp. 100, 195; Maynard Geiger, O.F.M., *The Franciscan Conquest of Florida* (Washington, D. C.: Catholic University of America, 1937), p. 21; Bolton, "Mission as a Frontier Institution," p. 45.

14. David P. Quinn, ed., *New American World*, 5 vols. (New York: Arno Press, 1956), vol. 5, p. 70; Charles W. Hackett, ed., *Revolt of the Pueblo Indians of New Mexico* (Albuquerque: The University of New Mexico Press, 1942), p. 25.

The priests spent their lives within the bounded world of the isolated missions, struggling against traditional Native American ritual leaders for the loyalty of converts and exercising an authority that elicited both hostility and obedience and veneration. They presided over local kingdoms, and when all went well, they ruled as monarchs of the spirit. But they occupied an uneasy throne.

Ministry

Like the Spanish missionaries, other seventeenth-century clergy viewed their principal aim as the salvation of souls. Catholic promoters defined the purpose of the mission to Maryland in 1634 as "aiding and saving souls," and the earliest Jesuits in the colony described their aim as "the conversion of poore Indians" as well as of Protestants in the colony so that their "immortal souls" might "return back to [their] Creator." The Protestant clergy also aimed, as Thomas Hooker of Connecticut explained, at "spirituall and supernaturall ends," especially "the conversion, sanctification, and salvation" of souls, which meant eternal bliss in a heavenly domain in contrast to indescribable suffering in an endless hell. The Puritan preacher Increase Mather reminded the second-generation ministers of New England that their "main design" was "converting work."[15]

His son Cotton Mather listed the typical cleric's duties: he "must preach, catechize, administer the Sacraments, visit the afflicted, and manage all the parts of Church Discipline." From colony to colony, the priests and ministers weighted these duties differently. For Andrew White, the chief of the Catholic mission in Maryland, the main concern was "attendance on the sacraments," and the proof of faithful ministry was that none of the sick had died without them. For Anglicans in Virginia, the symbolic center was the liturgy: the first Virginia Assembly in 1619 stipulated that ministers "read divine service" from the Book of Common Prayer every Sunday. For Lutherans in New Sweden on the Delaware River, the main duty was the sermon, though ministers there also had to see that "divine service be zealously performed" in accord with "the ceremonies of the Swedish Church."[16]

The Dutch Calvinists in New Netherland believed that ceremonies obscured

15. Curran, ed., *American Jesuit Spirituality,* pp. 8, 63, 65; Thomas Hooker, *A Survey of the Summe of Church Discipline* (London: John Bellamy, 1648), p. 44; Hall, *Faithful Shepherd,* p. 249.

16. Cotton Mather, *Magnalia Christi Americana, Books I and II,* ed. Kenneth B. Murdock (Cambridge: Harvard University Press, 1977), Book 1, p. 102; Curran, ed., *American Jesuit Spirituality,* p. 63; William H. Seiler, "The Church of England as the Established Church in Seventeenth-Century Virginia," *Journal of Southern History* 15 (1949): 482; Israel Acrelius, *A History of New Sweden* (Philadelphia: Historical Society of Pennsylvania, 1874), p. 40.

their mandate, which was "to preach God's Holy Word, as embraced in the Scriptures of the Old and New Testament." And in New England, as well, ministers viewed themselves, above all, as preachers. They preached at least two sermons every week, each lasting an hour to two hours or longer, in addition to sermons in private homes and at public executions, election days, artillery drills, thanksgiving and fast days, and ordinations.[17]

All the colonial clergy performed all the duties on Mather's list — and more. All of them preached. White reported in 1638 that Catholic priests gave "catechetical lectures" every Sunday and delivered sermons on feast days. The Virginia Assembly ruled that Anglican ministers had to "preach one sermon every Sunday in the yeare." The Dutch expected their clergy to preach weekly. The church in Brooklyn protested when the minister delivered no sermon but only a prayer "from which we learn and understand little." Nowhere did the sermon define the ministry more than in New England, where faithful church members might well hear seven thousand sermons before they died.[18]

The sermons in New England were extended discourses in which the preacher clarified a biblical text, drew the doctrine from it, and then presented the uses, or applications, that could edify and guide the listener. Thomas Shepard in Cambridge preached a four-year series on a single New Testament parable. Thomas Hooker devoted ten sermons to "the application of redemption." New Englanders contrasted their "plain style" of preaching with Anglican "Ornaments of Rhetoric," but they disagreed among themselves about the extent to which sermons should "pound . . . hearts all to pieces" in order to humble the unregenerate listener. Some thought that a good sermon should shatter human presumption before announcing divine mercy; others considered it unwise to preach of "such dreadful legal terrors, deep sorrow, and humblings, as being the common road through which men go that come to Christ." But the New England Calvinists agreed that the most important thing a minister did was preach.[19]

---

17. Hugh Hastings, ed., *Ecclesiastical Records, State of New York*, 7 vols. (Albany: James B. Lyon, 1901), vol. 1, p. 93; Harry S. Stout, *The New England Soul: Preaching and Religious Culture in Colonial New England* (New York: Oxford University Press, 1986), pp. 4, 13-85; Ola Elizabeth Winslow, *Meetinghouse Hill 1630-1783* (New York: Macmillan, 1952), p. 93.

18. Curran, ed., *American Jesuit Spirituality*, p. 63; William Waller Hening, ed., *The Statutes at Large: Being a Collection of all the Laws of Virginia*, 12 vols. (New York: Bartow, 1823), vol. 1, p. 157; Gerald F. DeJong, *The Dutch Reformed Church in the American Colonies* (Grand Rapids: Eerdmans, 1978), pp. 11, 14, 30; Stout, *New England Soul*, p. 4.

19. Shepard, *Parable of the Ten Virgins* n.p.; Thomas Hooker, *The Application of Redemption by the Effectual Work of the Word . . . the Ninth and Tenth Books* (London: Peter Cole, 1657), p. 1; John Norton, *Abel Being Dead Yet Speaketh* (London: L. Lloyd, 1658), p. 13; John A. Albro,

Sacramental practice varied from place to place. Priests in Maryland maintained the mass, baptism, penance, marriage, and extreme unction for the dying. (They had no bishops to confirm and ordain.) Protestants recognized only two sacraments — baptism and the Lord's Supper — and normally the clergy alone could administer them, though Lutherans permitted lay baptisms in emergencies. Protestant clergy administered the Lord's Supper three or four times a year, though some New England churches communed once a month. By law, New York required, after 1665, at least one annual observance. In New England, the clergy emphasized that marriage was no sacrament by turning over the ceremony to the magistrates. Not until late in the century did they decide that it was fitting for them to participate. In reaction against Catholic rituals at the time of death, some New Englanders also decided against funeral sermons or any prayers or readings at the graveside, though sermons on the day of the funeral became more common in New England culture by mid-century.[20]

All colonial pastors sought spiritual conversation with the faithful and the faithless. The law in Virginia in 1610 specified that every colonist should seek "conference" with the minister, and private conferences, often at the minister's initiative, became a standard practice. Ministerial manuals in England recommended that believers seek out "much conference" with their clergy, and in New England, ministers "conferred" with applicants for membership, with the sick, with persons suffering spiritual maladies, with couples having marital conflicts, with the dying, with people in mourning, and with feuding neighbors. They acceded to parental requests to confer with their children. Some clergy preferred to have people come to their homes; others rode on horseback from house to house. John Cotton Jr. regularly visited every house in Plymouth; Samuel Phillips and his wife rode to each Andover home once a year.[21]

---

ed., *Life of Thomas Shepard, The Works of Thomas Shepard,* 3 vols. (New York: Georg Olms, 1971), vol. 1, p. clxxvii; Thomas Hooker, *The Soules Preparation for Christ, Or, A Treatise of Contrition* (London: Dawlman, 1632), p. 40; Giles Firmin, *The Real Christian* (London: Dorman Newman, 1670), p. 2.

20. Hastings, ed., *Ecclesiastical Records,* p. 571; John K. Nelson, *A Blessed Company: Parishes, Parsons, and Parishioners in Anglican Virginia, 1690-1776* (Chapel Hill: University of North Carolina Press, 2001), p. 194; Thomas Lechford, *Plain Dealing or News from New England* (1st. ed, 1642; Boston: Wiggin and Lunt, 1847), pp. 46, 86-87.

21. H. Shelton Smith, Robert T. Handy, and Lefferts A. Loetscher, eds., *American Christianity,* 2 vols. (New York: Charles Scribner's Sons, 1960), vol. 1, p. 44; Charles E. Hambrick-Stowe, *The Practice of Piety* (Chapel Hill: University of North Carolina Press, 1982), pp. 150-55; Sacvan Bercovitch, ed., *Puritan Personal Writings: Diaries* (New York: AMS Press, 1982), p. 180; Lechford, *Plain Dealing,* pp. 125-26; George Selement, *Keepers of the Vineyard* (Lanham: University Press of America, 1984), pp. 25, 44-46.

Catholic priests in Maryland visited the sick and dying and also led the "spiritual exercises" of the Jesuits in private homes, resolved disputes, and heard confessions. Anglicans in the same colony wrote of riding "all over" their parishes to visit the sick. When Cotton Mather in Boston wrote, at the end of the century, that his motto was to "visit, visit, visit — more frequently, more fruitfully," he was giving expression to a widely held expectation about the work of the clergy.[22]

Ministers had special duties with children. A 1610 law in Virginia required weekly catechizing on Sunday afternoons, and in 1631 the Virginia Assembly instructed the ministers again to "catechize the youth." The Prayer Book stipulated that the rector teach youth and adults from the catechism every Sunday evening, but by the end of the century the instruction seems to have occurred only during Lent and Easter and only in some parishes. The absence of a bishop, who normally tested children on the catechism before confirming them, doubtless led some to minimize the instruction, but the goal was that the children be taught at least the rudiments of the faith.[23]

Ministers in every other large colony had the same goal. The Dutch in New Netherland taught from the Heidelberg Catechism not only in sermons and classes but also in the schools. Even though Johann Megapolensis wrote his own catechism, the Classis of Amsterdam ruled that he could teach from "no other catechisms besides the Heidelberg and the Compendium of the same." After the English took over the region, the Dutch clergy redoubled their efforts at catechizing, and the English also "strictly" required the catechism for children and servants. In Maryland, Catholic priests gave "catechizings" every Sunday and "catechetical lessons" before sermons, aiming to reach both children and adults, and in 1700 Maryland's seventeen Anglican clergy passed a resolution in support of the practice.[24]

Initially the New Englanders expected parents to catechize, and a 1642 law in

22. Andrew White et al., *A Relation of the Colony of the Lord Baron of Baltimore, in Maryland*, in Peter Force, ed., *Tracts and Other Papers Relating Principally to the Origin, Settlement and Progress of the Colonies in North America*, 5 vols. (Gloucester, Mass.: Peter Smith, 1963), vol. 4, pp. 25-28; Edwin S. Gaustad, ed., *A Documentary History of Religion in America*, 2 vols. (Grand Rapids: Eerdmans, 1982), vol. 1, p. 146; Selement, *Keepers of the Vineyard*, p. 104.

23. "Lawes Divine, Morall, and Martiall," in Force, ed., *Tracts and Other Papers*, vol. 3, p. 11; Hening, ed., *Statutes at Large*, p. 157; George Maclaren Brydon, *Virginia's Mother Church and the Political Conditions Under Which It Grew* (Richmond: Virginia Historical Society, 1947), p. 381.

24. Hastings, ed., *Ecclesiastical Records*, p. 349; DeJong, *Dutch Reformed Church*, p. 163; J. Franklin Jameson, ed., *Narratives of New Netherland 1609-1664* (New York: Charles Scribner's Sons, 1909), p. 34; Smith, Handy, and Loetscher, eds., *American Christianity*, p. 70; Nelson Waite Rightmyer, "The Character of the Anglican Clergy of Colonial Maryland," *Historical Magazine of the Protestant Episcopal Church* 19 (1950): 115.

Massachusetts Bay required them to do it every week, but ministers selected the catechism and some began to teach it themselves. Some parents resisted on the grounds that they could find no "direct Scripture for Ministers catechizing" — and a few ministers, including John Cotton, also had qualms — but by the 1650s catechetical duties were falling to the ministers. Between 1641 and 1663, they wrote at least fourteen catechisms, including John Cotton's *Milk for Babes, Drawn Out of the Breasts of both Testaments.* His grandson Cotton Mather later described it as the catechism with which the children of New England were "usually fed."[25]

The colonial clergy also had disciplinary duties. They maintained a watch over the moral behavior of church members, whom they called to account for everything from drunkenness, sexual misdeeds, and slander to disrespect for parents and ministers and greedy business practices. Their options ranged from private admonition and public rebuke to church trials that could lead to ex-communication or even to legal punishment. In New Netherland, the law required ministers to maintain "good discipline and order" in their churches. In Virginia, clergy and lay church wardens worked side by side, and discipline could take the form of public shaming in the churchyard or presentation to county courts. In early New England, discipline was entirely a congregational activity, but by 1642 the clergy were assuming the power to examine offenders privately and determine if their misdeeds were "public" enough to require a church trial. In some churches, the clergy claimed the right to pronounce sentence and determine the penalty even if the congregation disagreed.[26]

To preserve order meant more than ensuring the purity of the church. Colonial clergy served as public figures with responsibility for the moral goods of the society. In Virginia, the churches oversaw the care of the poor, including orphans and widows. In New England, the towns assumed that duty, but the churches took collections for the poor, and some ministers made it part of their duty to care for them. Cotton Mather kept lists of the poor, gave away much of his salary, and distributed gifts from others. The Boston clergy organized charity schools for poor children, and a few of the ministers took on special projects, such as

---

25. Hall, *Faithful Shepherd*, p. 168; Lechford, *Plain Dealing*, p. 53; Daniel Dorchester, *Christianity in the United States from the First Settlement Down to the Present Time* (New York: Hunt and Eaton, 1890), p. 168.

26. Hastings, ed., *Ecclesiastical Records*, p. 93; Philip Alexander Bruce, *Institutional History of Virginia in the Seventeenth Century*, 2 vols. (New York: G. P. Putnam's Sons, 1910), vol. 1, pp. 47-52; William H. Seiler, "The Anglican Parish in Virginia," in *17th-Century America: Essays in Colonial History*, ed. James Morton Smith (Chapel Hill: University of North Carolina Press, 1959), p. 128; Lechford, *Plain Dealing*, pp. 20, 29; Hall, *Faithful Shepherd*, p. 111; Theodore Dwight Bozeman, *The Precisionist Strain: Disciplinary Religion and Antinomian Backlash in Puritanism to 1638* (Chapel Hill: University of North Carolina Press, 2004).

places of "hospitality" for the indigent. They distributed books and tracts on religious and moral topics, accompanied military missions as chaplains, published treatises on government, and lobbied in the general court.[27]

Even before he came to America, John Cotton expressed a common clerical sentiment when he designated the magistrate as the left hand and the minister as the right hand of Christ. The image meant that ministers and magistrates worked together to uphold the reign of Christ in the world, and in several of the colonies the clergy served both as advisers and as agents for rulers of the state. In New Netherland, they offered "useful advice" to the Council. In Virginia, the parish vestries, in which the ministers presided over eleven of "the most sufficient and selected men" of the parish, assumed civil as well as religious responsibilities, and each year the ministers and church wardens were expected to report to the county courts on disciplinary cases. Clergy in Virginia and New England read civil legislation and proclamations from the pulpit, and in Massachusetts Bay, the preachers delivered sermons at each session of the general court. In the ritual processions of colonial governments, a minister often walked alongside the governor, symbolically depicting the alliance of church and state.[28]

The New England colonies forbade ministers to assume political office, but Puritan preachers wrote drafts of legislation, helped shape criminal law, represented the colonies in diplomatic missions abroad, attended sessions of the general court as official advisers, and met as a group with magistrates during the year. In two New England colonies — Massachusetts Bay and New Haven — only church members held the civic franchise, and since ministers presided over admission to the churches, some feared that the clergy exercised too much control over political decisions. The ministers could assume special prerogatives in the political sphere. Cotton told Governor John Winthrop in Massachusetts Bay that rulers should "consult with the ministers of the churches" about any "weighty business," and his colleague Thomas Cobbett felt emboldened to say that godly rulers should "lick the dust of the Churches feet, in attending faithfully to the well grounded Counsels of their Pastors."[29]

---

27. Bruce, *Institutional History,* pp. 85-87; Stephen Foster, *Their Solitary Way: The Puritan Social Ethic in the First Century of Settlement in New England* (New Haven: Yale University Press, 1971), pp. 149-50; "An Abstract of the Lawes of New England," in *Tracts and Other Papers,* ed. Force, p. 3:17; Johnson, *Wonder-Working Providence,* p. 112.

28. John Cotton, *A Brief Exposition of the Whole Book of Canticles, or Song of Solomon* (London: Philip Nevil, 1642), p. 238; Jameson, ed., *Narratives of New Netherland,* pp. 112, 126; Hening, ed., *Statutes at Large,* pp. 240-42; "Lawes Divine, Morall, and Martial," in *Tracts and Other Papers,* ed. Force, p. 19.

29. Hall, *Faithful Shepherd,* pp. 15, 130-31; Norton, *Abel Being Dead,* p. 22; Lechford, *Plain Dealing,* pp. 58-59; Bercovitch, ed., *Puritan Personal Writings,* p. 168.

Magistrates were not quite so compliant. In New England, they would not allow ministers to form new churches without their approval; they intervened in church disputes, sometimes in opposition to the local pastor; and they occasionally resisted ministerial requests. By the 1640s, some New England ministers welcomed state control, but others were growing wary. Richard Mather in Dorchester worried that "the power of magistrates" was being used to "hinder the saints of God" from "observing the ordinances of Christ according to the rule of his word." But when the synod of 1648 produced the Cambridge Platform, the document in which the New Englanders worked out their doctrine of the church and ministry, the delegates felt obliged to submit it to the magistrates for approval. Only in subsequent years did the clergy gradually reduce the scope of state control.[30]

Their functioning in the society drew them in other ways beyond the walls of the churches. They conducted private neighborhood schools and taught in New England grammar schools. Because the ministers were educated, colonists turned to them for medical care as well as spiritual guidance. Almost 10 percent of the clergy in seventeenth-century New England practiced as physicians. The dual role aroused some opposition — the Synod of Holland in 1633 forbade the Dutch Reformed clergy to engage in medical practice — but in an era of limited medical knowledge, a university education and a small library could qualify a minister to give as good advice as anyone else, especially in colonies on the periphery of the cosmopolitan centers.[31]

Just as they moved outside the boundaries of the churches, so also the clergy — at least some of them — moved back and forth across the divide between European and Native American cultures. The clergy of the eastern seaboard never ventured as deeply into the native cultures as the Catholic missionaries of New France and New Spain, but the English Jesuits in Maryland had successes with the Patuxents, the Piscataway, and the Anacostians. While English Protestants gave only rhetorical support to the mission until 1646, a number of New England ministers preached to the Narragansett, Mohegans, and Pequots. The first Bible printed in America was John Eliot's Algonquian translation in 1663.[32]

About 6 percent of the New England clergy in the seventeenth century became missionaries. Their missions became entangled in the exploitation and destruction of Native American cultures, and some of the clergy invoked divine

30. B. R. Burg, *Richard Mather* (Boston: Twayne Publishers, 1982), pp. 84, 91.

31. Selement, *Keepers of the Vineyard*, p. 28; Hastings, ed., *Ecclesiastical Records*, p. 85.

32. James Axtell, *The Invasion Within: The Contest of Cultures in Colonial North America* (New York: Oxford University Press, 1985), pp. 218-41.

wrath — and military violence — against Indian resistance, but a few of the ministers rebuked the exploiters, and some Native American converts became ministers themselves. The clergy also wrote descriptions of native societies for European and colonial readers, and some of their productions, such as the copious *Relations des Jésuites* that fifty-four Catholic priests and two Ursuline nuns sent to France between 1632 and 1673, contained a treasure of detailed ethnographic information.[33]

Like the Spanish missionaries, the colonial clergy and their parishioners lived in an "enchanted universe" of special providences, satanic emissaries, inexplicable miracles, and apparitions. They found in every unusual event — and in ordinary events as well — signs of providential intervention. Catholics in Maryland spoke of them as miracles; Protestants in New England normally designated them as providences. Death, rain, military victory, rescues, comets, earthquakes, and frightening events — all required interpretation by experts on the "invisible world."[34]

The clergy did battle with Satan and joined in skirmishes against witches and warlocks. In 1672, Samuel Willard, pastor of the church in Groton, returned to his house to find his sixteen-year-old servant, Elizabeth Knapp, in a "strange frame," throwing herself on the floor, leaping, roaring, and screaming. The girl intimated that she suffered from satanic intrusions, and she began to show signs that the devil had inhabited her body. Willard worked with her for days, questioning, praying, and comforting. Her behavior seemed suspicious in the extreme; she barked, bleated, and sobbed, and then in moments of relative calm, she told him of Satan's assaults and blandishments.

Willard sought guidance from a physician, but it became clearer by the day that her plight required more than medication. She confessed to satanic compacts and then recanted her confessions, falling again into fits, her tongue drawn out of her mouth "into extraordinary length and greatness." And then the devil began to speak through Knapp directly to Willard in a "low, yet audible voice," charging that he was a rogue and a liar. Willard responded with equal directness: "Satan, thou art a liar and a deceiver, and God will vindicate His own truth one day." The drama continued for days, finally leaving Elizabeth Knapp speechless and Willard baffled, unsure whether the distemper was "real or counterfeit," natural or "diabolical," hoping for the best and resolved that "all

---

33. Selement, *Keepers of the Vineyard*, p. 52.

34. David D. Hall, *Worlds of Wonder, Days of Judgment: Popular Religious Belief in Early New England* (New York: Alfred A. Knopf, 1989), p. 70; Andrew White, *A Narrative of the Voyage to Maryland*, in *Tracts and Other Papers*, ed. Force, vol. 4, pp. 21, 41; Johnson, *Wonder-Working Providence*, p. 107.

means ought to be used for her recovery." Invasions from strange worlds complicated the lives of seventeenth-century clerics.[35]

Authority

Catholics grounded the authority of the clerical office on scripture and tradition. Most Protestants turned solely to scriptural argument, but differing interpretations divided them. Beginning in the late sixteenth century, Anglicans placed renewed emphasis on the threefold ordering of the ministry — the offices of bishops, elders, and deacons — and the apostolic succession of the bishops, and these became for some Anglicans the necessary condition of a true church. Early Virginia clergy were of "low church" sentiment, which meant that they probably viewed the three offices as needful merely for the optimal ordering, not for the existence, of a true church. In contrast to both varieties of Anglicans, the Congregational clergy of New England denied that "proud Bishops" of the Anglican variety could even be found in the New Testament, and when they sought the scriptural "pattern" for the ordering of the ministry, they concluded that the "bishop" was no more than the overseer of a congregation.[36]

In the Congregational ordering, which the Puritan theologians tried to model on the New Testament church, the eldership included the pastor, responsible for preaching, sacraments, and discipline, and the teacher, charged with interpreting biblical doctrine. A "ruling elder," not ordained, was to assist the teaching elders and help maintain congregational discipline. Deacons, also not ordained, handled the treasury and assisted the poor, while deaconesses, or "widows," ministered to the poor and the sick. Only the pastors and teachers were to "labor in word and doctrine," whether from the pulpit or in administering the sacraments.[37]

The ideal New England order proved impossible to maintain. By mid-century, few congregations tried to distinguish between pastors and teachers or to support both offices. Few laymen assumed the onerous chores of the ruling

---

35. John Demos, ed., *Remarkable Providences* (Boston: Northeastern University Press, 1991), pp. 432, 435-36.

36. Norman Sykes, *Old Priest and New Presbyter: Episcopacy and Presbyterianism Since the Reformation* (Cambridge: Cambridge University Press, 1956), p. 39; Johnson, *Wonder-Working Providence*, p. 104; Cotton, *True Constitution*, p. 2.

37. Cotton, *True Constitution*, pp. 2-3; Thomas Hooker, *A Survey of the Summe of Church-Discipline* (London: John Bellamy, 1648), pp. 4, 10, 19, 21, 32. For Puritan primitivism, see Theodore Dwight Bozeman, *To Live Ancient Lives: The Primitivist Dimension in Puritanism* (Chapel Hill: University of North Carolina Press, 1988).

elders, and deaconesses also disappeared. Most churches had only a single pastor, though they continued to idealize the older pattern. The reforming synod of 1680 in Massachusctts Bay called for "a full supply of officers in the churches, according to Christ's institution," which meant, at a minimum, pastors, teachers, and ruling elders. But the synod recognized that "most of the churches" had "only one Teaching officer, for the burthen of the whole Congregation to lie upon" because they could not afford two teachers. The New England congregations could only partially realize their biblical ideal, but the pastors still argued that they held an office established "according to the pattern" of the biblical word.[38]

The colonial churches continued to signify the authority of the office through a rite of ordination, though it proved also to be problematic. In Catholic and Anglican traditions, only bishops could ordain, and the mainland colonies had no bishops. New England Congregationalists could ignore that problem, but ordination remained troublesome for them. Some protested against any imposition of hands. Most retained the ritual but insisted that the minister's authority came from a divine inward call and the vote of a congregation, not from the ordination rite. "The election of a pastor," wrote John Cotton in Boston, "is a higher act than their ordination is." The Cambridge Platform taught that "the essence" of the outward calling consisted not in ordination but in "voluntary and free election by the Church." It permitted the lay members to ordain ministers when elders were unavailable. A minister could exercise ministry only in "his own congregation," though he could preach, by invitation, in neighboring villages. If he moved to another church, he submitted to another ordination and preached his own ordination sermon.[39]

By the 1660s, some of the clergy began to argue against the lay ordination of ministers and to assume that ordination conferred a permanent status that a minister took with him even if he moved to another church. Cotton Mather reported in his *Magnalia Christi Americana* (1702) that the "very judicious" clergy had gradually concluded that ordination admitted them "into the order of pastors" (rather than merely binding them to a congregation) and "that they could not allow the rites of this order to be regularly and conveniently performed by

---

38. Lechford, *Plain Dealing*, pp. 12, 40; Williston Walker, ed., *The Creeds and Platforms of Congregationalism* (1st ed., 1893; Boston: Pilgrim Press, 1960), p. 434; Hall, *Faithful Shepherd*, p. 95; Hooker, *Survey of the Summe*, p. 1.

39. Hooker, *Survey of the Summe*, pp. 22, 49-52; John Cotton, *The Way of Congregational Churches Cleared* (London: Matthew Simmons, 1648), p. 24; Richard Mather, *Church-Government*, pp. 67-71; Walker, ed., *Creeds and Platforms*, p. 216; Thomas Shepard, *Defence*, pp. 132-33.

any but such as were themselves of the same order." The Boston association of ministers agreed that only the ordained could ordain.[40]

Mather thought that ordination solely by ordained elders had become general throughout New England, and ordination services became increasingly elaborate. In 1688, for example, Governor Bradstreet and his party rode in a hackney coach to Roxbury to watch as four elders laid hands on Nehemiah Walter, extended to him the "right hand of fellowship," pronounced a formal blessing, and then retired for a celebratory dinner. Such moments signaled a growing effort to elevate the authority of the office.[41]

Authority rested, as well, on educational attainment. Puritans founded Harvard College in 1636 partly because leading colonists "dreaded" to "leave an illiterate Ministry to the Churches, when our present Ministers should lie in the dust." In an era when Harvard, the sole college in the colonies for more than half a century, graduated only about eight students a year, the clergy were the best-educated group in America. Most attained degrees from schools across the Atlantic; a smaller number graduated from Harvard, and in the course of the seventeenth century, half the Harvard graduates entered the ministry. Of the 250 ministers known to have been ordained in Congregational churches in New England between 1640 and 1740, at least 90 percent, and probably more, had college degrees.[42]

In Virginia, most of the early Anglican clergy had graduated from Oxford or Cambridge, and by 1693 the colony chartered William and Mary so that "the Church of Virginia may be furnished with a Seminary of Ministers." The Dutch Reformed classis of Amsterdam made it a point to assure colonists in New York that it would continue to send "learned" ministers, in the tradition of the first Dutch clergy, Jonas Michaelius and Johannes Megapolensis. Both men had a classical education, wrote easily in Latin, and read widely in history and theology.[43]

40. Hall, *Faithful Shepherd*, p. 221; Cotton Mather, *Magnalia Christi Americana*, 2 vols. (New York: Russell and Russell, 1852), vol. 2, p. 242.

41. Walter Eliot Thwing, *History of the First Church in Roxbury, Massachusetts, 1630-1904* (Boston: Butterfield, 1908), p. 72; Mather, *Magnalia Christi Americana* (1852), vol. 2, p. 242.

42. Samuel Eliot Morison, *Builders of the Bay Colony* (Boston: Houghton, Mifflin, 1964), pp. 120, 188; Samuel Eliot Morison, *The Intellectual Life of Colonial New England* (New York: New York University Press, 1956), p. 57; William T. Youngs Jr., *God's Messengers: Religious Leadership in Colonial New England, 1700-1750* (Baltimore: Johns Hopkins University Press, 1976), p. 14; Mary Latimer Gambrell, *Ministerial Training in Eighteenth-Century New England* (New York: Columbia University Press, 1937), pp. 21-22.

43. Susan Godson et al., *The College of William and Mary*, 2 vols. (Williamsburg: King and Queen Press, 1993), p. 1:12; Robert W. Prichard, *A History of the Episcopal Church* (Harrisburg: Morehouse, 1991), p. 6; DeJong, *Dutch Reformed Church*, p. 26; Hastings, ed., *Ecclesiastical Records*, p. 1:155.

The New England clergy guarded the high educational standards of their office. "No calling (besides Divine requisites)," John Norton wrote in 1658, "calleth for more Abilities, or a larger measure of humane knowledge than the Ministery." He said that some New England ministers spent ten hours a day in their studies, mastering Hebrew, Greek, Latin, history, patristics, and theology. Increase Mather claimed to devote sixteen hours a day to study, and he boasted a library of more than a thousand books. His son Cotton had more. Such assertions constituted a form of myth making. Clergy who had to manage farms as well as serve their congregations could hardly afford such a scholarly regimen. But the descriptions illustrate the idealized conception of a minister as learned. When Samuel Willard, acting president of Harvard, wrote, sometime around 1701, his *Brief Directions to a Young Scholar Designing the Ministry,* he devoted the entire treatise to the learning required for the ministerial calling.[44]

In New England, ministers distinguished themselves by their extensive writing on theological and devotional topics. About 34 percent of them — 180 of the 531 ministers in the region in the seventeenth century — published books, treatises, or sermons. Twenty-seven ministers accounted for 70 percent of the publications, most of which were sermons, popular homilies, or devotional treatises, and 11 percent of the ministers published only a single item. A few wrote complex theological tomes, a tradition climaxed by Samuel Willard's *Compleat Body of Divinity,* the fruition of 246 lectures on the Westminster Shorter Catechism. In no other period of American history, and in no other region, would such a substantial percentage of the clergy entertain — and realize — the ambition to publish their reflections.[45]

In addition to all these emblems of authority, they enjoyed authorization from the state. Following a precedent set in the original charter, Virginia assemblies required the churches to uphold public worship "according to the form and discipline" of the Church of England, excluding any minister who would not conform to the Anglican canons. The West India Company attempted to reserve the pulpits of New Netherland only for clergy of the Dutch Reformed Church, while neighboring New Sweden expected its governor to support clergy who upheld the Lutheran confessions and "the ceremonies of the Swedish Church." In New England, the general courts protected the Congregational churches from competition from other Christian groups even though the

44. Norton, *Abel Being Dead,* pp. 24-25; M. G. Hall, ed., "The Autobiography of Increase Mather," *American Antiquarian Society Proceedings,* n.s. 71 (1961): 303; Selement, *Keepers of the Vineyard,* p. 14; Samuel Willard, *Brief Directions for a Young Scholar Designing the Ministry* (Boston: John Draper, 1735), pp. 1-6.

45. Selement, *Keepers of the Vineyard,* p. 61; George Selement, "Publication and the Puritan Ministry," *William and Mary Quarterly* 37 (1980): 223.

charters were silent about establishment. Church monopolies, in turn, produced laws to shield the clergy from public criticism. Beginning with Dale's
Laws in 1610 in Virginia, one colonial government after another demanded that
their subjects hold ministers in "all reverent regard" and restrain any impulse to
"demeane" them.[46]

The sphere in which the clergy sought distinctive authority was not the
state but the congregation, and the most extensive discussion of clerical power
within the congregation occurred in New England, where the earliest settlers
assumed that the local church was the "first subject" of the "keys of the kingdom." This meant that the laity shared with the ministers the right to admit and
to discipline members; that male lay members could publicly exhort in the
churches; and that the lay "brethren" could choose and depose their ministers.
The first New England churches symbolized these prerogatives by permitting
the laity to participate in the ritual of ordination.[47]

After a doctrinal crisis in 1636 threatened ministerial authority and social order, the clergy began slowly to elevate their office. They insisted that the government of the church was properly a mixture of monarchy, aristocracy, and democracy. Christ was the monarch. The laity held a "democratic" right to choose their
pastors. And the clergy were the aristocrats who occupied a position "superior to
the Fraternity [of laity] in regard of office, Rule, Act, and Exercise, which is proper
only to them." What this meant, in practice, was that a congregation, having chosen a pastor, was to "become subject, and most willingly submit" to him.[48]

The 1648 Cambridge Platform, which protected some of the customary
rights of the laity, also gave the clergy the sole right to preach, administer sacraments, call church meetings at which attendance was mandatory, determine
which laity could speak in such meetings, examine new applicants for membership, and "pronounce sentence" in disciplinary cases, needing only the "consent" of the church. The Platform concluded with an assurance that this power
"in the Elders" prejudiced none of the privileges of the "brethren." For good
measure, its provisions paved the way for ministers to assume a more prominent place in the rite of ordination. Like clergy in other colonies, the ministers

---

46. Hening, ed., *Statutes at Large*, pp. 144, 149, 155, 156; DeJong, *Dutch Reformed Church*,
p. 34; Hastings, ed., *Ecclesiastical Records*, pp. 343-44; Hall, *Faithful Shepherd*, p. 125; "Lawes Divine, Morall, and Martiall," in Force, ed., *Tracts and Other Papers*, p. 10; "Abstract of the Lawes of
New England," in Force, ed., *Tracts and Other Papers, p. 13.*

47. Hooker, *Survey of the Summe*, Preface, p. 187; Shepard, *Defence*, 48; Lechford, *Plain
Dealing*, p. 129; John Cotton, *The Keyes of the Kingdom of Heaven, and Power Thereof, According
to the Word of God* (London: M. Simmons, 1644), p. 40; Hall, *Faithful Shepherd*, pp. 78, 93, 106.

48. Hooker, *Survey of the Summe*, p. 191; Cotton, *Keyes of the Kingdom*, p. 56; Shepard, *Subjection to Christ*, p. 96; Walker, ed., *Creeds and Platforms*, pp. 214, 217.

of New England called, as a requisite of faithful ministry, for the right to "Rule."[49]

One mode of clerical influence took shape through the formation of ministerial associations. Such meetings occurred regularly after 1632 despite fears that they opened the way to "presbyterial" government of the churches. In 1641 the general court passed a "Body of Liberties" that codified the rights of the colonists and guaranteed the ministers "free libertie to meete . . . for conferences and consultations about Christian and Church questions and occasions." The Cambridge Synod declined to give these ministerial meetings its imprimatur, but the general court approved a set of "Laws and Liberties" that approved the practice. By insisting on their right to meet as a separate group — despite resistance from purists who worried about any authority outside the local church — the New England ministers spoke up for clerical rule.[50]

And finally, the clergy bore authority simply because they were so often the source of information about the wider world and of colonial influence within it. The ministers in New England, for example, maintained a steady correspondence with clerical friends across the Atlantic, sending and receiving books and letters with every ship that set sail, and they occasionally served as agents for colonial business. When Massachusetts Bay sent Hugh Peter and Thomas Welde to England as agents in 1641, they worked to secure economic aid, lower customs duties, and defend New England churches. Networks of friends in the mother country kept the ministers informed about politics, ideas, and the changing fortunes of the English churches, and they passed this information on to the members of their congregations.[51]

Colonial laypeople could have vehement disputes with their ministers, but they could also accord them unstinting praise, respect, and affection. One example: in Boston, the parishioners of Samuel Willard, the pastor of Third Church from 1678 to 1707, often took careful and detailed notes when he preached, called upon him at every crisis, and voted to give munificent gifts to him, his wife, and his children, setting up a trust fund for their college education. The congregation paid him well, and merchants in his church often subsidized the printing of his books and sermons. Not every minister received the same adulation — and even Willard had his detractors — but his ministry gave

---

49. Walker, ed., *Creeds and Platforms*, pp. 211, 216, 219, 220.

50. Edmund S. Morgan, ed., *Puritan Political Ideas* (Indianapolis: Bobbs-Merrill, 1965), p. 200; Robert F. Scholz, "Clerical Consociation in Massachusetts Bay: Reassessing the New England Way and Its Origins," *William and Mary Quarterly*, 3d ser., 29 (1972): 404, 409-14.

51. Francis J. Bremer, *Congregational Communion: Clerical Friendship in the Anglo-American Puritan Community* (Boston: Northeastern University Press, 1994), pp. 111-13, 121, 146, 158, 236-38.

him an authority that made him one of the most influential figures in the city. His office gave him respect, but his authority rested on the response of his congregation.[52]

Boundaries

Colonial clergy ruled without the benefit of the institutional arrangements and settled practices that elevated the clerical office in Europe. The Anglicans in America lacked bishops and ecclesiastical courts. The four Catholic priests who upheld the mission in early Maryland had to wend their way between the demands of an absentee proprietor and the admonitions of equally distant Jesuit superiors. The Dutch Reformed *domines* who by 1650 served the nine congregations of New Netherland could communicate with the Classis of Amsterdam only through letters that traveled slowly back and forth across the ocean. New England Congregationalists had, on principle, repudiated the authority of supra-local institutions over their congregations. As a result, the conditions of religious life in the colonies would, despite all the ministerial self-assertion, tilt the balance of power in the direction of the laity.[53]

By 1650, the colonial clergy oversaw 110 congregations, sixty-one of them consisting of Congregationalists in New England, twenty-seven of Anglicans in Virginia. The colonial population in 1650 has been estimated at 50,368, so the colonies might have had one congregation for every 458 settlers. In Virginia, the twenty-seven Anglican congregations drew their communicants from a population of about 18,731, which meant about 694 people for each Anglican church. In New England, the population was around 20,065, or about 328 settlers for each Congregational church.[54]

The colonial preachers filled their churches, but by 1650, despite colonial laws mandating church attendance, they probably preached each Sunday to less than half the population. Churches built in the middle of the seventeenth century seated, on average, about 144 people; only 40 percent of the population could have found a seat in a colonial congregation on a Sunday morning. Women and servants often stayed at home to tend to infants and young children. At the end of the century, the number of congregations rose to four hundred for a population of about 250,888 — one church for every 627 souls —

---

52. Mark A. Peterson, *The Price of Redemption: The Spiritual Economy of Puritan New England* (Stanford: Stanford University Press, 1997), pp. 79, 124.

53. Curran, ed., *American Jesuit Spirituality*, p. 63.

54. Edwin S. Gaustad, *Historical Atlas of Religion in America* (New York: Harper and Row, 1962), p. 167.

so the formation of new congregations did not quite keep up with population growth.[55]

One reason for the relatively slow expansion was that the southern and middle colonies suffered from shortages of ministers. By 1662, Virginia had laid out forty-five parishes, but it had only ten ministers available for service. The number of clergy increased to thirty-five by 1680, but they were still unable to supply the growing number of parishes, and the government issued repeated requests to England for more. In 1697, the commissary, James Blair, claimed that the colony had only enough ministers to fill half its parishes.[56]

In neighboring Maryland, the Anglican John Yeo complained in 1676 that the colony had a population of twenty thousand served by only three Protestant ministers "conformable to the doctrine and discipline of the Church of England," and the Catholic proprietor of the colony felt dismay that the Holy See had sent so few missionary priests. The lack of clergy accounts for part of the strength of the Quakers in Maryland. After the English conquered New Netherland in 1664, the new government discovered that the colony suffered a "want of painful & able Ministers," either Anglican or Reformed. For most of the last decade of the century, no Lutheran minister could be found in the whole of North America. Only New England had enough ministers to fill every church; by 1642, some Harvard graduates began to return to England to find churches to serve.[57]

The shortage of clergy outside New England created a temptation for con-

---

55. I arrived at the average of 144 seats per church in this way: (1) The church in Hingham, Massachusetts, built in 1681, designed a 2,475 square foot building for 335 people, or one person for each 7.4 square feet. (2) A sample of 15 New England churches built around 1650 shows an average of 1,039 square feet for each building. If the Hingham ratio is even roughly representative, these buildings seated, on average, 144 people. For Hingham, see Edmund W. Sinnott, *Meetinghouse and Church in Early New England* (New York: McGraw Hill, 1963), pp. 32-33. See also Marian Card Donnelly, *The New England Meetinghouses of the Seventeenth Century* (Middletown, Conn.: Wesleyan University Press, 1968), pp. 15, 46, 154. See Sarah Goodhue, "A Valedictory and Monitory Writing," *Puritans in the New World: A Critical Anthology*, ed. David D. Hall (Princeton: Princeton University Press, 2004), p. 186. The population estimates come from *Historical Statistics of the United States: Colonial Times to 1970, Part 2* (Washington, D.C.: U.S. Bureau of the Census, 1975), p. 1168.

56. Seiler, "Anglican Parish in Virginia," pp. 129-30; Bruce, *Institutional History*, p. 124; James Blair et al., *The Present State of Virginia, and the College*, ed. Hunter Dickinson Farish (Williamsburg: Colonial Williamsburg, 1940), p. 67.

57. Smith, Handy, and Loetscher, eds., *American Christianity*, pp. 54, 331; John D. Krugler, "With Promise of Liberty in Religion: The Catholic Lords Baltimore and Toleration in Seventeenth-Century Maryland, 1634-1692," *Maryland Historical Magazine* 79 (1984): 37; Theodore Tappert, "The Church's Infancy," *The Lutherans in North America*, ed. E. Clifford Nelson (Philadelphia: Fortress Press, 1975), p. 13; Hall, *Faithful Shepherd*, p. 111.

gregations to lower their standards. In 1631, Virginians had to pass a law that no ministers were to indulge in "excess in drinking or riot" or spend their time idly "by playing at cards or dice." James Hammond, writing in 1656, conceded that for a period the colony had been compelled to accept too many ministers who "could babble in a Pulpit, roare in a tavern, exact from their Parishioners, and rather by their dissoluteness destroy than feed their Flocks." John Yeo also complained of disruptive and unlearned preachers in Maryland, and the first English governor in New York issued warnings against "Scandalous and Ignorant pretenders to the Ministry." The minister in New Amsterdam described the Lutheran pastor in New Sweden as "a wild drunken unmannerly clown." Swedish congregants removed this man from his office, but they restored him after he amended his life. The shortage made it imprudent to insist on too high a standard.[58]

Across the colonies, the clergy did not think of themselves as sharing a common enterprise. Doctrinal divisions cast them into opposition to each other. Anglicans in Virginia supported legislation that barred dissenting ministers from the colony, and the New England clergy also had no tolerance for dissenters. The Dutch Reformed resisted the entry of Lutheran clergy into New Netherland on the grounds that toleration would open the way for "Papists, Mennonites, and others" to create a "Babel of confusion." Despite early efforts at toleration in Maryland, Protestants were soon able to suppress any public activity by Catholic priests, and when John Yeo, two decades later, bemoaned Maryland's lack of ministers, he dismissed dissenting preachers and priests in the colony — who would have included Catholics, Presbyterians, Congregationalists, Baptists, and Quakers — as pretenders who did nothing but sow seeds of division. From the outset, the diversity prevented any recognition of the clergy as a unified vocational group.[59]

Still another challenge came from a religious populism that bedeviled the educated ministers almost from the beginning. As early as 1636, the New England clergy had to listen to critics who said that lay exhorters, including women, preached "better Gospel than any of your black-coates that have been at the Ninneversity." After the 1640s, lay preaching became common in New England. Cotton reported that "deluded sectaries" scoffed at the "Scholler-like"

---

58. Hening, ed., *Statutes at Large*, p. 158; John Hammond, *Leah and Rachel, Or the Two Fruitful Sisters Virginia and Maryland*, in *Tracts and Other Papers*, ed. Force, vol. 3, p. 9; Smith, Handy, and Loetscher, eds., *American Christianity*, pp. 54, 158, 331; Christopher Ward, *The Dutch and Swedes on the Delaware 1609-1664* (Philadelphia: University of Pennsylvania Press, 1930), p. 218; Rightmyer, "Character of the Anglican Clergy," p. 113.

59. Hastings, ed., *Ecclesiastical Records*, p. 386; Smith, Handy, and Loetscher, eds., *American Christianity*, p. 54; Krugler, "With Promise of Liberty," p. 36.

preaching of the educated clergy and gave allegiance to "ignorant and unlettered" preachers, both male and female. In 1653, Massachusetts Bay passed the first of a number of laws designed to stamp out such interloping, but the laws never entirely succeeded, and the exhorters sometimes simply moved to neighboring Rhode Island.[60]

Samuel Gorton spoke for the interlopers in Rhode Island when he announced his "call to preach the Gospel" and rejoiced that he had not been "bred up in the Schooles of human learning" that exalted Aristotle over Christ. But not every populist moved away from the Bay Colony. Urian Oakes, president of Harvard, complained in 1677 about the prevalence of "good-for-nothings" who despised academic training and thought they could "make themselves Doctors of Theology in three days." Nor did the populist impulse reside solely in New England: Mennonites in New Netherland also rejected "the office of preacher" as the Lutherans and Dutch Reformed understood it, and lay exhorters infiltrated all the colonies.[61]

Challenges to clerical authority could be both explicit and implicit, both populist and pragmatic. No group pursued the populist agenda more wholeheartedly than the Quakers, who invaded the colonies during the 1650s with the message that God had "no need for the ministry." The Quakers had the audacity to feature women preachers claiming an "inward word of truth." Marching into Rhode Island, Maryland, and Virginia, and then flooding into Pennsylvania and the Jersey colonies, they proclaimed that learned clergy did nothing but impede the spread of the gospel. In Virginia, meanwhile, the Assembly dealt with clerical shortages in 1661 by empowering lay readers to conduct services in the absence of a minister. It had no intention of diminishing the position of the clergy, but by 1680 the Anglican minister Morgan Godwyn lamented that some congregations preferred lay readers to regular ministers.[62]

No trend affected the status of the clergy in early America more than the resolve of congregations to set the terms of employment. In the absence of a bishop, the Virginia assembly in 1643 authorized local vestries to choose their rectors and then present them to the governor for induction. Since induction virtually ensured tenure, the parishes soon learned to offer ministers annual

60. Johnson, *Wonder-Working Providence*, pp. 95-96; John Cotton, *Of the Holiness of Church Members* (London: F. N., 1650), 25.

61. Cotton, *Holiness of Church Members*, p. 25; Samuel Eliot Morison, *Harvard College in the Seventeenth Century*, 2 vols. (Cambridge: Harvard University Press, 1936), vol. 1, p. 433.

62. John Norton, *The Heart of N-England Rent at the Blasphemies of the Present Generation* (Cambridge: Samuel Green, 1659), p. 14; George Bishop, *New England Judged, Not by Man's, but the Spirit of the Lord* (1st ed., 1661; London: T. Sowle, 1703), p. 132; Bruce, *Institutional History*, vol. 1, pp. 225, 512; vol. 2, p. 43.

contracts, ignoring the governor and keeping the clergy under their control. In 1662, the vestries became self-perpetuating institutions, and although the rector usually presided over vestry sessions, the twelve-member boards still represented an assertion of lay power.[63]

Not all the clergy found the arrangement satisfactory. Morgan Godwyn protested in 1680 that the vestries reduced the ministers "to their own Terms; that is, to use them how they please, pay them what they list, and to discard them whensoever they have a mind to it." Commissary James Blair bemoaned the "contrary Custom of making annual Agreements with the Ministers, which [the parishes] call by a Name coarse enough, viz. Hiring of the Ministers, that they may by that Means keep them in more Subjection and Dependence." He thought that the practice drove good ministers away and dissuaded them from preaching "against the Vices that any great Man of the Vestry was guilty of." He saw the vestries acting in a "high-handed" manner, turning out ministers without proof of any charges against them. This explained, he contended, why "the Country is very badly provided with Ministers." The system was less capricious than Blair implied, for most Virginia clergy enjoyed long tenures, but they had to please their congregations in order to do it.[64]

Soon enough the preachers in New England faced similar constraints. Although the ministers expanded their authority within the congregations, the laity preserved the right to have the last word. During the late 1640s, the hiring of ministers became contractual, a process that could protect a minister but empower the congregation. John Woodbridge told Richard Baxter in the 1660s that "the people are grown so rude, insolent, and Coltish . . . that the Ministers that have most Authority have not enough." Congregations could keep a minister on trial for months or even years while the town meetings deferred signing a permanent contract.[65]

The system tempted laymen to lord it over young applicants. In Barnstable in Plymouth Colony, Elder Chipman boasted in 1680 that he and Thomas Hinckley could "make or break" any minister, a bit of swagger that convinced the young Peter Thacher to decline the invitation to settle there. Other ministers had congregations that wanted to grant them "no more authority than any

63. Bruce, *Institutional History,* vol. 1, pp. 240-42; Robert Beverley, *The History and Present State of Virginia,* ed. Louis B. Wright (1st ed., 1705; Chapel Hill: University of North Carolina Press, 1947), p. 263.

64. Morgan Godwyn, *The Negro's and Indians Advocate, Suing for the Admission to the Church* (1680), printed in Brydon, *Virginia's Mother Church,* p. 512; Blair, *Present State of Virginia,* pp. 66-67; Seiler, "Anglican Parish in Virginia," p. 133; Beverley, *History and Present State,* p. 264.

65. Quoted in Hall, *Faithful Shepherd,* pp. 187, 193.

particular Brother." New England's second clerical generation sometimes expressed a feeling that their "Democratical" church order was sliding into "Anarchy." Similar issues emerged in other regions. In New Netherland, the system of lay patronage gave the "patroon," essentially a feudal lord, even more power over the minister.[66]

On the whole, most ministers adapted themselves quite easily to the balance of power between themselves and the laity. The primary sign of their success was their long tenure in their parishes. In New England, 79 percent of the seventeenth-century ministers served in one congregation throughout their careers; 8 percent served in two. It was not unusual for a minister to spend twenty or thirty years in one congregation. Clergy in Maryland and Delaware were more mobile; 71 percent in Maryland and 77 percent in Delaware worked in two or more congregations, but this was mainly because the Jesuits in Maryland rotated back and forth from St. Mary's City, St. Inigoes, and other mission stations while the tiny number of Episcopal, Reformed, and Lutheran clergy were in such high demand that new opportunities continually opened up for them.[67]

Colonists wanted able ministers, and they were willing to pay, but their willingness had limits. The first ministers of New England preferred voluntary contributions, and most found that their congregations were willing to provide an "honorable and comfortable" living through weekly offerings. Each Sabbath day the members ritually handed their gifts to the deacon of the church. Voluntary contributions continued in the Boston churches throughout the century, but they did not always produce the desired results. By 1672, Increase Mather, one of the most celebrated ministers of the city, wrote in his diary that he was "miserably perplexed still with sad thoughts of my debts, and the unworthy spirit which is in some of my people, that have no Heart to relieve mee in these my sorrows."[68]

Outside Boston, the voluntary system gave way to state taxation. The general court in Massachusetts ruled in 1638 that the towns could compel contribu-

66. Increase Mather, "To the Reader," in Samuel Torrey, *An Exhortation unto Reformation* (Cambridge, Mass, 1674), n.p.; Cotton Mather, *Magnalia*, vol. 1, p. 313; Edward Pierce Hamilton, ed., "The Diary of a Colonial Clergyman: Peter Thacher of Milton," *Proceedings of the Massachusetts Historical Society* 71 (1953-57): 55; Major Denison, "Irenicon," in William Hubbard, *The Benefit of a Well-Ordered Conversation* (Boston: Samuel Green, 1684), p. 182.

67. See the lists in Frederick Lewis Weis, *The Colonial Clergy and the Colonial Churches of New England* (Lancaster: Weis, 1936) and Frederick Lewis Weis, *The Colonial Clergy of Maryland, Delaware, and Georgia* (1st ed., 1950; Baltimore: Genealogical Publishing, 1978).

68. Lechford, *Plain Dealing*, p. 49; Hooker, *Survey of the Summe*, p. 28; M. G. Hall, ed., "The Autobiography of Increase Mather," *American Antiquarian Society Proceedings*, n.s. 71 (1961): 298.

tions, and one after another, townships voted a fixed amount. When it proved difficult to raise the promised sum, they taxed the townspeople, church members and non-members alike. By 1648, the Cambridge Platform declared the magistrates responsible for seeing that the "ministry be duly provided for," and in 1654 the general court in Massachusetts commanded due payment of ministerial salaries.[69]

The law should have sufficed. New England clergy received from sixty to a hundred pounds a year, payable largely through produce, cattle, and labor, along with the right to occupy a farm and receive such incidentals as wood for cooking and heating. As early as the 1640s, however, complaints could be heard that the towns sometimes failed to keep their promises, and a regional synod in 1680 reported that ministers had been forced "into the Field" as farmers. By no means did the New England clergy suffer; they usually stood among the wealthiest 15 percent of colonists in their towns, and their social standing allowed some of them to marry into affluent mercantile families. Peter Thacher of Milton combined an inheritance, a good marriage, and his salary to ascend into the upper class, managing in 1675 to be the only person in the county with a coach. But some ministers had difficulty collecting the promised sums.[70]

The clergy of Virginia received for their salaries an allotment of tobacco. The legislature in 1662 set the amount at 13,333 pounds, collected by the church wardens and delivered to the ministers in hogsheads convenient for shipping. In addition, the Assembly in 1642 gave each of the clergy two hundred acres of land (known as a "glebe"), and in 1661 it added a parsonage for each rector. The ministers also received fees for funerals, marriages, and the posting of the banns that announced a forthcoming wedding. After the Assembly raised the tobacco allotment to 16,000 pounds, it amounted to between £80 and £160 sterling. The clerical stipend, combined with the earnings from the glebe lands, made possible a life of moderate gentility.[71]

The only problem was that the value of the payment depended on the quality of the tobacco and the vagaries of the market, so clerical salaries could fluctuate wildly. Some attempted to ensure that payment always be made in "the best Tobacco," arguing that ministerial livelihood was "very uncertain," but the

69. Walker, ed., *Creeds and Platforms*, p. 221; Hall, *Faithful Shepherd*, p. 147; John Childe, *New Englands Jonas Cast up at London* (London: T. R., 1647), in Force, ed., *Tracts and Other Papers*, vol. 4, p. 13; Peter Oliver, *The Puritan Commonwealth* (Boston: Little Brown, 1855).

70. Joseph B. Felt, *The Ecclesiastical History of New England*, 2 vols. (Boston: Congregational Library Association, 1862), p. 160; Walker, ed., *Creeds and Platforms*, p. 434; Hall, *Faithful Shepherd*, pp. 182-83; Thacher, "Diary," p. 59.

71. Beverley, *History and Present State*, pp. 262-63; Nelson, *A Blessed Company*, p. 50; Blair, *Present State of Virginia*, p. 67.

best tobacco was not always forthcoming. In 1642 the Virginia Council expressed dismay about the "many controversies [that] do daily arise between Parishioners and their ministers throughout the colony concerning the payment of their duties." Some ministers brought suits against their parishioners, and by 1662 one could hear warnings that failures to ensure "the maintenance of the ministery" ran the risk of bringing Virginians under the "curse of God."[72]

Outside New England and Virginia, the clergy often lived a precarious existence. Ministers in Rhode Island farmed and depended on voluntary contributions. In New Netherland, voluntary contributions were supposed to supplement the stipend paid by the West India Company, but Megapolensis said that people crowded into his church while refusing to pay. After England seized the colony in 1664, the government taxed each town to support the minister, but he said that the salaries were "limited" and that they came in slowly. The preachers appealed to secular courts to enforce the requirement, but sometimes the courts could only ask wealthy Dutch Christians to subsidize the salaries.[73]

By the end of the century, the Dutch Reformed ministers in the region received from £40 to £100 a year in quarterly payments, depending on their location, but they had no guarantee of payment. Four communities refused to pay anything, insisting that they could "live well enough without ministers or sacraments." A Dutch minister lamented in 1691 that "we ministers are treated with scorn, and paid in insults, and deprived of what is justly our dues, receiving no salary worth mentioning." In Maryland, the three Anglican clergy serving in 1696 could not "get the half and sometimes not a fourth part" of the amount subscribed for their support, and they feared that they could not afford to keep the horses that enabled them to ride to their churches and visit their parishioners.[74]

The colonial clergy made claims to high authority, and they occupied eminent positions in the society, but they also encountered resistance and labored

72. Anonymous, *Virginia's Cure: Or an Advisive Narrative Concerning Virginia* (London: W. Godbid, 1662), in Force, ed., *Tracts and Other Papers,* vol. 3, pp. 5, 17; Jon Butler, *Awash in a Sea of Faith: Christianizing the American People* (Cambridge: Harvard University Press, 1990), p. 43.

73. Randall H. Balmer, *A Perfect Babel of Confusion: Dutch Religion and English Culture in the Middle Colonies* (New York: Oxford University Press, 1989), p. 11; DeJong, *Dutch Reformed Church,* p. 49; Randall H. Balmer, "The Social Roots of Dutch Pietism in the Middle Colonies," *Church History* 53 (1984): 191.

74. Balmer, *Perfect Babel,* p. 64; Balmer, "Social Roots," p. 191; "An Act for Settling a Minister and Raising a Maintenance for them in the City of New York County of Richmond, Westchester, and Queens-County," in Force., ed., *Tracts and Other Papers,* vol. 4, pp. 47-48; W. S. Perry, ed., *Historical Collections Relating to the American Colonial Church,* 4 vols. (1st ed., 1878; New York: AMS Press, 1969), vol. 4, p. 8.

under the expectations of parishioners who felt no compunction about exercising their own power in religious matters. The ministry was an "office," honored and respected, and the office conferred authority, but charisma and competence — the personal and rational dimensions of authority — functioned even in the seventeenth century to enhance the influence of the ministry, while their absence could diminish it. The proof of the calling, at least for the colonial laity, came in the ordinary routines of ministry that defined a clerical life.

CHAPTER 3

Association, Revival, and Revolution

1700-1791

In October 1724, Ebenezer Parkman, a twenty-one-year-old graduate of Harvard College, celebrated the "greatest day" he "ever yet saw": his ordination "to the Work of the Gospel Ministry." He spent the next fifty-eight years as a Congregational minister in Westborough, Massachusetts, preaching twice every Sabbath day, a regimen of six thousand regular sermons in addition to others in private homes and on special occasions. He baptized and catechized the village children, administered the Lord's Supper, visited twenty families a month, and welcomed visitors for spiritual conversation and casual hospitality. Although he saw himself as "unable to manage a Quarrell and very much indispos'd towards it," he spent hours reconciling neighbors, dealing with cantankerous parishioners, and helping his clerical association restore peace between ministers and laity. He mostly approved the revivals of the 1740s but regretted the conflict they produced. He oversaw discipline in his congregation, and he maintained a watch over his own heart, chastising himself for his "iniquities before God." In his remaining hours, he studied his Bible, read theology, and farmed his land.[1]

In October 1762, Devereux Jarratt, a native of Kent County, Virginia, sailed to London to receive priestly orders from the Anglican bishop of Chester authorizing him to assume "the pastoral charge of some thousands of souls, in the county of Dinwiddie, and parish of Bath." For the next thirty-eight years, he preached two times each Sunday in one or another of the three churches of his parish, and he delivered additional sermons in other congregations, at private

---

1. Francis G. Wallet, ed., "The Diary of Ebenezer Parkman," *Proceedings of the American Antiquarian Society* 71 (1962): 117, 206, 368; vol. 72 (1963): 149, 152.

homes, or "in the open air, under trees, arbors, or booths." He claimed that for several years he preached 270 sermons annually. Believing that the Anglican *Book of Common Prayer* contained "a system of doctrine and public worship . . . equal to any other in the world," he embedded his Sunday sermons within the liturgy. He baptized children, tried to increase the numbers receiving the Eucharist, convened religious meetings in private homes, counseled with parishioners, presided at weddings and funerals, reconciled disputes, and made sporadic efforts to maintain "the Godly discipline of the church." Like Parkman, he ran a farm, though unlike Parkman he oversaw the labors of twenty-four slaves.[2]

The two ministers illustrate the transitions of the eighteenth-century clergy. They shared an interest in clerical solidarity: Parkman joined an association and Jarratt attended ministerial conventions. They both felt the force of revivalism. Parkman viewed the revivals with sympathetic interest but maintained his distance. Jarratt, unlike most other Anglicans, endorsed a revivalist piety. Both men honored learning and worried about unlearned clergy. Parkman was a college graduate, and Jarratt learned Latin and Greek from a tutor and took pride in his "considerable knowledge of Divinity." He looked askance at preachers who felt "called to preach" without "qualifications and credentials." Both received salaries mandated by the government, but both witnessed successful protests against exclusive state privileges for any one religious group. In Massachusetts, the Congregational clergy lost their monopoly on tax support, and in Virginia the assembly cut off the church tax in 1776, subjecting Anglican clergy "to the caprice of the multitude."[3]

The two men worried about new forms of clerical itinerancy and about increasing religious pluralism. Jarratt frequently traveled, preaching in twenty-three counties in Virginia and five more in North Carolina, but he, like Parkman, disliked self-initiated itinerancy, believing that "peripatetic pastors" subverted "the unity of the Christian Church" by "continually intruding," uninvited, on the province of the local clergy. Both men had to find ways of dealing with diversity. Parkman fretted about Baptists and Anglicans. Jarratt suffered frequent "interruption" from Baptists, worried about Deists, and quarreled with the Methodists, whom he initially assisted but came to consider "a designing people" whose professed Anglican allegiance was "disingenuous."[4]

The two careers illustrated the three trends that altered the work of the

2. Devereux Jarratt, *The Life of the Reverend Devereaux Jarratt: An Autobiography,* ed. David L. Holmes (1st ed., 1806; Cleveland: Pilgrim Press, 1995), pp. xviii, 47, 55, 56, 58-59.

3. Jarratt, *Life,* pp. 27-29, 73, 111.

4. Jarratt, *Life,* pp. 55, 74, 86-87.

minister during the eighteenth century. The participation of the clergy in new forms of association represented, among other things, an effort to enhance clerical authority. Revivalism introduced distinctive styles of communication, created tensions over clerical education, and displayed the potential and peril of itinerancy in ways that threatened the "authority of the office" but elevated the minister's charismatic authority. Denominational diversity hastened a shift that gradually disentangled the clergy from the authority of the state.

Association

The Congregational clergy of New England had long gathered informally to discuss theology and strategy. In 1690 the ministers near Boston, following English precedents, regularized the practice by forming a Cambridge-Boston Association, which met at Harvard College every six weeks, and several groups outside Boston followed their example. In 1704, the Boston-area clergy issued a circular letter urging that "the Association of the Ministers in the several Parts of the Country . . . be strengthened" as one means to counter the "decay" of religion. The next year, some of them offered a set of proposals for creating associations to deliberate on "Cases of importance," hear accusations of clerical scandal or heresy, examine candidates, and recommend pastors to congregations. The idea drew support, but many of the laity and some powerful clergy feared that it threatened congregational autonomy, and the royal government remained aloof, so it never received formal approval.[5]

By the middle of the century, the clergy in Massachusetts had formed more than sixteen associations. Even though the groups lacked the authority envisioned in the 1705 proposals, they could examine candidates, oversee disputes, discuss theology, discipline errant clergy, and provide clerical fellowship. Cotton Mather reported in 1725 that "the Country is full of Associations, formed by the Pastors in their Vicinities, for the Prosecution of Evangelical Purposes." Some evidence suggests that they augmented ministerial power at the expense of the laity; other evidence suggests that they never attained much power over local churches. In any event, they signified a desire on the part of the ministers to strengthen the profession.[6]

5. William T. Youngs Jr., *God's Messengers: Religious Leadership in Colonial New England, 1700-1750* (Baltimore: Johns Hopkins University Press, 1976), pp. 69, 71; Williston Walker, ed., *Creeds and Platforms of Congregationalism* (Boston: Pilgrim Press, 1960), pp. 649-70, 484, 489, 493; Robert F. Scholz, "Clerical Consociation in Massachusetts Bay: Reassessing the New England Way and Its Origins," *William and Mary Quarterly*, 3d ser., 29 (1972): 391-414.

6. Youngs, *God's Messengers*, 73-75; Mary Latimer Gambrell, *Ministerial Training in*

In Connecticut, their proponents won a victory when the general court urged the churches to support the 1708 Saybrook Platform, which formed associations of the clergy and consociations of churches in each county. The platform authorized the associations to discuss "the duties of [the clerical] office and the common interests of the churches," examine and recommend candidates for ministry, and deal with clerical scandal or heresy. It assigned to the consociations, which had both clerical and lay members, the power to settle disputes in local churches and to ordain, dismiss, and try ministers. Since Saybrook required a clerical majority before any ruling of the consociation would go into effect, it strengthened the ministerial "elders." It moved the Connecticut churches closer to a presbyterial polity, so some churches resisted, but most accepted it.[7]

In 1706, seven Presbyterian clergy of the middle colonies, led by the Scottish itinerant Francis Makemie, created the Presbytery of Philadelphia. They planned to meet annually to "advance religion," improve "ministerial ability," and recruit more preachers. When the presbytery met the following year, it consisted of equal numbers of ministers and lay elders, but in later years the ministers usually constituted a majority, so they took the lead in questions about recruitment, discipline, and ordination. The presbytery dispensed advice about worship, sought funds for ministerial support, and oversaw disciplinary cases. It also had the power to license and ordain new ministers, approve ministerial calls from congregations, and dismiss local pastors. In 1716, it helped form the Synod of Philadelphia, which expanded the organization of presbyteries into Long Island and Delaware. As presbyteries multiplied, the ordained ministers outnumbered the lay elders, and committees of ministers alone examined, ordained, and installed pastors.[8]

In 1707, Baptist preachers in the Delaware Valley formed the Philadelphia Baptist Association in order to encourage cooperation among Baptist churches. These early Baptists had a flexible notion of ministry, with no sharp distinctions between ordained and lay ministers, but the Association sought clearer

Eighteenth-Century New England (New York: Columbia University Press, 1937), p. 42; David Harlan, *The Clergy and the Great Awakening in New England* (Ann Arbor: UMI Research Press, 1980), p. 15.

7. Walker, ed., *Creeds and Platforms*, pp. 503, 506; Harlan, *Clergy and the Great Awakening*, pp. 19-20.

8. Boyd Schlenther, ed., *The Life and Writings of Francis Makemie* (Philadelphia: Presbyterian Historical Association, 1971), pp. 252, 259-60; Jon Butler, *Power, Authority, and the Origins of American Denominational Order* (Philadelphia: The American Philosophical Society, 1978), pp. 55, 60; Charles Hodge, *The Constitutional History of the Presbyterian Church in the United States of America* (Philadelphia: William S. Martin, 1839), pp. 11-12, 125-25.

definitions, deciding that only the "pastor" had the authority to preach. Focusing its energies on the preaching ministry, it oversaw recruitment and discipline and established rules for examining "gifted brethren." Its guiding light, the Welsh Calvinist Morgan Edwards, became known as an advocate of pastoral authority after he defined the office of the ordained minister as necessary for a "complete" church. He proposed to symbolize that authority by requiring that an already ordained pastor participate in the ordination of any new pastor. The Philadelphia group became a model for similar associations in other colonies.[9]

Early eighteenth-century Anglicans formed no permanent associations, but in 1701 officials in England, convinced of the need for "good, substantial, well studied Divines" in America, created the Society for the Propagation of the Gospel in Foreign Parts (SPG). Led by Thomas Bray, who had lived in Maryland, the SPG collected funds, defined standards, and appointed clergy to mission fields in the northern colonies. Anglicans also experimented with other forms of association. The commissaries in Virginia, beginning with James Blair, convened occasional clerical assemblies, and in the 1720s SPG missionaries organized semi-annual gatherings in the middle colonies to discuss common problems. In 1754, Commissary Thomas Dawson initiated a gathering of Virginia clergy who met every year at William and Mary to handle business, share strategies, and listen to each other's sermons. By 1758, Anglicans in other colonies had organized similar conventions, partly to campaign for an Anglican bishop in America but also to hear sermons and discuss parish problems.[10]

In one Protestant denomination after another, the clergy organized themselves. Quakers had no ordained ministers, but they had Public Friends who assumed clerical functions, and after 1685 they met four times a year and garnered power in the Philadelphia Yearly Meeting. Lutherans created something like a presbyterial system after 1725 in New York and New Jersey, and by 1748 the Lutheran patriarch Henry Melchior Muhlenberg succeeded in organizing the Ministerium of North America, a body of ministers (with laymen as nonvoting consultants) who would examine, ordain, and assign clergy to the churches.[11]

9. Butler, *Power, Authority, and the Origins*, p. 51; Morgan Edwards, *The Constitution of Particular Churches* (Philadelphia: by the author, 1744), p. 15.

10. Butler, *Power, Authority, and the Origins*, p. 73; John K. Nelson, *A Blessed Company: Parishes, Parsons, and Parishioners in Anglican Virginia, 1690-1776* (Chapel Hill: University of North Carolina Press, 2001), pp. 141-42; Robert W. Prichard, *A History of the Episcopal Church* (Harrisburg: Morehouse, 1991), pp. 62-63; Carl Bridenbaugh, *Mitre and Sceptre: Transatlantic Faiths, Ideas, and Personalities, 1769-1775* (London: Oxford University Press, 1962), pp. 179-80.

11. Butler, *Power, Authority, and the Origins*, p. 30; Theodore Tappert, "The Church's Infancy," *The Lutherans in North America*, ed. E. Clifford Nelson (Philadelphia: Fortress Press,

The impulse to organize extended through the middle colonies. In the late 1740s, Dutch Reformed ministers in New York and New Jersey began to unite, and by 1754 they created, despite opposition, a "classis" with the right to examine and ordain new clergy. In 1747, the German Reformed itinerant Michael Schlatter organized a "coetus," consisting of ministers and lay elders who solicited funds and recruited new clergy. Imitating English models, Methodist preachers, mostly laymen, formed themselves into quarterly and annual conferences. When they broke away from the Church of England in 1784, one of their first actions was to safeguard the annual conference for their newly ordained preachers.[12]

The Catholic clergy sought similar forms of organization. In 1784, the former Jesuit priests in America organized a "Select Body of Clergy" and created a corporation to administer the properties held by Jesuits when the papacy suppressed the society in 1773. The group hoped to influence Rome's decisions about the administration of the church in America, but the Vatican appointed John Carroll as superior of the mission in America without consulting them. The pope eventually permitted the American clergy to nominate a bishop, and they chose Carroll. They never again had that kind of influence, but in forming the "Select Body" they aligned themselves with the trend toward clerical organization.[13]

At one level, the new organizations represented no more than a transfer of British and European institutions to America. The clergy replicated models that had proved to be effective in the homelands. Associations, presbyteries, conventions, and conferences had antecedents in Britain and Europe, and their introduction to America represented in part the sheer weight of tradition. The organizers were often recent immigrants with experience in similar institutions in their home countries. But nostalgia for familiar institutions did not entirely explain why the clergy imported the older forms.

The associations and convocations reflected, on the one hand, the self-consciousness of an honored group and, on the other, a perception of threat. They symbolized the clerical sense of standing apart from the laity as a com-

1975), p. 50; Patricia U. Bonomi, *Under the Cope of Heaven: Religion, Society, and Politics in Colonial America* (New York: Oxford University Press, 1986), p. 76; Henry M. Muhlenberg, *The Journals of Henry Melchior Muhlenberg*, ed. Theodore G. Tappert and John W. Doberstein, 3 vols. (Philadelphia: The Muhlenberg Press, 1942), vol. 1, p. 200.

12. Richard W. Pointer, *Protestant Pluralism and the New York Experience* (Bloomington: Indiana University Press, 1988), p. 22; Russell E. Richey, *The Methodist Conference in America: A History* (Nashville: Abingdon Press, 1996), pp. 21, 36.

13. Sydney E. Ahlstrom, *A Religious History of the American People*, 2 vols. (Garden City: Doubleday and Yale University Press, 1975), vol. 1, pp. 637-38.

pany of men dignified by a sacred calling, special education, and a widely acknowledged authority to assume leadership in the culture. They signified an
implicit assertion of the "rational authority" of the ministry: a declaration of
collective expertise that promised more efficient administration of the
churches. At the same time, they registered worries and anxieties. Ministers
formed associations — and strengthened them throughout the century —
partly because they had concerns about the supply of clergy, the assertiveness of
the laity, the competence and integrity of the ministry, and the status of the
profession. We can understand the organizing impulse only by looking at the
ways in which ministers viewed their callings and laity viewed their ministers.

Authority

Jonathan Edwards employed a time-honored trope when he taught his Congregational church in Northampton, Massachusetts, that "the Honour that is put
upon faithful ministers is in some respects greater than that of Angels." The
clergy still thought of themselves as "Sacred Persons," called and set apart by
Christ. This claim permitted them to assert their authority against both congregations and magistrates: "They Represent Christ, Act in his Stead, and by his
Authority." They employed familiar biblical images to describe themselves as
ambassadors for Christ, shepherds of the flock, watchmen on the walls, and
stewards of the mysteries of God. And this made the clerical office "a great and
important work, Greater & of more Importance than that of other Professions."
Thomas Clap wrote in 1732 that the work of the ministry was the "greatest business that any men are employed in."[14]

The "sovereign aim" of the minister — almost everyone agreed — was
still "the conversion and edification" of men and women "in Christ." Ministers were responsible for "the Souls of their People," which meant that they
were to promote "the Work of Salvation." The office therefore had awesome
responsibilities, even dangers. If church members fared ill in the final judgment, warned Clap, and if their ministers could not provide God with a "fair"
explanation, then "the Blame thereof will lye upon" the ministers. This warning became a standard theme in ordination sermons: God would call min-

14. Youngs, *God's Messengers*, pp. 130-31; Azariah Mather, *The Gospel Minister Described*
(New London: Green, 1725), pp. 2, 12; Benjamin Moore, *A Sermon Preached in St. George's Cha-
pel* (New York: Gaines, 1787), pp. 7-8; Eliphalet Adams, *The Gracious Presence of Christ with the
Ministers of the Gospel* (New London: Green, 1730), p. 9; Thomas Clap, *The Greatness and Diffi-
culty of the Work of the Ministry* (Boston: John Eliot, 1732), p. 4; Morgan Edwards, *A Sermon
Preached in the College of Philadelphia* (Philadelphia: Stewart, 1763), p. 5.

isters to account for any "Souls that perish through their neglect." Peter Thacher said that his heart "trembled" at the "infinite weight and importance" of his calling.[15]

Despite consensus about basics, the clergy found ample ground for disagreement about the theological basis for their calling. In 1719, for example, the Anglican John Checkley caused a tempest in Boston by publishing a work on the apostolic origins of the office of the bishop. (Boston Congregationalists deplored Anglican bishops.) Three years later, the Congregational rector and tutor at Yale College, along with five nearby ministers, shocked New England by announcing that they planned to conform to the Church of England because they could no longer accept the validity of ordination by mere presbyters. The Yale apostasy helped spark an incessant dispute. Anglicans said that according to the New Testament only bishops *(episkopoi)* could ordain. Congregationalists and Presbyterians responded with arguments for "the Right and Authority of Presbyters" to perform the rite. In 1734, the Hampshire Association complained that missionaries of the SPG were "insinuating that our Ministry is no Ministry, not having had Episcopal Ordination."[16]

The struggle flared up not only in New England but also in the middle colonies, where Anglicans and Presbyterians competed with each other. Anglicans viewed bishops as the successors of the apostles, and many thought that no ministry was valid that stood outside the ordination conveyed through this "apostolic succession." Their Presbyterian opponents adduced evidence in the New Testament epistles that the presbytery of elders had the authority to ordain and that the succession of bishops rested on a Roman error.[17]

The clergy who published — or read — treatises on such issues were the most highly educated group in the colonies. At a time when few colonists even thought of attending college, Cotton Mather assured ministerial students in New England that their learning distinguished them "from the more uncultivated part of mankind" and gave them a "place among them, who are the blessings and beauties of their generation." By 1767, the Boston minister Charles Chauncy could claim, with only a degree of exaggeration, that all the clergy of New England had received an education "at one or another of our colleges."

---

15. Thomas Foxcroft, *A Practical Discourse Relating to the Gospel Ministry* (Boston: Buttolph, 1718), pp. ii, 44; Jonathan Edwards, *Christ the Great Example of the Gospel* (Boston: Fleet, 1750), pp. 16-17; Clap, *Greatness and Difficulty*, pp. 6-7; Peter Thacher, *A Sermon Preached October 1788* (Portland: T. B. Wait, 1788), pp. 7, 19.

16. Bridenbaugh, *Mitre and Sceptre*, pp. 68, 85-90; Joseph Parsons, *The Validity of Presbyterian Ordination* (Boston: Kneeland and Green, 1733), p. 2.

17. Jeremiah Leaming, *A Defence of the Episcopal Government of the Church* (New York: Holt, 1766), pp. 3-4, 10.

About 95 percent of the New England Congregationalist clergy in the eighteenth century had college degrees.[18]

Anglicans and Presbyterians shared the assumption that ministers would be men of higher education. Anglicans had a smaller percentage of graduates than the Congregationalists, but the Church of England required that candidates for Holy Orders have a university degree or give an account of their faith in Latin. The records are incomplete, but by 1750 the majority of Anglican clergy in Virginia — as many as 70 percent and probably more — had studied in English, Scottish, or American universities. In 1789, the Presbyterian General Assembly reported a total of 188 ministers. Almost all held college or academy degrees, of which more than half came from the College of New Jersey (Princeton). Lutherans relaxed educational standards, but they still insisted that candidates receive tutoring from knowledgeable clergy, and in the latter part of the century they founded academies to prepare candidates.[19]

To a marked degree American colleges served as training schools for ministers. During the first fifty years of the century, over half the graduates of Harvard and Yale went into the ministry. The proportion fell to roughly a third by mid-century, but even then more graduates entered ministry than law or medicine. The story was similar at the College of New Jersey, founded by Presbyterians in 1746 to ensure a supply of educated clergy. In its first twenty-two years, 47 percent of its 313 graduates chose ministerial careers. The number fell to 13 percent in the two decades after the Revolution, but by that time Presbyterians had founded sixty-five other academies that offered classical training. In the first two decades of the century, 65 percent of the graduates of all the colonial colleges entered the ministry. The number fell to 40 percent between 1741 and 1760.[20]

In the colleges, many of the teachers — and most of the presidents — were themselves ministers. Six of the seven presidents of Harvard during the century were clergy, as were all the presidents of Yale, the College of New Jersey, King's

18. Cotton Mather, *Manuductio ad Ministerium,* ed. John Ryland (London: Charles Dilly, 1781), pp. 25-26; Bonomi, *Under the Cope,* p. 70; Youngs, *God's Messengers,* p. 110; Gambrell, *Ministerial Training,* p. 52; Charles Chauncy, *A Letter to a Friend, Concerning Certain Remarks on Certain Passages in a Sermon* (Boston: n.p., 1767), p. 8.

19. Bonomi, *Under the Cope,* p. 45; Nelson, *A Blessed Company,* p. 111; Elwyn Allen Smith, *The Presbyterian Ministry in American Culture* (Philadelphia: The Westminster Press, 1962), p. 92; Tappert, "The Church's Infancy," p. 46.

20. Bonomi, *Under the Cope,* p. 70; Youngs, *God's Messengers,* p. 14; Smyt, *Presbyterian Ministry,* pp. 81, 93; James W. Fraser, *Schooling the Preachers: The Development of Protestant Theological Education in the United States 1740-1875* (Lanham: University Press of America, 1988), p. 7; Mark A. May, *The Education of American Ministers,* 4 vols. (New York: Institute of Social and Religious Research, 1934), vol. 2, pp. 23-24.

College (Columbia), William and Mary, Queen's College (Rutgers), Georgetown, and the College of Rhode Island (Brown), along with all the provosts at the College of Philadelphia. Only one layman held a college presidency during the colonial period, and he had clerical training. And the clergy also dominated the faculties. Half the teachers at King's College were ministers, and even in the three decades after the Revolution they held 40 percent of the faculty positions. During some periods at William and Mary, every instructor was an Anglican clergyman.[21]

The colleges therefore taught subjects deemed useful to the ministry. Students learned Greek, Latin, rhetoric, logic, ethics, the Bible, and divinity, but ministers were also expected to know more. Cotton Mather urged ministerial students to learn the standard religious subjects and then explore natural science, philosophy, mathematics, geography, astronomy, poetry, and history. We should not exaggerate the depth of an eighteenth-century collegiate education; students entered in their early teens, and they learned partly through rote memory and recitation. Yet the training prepared boys for the pulpit. A Yale student began the day with morning prayers, took morning and afternoon classes, and recited twice a day. He memorized sermons and learned oratorical skills in weekly disputations (defending propositions in ethics, natural philosophy, and logic) and in declamations before the faculty. Colleges were more than seminaries, but they were solicitous of the needs of the pulpit.[22]

For some, the training continued after graduation. They remained at the college to "read divinity" for up to three years, receiving a master's degree if they stayed the whole period. In addition, the churches had their own programs of education. Presbyteries adopted reading lists and examined young ministers on their reading. Equally popular were the "field schools," in which pastors received students into their homes for theological study. Jonathan Edwards trained several students through readings, examinations, and apprenticeship at Northampton. His disciple Nathaniel Emmons taught nearly ninety students in fifty years. Joseph Bellamy in Connecticut made reading and writing assignments and discussed theological questions with his students almost every evening while guiding them in public speaking and parochial duties. The Dutch

21. George P. Schmidt, *The Old Time College President* (New York: Columbia University Press, 1930), p. 184; John S. Brubacher and Willis Rudy, *Higher Education in Transition: A History of American Colleges and Universities, 1636-1968* (New York: Harper and Row, 1968), pp. 8, 28; Susan Godson, et al., *The College of William and Mary: A History,* 2 vols. (Williamsburg: King and Queen Press, 1993), vol. 1, p. 114; Robert A. McCaughey, *Stand, Columbia: A History of Columbia University in the City of New York, 1754-2004* (New York: Columbia University Press, 2003), p. 59.

22. Mather, *Manuductio,* pp. 29-91; Richard Warch, *School of the Prophets: Yale College, 1701-1740* (New Haven: Yale University Press, 1973), pp. 191-95.

Reformed minister J. H. Goetschius in New York attracted fourteen students through advertisements in newspapers. In return, the students did farm work and tutored children.[23]

One result of such learning was that the clergy dominated the world of publication. The books most frequently reprinted up to 1770 came from clerical authors. From 1701 to 1730, American publishers reprinted Cotton Mather's books more frequently than any others. During the next twenty years, the revivalist George Whitefield moved into the front rank. In the 1750s, the Philadelphia Anglican William Smith had more reprints than anyone else. But even this ranking does not convey the full sense of clerical domination. In every decade between 1700 and 1770, clerical writers — American and European — held all but one or two of the top eight positions in the listing of reprinted books. Only in the years of revolutionary ferment did political works or literary writings outrank theological and devotional books.[24]

A few prolific authors were responsible for most clerical publishing, and the sermon was the genre of preference. Between 1750 and 1770 in New England, for example, eleven authors accounted for 62 percent of the religious books. Yet over a third of the New England clergy during those years published at least one sermon, and until 1790 sermons appeared from the New England presses more frequently than any other form of writing. The middle colonies produced fewer sermons, with almanacs and poetry ranking above the homilies, and in the South, too, the almanacs outpaced the sermons. But in the first 150 years of colonial publishing, sermons outranked every other genre apart from government documents.[25]

Some ministers published intricate theological treatises; others ventured outside the boundaries of theology. No theologian wrote with more subtlety and breadth than Jonathan Edwards. The Presbyterian Jonathan Dickinson attained an international reputation for blending Calvinism and revivalist piety. Samuel Johnson in Connecticut was equally at home with Anglican sacramental theology, British moral thought, and philosophy. Cotton Mather wrote the history of New England, James Blair and William Stith the history of Virginia, and Jeremy Belknap the history of New Hampshire. Jedidiah Morse was America's leading geographer. Francis Allison and John Witherspoon popularized Scottish philosophy. John Clayton and John Bannister in Virginia prepared botanical reports,

23. Gambrell, *Ministerial Training,* pp. 14, 131-32, 139; Randall H. Balmer, *A Perfect Babel of Confusion: Dutch Religion and English Culture in the Middle Colonies* (New York: Oxford University Press, 1989), p. 129.

24. Hugh Amory and David D. Hall, eds., *The Colonial Book in the Atlantic World* (Cambridge: Cambridge University Press, 2000), pp. 517-18, 520-21.

25. Amory and Hall, *Colonial Book,* p. 55.

while Jared Eliot wrote on iron and field husbandry in New England. Edward Taylor, Timothy Dwight, and Conowry Owen stand out as colonial poets. Toward the end of the century, lawyers and political theorists took the lead, but for most of the period the clergy were America's intellectuals.

The landscape symbolized their high standing, especially in the cities, where church steeples loomed over every other building. In 1771, eighteen steeples dominated the skyline of New York City. In New England, meetinghouses in the High Georgian style — such as Old North and Old South in Boston — became large and elaborate. St. Michael's Church in Charleston, with its columnar portico, was the most impressive building in South Carolina. The brick Anglican churches of Virginia were the largest buildings in most counties. Their plastered interiors, arched ceilings, round-headed windows, and interior ornamentation set them apart, and their elevated pulpits provided a privileged place of address. Many a preacher proclaimed the gospel in a ramshackle building, but for others the sacred architecture symbolized cultural power.[26]

The more eminent urban clergy presided over congregations of as many as 1500 people. The most convincing study of churchgoing suggests that 80 percent of the white population should be accounted as church adherents in 1700, and perhaps 59 percent even during the Revolutionary War. Some were communicants who received baptism and communion, and others were attenders who worshiped regularly without becoming communicant members. Both groups — along with their children — constituted the adherents. A report from Anglican clergy in Virginia in 1724 indicated that attenders outnumbered communicants by more than four to one. The clerics said that the church buildings often could not hold all who came on the Sundays when the minister preached. In Boston, Cotton Mather preached to as many as 1600 people and once in 1723 described an attendance of 1,000 as "Thinner . . . than ordinary."[27]

Attendance varied widely, depending on local circumstances. Brookline, Massachusetts, in 1714, had 360 inhabitants, but the meetinghouse would hold only 65 of them. Anglican reports in 1724 revealed that, from one parish to another, 10 to 70 percent of the parishioners might be absent on any given Sunday.

---

26. Bonomi, *Under the Cope*, p. 2; Dell Upton, *Holy Things and Profane: Anglican Parish Churches in Colonial Virginia* (New York: The Archaeological History Foundation, 1986), pp. 39, 114, 133-38, 172.

27. Patricial U. Bonomi and Peter R. Eisenstadt, "Church Adherence in the Eighteenth-Century British American Colonies," *William and Mary Quarterly*, 3d ser., 39 (1982): 245-86; Bonomi, *Under the Cope*, p. 90; George Maclaren Bryden, *Virginia's Mother Church and the Political Conditions Under Which It Grew* (Richmond: Virginia Historical Society, 1947), pp. 372-73; Cotton Mather, *Paterna: The Autobiography of Cotton Mather*, ed. Ronald A. Bosco (Delmar: Scholars' Facsimiles and Reprints, 1976), p. 72.

In Germantown, Pennsylvania, around 56 percent of the inhabitants in 1770 attended regularly. William Shurtleff in Portsmouth, New Hampshire, complained that it had been the habit of some to attend only "when the Season was inviting, and there was nothing in the Way." The churches touched the lives of most white Americans, but an adherence rate of 80 percent might suggest a regular attendance of closer to 40 percent of the population.[28]

Whether they attended or not, they usually accorded the educated clergy a high standing in society. In Virginia, the gentry accepted the Anglican ministers into the ranks of "gentlemen," even if their lack of wealth made them "gentlemen of a subordinate sort." Anglican ministers married into the families of the powerful, dined with the wealthy planters, and associated with the "best people." In St. Anne's Parish, Robert Rose's schedule included social visits with the

---

28. Upton, *Holy Things*, pp. 185-86; William H. Lyon, *The First Parish in Brookline* (Brookline: Riverdale, 1898), p. 8; Brydon, *Virginia's Mother Church*, pp. 372-73; Stephanie Grauman Wolf, *Urban Village: Population, Community, and Family Structure in Germantown, Pennsylvania, 1683-1800* (Princeton: Princeton University Press, 1976), p. 215; William Shurtleff, "A Letter" (1745), in Alan Heimert and Perry Miller, eds., *The Great Awakening* (Indianapolis: Bobbs-Merrill, 1967), p. 357.

The debate over adherence has had conflicting definitions and assumptions. Bonomi and Eisenstadt defined "adherents" as attenders and their children, assumed that each congregation had, on average, 80 families (400 to 480 persons), calculated the population in 1780 as 2,204,949, and concluded that 80 percent were "churched" in 1700, 59 percent in 1780. Rodney Stark and Roger Finke, "American Religion in 1776: A Statistical Portrait," *Sociological Analysis* 49 (1988): 39-51, argued that 10 percent of Americans were "members" of churches. They assumed that each of 3,228 congregations had, on average, 75 members and that the colonial population in 1776 stood somewhere between 2,421,000 and 2,524,000. In *The Churching of America* (New Brunswick: Rutgers University Press, 1992), p. 26, they factor in the children of members to get the number of "adherents." For them, therefore, adherents are members and their children rather than attenders and their children, and they calculate the national adherence rate as 17 percent of the population. Jon Butler, *Awash in a Sea of Faith*, p. 4, defined adherence as "regular or steady attachment to institutional Christianity," but he tended to interpret it as communicant membership, and he saw it as varying from place to place, ranging from 8 percent to 40 percent, with a pattern of religious indifference. James Hutson, "The Christian Nation Question," *Forgotten Features of the Founding* (Lanham: Lexington Books, 2003), pp. 111-32, cites evidence that the population in 1770 was only 2,100,000 (2,204,500 in 1775) and that churches had on average 500 to 800 adherents (defined as regular attenders and their children). He concludes that the adherence rate in New England and Virginia in 1750-60 was 71 percent, a conclusion close to that of Bonomi and Eisenstadt. His definition included adherents who might have attended only infrequently. My figure of 40 percent attendance — an informed guess — assumes that in a family of five persons, some were often too young to attend, and someone had to stay home with them; that weather, old age, and illness kept others away; that distance and poor transportation sometimes made attendance difficult; that clerical shortages, especially on the frontiers, reduced attendance, and that some adherents in the eighteenth century, as in the twenty-first, simply felt no compelling reason to attend every Sunday.

Beverleys, the Blands, the Randolphs, and the Spotswoods, the families that dominated colonial government. In New England and the middle colonies, the upper levels of the clergy enjoyed a similar proximity to the powerful, mingling easily with affluent merchants and magistrates.[29]

Challenges

Not every preacher had entry into the circles of power. The lower levels of society produced a host of preachers who ridiculed the pretensions of the elites. Some of the New England revivalists kept a suspicious distance from wealthy merchants, criticizing their greed and complicity in the slave trade. During the struggles over religious taxation in New England, the Baptist clergy scorned the magistrates as persecuting "Pharaohs." Baptist preachers in Virginia after 1754 defied the magistrates and deplored genteel pastimes, dress, and haughtiness. Preachers in the small German churches — Moravians, Mennonites, and Dunkers — lacked access to the powerful. Working-class Universalist preachers in the New England hill country after 1774 voiced suspicions of social hierarchies. At least 36 percent of the congregations in 1776 represented denominations in which the clergy had little chance of attaining a high social standing.[30]

Whether eminent or lowly in status, the clergy were in high demand and short supply. In sparsely populated areas, churches in New England had to content themselves with lay exhorters or occasional itinerants while waiting for a regular minister. By 1785, Ezra Stiles found 120 churches with vacant pulpits. Few educated clergy sought congregations in regions where the population was sparse, salaries low, and pulpits undistinguished. The southern colonies had similar problems with supply. In 1703, Virginia had forty ministers to serve fifty parishes; in 1735, seven parishes were vacant; in 1744, the parishes had ten vacancies. In the half century before the Revolution, about 11 percent of Virginia parishes each year had no ordained clergy to serve their congregations.[31]

29. Upton, *Holy Things*, p. 172; Robert Rose, *The Diary of Robert Rose: A View of Virginia by a Scottish Colonial Parson 1746-1751*, ed. Ralph Emmett Fall (Verona: McClure Press, 1977), pp. 107, 112, 120; Samuel P. Fowler, ed., "Biographical Sketch and Diary of the Rev. Joseph Green of Salem Village," *Essex Institute Historical Collections* 8 (1866): 220.

30. Isaac Backus, *A History of New England with Particular Reference to the Baptists* (New York: Arno Press, 1969), p. 518; Rhys Isaac, *The Transformation of Virginia, 1740-1790* (Chapel Hill: University of North Carolina Press, 1982), pp. 163-77; Ann Lee Bressler, *The Universalist Movement in America 1770-1880* (New York: Oxford University Press, 2001), pp. 19-22. For the basis of the percentage, see note 71.

31. Ezra Stiles, *The Literary Diary of Ezra Stiles*, ed. Franklin B. Dexter, 3 vols. (New York:

In the Anglican churches, few congregations had a full-time minister. Virginia's parish clergy normally served from two to eight congregations. In 1724, twenty-seven clergy in Virginia reported to the bishop of London that they served fifty-three congregations. Half a century later, Jarratt served three churches in Bath Parish. The minister in St. James Parish in South Carolina preached in ten churches, with occasional sermons in twelve others. In 1705, John Brooke in New Jersey preached in seven congregations in a parish over fifty miles long. In the 1720s, Samuel Johnson in Connecticut traveled a circuit of more than sixty miles to reach the four congregations of his parish.[32]

Some denominations had even more severe shortages. In 1741, New York, Pennsylvania, and Delaware had fifteen thousand German Reformed settlers but only four ordained ministers, who stretched themselves to maintain any pastoral presence. John Philip Boehm ministered to congregations over one hundred miles apart. German Lutherans faced similar strains. When William Berkenmeyer came to New York in 1725, he cared for fourteen congregations scattered over 150 miles of the Hudson Valley. After arriving in Pennsylvania in 1742, Muhlenberg urged the authorities in Halle to "find preachers." He wore out three horses in one year and answered plaintive letters from isolated congregations "anxious to have a faithful pastor." Lutheran pastors in New York typically served three to six congregations; in 1784, seven of them were serving twenty local churches. The Lutherans were better off than the Dutch Reformed, who had only fifteen ministers for ninety churches.[33]

Catholics barely maintained a presence in the eastern coastal colonies. In the early part of the century, most New England governments still had laws banning Catholic priests, as did Virginia and Maryland. In 1700, New York required all priests to emigrate or face life imprisonment. In the same year, the government in Maryland threatened lifetime imprisonment for any priest who exercised clerical functions publicly. Public opinion softened in Maryland, but as late as 1785 it had only nineteen priests to serve around 15,800 Catholics, prompting Bishop John Carroll to complain of an "extreme want of priests." Many congregations, he wrote, "hear the word of God only once a month, and

Scribner's, 1901), vol. 3, p. 147; Stephen A. Marini, *Radical Sects of Revolutionary New England* (Cambridge: Harvard University Press, 1982), p. 36; E. Brooks Holifield, "Toward a History of American Congregations," in *American Congregations*, ed. James P. Wind and James W. Lewis, 2 vols. (Chicago: University of Chicago Press, 1994), pp. 36-39; Nelson, *A Blessed Company*, p. 4.

32. Nelson, *A Blessed Company*, p. 28; Bonomi, *Under the Cope*, pp. 55-56; Butler, *Power, Authority, and the Origins*, p. 70.

33. John B. Frantz, "The Awakening of Religion Among the German Settlers in the Middle Colonies," *William and Mary Quarterly*, 3d ser., 33 (1976): 271; Tappert, "The Church's Infancy," p. 15; Muhlenberg, *Journals*, vol. 1, pp. 121, 408; Pointer, *Protestant Pluralism*, pp. 13, 106.

sometimes only once in two months. We are reduced to this by want of priests, by the distance of congregations from each other and by difficulty of traveling." By that time, Pennsylvania had five priests for seven thousand Catholics. New York, with 1,500 Catholics, could attract only one Irish Franciscan. These twenty-five priests were, Carroll reported, the only Catholic clergy in the American republic. They served congregations "far apart" and spent their time "riding constantly and with great fatigue, especially to sick calls." Several were too old or ill to travel. Carroll worried that "the Vineyard of the Lord" in America could not be cultivated.[34]

In Spanish and French regions of the continent, Catholics maintained their mission to Native Americans, but they complained that they lacked the priests to accomplish their ends, and the missions declined. Only in California, where Junípero Serra founded in 1769 the first of a chain of mission stations stretching from San Diego to San Francisco Solano, did the Spanish Catholic mission prosper. But even there it suffered from a shortage of priests.[35]

From one perspective, the shortages elevated clerical authority: they created a high demand for ministers. But the demand could be so insistent that it could subvert the standing of the educated pastors. In Protestant areas, the shortages meant that isolated or dissenting churches sometimes turned to lay exhorters who claimed a divine call. In 1714, Governor John Hart in Maryland expressed astonishment at finding several "illiterate men" preaching in the colony. In the next thirty years it became more common to find preachers without the usual collegiate training. On the frontiers of New England, unlearned ministers found a welcome among settlers unable to afford an educated preacher. In the middle colonies, the smaller religious groups — Dunkers, Seventh-day Baptists, and Mennonites — expected no higher education from their clergy, and they scorned the Lutheran preference for trained ministers as spiritual snobbery.[36]

Unlettered Dutch Reformed preachers claimed that the Holy Spirit alone authorized their calling. "The single question now," complained one educated Dutch minister, "is as to whether they have the Spirit." The Baptist movement objected in principle to any requirement for a learned ministry. The New England Baptist Isaac Backus argued in 1754 that the internal call of the Spirit produced better biblical interpretation than human learning. Morgan Edwards in

34. John Tracy Ellis, *Catholics in Colonial America* (Baltimore: Helicon Press, 1965), pp. 335, 369; Peter Guilday, *The Life and Times of John Carroll* (1st ed., 1922; Westminster: The Newman Press, 1954), pp. 225-27.

35. Ellis, *Catholics in Colonial America*, pp. 45, 67, 75, 114.

36. Nelson Waite Rightmyer, "The Character of the Anglican Clergy of Colonial Maryland," *Historical Magazine of the Protestant Episcopal Church* 19 (1950): 120.

Pennsylvania explained that God's "inward call" endowed the preacher with all necessary qualifications.[37]

The uneducated preachers troubled ministers who saw learning as necessary for faithful interpretation of the Bible. Increase Mather, who believed that the minister must have "more wisdom and knowledge than what the generality of Believers have attained unto," insisted that an uneducated man was "not qualified to be a Publick Interpreter of the Divine Law." John Hancock added that an "ignorant" and "unqualified ministry" would bring "contempt" on the profession. "Should an Unlearned Ministry prevail generally in the Land," said Azariah Mather in Connecticut, "farewell Religion." To the learned Dutch Reformed clergy in New York, it was a disaster that learning seemed no longer "of much consequence." Convinced that the "minister's work" was to "teach wholsom[e] Doctrine," the educated clergy emphasized that only men of "Wisdom and Knowledge" could interpret the Bible rightly.[38]

The uneducated claimed a divine call; the educated insisted not only on an internal call but also on a providential call, a call from the church, and ordination. A providential call meant that the minister would have natural gifts and the opportunity to improve them through education. The call from the church included the necessity for approval from other ministers. And the demand for ordination suggested that the ritual signified a conferring of authority. In Catholic and Anglican traditions, ordination conveyed the gifts of the Spirit. In other traditions, it constituted a public recognition that confirmed the inward and providential call. For most clergy, a simple claim to have received God's call was insufficient.[39]

The shortages meant that the churches often had to accept mediocre leadership. Governor William Gooch in Virginia thought in 1728 that the Anglicans had "some very good men, some very bad, and many indifferent." Muhlenberg bemoaned mediocrity among the German and Swedish Lutherans: Mr. Wolf lacked "gifts" and "failed to discharge the duties of his office." Mr. Falck "appeared to mean well but had poor judgment." Mr. Andrea was "more drunk than sober." Mr. Nyberg was "shameless." Mr. Schrenck fell into "violent, furious fits

---

37. Balmer, *A Perfect Babel,* p. 134; Amory and Hall, eds., *Colonial Book,* p. 431; Edwards, *Constitution of Primitive,* p. 15.

38. Increase Mather, *Practical Truths* (Boston: Green, 1718), pp. 105, 119-20; John Hancock, *The Danger of an Unqualified Ministry* (Boston: Rogers and Fowle, 1743), pp. 16, 20; Azariah Mather, *Gospel Minister Described,* pp. 19-20; Balmer, *Perfect Babel,* p. 134; Joseph Morgan, *The Great Concernment of Gospel Ordinances* (New York: Bradford, 1712), pp. 15-16; Foxcroft, *Practical Discourse,* p. ii.

39. Isaac Eaton, *The Qualifications, Characters, and Duties of a Good Minister of Jesus Christ, Considered* (Philadelphia: Franklin and Hall, 1755), p. 18.

of temper." Mr. Hartwich "did not have the talent for visiting and attracting people." Muhlenberg admired some of his colleagues, but he noted privately that
"the lack of faithful, steadfast, and experienced laborers is a great hindrance to
the spread of the Kingdom of Jesus Christ."[40]

Even more troubling than the uneducated and the ungifted were the fraud-
ulent. As early as 1700, Cotton Mather and a dozen colleagues warned the
churches not to be fooled by "imposter ministers," and they recounted tales of
"wretches" who pretended to knowledge they did not have, preached sermons
written by others, and cheated the people out of their money. A Dutch Reformed minister in New York in 1713 took note of "imitators," and the flow of
immigrants into the middle colonies created opportunities for pretenders. The
desire for preaching and sacraments led German settlers to accept self-attested
clerics who lied about their credentials. When Muhlenberg arrived in Pennsylvania in 1742, he found "pretenders" and "vagabonds" who traveled about trying to "get a few shillings for a baptism and the offerings at the Lord's Supper."
He told Governor Morris that there were "many more of the same sort whom
we shall never get rid of" until someone could "demand proper credentials of
all who exercise the ministry and no longer suffer vagabonds to laugh at us who
are regular clergymen by saying it is a free country and by turning liberty into
licentiousness." One reason for founding the Lutheran ministerium was a desire
to verify credentials for pastors.[41]

Even when ministers had legitimate ordination, the unity of the brotherhood could suffer as a result of doctrinal deviation. Ministerial associations in
New England assembled periodically to examine charges of heresy. The charges
could be trivial. In 1726 a Massachusetts association cleared one minister who
angered his congregation by preaching that they ought to give thanks to God
for both prosperity and affliction. But in some circles theology was changing in
the eighteenth century. While many ministers still dwelt within the cosmos of
wonders that they inherited from the past, others were becoming accustomed
to a more rational universe. For many, talk of witches and demons was now an
embarrassment. And in New England some of the more rationalist clergy also
began to have second thoughts about Calvinism.[42]

When the clergy accused each other of deviations from Calvinist ortho-

---

40. Joan Gunderson, "The Anglican Ministry in Virginia 1723-1776: A Study of Social
Class" (Ph.D. dissertation, University of Notre Dame, 1972), p. 133; Muhlenberg, *Journals*, vol. 1,
pp. 106, 107, 186, 212, 246, 395, 403, 238.

41. Cotton Mather, *A Warning to the Flocks* (Boston: B. Green and J. Allen, 1700), pp. 15-16,
17-24, 26-27; Bonomi and Eisenstadt, "Church Adherence," p. 247; Tappert, "The Church's Infancy," p. 45.

42. Parkman, "Diary," *Proceedings*, vol. 71, p. 133.

doxy during the 1730s, the associations became involved in those more serious struggles. A good number of eighteenth-century ministers abandoned strong statements of the doctrine of election, accentuated good works, and suggested that human striving might contribute to salvation. Shocked colleagues thought they subordinated divine grace to human morality. The split led to inquiries and church trials in which the associations assumed the lead. Some Calvinistic Presbyterians saw it as one purpose of the new presbyteries "to keep out of the ministry those who are corrupt in doctrine."[43]

More damaging than even doctrinal disputes were charges of misconduct. Critics pounced on any sign of ethical lapse. As early as 1697, the Board of Trade in England charged that Virginia's Anglican clergy were "too commonly vitious and scandalous in their lives." Alexander Forbes in 1724 described some of the Virginians as men of "scandalous carriage" and "vicious practice." John Long accused others of debauchery and drunkenness. In Maryland, Governor Hart found clergy whose morals were "a scandal to their profession." The Presbyterian George Gillespie charged in 1723 that six of the thirty ministers and probationers in the Synod of Philadelphia had proven to be "grossly scandalous."[44]

Such charges sometimes turned out to be false. The Rhode Island Presbyterian John Adams pointed out that clerical opponents invented "malicious Stories of Faults never committed." But misconduct still worried conscientious clergy who insisted on "unspotted Piety of Life." Fifteen percent of the two hundred Anglican clergy who served in Maryland between 1692 and 1776 faced charges of moral lapse, usually of alcohol abuse, though one study has concluded that the cases of "undoubted scandalous behavior" in that colony might not have exceeded 3 percent. In Virginia, 10 percent of the Anglican clergy between 1690 and 1776 fell into moral difficulty, usually with alcoholism, though occasionally with sexual lapses or inability to pay debts. In South Carolina, about 10 percent of the Anglican ministers who served churches between 1696 and 1775 suffered some form of scandal. Of the four hundred Congregational ministers in New England between 1680 and 1740, however, only 3 percent became involved in scandal, which again typically meant alcoholism in a society that viewed it simply as a moral failing.[45]

Even the most respected ministers could face harsh criticism. Cotton Mather warned young clergy in 1726 that they should "be prepared for obscurities, and

---

43. Butler, *Power, Authority, and the Origins*, p. 63.

44. Nelson, *A Blessed Company*, p. 151; Rightmyer, "Character," p. 120; Butler, *Power, Authority, and the Origins*, p. 61.

45. John Adams, *Jesus Christ an Example* (Newport: Franklin, 1728), p. 50; Foxcroft, *Practical Discourse*, p. 20; Bonomi, *Under the Cope*, p. 48; Rightmyer, "Character," p. 128; Nelson, *A Blessed Company*, pp. 155-56; Youngs, *God's Messengers*, p. 47.

indignities," and Daniel Lewes attested to the aptness of Mather's warning when he complained of the "Contempt" cast upon "the Gospel Ministry." Eighteenth-century clergy repeatedly complained of disrespect, prejudice, disregard, ingratitude, and misunderstanding. Thomas Foxcroft saw the profession as "reviled, despised, [and] buffeted." It would seem, Thomas Clap said, that "all the Powers of Darkness" combined themselves against the ministry. If anti-clericalism is defined as a sustained opposition to the existence of a clerical class, eighteenth-century America had no strong anti-clerical movement, but anti-ministerial sentiment could still create dismay.[46]

In Congregational and Baptist churches, anti-ministerial rhetoric sometimes represented no more than a zealous solicitude for lay initiative. When the young Timothy Cutler in Connecticut complained in 1717 of "Vile Words that are cast about, of Priest-Craft, and Priest-Ridden, and an Ambitious and Designing Clergy," he was referring to grassroots lay suspicions of clerical authority. Many of the laity — and some of the clergy — in New England Congregational churches resisted efforts by the minister to govern the church "without the consent of the brethren." Ministers who tried to do that could not escape criticism.[47]

The ministers in state church establishments — or in denominations that insisted on an educated and salaried clergy — became objects of ridicule from separatist or dissenting groups. The Anglican Charles Woodmason reported in the 1760s that "New Light Baptists" in the Carolinas mocked the established clergy as "Children of Hell" and that he had to endure their insults "where ever I Go": "They call'd Mr. Turquand a Turkey Cock (because he has a rosy Complexion) and Mr. Richardson (who is a Pale man) The Pale or White Horse of Death, for his People to ride on to Hell." The German Reformed leader Michael Schlatter told authorities in Germany to send only young ministers who could have "sympathy toward those who oppose them." The learned clergy, in turn, could be equally contemptuous of upstart preachers; Woodmason ridiculed the "Wretches," "unholy Apostles" and "Pretended Prophet[s]" of the New Lights.[48]

Beneath the surface of society bubbled a latent resentment of authority,

---

46. Cotton Mather, *Manducatio ad Ministerium*, p. 27; Daniel Lewes, *Of Taking Heed To, and Fulfilling, the Ministry* (Boston: S. Kneeland, 1720), p. ii; Clap, *Greatness and Difficulty*, pp. 15-16; Youngs, *God's Messengers*, p. 97; Harlan, *Clergy and the Great Awakening*, pp. 39-40; Foxcroft, *Practical Discourse*, p. 4.

47. Timothy Cutler, *The Firm Union of a People Represented* (New London: Green, 1717), 53; Harlan, *Clergy and the Great Awakening*, 40.

48. Charles Woodmason, *The Carolina Backcountry on the Eve of the Revolution*, ed. Richard J. Hooker (Chapel Hill: The University of North Carolina Press, 1953), pp. 78, 79, 111, 114; Bonomi, *Under the Cope*, p. 80.

and the clergy were symbols of authority. The resentment could flare up without much warning. When several ministers in Boston in 1721 supported small-pox vaccination in the face of community opposition, the bitter feelings against "Conscience Directors" led to an outpouring of anti-ministerial sentiment in the newspapers. Later New England clergy warned each other about "gentlemen not over-tender of ministers of the churches."[49]

Conflicts between clergy and their congregations could be especially unsettling. Some ministers found their congregations "critical, rigid, [and] censorious." Between 1680 and 1740, for instance, 112 of 400 Congregationalist and Presbyterian ministers in New England and on Long Island had serious trouble with their congregations: forty-eight had financial disputes, thirty-two became embroiled in conflict over the division of a parish or the building of a new meetinghouse, twenty fought theologically with their members, and the rest had personality conflicts. Thirty-two of the four hundred had to leave their churches. A number of clergy fell into trouble with their congregations in the 1720s when they tried to change worship by having their congregations sing by note and in harmony.[50] Later in the century, Ebenezer Parkman listed fifty-five of his colleagues whose congregations had dismissed them. Theological fame could not offer protection; after disputes about membership criteria, communion, church discipline, and salary, the Northampton, Massachusetts, congregation dismissed Jonathan Edwards. Some ministers felt that parishioners viewed them as "unnecessary" and disparaged them as "unprofitable burdens."[51]

Some worried that the laity had too much power over them. Mittelberger remarked that Pennsylvania churches hired their ministers by the year, "like cowherds in Germany," making that colony "hell for . . . preachers." Some middle colony Lutherans feared that such annual contracts would permit the laity "to drive out pious pastors when the year is up." Worries about the power of vestries continued also to trouble Anglican ministers. The barons of the Virginia plantations could sometimes expect "mean, low, and humble obedience" from their ministers, and they could use the vestries to get their way. In 1747, planter Landon Carter physically assaulted Rev. William McKay, who had preached on pride; then Carter convinced the vestry to dismiss the

---

49. Robert Middlekauff, *The Mathers: Three Generations of Puritan Intellectuals, 1596-1728* (New York: Oxford University Press, 1971), pp. 354-59; George Marsden, *Jonathan Edwards: A Life* (New Haven: Yale University Press, 2003), p. 359.

50. John Callender, *A Sermon Preached at the Ordination of Mr. Jeremiah Condy* (Boston: Kneeland and Green, 1739), p. 10; Clifford K. Shipton, "The New England Clergy of the 'Glacial Age,'" *Colonial Society of Massachusetts Publications* 32 (1933): 36, 50.

51. Youngs, *God's Messengers*, p. 104; Marsden, *Jonathan Edwards*, pp. 357-74; Harlan, *Clergy and the Great Awakening*, 39-40.

pastor. The vestries maintained control even after the House of Burgesses passed a 1749 statute granting tenure to Anglican rectors whom the parish had formally accepted.[52]

The hiring of a minister in New England became an intricate dance that could keep candidates waiting for months. In the 1720s, Ipswich nominated eight candidates and expected each to preach at the church for three months before the congregation chose one of them. The churches then usually required a trial period before the signing of a final contract, and the congregation always retained the power to dismiss the minister.[53]

The ministerial associations served to help the clergy handle this whole array of privileges and problems. No single motive accounts for their creation or their persistence. Some saw them as expressions of biblical mandates; others supported them because they represented familiar ways of organizing clerical work, or simply because they appeared useful. Clergy used them to work out their relationships with lay leaders, but they also used them to discipline each other, to maintain doctrinal unity, and to guide younger ministers into the profession. They were about power and status, but they were also about settling disputes, providing mutual support, and spreading the gospel.

Ministry

Eighteenth-century Congregationalist and Presbyterian ordination sermons contained a standard list of clerical duties. They told the new clergy to preach, administer the sacraments, teach, counsel, discipline, visit, comfort, catechize, reconcile, and evangelize. Anglicans added admonitions to "perform every Part of Divine Service" with decorum. Lutherans recited the standard list but emphasized catechizing, confirming children, and hearing confessions (sometimes private and sometimes collective) before administering the Lord's Supper. Catholics elevated the sacramental duties, the celebration of the "divine Mysteries." The lists were familiar, but the eighteenth century brought changes in tone and emphasis.[54]

52. Gottlieb Mittelberger, *Journey to Pennsylvania*, ed. Oscar Handlin and John Clive (Cambridge: Harvard University Press, 1960), pp. 47, 48; Simon Hart and Jarry J. Kreider, eds., *Protocol of the Lutheran Church in New York City, 1702-1750* (New York: New York Synod, 1958), p. 311; Bonomi and Eisenstadt, "Church Adherence," p. 247; Tappert, "Church's Infancy," pp. 55, 61; Isaac, *Transformation*, pp. 143-44; Bonomi, *Under the Cope*, p. 44.

53. Youngs, *God's Messengers*, p. 27.

54. Adams, *Gracious Presence*, pp. 11-12; Morgan, *Great Concernment*, p. 29; Increase Mather, *Practical Truths*, p. 106; Shelton Smith, Robert Handy, and Lefferts Loetscher, eds.,

Preaching could make strenuous demands on congregations. The New England sermon was anywhere from forty-five minutes to two hours long. Cotton Mather preached a two-hour sermon at a hanging in Boston, and at Mather's ordination, his prayer and sermon together lasted three hours and a quarter. (Cotton Mather was a man of many words.) John Barnard typically preached for an hour and a quarter. Charles Chauncy in Boston tried to limit his sermons to forty-five minutes. Anglican sermons were shorter because they were part of the liturgy. The New Englander Philip Fithian, who tutored children in Virginia and regularly heard the sermons of Thomas Smith in Cople Parish, found several too short. It was not unusual for a southern Anglican sermon to last only twenty minutes.[55]

Reliance on notes — or even manuscripts — became a common practice. Some Puritan preachers had frowned on it, and some revivalists criticized it, but increasingly ministers read their sermon manuscripts from the pulpit. In Baptist churches and among Congregational separatists, Methodists, and smaller German groups, the extemporaneous sermon, preached without either manuscript or notes, conveyed greater spiritual force. In New England it had always been considered "disreputable, if not criminal" for a minister to preach a sermon stolen from another preacher, but some Anglicans considered it permissible to preach the published sermons of others, and several freely borrowed from the English archbishop John Tillotson and others.[56]

Ministers in New England changed their minds about funeral sermons and weddings. European clergy had traditionally presided at weddings and officiated at funerals, and Catholics, Anglicans, and Lutherans maintained the practice. In Virginia, Anglican priests alone could conduct marriage ceremonies. In New England, seventeenth-century preachers had found no biblical precedent for church weddings, but by the eighteenth century the clergy began to replace the magistrates at weddings. They also reassessed their attitudes toward funerals. At the earliest New England burials, ministers attended but read no liturgy and preached no sermon. They permitted funeral sermons later in the day or week, however, and by the mid-1670s they began to preach sermons before the

American Christianity: An Historical Interpretation with Representative Documents, 2 vols. (New York: Scribner's, 1963), vol. 1, p. 251; Muhlenberg, *Journals*, vol. 1, pp. 118-19; 145, 177, 295, 415, 449, 497, 522; John Tracy Ellis, ed., *Documents of American Catholic History* (Milwaukee: Bruce, 1956), p. 188.

55. Horton Davies, *The Worship of the American Puritans* (New York: Peter Lang, 1990), pp. 101-02; Harry S. Stout, *The New England Soul: Preaching and Religious Culture in Colonial New England* (New York: Oxford University Press, 1986), p. 153; Bonomi, *Under the Cope*, p. 101.

56. Youngs, *God's Messengers*, pp. 61-62; Davies, *Worship*, p. 103; Peter Oliver, *The Puritan Commonwealth* (Boston: Little Brown, 1855), p. 159.

burial. In Virginia, Anglican clergy preached funeral sermons for pay when families sought their services.[57]

For everyone, it was more important to talk with the dying than to bury the dead. Catholics made these final moments sacramental, employing oils and prayers in the rite of extreme unction. Protestants concentrated on preparing the dying for their death. The aim was to "set them in the direct Course to Heaven." In 1727, Ebenezer Parkman attended at the bedside of Mistress Forbush, to whom he addressed pointed questions in order to assist her "in preparing actually to give up her account to the great judge" after she passed from this world. "We act most wisely," he said, "to look all over as carefully as possible to find out whatever escapes or flaws there may be, since it can never be done after throughout Eternity, and Eternity depends upon this account." No pastoral visit was more important than the final one.[58]

The main means of pastoral care was still the visit to the home. Parkman made as many as six visits a day, and in some cases of sickness he remained at the house overnight. The purpose of such visiting, as Cotton Mather wrote, was to inquire into the state of the soul and to offer lessons in piety. Thomas Clap in Windham, Connecticut, used visits to prepare notes on the spiritual condition of his 700 parishioners. Lutheran Pietist pastors asked for narratives of conversion and evidence of grace. Muhlenberg objected when one pastor allowed lay elders to join him on his visits, complaining that they would inhibit members from disclosing to the pastor "in confidence" matters on which they desired "counsel and comfort." Some visits remained at the level of casual conversation. One minister argued in 1772 that visits should help people overcome their fear of the clergy and learn to converse freely with them. But the overriding purpose was spiritual inquiry and guidance.[59]

Lutheran clergy put in long hours working with children. Berkenmeyer in New York complained in 1725 that his parishioners knew "little of catechisms," so he distributed thirty copies of Luther's Small Catechism and began, like

57. Nelson, *A Blessed Company*, pp. 223, 228; Bonomi, *Under the Cope*, p. 69; Davies, *Worship*, pp. 193-95, 219; Thomas Lechford, *Plain Dealing or News from New England* (1st. ed, 1642; Boston: Wiggin and Lunt, 1847), p. 94; Daniel Dorchester, *Christianity in the United States* (New York: Hunt and Eaton, 1890), p. 154; David E. Stannard, *The Puritan Way of Death* (New York: Oxford University Press, 1977), pp. 109-22.

58. Clap, *Greatness and Difficulty*, p. 17; Parkman, "Diary," in *Proceedings*, vol. 71, p. 189.

59. Parkman, "Diary," in *Proceedings*, vol. 71, p. 369; Cotton Mather, *A Brief Memorial of Matters and Methods for Pastoral Visits* (Boston: n.p., 1723), pp. 1-3; Youngs, *God's Messengers*, p. 49; Tappert, "The Church's Infancy," p. 71; Muhlenberg, *Journals*, vol. 1, p. 434; Samuel Stilman, *The Substance of a Sermon Preached at the Ordination of the Reverend Samuel Shepard* (Boston: Kneeland, 1772), pp. 15-16.

other Lutherans, to make catechetical instruction a necessary prelude for admission to the Lord's Supper. By 1745, Muhlenberg could write that "a catechism is as much a necessity for us as our daily bread." Lutherans in Pennsylvania employed lay catechists in the schools, but Muhlenberg spent much of his time catechizing children — sometimes alongside adults — on Sundays, and he worked to secure one catechism for all the congregations. In 1785 the Pennsylvania Ministerium adopted an official text of Luther's shorter catechism.[60]

In other traditions, ministers devoted varying amounts of time to catechizing. Cotton Mather believed that it accomplished "great things," and some Calvinist clergy led classes twice a week. Others taught only once a month, and still others allowed catechetical work to lapse for long periods. Eleven-year-old Anna Green Winslow in Boston wrote in her journal in 1771 that several of the ministers had agreed "during the long evenings to discourse upon the questions . . . in the [Westminster] assembly's shorter catechism," and she also mentioned sermons on the catechism. In Virginia, it was customary to catechize in the summer and during Lent. In the 1720s, 92 percent of the Virginia clergy responding to the bishop of London reported that they taught the catechism for a period each year. Some dropped the practice because parents objected to sending their children long distances.[61]

They included adults in catechism classes and preached from the catechism on Sunday mornings, but efforts to teach could seem fruitless. Parkman bemoaned "the irreligion and ignorance of many (professedly Christian) Families among us of this Country, notwithstanding the Care universally taken for their instruction." Jarratt found his parishioners "extremely ignorant of divine things," but he believed that his group meetings let him teach the "evangelical truths" about which his congregations were confused. No one could make any assumptions about religious knowledge.[62]

Most ministers had plenty of time to educate a congregation. Ministers in New England normally began their pastorates when they were between twenty-one and twenty-five years old. Anglicans could not assume a pastorate until they were twenty-four. A small number entered the ministry from other careers, but the norm was for ministers to begin young and to stay with one congregation. The average New England minister filled his pulpit for more

60. Arthur C. Repp Sr., *Luther's Catechism Comes to America* (Metuchen: Scarecrow and the American Theological Library Association, 1982), pp. 23, 24, 26, 40; Muhlenberg, *Journals,* vol. 1, pp. 77, 99, 329, 446.

61. Mather, *Manuductio ad Ministerium,* p. 115; Youngs, *God's Messengers,* p. 48; Alice Morse Earle, ed., *Diary of Anna Green Winslow* (Boston: Houghton Mifflin, 1894), pp. 24, 63; Brydon, *Virginia's Mother Church,* pp. 372-73; Nelson, *A Blessed Company,* p. 219.

62. Parkman, "Diary," in *Proceedings,* vol. 71, p. 155; Jarratt, *Life,* pp. 52-53.

than twenty-five years, and it was not uncommon to remain in one church for half a century. Eighty percent of the Anglican clergy in Virginia remained in a single parish throughout their ministry, and almost half held their posts for more than twenty years. Muhlenberg's journals did, however, record frequent moves among Lutheran pastors, and Methodists moved around as a matter of policy.[63]

The long tenure of the clergy reflected a high degree of local authority. Once appointed to a church, most retained sufficient respect and affection to occupy a lifelong office. In practice, ministers gained authority when they performed the duties of the office in a way that drew the assent of their parishioners. But clergy in the eighteenth century also endured two of the most significant challenges to traditional views of clerical authority that ministers in America had ever had to face: first Revival, then Revolution.

Ambiguous Awakening

Periods of religious excitement could upset normal expectations. In seven of the colonies, the revivals that followed in the wake of George Whitefield's tours of America after 1739 brought severe challenges to habitual patterns. Whitefield was a star, and he attracted lay devotees and clerical imitators. Traveling from colony to colony, he appeared to represent the height of clerical power and influence, conducting services that could fill churches and draw thousands of people to his outdoor meetings. But he set the clergy against one another and positioned many of the laity against their ministers. Congregationalists divided into "New Light" supporters of the revivals and "Old Light" opponents. Presbyterians had similar "New Side" and "Old Side" factions. The revivals threw the ministry off balance.

Whitefield popularized an "extempore Manner of preaching" with earthy and dramatic language and theatrical flair. To his opponents, the sermons seemed little more than "harangues" — "profane Reveries" — that employed "a Manner of Diction or Phraseology" that brought "downright Disgrace to the sacred Function of the Ministry." To his many imitators, Whitefield brought a welcome alternative to "the learned and elaborate Discourses" of clergy whose sermons now appeared as "without life or Power." Charles Chauncy complained that they appealed only to the emotions, but the revivalists attacked "the dull and lifeless manner of delivering of Sermons" that they

---

63. Gunderson, "Anglican Ministry," pp. 49-50; Youngs, *God's Messengers*, p. 29; Nelson, *A Blessed Company*, pp. 131-32.

heard in most pulpits. Never had so many colonial preachers been so divided about preaching.[64]

The content of sermons caused as many disputes as their style. The revivalists preached "the Terrors of the Law" to convict their hearers of sinfulness; their opponents thought they overdid it. Revivalists proclaimed justification by faith alone; their critics thought they went to the extreme of disparaging moral actions. Revivalists demanded experiences of conversion; anti-revivalists worried that they left the impression that regeneration always occurred in a set manner. Some revivalists insisted that converts have an immediate witness of the Spirit, assuring them of salvation; anti-revivalists thought that this sounded fanatical. No vast doctrinal differences separated the two factions, but the revivals made the ministers suspicious of one another.[65]

Critics felt shock when women stood before congregations and witnessed to the work of the Spirit or when Africans — slave and free — exhorted the unsaved. Chauncy complained that lay preachers — male and female — claimed to need "no books but the Bible." Possessing the Spirit, they desired no learning. For a half century after Whitefield's tour, populists still repeated the awakening's challenge to "a learned ministry." The illiterate, they said, make more converts than the learned.[66]

Then there was the problem of itinerancy. Imitating Whitefield, scores of lay and clerical itinerants began after 1740 "to travel about Preaching" in "other Men's pulpits or at least into their especial charge, without their desire or consent." In the eyes of the critics, they were "Pedlars in Divinity," intruding into the territory of others "to the Disturbance of the Peace of the Church." The Presbyterian Synod of Philadelphia declared that no minister should preach "in another's Bounds," and the Congregationalist Old Lights in Connecticut turned to the General Assembly to curb the practice. When Whitefield returned in 1744, the Harvard faculty declared that his itinerating was his "most pernicious Tendency" because he and his imitators "thrust themselves into Towns

64. John Thomson, "The Government of the Church of Christ" (1741), in *Great Awakening*, pp. 124-25; "The Testimony of the Professors, Tutors, and Hebrew Instructors of Harvard College, Against George Whitefield," in *Great Awakening*, p. 350; Samuel Finley, "Christ Triumphing and Satan Raging" (1741), in *Great Awakening*, p. 155.

65. Gilbert Tennent, "Remarks Upon a Protestation" (1741), in *Great Awakening*, p. 170; E. Brooks Holifield, *Theology in America: From the Era of the Puritans to the Civil War* (New Haven: Yale University Press, 2003), pp. 95, 97.

66. Timothy D. Hall, *Contested Boundaries: Itinerancy and the Reshaping of the Colonial American Religious World* (Durham: Duke University Press, 1994), p. 38; Charles Chauncy, *Seasonable Thoughts on the State of Religion in New England* (Boston: Rogers and Fowle, 1743), p. 259; Benjamin Trumbull, *A Sermon Delivered at the Ordination of the Rev. Lemuel Tyler* (New Haven: Green, 1793), p. 9.

and Parishes" in an unprecedented way that made people ready to "despise their own ministers," but the new practice was hard to stop.[67]

In the 1750s, itinerant preachers imported the revival into the South. Baptist itinerants — former Congregationalists — moved into Guilford County in central North Carolina and from there radiated outward, prompting complaints that "vagrants" were trying to "subvert all order." In 1767, Charles Woodmason complained about "Itinerant Teachers, Preachers, and Imposters from New England and Pennsylvania — Baptists, New Lights, Presbyterians, Independents, and an hundred other Sects." In 1773, Methodist itinerants were traveling through the colonies from New York to Virginia, stirring emotions and forming "class meetings" for fellowship and discipline. Virginians passed laws that restricted preaching to "qualified teachers" meeting in "licensed houses," but itinerancy eroded boundaries. It spread the message but divided the messengers.[68]

The divisions were deep and bitter. When Gilbert Tennent traveled from Pennsylvania into New England to denounce the "unconverted" clergy of the region, he unleashed a rhetoric of abuse that conveyed, as Chauncy complained, sheer "contempt." Tennent claimed that ministers unwilling to testify to an experience of conversion lacked all authority: "Is a blind Man fit to be a Guide in a very dangerous Way? Is a dead Man fit to bring others to Life?" Accusing these men of "Rottenness, and Hypocrisie," he urged their parishioners to abandon them, and many followed his advice. In New England, they formed more than a hundred separatist congregations.[69]

Jonathan Edwards defended the revivals, but he lamented the disposition to "give ministers over as reprobates." Such accusations, he noted, had "stirred up great contention, and set all in a flame." Clergy had disagreed in the past, often vigorously, but never had so many laity been exposed, for such an extended period, to such a bitter rupture within clerical ranks. The awakenings produced a sustained attack on clerical authority, and the assailants were other clergy, though the laity also felt free to offer their own negative judgments. The dis-

67. Hall, *Contested Boundaries*, pp. 37-38, 49, 60, citing the *Boston Weekly Post-Boy*, Sept. 28, 1741; John Thomson, *The Government of the Church of Christ* (Philadelphia: Bradford, 1741), pp. 7-8; "The Testimony," in *Great Awakening*, pp. 351-52.

68. William Lumpkin, *Baptist Foundations in the South* (Nashville: Boardman, 1961), p. 55; Woodmason, *Carolina Backcountry*, p. 13; Russell E. Richey, Kenneth E. Rowe, and Jean Miller Schmidt, eds., *The Methodist Experience in America: A Sourcebook*, 2 vols. (Nashville: Abingdon, 2000), vol. 2, p. 57; Hall, *Contested Boundaries*, p. 126.

69. Charles Chauncy, "Enthusiasm Described and Cautioned Against" (1742), in *Great Awakening*, p. 236; Gilbert Tennent, "The Dangers of an Unconverted Ministry" (1740), in *Great Awakening*, pp. 80, 95; C. C. Goen, *Revivalism and Separatism in New England* (New Haven: Yale University Press, 1962).

putes also represented a shift, among the revivalists, from an appeal to the authority of office toward even greater reliance on personal charisma. Several colonies remained indifferent to the revivals, but in the regions swept by revival fervor, the profession felt the shock they produced.[70]

Crumbling Establishment

The growth of the American population changed the ministry in America. In 1700, the colonies contained 250,000 people, a third of them clustered in New England. By 1790, the number grew to 3,929,000, scattered from the northern tip of Maine to southern Georgia. The expansion increased the number of congregations, and it also increased denominational pluralism, which would eventually alter the status and authority of the clergy, especially as the agitation for colonial independence began to advance revolutionary ideas that encouraged the colonial governments to abandon their financial support of ministers.

In 1700, the regions that would eventually comprise the thirteen colonies probably had about four hundred local churches. By 1776, the number had risen to more than 3,228. In 1700, roughly 36 percent of the churches were Congregational and 27 percent were Anglican. In 1776, the Congregational churches had only about 21 percent, while the Anglicans fell to 15 percent. The Presbyterians, enrolling immigrants from Northern Ireland, moved into second place, with about 18 percent, while the Baptists, buoyed by revivalist piety, rose to about 15 percent. Quakers remained strong with 10 percent of the churches, and the German Reformed and Lutheran denominations had roughly 5 percent each. A variety of smaller groups shared the remainder. When Gottlieb Mittelberger arrived in Pennsylvania, he marveled at finding "so many varieties and doctrines of sects that it is impossible to name them all."[71]

70. Jonathan Edwards, "Some Thoughts Concerning the Present Revival," in *Great Awakening*, p. 286; Frank Lambert, *"Pedlar in Divinity": George Whitefield and the Transatlantic Revivals, 1737-1770* (Princeton: Princeton University Press, 1994); Frank Lambert, *Inventing the "Great Awakening"* (Princeton: Princeton University Press, 1999), pp. 125-38.

71. In 1700, 9 percent were Baptist, 7 percent Presbyterian, 7 percent Quaker, 6 percent Dutch Reformed, 6 percent Catholic, and 2 percent Lutheran. In 1776, the Dutch Reformed dipped to 4 percent. The Methodists, not yet separated from the Church of England, had a sufficient number of "societies" in 1776 to give them slightly less than 2 percent of the total. The Catholics also stood at less than 2 percent, though the addition of Catholic missions in the west would slightly raise the percentage. The remaining 7 percent of churches were divided among Moravians, Congregational Separates, Dunkers, Mennonites, French Protestants, Sandemanians, Rogerenes, and Independents.

The numbers are informed estimates, and different historians reach different conclusions.

Dissenters disliked paying taxes to support a minister of another church. In four colonies, that was no problem. In Pennsylvania, New Jersey, and Delaware, Quakers blocked any governmental maintenance for preachers. The Quakers, Baptists, Separatists, and assorted radicals who settled in Rhode Island also had no liking for religious taxes. In these regions, the clergy depended on voluntary contributions, funding from mission societies, and farming. But in nine of the colonies, the clergy received salaries mandated by the state.[72]

In the southern colonies the state money went to Anglicans. Virginia parishes paid with a fixed quantity of tobacco, often supplemented by a glebe, a residence, and two hundred or more acres of land that they could farm or lease. In Maryland, the Anglican clergy received a fixed weight of tobacco for each taxable person in the parish. In 1706, the South Carolina provincial assembly voted to support Anglican ministers from import duties and a tax on slaves instead of from parish assessments. After 1758 Georgia provided glebe lands and modest financial support from appropriations and liquor duties, though some of the money went to dissenters. In North Carolina, with only six Anglican clerics in 1764, the act of establishment had little force.[73]

In New England, state-mandated funds went to Congregationalists. In 1629, Massachusetts required each town to support an "able, learned, and orthodox minister," and the law survived into the eighteenth century. New Hampshire and Connecticut passed similar acts. The New England laws did not specify the amount of the salaries, which varied from town to town, and the arrangement did not always work. The Connecticut General Assembly in 1735 had to decree that no town could legally fall more than two months behind in paying the minister. But by then every New England taxpayer outside Boston helped maintain the Congregationalist clergy.[74]

E. S. Gaustad, *Historical Atlas of Religion in America* (New York: Harper and Row, 1962), pp. 3-4, 33, found 373 congregations in seven denominations, not including Quakers, in 1700. He found 2,731 congregations from eight groups, again not including Quakers, in 1780. Charles O. Paullin, *Atlas of the Historical Geography of the United States* (Baltimore: Carnegie Institution of Washington and the American Geographical Society of New York, 1932), pp. 50, 245-86, found 2,637 among the same eight groups in 1776. John K. Nelson, *A Blessed Company*, p. 29, and Bonomi and Eisenstadt, "Church Adherence," pp. 245-86, found more Anglican congregations than Gaustad. Paullin estimated that he missed at least 150 churches. Still, the estimates illumine general patterns of distribution.

72. Thomas J. Curry, *The First Freedoms: Church and State in America to the Passage of the First Amendment* (New York: Oxford University Press, 1896), p. 73.

73. Bonomi, *Under the Cope*, pp. 47, 49, 50; Nelson, *A Blessed Company*, pp. 48, 50.

74. Leonard W. Levy, *The Establishment Clause: Religion and the First Amendment* (New York: Macmillan, 1986), pp. 15, 23; Shipton, "New England Clergy," p. 48; Youngs, *God's Messen-*

New York was a special case. In six of its ten counties, it collected no church tax, but despite the Dutch Reformed majority, the Anglican Governor Benjamin Fletcher persuaded the Assembly in 1693 to require the other four counties to support "a good sufficient Protestant Minister." Anglicans — including the governor — thought that the law restricted the money to Anglican clergy. Most of the Assembly — and the clergy of other denominations — thought that local communities ought to decide. Disputes flared when dissenters appointed their ministers to the churches and made a claim to public support. The local communities interpreted the law as they pleased.[75]

By the 1720s, the establishments began to crumble. Anglicans convinced the general court in Massachusetts in 1727 that they should not have to pay for Congregational ministers. Their tax could go to Anglicans if they could prove that they attended an Anglican church near their homes. But Baptists and Quakers objected in principle to tax money for any clerical salaries. In 1728, the court exempted them if they could offer the same proof as the Anglicans, but they remained dissatisfied. The disputes resumed in the 1740s when New Light separatists objected to paying for Old Light ministers. The Separate Baptist minister Isaac Backus led a thirty-year struggle against Congregational establishment. Complaining of magistrates who imprisoned Baptists and confiscated their property, Backus insisted that ministers who preached the gospel should "live of the Gospel." His campaign ended in failure when the Massachusetts constitution of 1780 assessed every taxpayer for the support of Protestant ministers.[76]

Connecticut granted dissenters liberty to worship, but it still made them pay taxes to support Congregational clergy. An act of 1727 permitted Anglicans to assign their church tax to their own ministers, and two years later the assembly exempted Baptists and Quakers, but they had to prove membership in congregations with resident ministers and church buildings, and only one Baptist and one Anglican group could prove it. The state constitution of 1784 still mandated taxation on behalf of all Protestant ministers, so while Congregationalists lost their monopoly they held on to state funding. New Hampshire's state constitution of 1784 also created a general Protestant establishment, allowing each town to decide which minister to support.[77]

---

gers, p. 26; H. James Henderson, "Taxation and Political Culture: Massachusetts and Virginia, 1760-1800," *William and Mary Quarterly* 47 (1990): 98.

75. Smith, Handy, and Loetscher, eds., *American Christianity,* vol. 1, p. 248; Frantz, "Awakening of Religion," p. 273; Curry, *First Freedoms,* pp. 67, 71.

76. William McLoughlin, ed., *Isaac Backus on Church, State, and Calvinism: Pamphlets, 1754-1789* (Cambridge: Harvard University Press, 1968), p. 318; Levy, *Establishment Clause,* pp. 15-20, 26-28.

77. Bonomi, *Under the Cope,* p. 66; Levy, *Establishment Clause,* pp. 38-44.

Outside these three New England states, the clergy lost their tax support. In 1750, about 39 percent of American congregations paid state-mandated salaries. When the states adopted new constitutions after the Revolution, only about 23 percent stood under state regulation. In 1776, Pennsylvania and New Jersey determined that no person could be required to "maintain any ministry," and within two years eight other colonies followed their lead. Virginia suspended taxes for ministers in 1776, and three years later the suspension became permanent. Thomas Jefferson's Bill for Establishing Religious Freedom in 1786 declared that no one could be compelled to support "any . . . ministry whatsoever." Even before the passage of the First Amendment to the U.S. Constitution in 1791, most states decided that financial support for the clergy should not be a responsibility of government.[78]

Even with state support, the clergy had no assurance of an "honourable maintenance." John Tufts believed that too many congregations gave the minister "just enough to maintain a Middling Tradesman's or Farmer's Family decently," without regard to the minister's "Place and Station in the World." In the 1730s, clergy in New England received about £60 a year, paid in cash and produce, along with firewood and some assistance on the farm. This was about twice the salary of schoolteachers, and it would have sufficed for a comfortable "middling" life had the towns regularly paid on time.[79]

Inflation ate away at incomes, and disparities marked the salary scales. The Hampshire Association in Connecticut reported in 1734 that some salaries were worth no more than £40 a year "as our Bills are now sunk." After 1770, ministers could receive anywhere from £40 to £260, but the average was about £100, which hardly kept pace with inflation, but it kept ministers near the middle of the scale. Physicians received about the same income, but elite lawyers took in as much as £2000, while the highest paid minister in Boston received £260. Laborers earned little more than £18 a year, while artisans had incomes of £25 to £45 and schoolteachers lived on £20 to £75.[80]

The problem was that towns fell behind in payments, or divided into two

78. For the percentages, see Holifield, "Toward a History," pp. 31, 49, n. 24; for the state constitutions, see B. P. Pore, ed., *The Federal and State Constitutions, Colonial Charters, and Organic Laws, Part I* (Union: The Lawbook Exchange, 2001), pp. 258-1859; Smith, Handy, and Loetscher, eds., *American Christianity,* vol. 1, p. 447.

79. John Tufts, *Anti-Ministerial Objections Considered, Or, The Unreasonable Pleas Made by Some Against their Duty to their Ministers* (Boston: B. Greene, 1725), pp. 8, 12; Shipton, "New England Clergy," p. 52.

80. Bonomi, *Under the Cope,* p. 70; Bridenbaugh, *Mitre and Sceptre,* p. 81; Henderson, "Taxation," p. 98; Jackson Turner Main, *The Social Structure of Revolutionary America* (Princeton: Princeton University Press, 1965), pp. 68-114.

parishes and reduced the salaries for both, or paid less than the promised amount. Parkman complained of "ingratitude," asserting that few pastors could support themselves with what they received from their congregations. In 1746 he pointed out to the town meeting that for five months he had received none of the money that was due him, and 12 percent of the New England clergy in the first half of the century had similar conflicts over salary with their congregations. Ordination sermons implored the laity to help the minister avoid "Poverty" and to devote full time to the work of the church.[81]

Anglicans in the South fared slightly better. The Virginia legislature set the rate in 1727 at sixteen thousand pounds of tobacco, which could have a value of £50 to £120, depending on the quality. By 1770, the average allotment brought in £100 to £150. The clergy in Maryland received thirty-five pounds of tobacco for each taxable person, which made them the highest paid ministers in the colonies, with incomes sometimes exceeding £200 a year. Only Charleston, South Carolina, which paid a salary of more than £300, could compete with the higher-paying Maryland parishes. The southern coastal parishes therefore drew Anglican clergy from other colonies. Evan Evans departed from Pennsylvania for Maryland with the observation that "nobody will serve the Church for Nought."[82]

The governing class in Virginia had no intention of creating a class of wealthy vicars. In the 1750s, when it appeared that tobacco values would rise, the Assembly allowed parishioners to replace the tobacco payment with a cash amount. Some of the clergy appealed to England and won their case — it became known as the Parsons' Cause — but county courts ignored the English decision, and Virginia politicians excoriated the offending pastors. For Anglicans outside the South, salaries could be insecure. The SPG paid anywhere from £20 to £70 a year, but the stipends did not always arrive, and they induced congregations to reduce their own payments. Anglicans in New England usually served poor congregations and depended on the supplements. The vicar in Lewes, Delaware, relied on "the Precarious Contribution of a very poor People," tempting him to "Connive at many of their irregular actions."[83]

In the German and Dutch churches, ministers had an even harder time. The German sects denounced "hireling ministers" and expected their clergy to support themselves. German Reformed congregations sometimes lacked funds

---

81. Parkman, "Diary," in *Proceedings*, vol. 71, pp. 144, 212, 418; Youngs, *God's Messengers*, p. 107; Joseph Parsons, *The Validity of Presbyterian Ordination* (Boston: Kneeland and Green, 1733), p. 20; Jeremiah Wise, *Prayer for a Succession* (Boston: Fleet, 1731), p. 20; Ebenezer Thayer, *Ministers of the Gospel* (Boston: Gerrish, 1727), p. 27.

82. Gunderson, "Anglican Ministry," pp. 11, 16; Henderson, "Taxation," p. 98; Nelson, *A Blessed Company*, p. 48.

83. Nelson, *A Blessed Company*, p. 49; Butler, *Power, Authority, and the Origins*, pp. 70, 72.

to pay. Salaries for Lutherans after 1750 ranged from £50 to £100 a year, but the preachers often failed to receive their full pay. They charged fees for services like funerals and weddings, but these small amounts made little difference. Eric Bjork in Delaware wrote that he lived "worse than a common laborer." The Germans took a large part of their pay in produce and firewood, and few of them attained even a "middling" status.[84]

The magistrates abandoned the ministers, but the ministers remained involved with the state. In New England election and militia sermons — and sometimes in Sunday sermons — they presented Christian theories of political order and interpreted political and military events. During the French and Indian War (1754-1763), they depicted the colonies as citadels of liberty against satanic political power, and they also recruited for the army. New England ministers opposed the English Stamp Act in 1765 so vigorously that one loyalist judge labeled them the "black regiment" that sounded "the Yell of Rebellion." An Anglican vicar disparaged "the dissenting clergy" as the "chief instruments" of "Tumult, and Disaffection." By contrast, the northern Anglican clergy favored the Stamp Act and counseled obedience.[85]

In the 1770s, the clergy took sides for and against the royal governors. Loyalists charged that New England clerical critics of English policy "had quite unlearned the Gospel, & had substituted Politicks in its Stead." During the Revolution, ministers spoke for and against separation from England, served on local committees of correspondence, helped organize the state conventions, and served as delegates to provincial congresses. A good many ministers resisted political involvement, but clergy in the larger denominations sometimes performed political duties and negotiated with Native Americans and backcountry settlers on behalf of revolutionary governments.[86]

Struggles over ministry fed into the battles over politics. An insistent company of Anglicans wanted a bishop in the colonies. By the 1760s, non-Anglican clergy feared that the Church of England intended to send bishops with secular powers, and they suspected a plot to expand Anglican establishment. Every move the Anglicans made — from trying to control King's College in New York to building an elaborate house for the minister in Cambridge — aroused new suspicions, and the newspapers gave the issue so much attention that some readers became "tired of the dispute." Most southern Anglicans were indiffer-

84. Frantz, "Awakening of Religion," p. 268; Bonomi, *Under the Cope,* p. 96; Tappert, "Church's Infancy," pp. 61-62; Horace Burr, ed., *The Records of Holy Trinity (Old Swedes) Church* (Wilmington: Historical Society of Delaware, 1890), pp. 114, 116.

85. Alice M. Baldwin, *The New England Clergy and the American Revolution* (1st ed., 1928; New York: Frederick Ungar, 1965), pp. 40-41, 98; Bridenbaugh, *Mitre and Sceptre,* pp. 255, 257.

86. Baldwin, *New England Clergy,* pp. 116, 122.

ent on the issue, but non-Anglicans feared Anglican intentions everywhere. The controversy intensified the revolutionary fervor.[87]

The Revolution altered the balance of denominational power. During the war, more than half the Anglican clergy left their parishes. In some regions, especially in the South, a majority of Anglican priests supported the patriot cause, but others, feeling bound by their oaths to the English crown, opposed it and left. By one estimate, the number of Anglican clergy fell from 325 in 1775 to 100 only eight years later. The Methodists and Baptists rushed in to fill the void. But the Revolution did not drive the clergy out of politics. Of the 1,420 delegates to the conventions that ratified new state constitutions in 1787-88, more than 100 were clergymen. Yet the constitutions symbolized a changing relationship of the clergy to the public order. Seven constitutional conventions thought it necessary to declare that ministers could not hold political office. New Yorkers exemplified the trend when they declared that ministers were "dedicated to the service of God" and could therefore hold no "civil or military office."[88]

Despite the political concerns of many eighteenth-century clergy, they led few movements for social reform. For most of the century, most of them ignored slavery. Many held slaves and upheld the institution. Jonathan Edwards was a slave owner. In his late years, Whitefield schemed to get slavery into Georgia. Cotton Mather urged slaves to submit to their masters; Anglican missionaries instructed them to accept their bondage and secured a ruling from England that baptism would not alter their civil status.

Not all ministers argued for slavery. In the 1770s, a handful of anti-slavery sermons found their way into print. By the 1780s, Presbyterians were urging members to let their slaves purchase their freedom; Baptist associations in Kentucky and Virginia denounced slavery; and the conference of Methodist preachers in 1784 told slaveholding members to accept emancipation. But the reaction was so inflamed that the Methodists rescinded their decree within six months, and the anti-slavery enthusiasm in the other churches also faded away.[89]

In the new nation, the clergy would have to adapt to a society far different from the one to which their predecessors had been accustomed. The immediate task of groups previously part of British and European state churches was

87. Bridenbaugh, *Mitre and Sceptre,* pp. 75, 321.

88. Stephen A. Marini, "Religion, Politics, and Ratification," in *Religion in a Revolutionary Age,* ed. Ronald Hoffman and Peter J. Albert (Charlottesville: University Press of Virginia, 1994), pp. 190, 194; Pore, ed., *Federal and State Constitutions,* pp. 277-78, 287, 385, 825, 1338-39, 1624, 1630, 1911.

89. Lester B. Scherer, *Slavery and the Churches in Early America, 1619-1819* (Grand Rapids: Eerdmans, 1975), pp. 75, 76, 90, 126-49.

to organize their traditions into American denominations — the Methodists in 1784, the Episcopalians in 1789, the Presbyterians in 1789, and others later — that had a national reach and ambition. Loosely organized confederations, the new denominations extended the principles implicit in the earlier clerical associations. For the most part, they confirmed the authority of the ministers even when the laity were part of the governance. But they established the frameworks within which new claims to authority would compete with old ones, and new forms of ministry would alter the clerical office. The clerics of the republic proved to be eminently adaptable, but the Revolution had changed forever some of the older assumptions about the place of the ministry in the society.[90]

90. Craig Dykstra and James Hudnut-Beumler, "The National Organizational Structures of Protestant Denominations: An Invitation to a Conversation," in *The Organizational Revolution: Presbyterians and American Denominationalism*, ed. Milton J. Coalter, John M. Mulder, and Louis B. Weeks (Louisville: Westminster/John Knox Press, 1992), pp. 306-11.

CHAPTER 4

Professionals, Populists, and Immigrants

1791-1861

British and European visitors to the new American republic were curious about the clergy, and they offered a perplexing variety of opinions about them. One traveler thought that they enjoyed "unbounded influence"; another thought that their influence was "merely apparent" — that "at bottom nobody cares for it" — and that only a "feeble minority" recognized clerical authority. The English Unitarian Harriet Martineau called the American clergy "the most backward and timid class in the society in which they live; self-exiled from the great moral questions of the time; the least informed with true knowledge; the least efficient in virtuous action." But the English writer Isabella Lucy Bird Bishop concluded that no ministers were "more deserving of respect" and that their "vast influence" had helped to secure both "the morals of the community and the stability of the government."[1]

Some travelers found a weakened clerical office; others saw an eminent professional group. The English author Frances Trollope wrote that the clergy alone had "distinction and preeminence," but the French refugee Achille Murat saw little distinction and even less eminence. Anybody could become a preacher in America, he argued, simply by finding auditors. The Swiss immi-

---

1. Frances Trollope, *Domestic Manners of the Americans*, ed. Pamela Neville-Sington (1st ed., 1832; London: Penguin, 1997), pp. 15, 212; Achille Murat, *A Moral and Political Sketch of the United States of North America* (1832), in Milton Powell, ed., *The Voluntary Church: American Religious Life Seen Through the Eyes of European Visitors* (New York: Macmillan, 1967), p. 56; Harriet Martineau, *Society in America* (1837), in *Voluntary Church*, p. 119; Isabella Lucy Bird Bishop, *The Aspects of Religion in the United States of America* (1st ed., 1859; New York: Arno Press, 1972), p. 170.

grant Philip Schaff, himself a Protestant minister, agreed with Murat. He wrote soon after his arrival in 1844 that "every theological vagabond and peddler may drive here his bungling trade, without passport or license, and sell his false ware at pleasure." To the Scottish lecturer George Combe, moreover, it seemed that the American clergy exhibited a fawning dependence on their congregations, and the French aristocrat Alexis de Tocqueville broadened the observation by arguing that they submitted to "the intellectual supremacy exercised by the majority" and allowed themselves "to be borne away without opposition in the current of feeling and opinion by which everything around them is carried along." But after living in America for ten years, Philip Schaff rejected the charges of unworthy dependence. Americans expected a minister "to do his duty," he told a German audience, and they admired the fearlessness and impartiality displayed by the best pastors. Every generalization seemed to collide with its opposite.[2]

Almost everyone agreed, however, that the clergy divided into three classes, and that the division exerted a relentless influence on their practice and self-understanding. The first group supported the ideal of the educated pastor and strove to enhance the standing of the clergy as a learned profession. A second group, scorning demands for ministerial education, called for a ministry drawn — if God so willed — from the ranks of the poor and the uneducated and authorized not by learning but by the zeal flowing from a sense of divine calling. In the first four decades after the Revolution, this divide between professionals and populists reshaped the landscape of ministry. Yet for a third group of ministers, the Irish and German immigrants, other issues took precedence over disputes about professionalism and populism. For the immigrants, questions of ethnic tradition and adaptation to American culture proved more pressing than struggles over education, office, and calling.

The Pulpit, the Pastorate, and the Public

The differences did not entirely overshadow a shared experience of ministry, especially among Protestants. By mid-century many of the Protestant clergy labored within "devotional congregations" that looked different from their

2. Trollope, *Domestic Manners*, p. 15; Murat, *Moral and Political Sketch*, p. 52; Philip Schaff, *The Principle of Protestantism* (Philadelphia: United Church Press, 1964), p. 150; George Combe, *Notes on the United States* (1841), in *Voluntary Church*, p. 132; Alexis de Tocqueville, *Democracy in America*, 2 vols. (1st ed., 1835-40; New York: Schocken, 1961), vol. 2, p. 32; Philip Schaff, *America: A Sketch of Its Political, Social, and Religious Character*, ed. Perry Miller (1st ed., 1855; Cambridge: Harvard University Press, 1961), p. 80.

eighteenth-century predecessors by virtue of their cultivation of small groups, usually for devotional purposes. In addition to Sunday services, they offered prayer meetings, Bible classes, Sunday schools, gatherings for testimony, and mission societies. "To give satisfaction in the new congregation," wrote the Congregationalist Heman Humphrey in 1842, ministers had to know how to conduct "private religious meetings." Enoch Pond at the Congregationalist Bangor Seminary advised young ministers that they should expect to hold at least three "extra religious meetings" each week, from gatherings for prayer or lectures to inquiry meetings and testimony sessions.[3]

Most Protestants would have agreed with Humphrey that the "three general heads" of ministry continued to be "the preaching of the word, the pastoral care, and those more public labors which are called for to promote the general interests of the Redeemer's Kingdom," both at home and abroad. They still believed, as Humphrey noted, that "preaching holds the first place." Sermons lasted an hour or longer, and the Protestant minister still considered them "the most important part of his public work." They were always to have a "practical" end, aiming at conversion or giving instruction in the Christian life. The "one great object" was "to win souls to Christ."[4]

Although Schaff thought it a weakness that some seemed to regard conversion as "the whole work of the church," a revivalist ethos filtered into most Protestant preaching. According to the "evangelical conception of the ministry," a shortage of conversions in a congregation called into question ministerial "faithfulness." Success in converting people gave evidence that the minister "preached the truth." Handbooks for ministers had long chapters on "revivals" — some contended that no topic was more important — and many clergy planned for a week of services every year. The best-known minister of the era was the Free Presbyterian Charles G. Finney, whose *Lectures on Revivals of Religion* (1835) popularized the "new measures" — such as services extending over several days and the use of "anxious seats" for sinners under conviction — that would promote a revival.[5]

Humphrey's second general duty — pastoral care — occurred mainly

---

3. Heman Humphrey, *Thirty-Four Letters to a Son in the Ministry* (Amherst: Adams, 1841), p. 17; Enoch Pond, *The Young Pastor's Guide* (Bangor: Duren, 1844), p. 125.

4. Humphrey, *Thirty-Four Letters*, p. 54; Samuel Miller, *Letters on Clerical Manners and Habits* (New York: Carvill, 1827), p. 270; Anonymous, "The Preacher," *The Southern Quarterly Review* 10 (1846): 62.

5. Schaff, *America*, p. 95; Sidney E. Mead, "The Rise of the Evangelical Conception of the Ministry in America (1607-1850), *The Ministry in Historical Perspectives*, ed. H. R. Niebuhr and D. D. Williams (New York: Harper and Row, 1956), pp. 207-49; Humphrey, *Thirty-Four Letters*, 92-93, 263.

through "religious conversation" during pastoral visits. "Ministers," wrote the Presbyterian Samuel Miller in 1827, "are visitors by profession." He urged visits to every family twice a year. Enoch Pond suggested that ministers visit three afternoons a week and talk to 150 families a year. The purpose of visiting remained unchanged. Pastors needed to know the "spiritual estate" of their members, and visits gave opportunities "to inquire freely into their spiritual estates, learn their doubts, their difficulties, their encouragements, their consolations, and give such advice as circumstances require." Some kept notebooks on the spiritual condition of every member.[6]

In his *Pastor's Sketches* (1850), the Presbyterian Ichabod Spencer published verbatim reports of pastoral conversations that other ministers could use as a guide. He showed them how he corrected a member who claimed to have had visions, exhorted a woman suffering from despair, admonished a congregant who felt too ashamed to submit to baptism, instructed two sisters who felt unable to pray, and encouraged an abused wife to resist her husband's tyranny. Educated ministers like Spencer drew on "mental science" textbooks that taught them how to identify such states as mournfulness and melancholy, buoyancy and joy, self-centered anxiety and true conviction for sin.[7]

Among the more difficult acts of pastoral care was the occasional obligation to rebuke members guilty of transgression. Ministers had not only to "guard the door of the church against the intrusion of unworthy members" but also to protect the integrity of the fellowship. On occasion, they bore this burden alone; more frequently, standing committees of members under pastoral leadership ensured that offending members would be admonished, or even brought to trial and, if necessary, dismissed from the church. Bishop noted that membership made Christians "liable to strict discipline," and this required, as others argued, "pastoral vigilance." Baptists in the South, for example, excommunicated about 2 percent of their members every year. Churches were moral courts and on occasion had to make judgments.[8]

The goal was to nurture members who would never need discipline, and one means to this end continued to be the formation of children. The emer-

6. Henry Caswall, *America and the American Church* (London: Rivington, 1839), p. 300; Miller, *Letters*, p. 153; Pond, *Young Pastor's Guide*, pp. 53, 64, 66; Humphrey, *Thirty-Four Letters*, p. 199.

7. Ichabod Spencer, *A Pastor's Sketches*, 1st series (1st ed., 1850; New York: M. W. Dod, 1851); Miller, *Letters*, pp. 135, 138; James Spencer Cannon, *Lectures on Pastoral Theology* (New York: Board of Publication of the Reformed Protestant Dutch Church, 1859), p. 571.

8. Humphrey, *Thirty-Four Letters*, p. 249; Pond, *Young Pastor's Guide*, p. 100; Bishop, *Aspects of Religion*, p. 169; Gregory A. Wills, *Democratic Religion: Freedom, Authority, and Church Discipline in the Baptist South, 1785-1900* (New York: Oxford University Press, 1997), p. 22.

gence in the 1820s of the Sunday school competed with the older practice of catechetical instruction by the pastor. By 1844, Pond was lamenting the decline of "old fashioned catechizing," though Presbyterians and Episcopalians still taught the catechism, and Schaff wrote in 1855 that German Lutheran and Reformed pastors had "returned" to "the good old measures" of catechetical drill. Lutherans published new editions of the *Shorter Catechism,* and German Reformed clergy used the Heidelberg Catechism more generally "than ever before." Schaff charged that Methodists "dreadfully neglect all religious training of children," but well before his assessment, indeed by the 1820s, they too were printing catechisms and urging, with limited success, their use in the Sunday schools.[9]

In accord with Humphrey's third ministerial duty — "public labors" for the Redeemer's kingdom — Protestant clergy, working with the laity, organized local chapters of voluntary societies, some of them nationwide in scope, to propagate Christian virtues. These "benevolent societies" distributed Bibles, advocated temperance, combated dueling, and distributed tracts. They protected the Sabbath, rescued prostitutes, educated ministers, and reformed prisons. Ministers led societies to rehabilitate juvenile offenders, build Sunday schools, and promote world peace. They helped create agencies to fight slavery, ameliorate poverty, protect children, suppress vice, and support education. Critics charged that a few of the societies tried to control — even dominate — people more than help them, but most represented new forms of civic mobilization that relied on persuasion to shape a public ethos.[10]

These societies were a "disciplined moral militia," in the words of Congregationalist minister Lyman Beecher, and in the absence of state and federal programs of social welfare they were among the most important agencies of public benevolence in the nation. The tract and Bible societies were the country's largest publishing empires, and between 1789 and 1828, the thirteen leading benevolent societies spent $2.8 million to pursue their goals, almost as much as the federal government during that period spent on roads, canals, and the postal

9. Pond, *Young Pastor's Guide,* p. 226; Schaff, *America,* p. 163; Arthur C. Repp Sr., *Luther's Catechism Comes to America* (Metuchen, N.J.: The Scarecrow Press and the American Theological Library Association, 1982), pp. 220-38; George Washington Doane, "The Church's Care for Little Children," in *Sermons on Various Occasions, With Three Charges to the Clergy of his Diocese* (London: Rivington, 1842), pp. 671-72; James E. Kirby, Russell E. Richey, and Kenneth E. Rowe, *The Methodists* (Westport: Greenwood Press, 1996), p. 184.

10. Clifford S. Griffin, *Their Brothers' Keepers: Moral Stewardship in the United States, 1800-1865* (New Brunswick: Rutgers University Press, 1960), pp. 23-42, 119-74; John R. Bodo, *The Protestant Clergy and Social Issues, 1812-1848* (Princeton: Princeton University Press, 1954), pp. 10-54.

service. The clergy raised most of the money. The success of the societies, wrote one minister, depended on "the support of the pastors."[11]

The pastors provided ordinary Americans a link to the wider world. After the formation in 1810 by Congregationalists of the American Board of Commissioners for Foreign Missions — and of eight other denominational mission boards in the next twenty-five years — they threw themselves into the missionary movement. By 1860, the American Board alone had dispatched 567 men, most of them ordained clergy, along with 691 women, as missionaries to Hawaii, Burma, India, Africa, Ceylon, Micronesia, and East Asia. Other organizations supported missions to settlers in the Midwest and to the Native Americans. As evangelists, the missionaries enjoyed modest numerical success, but they also served as interpreters at boundaries where one cultural sphere touched another, whether by pleading the cause of the stranger, as Samuel A. Worcester did on behalf of the Cherokees in Georgia, or by introducing other cultures to American readers, as in the writings of Adoniram Judson on Burma or Hiram Bingham on Hawaii.[12]

To some it appeared that the political sphere was no longer the site of the minister's "public labors." When Tocqueville toured the country in 1831, he observed that preachers kept aloof "from parties and from public affairs." Harriet Martineau called them "a sort of people between men and women," possessing the right to vote but cut off from political culture. Some withdrew from political activity after the Revolution, partly because of otherworldly interests and partly because they shared a public unease with partisanship after the Jeffersonians challenged the ruling Federalists in 1800. Most agreed that they should remain neutral in the partisan debates, and some worried about whether they should even vote, but it was common knowledge that New England Congregational clerics favored the Federalists while clergy hostile to "established" churches gravitated toward the Jeffersonians.[13]

During the struggles between Whigs and Democrats in the 1820s, the clergy

11. Mark A. Noll, *America's God: From Jonathan Edwards to Abraham Lincoln* (New York: Oxford University Press, 2002), p. 198; Jean V. Matthews, *Toward a New Society: American Thought and Culture 1800-1830* (Boston: Twayne, 1991), p. 41; Pond, *Young Pastor's Guide*, p. 229; Andrew Reed and James Matheson, *A Narrative of the Visit to the American Churches, By the Deputation from the Congregational Union of England and Wales*, 2 vols. (New York: Harper and Brothers, 1835), vol. 2, pp. 37-43.

12. R. Pierce Beaver, *All Loves Excelling: American Protestant Women in World Mission* (Grand Rapids: Eerdmans, 1968), p. 70; William R. Hutchison, *Errand to the World: American Protestant Thought and Foreign Missions* (Chicago: University of Chicago Press, 1987), pp. 43-45.

13. Tocqueville, *Democracy in America*, in *Voluntary Church*, pp. 87, 90; Martineu, *Society in America*, p. 125; Pond, *Young Pastor's Guide*, p. 211; Richard J. Carwardine, *Evangelicals and Politics in Antebellum America* (New Haven: Yale University Press, 1993), pp. 25, 30, 122-24.

became more active. The political disputes had moral implications. Many mainline Protestant ministers saw the Whigs as more favorable than the Jacksonian Democrats to temperance reform, the curtailing of Sunday travel and mail delivery, and humane treatment of the Indians. The clerical populists, the German immigrants, and the Irish Catholics leaned toward the Democrats because they seemed more receptive to "outsiders." Though clergy rarely used the pulpit to support a candidate or a party, they discussed political issues in their sermons, wrote on politics, and commented on politicians.[14]

With the outbreak in 1846 of the Mexican War, which anti-slavery groups saw as an effort to extend the Southern "Slave Power," ministers from the North and the South slid toward a political collision. Some clergy, represented by the Presbyterian James Henley Thornwell in South Carolina, argued that the "spirituality of the church" required ministers and church assemblies to limit their official pronouncements to matters of eternal redemption rather than worldly justice, but the doctrine gained little support outside the South. Ministers spoke at political rallies, wrote in support of candidates, and even ran for political office.[15]

Before the politicians split the nation, the clergy split the churches. By 1860, slavery had divided the largest Protestant denominations into regional churches. Several Southern — and a few Northern — clergy defended slavery on biblical grounds; other Northern ministers replied with anti-slavery treatises. The issue severed congregations and disrupted national and regional church assemblies. When the Kansas-Nebraska bill of 1854 opened the territories to slavery, three thousand clergymen from New England petitioned Congress. With the founding of the Republican Party, which opposed the extension of slavery westward, some Northern ministers solicited Republican votes. The party hired the young Brooklyn pastor Henry Ward Beecher to speak weekly at rallies. But other clergy favored other parties, and some withdrew from it all in disillusion.[16]

Campaigns for moral reform had national repercussions, but mostly the clergy made a difference in local communities. Their preaching gave them a larger public audience of adults, week after week, than that of any other professional group. Their pastoral care of individuals — in a society without therapists or social workers — offered them more intimate access to other people's lives than any other profession enjoyed. Their leadership of congregations that

14. Carwardine, *Evangelicals and Politics,* pp. 29, 99.
15. Benjamin M. Palmer, *The Life and Letters of James Henley Thornwell* (Richmond: Whittett, Shepperson, 1875), p. 303; Carwardine, *Evangelicals and Politics,* pp. 99, 101-03, 117-18.
16. Carwardine, *Evangelicals and Politics,* pp. 236, 266-67.

had become more internally complex gave them a special expertise in a society that was beginning to turn toward voluntary organization to attain many of its aims. And their leadership in reform and social movements gave them public influence. Yet they remained divided, and politics was not the main reason for their divisions.[17]

Competition

The divisions occurred in part because church-state separation created a field for competition. The First Amendment did not affect religious establishments at the state level, but the states continued in the path set by the earlier state constitutions. In 1802, the Virginia legislature revoked governmental grants to the church, confiscating and selling the glebe lands that had supplemented clerical salaries. In 1807, Vermont repealed all laws that authorized churches to assess their members for ministerial support, and three years later, Maryland accomplished the same end with a constitutional amendment. In 1818, Connecticut rewrote its constitution to stipulate that the state could compel no one to support any religious society. Lyman Beecher said that it was "as dark a day" as he ever saw. He later changed his mind, but at the time he feared that "the odium thrown upon the ministry was inconceivable." A year later, New Hampshire ended tax support for clergy, and in 1833 the voters of Massachusetts ratified a constitutional amendment ensuring that ministers would receive their salaries only through the voluntary support of their parishioners. The old regime was gone.[18]

To Philip Schaff it seemed that the legal changes made America "the classic land of sects, where in perfect freedom from civil disqualification they can develop themselves without restraint." At the beginning of the Revolutionary War, 70 percent of the churches — and a similar proportion of the clergy — were Congregationalist, Anglican, or Presbyterian. By 1855, America had at least forty-eight Christian denominations, and visitors remarked on the "almost endless variety of religious factions." The three large colonial churches now contained only about 18 percent of the clergy. Enoch Pond believed that "the multiplication of sects" had "diminished the respect which was formerly

17. E. Brooks Holifield, "Toward a History of American Congregations," in *American Congregations*, ed. James P. Wind and James W. Lewis, 2 vols. (Chicago: The University of Chicago Press, 1994), pp. 36-39.

18. Leonard W. Levy, *The Establishment Clause: Religion and the First Amendment* (New York: Macmillan, 1986), pp. 38, 40, 44, 46, 48; Lyman Beecher, *The Autobiography of Lyman Beecher*, ed. Barbara M. Cross, 2 vols. (Cambridge: Harvard University Press, 1961), p. 252.

accorded to the sacred office." Schaff also deplored the "Sect system," but he thought that the competition at least promoted the work of religious conversion.[19]

Denominational differences produced incessant conflict as clergy relentlessly exposed the errors of other clergy. When they disagreed within their own denominations, they formed new ones. By 1855, Baptists divided into nine denominations, Methodists and Presbyterians into eight each. When they disagreed with clergy from other denominations, they depicted them as misguided, heretical, or dishonest. Trollope reported that the "innumerable shades of varying belief" had led to a "factious" sectarianism, and the clergy earned, in some quarters, a reputation for "intolerance," "unseemly strife," and "disagreeable collision."[20]

High-church Episcopalians, led by Bishop John Henry Hobart in New York, argued that the threefold order of bishops, priests, and deacons was "the institution of Christ and his disciples" and that no church could exist without it. They insisted, as well, on the apostolic succession of bishops. But "evangelical" Episcopalians argued that the three orders were necessary only for the perfection, not the validity, of the church. All Episcopalians agreed that Methodist bishops had no authority and that the Presbyterian synods were no substitute for the threefold order. In response, some Presbyterians argued that only their church order was faithful to scripture, and Methodists contended that their bishops were more consistent with the primitive churches than the Anglican variety.[21]

The Midwest became home to ethnic enclaves prone to disagree with each other and everyone else. Swedish, Norwegian, and German Lutheran clergy in the region sometimes refused fellowship with Lutherans in the East — and with each other — for reasons of doctrine and church order. Lutherans who were allied with Johannes A. A. Grabau in western New York defended clerical prerogatives that offended Lutherans who followed Carl F. W. Walther in Missouri in his defense of congregational authority. Walther's group also clashed with the theologians of the Iowa Synod, who objected to his congregationalism and his

19. Schaff, *America*, pp. 96, 98; Trollope, *Domestic Manners*, p. 69; Pond, *Young Pastor's Guide*, p. 325.

20. Trollope, *Domestic Manners*, pp. 16, 85-86; Rebecca Gratz, "Letter, 1844," *American Jewish Women: A Documentary History*, ed. Jacob R. Marcus (New York: Ktav, 1981), p. 1047.

21. John Henry Hobart, *An Apology for the Apostolic Order and Its Advocates* (New York: Stanford and Swords, 1844), p. 115; John Henry Hobart, *The Excellence of the Church* (New York: T. & J. Swords, 1810), p. 23; William Wilmer, *The Episcopal Manual* (Baltimore: E. J. Coale, 1859), p. 31; E. Brooks Holifield, *Theology in America: Christian Thought from the Age of the Puritans to the Civil War* (New Haven: Yale University Press, 2003), pp. 246-51, 370-94.

views about doctrine. Lars Esbjorn led a secession of Swedes and Norwegians who founded a separate Augustana Synod in Illinois to protest doctrinal laxity in the East.[22]

Onlookers wondered about the effect of the squabbling on clerical effectiveness. The British visitor Andrew Reed feared that the disputes, sometimes over "insignificant and perplexing distinctions," led the laity to "distrust their teachers." The church historian Robert Baird conceded that "the multiplication of sects" produced an "acrimony unbecoming the gospel."[23]

Baird noticed, however, that Protestants could set aside their differences to take common ground against "the errors of Rome." During the 1830s they formed associations and multiplied publications to expose Catholic "heresy." In 1844, clergymen helped create the American Protestant Society, which printed tracts, supported anti-Catholic newspapers, and sponsored speeches to counter Catholic influence. By 1855, Schaff observed that the antagonism — which he described as the "leading division" in American religion — generated a "fanatical hatred" that resembled "religious war." Fear of Catholicism drew some Protestant ministers into state and national politics on behalf of the new American Party — the "Know-Nothings." In 1855, twenty-four clerical Know-Nothing candidates gained seats in the Massachusetts legislature and twelve won positions in the United States Congress.[24]

Not all was conflict. The English visitor Isaac Candler found the harmony more impressive than the discord. Isabella Bishop noted that ministers exchanged pulpits and met in union prayer meetings. In some towns they met weekly to make "co-operative plans for the good of their location." In the 1850s, Protestants seemed "more harmonious in their feelings toward each other than they were formerly." Reactions against Catholic immigration in the 1840s generated a trend toward greater Protestant amity. And often the spirit of harmony extended across the Protestant and Catholic battlefields. When John England served as the bishop of Charleston, he received invitations from Protestant pastors to use their church buildings as he traveled across his diocese.[25]

22. Theodore Tappert, ed., *Lutheran Confessional Theology in America 1840-1880* (New York: Oxford University Press, 1972), pp. 25-35, 229-45, 252-78, 279-95.

23. Reed and Matheson, *Narrative*, vol. 2, p. 53; Robert Baird, *Religion in America*, ed. Henry W. Bowden (New York: Harper and Row, 1970), p. 254; Robert Baird, *Religion in the United States of America* (Glasgow: Blackie and Son, 1844), pp. 606, 611.

24. Baird, *Religion in the United States* (1844 ed.), p. 611; Baird, *Religion in America*, p. 255; Ray Allen Billington, *The Protestant Crusade, 1800-1860* (Chicago: Quadrangle, 1964), pp. 166-85; Schaff, *America*, pp. 77, 194; Carwardine, *Evangelicals and Politics*, p. 223.

25. Sándor B. Farkas, *Journey in North America, 1831*, ed. Arpod Kadarkey (Santa Barbara: A.B.C.-Clio, 1978), p. 152; Dixon, *Methodism in America*, p. 177; Bishop, *Aspects of Religion*, pp.

The sectarian competition altered the profession. Census takers found 28,993 ministers in 1850, but the editor of the census report admitted there were more. In 1860, they found 37,529, but again the census limited its denominational range and omitted part-time clergy. Baird, writing in 1855 from church reports, counted 32,640 full-time clergy in thirty-six denominations. Joseph Belcher, polling forty-six denominations, found around forty thousand. But both the census takers and the scholars agreed that the Baptists and Methodists had risen to numerical supremacy. By 1855, a third of the ordained clergy were Baptists and a fourth Methodists. Adding in the Methodist "local preachers" — or lay ministers — would give the various Methodist denominations 40 percent and the Baptists 26 percent.[26]

The census in 1850 found 38,061 congregations. Membership still had imposing requirements, and it is likely that only about 21 percent of Americans were members, but attendance greatly exceeded membership. When Andrew Reed toured in 1835, he observed the difference: six congregations in Lexington, Kentucky, had 3,200 attenders and 900 communicants; three in Danville, Pennsylvania, had 850 attenders and 325 communicants. In Danville, 22 percent of the inhabitants were communicants, but 57 percent attended; Morristown had 29 percent communicants, 71 percent attenders. If the average congregation still ministered to eighty families, then the rate of adherence (as defined earlier in the eighteenth-century count) would have been 72 percent by mid-century, and the attendance rate might have still been around 36 to 40 percent nationwide. Isabella Bird Bishop observed in 1859 that "the number of attendants on public worship is unusually large in proportion to the population, judging by the English standards." Ministers were still in high demand.[27]

166-67; Carwardine, *Evangelicals and Politics,* p. 130; John England, *Diurnal of the Right Rev. John England, D. D., First Bishop of Charleston, S.C. from 1820-1823* (Philadelphia: American Catholic Historical Society, 1895), p. 18.

26. J. D. B. DeBow, *Statistical View of the United States* (1st. ed., 1850; New York, Norman, 1990), pp. 132, 138; Harry Scarr, ed., *1990 Census of Population: Social and Economic Characteristics* (Washington, D.C.: U.S. Government Printing Office, 1993), p. lxix; Joseph C. G. Kennedy, ed., *Population in the United States in 1860* (Washington, D.C.: U.S. Government Printing Office, 1864), p. 661; Joseph Belcher, *The Religious Denominations in the United States* (Philadelphia: John E. Potter, 1857), pp. 213-840; Baird, *Religion in America* (New York: Harper and Brothers, 1856), pp. 462-557.

27. For definitions of adherence, see chapter 3, note 28; Reed and Matheson, *Narrative,* vol. 1, pp. 49, 99-176, 253; vol. 2, pp. 105-06, 283; Roger Finke and Rodney Stark, "Turning Pews into People: Estimating 19th-Century Church Membership," *Journal for the Scientific Study of Religion* 25 (1986): 180-92; Bishop, *Aspects of Religion,* pp. 141, 169. This assumes 5.5 members in a family. See Peter Laslett and Richard Wall, *Household and Family in Past Time* (Cambridge: Cambridge University Press, 1972).

Some of the churches worried about shortages. The Baptist Education Society reported in 1835 that 2,500 Baptist churches had no pastors, and Francis Wayland contended in 1853 that the number had risen to 4,000. Presbyterians had pastors for middle-class churches but not enough for poorer congregations. Episcopalians in the 1830s had an ample supply in the Eastern towns, but only fifteen clergy for the fifty parishes in Ohio. Lutherans had to provide "traveling preachers" to visit vacant congregations in the Midwest. Some denominations redoubled efforts at clerical education; others argued that educated pastors were a luxury the churches could not afford.[28]

The Professional Ideal

Ministers took pride in their accomplishments in the world of learning. Samuel Miller, writing in 1803, considered it "worthy of remark" that "among all the professions denominated *learned*, the *clerical* profession" had furnished as many "authors of distinction" as any other, "if not more." After another decade, some began to worry about a lack of clerical learning. In 1814, Lyman Beecher warned that illiterate preachers, "however pious, cannot command the attention of that class of the community whose education and mental culture is above their own," and he called for at least one educated pastor for every thousand souls in America. The nation needed, he thought, 8,000 educated ministers; it had only about 3,000, along with around 1,500 illiterate preachers. He could still assume that 67 percent of the clergy were among the most highly educated citizens of the nation, but he felt uneasy.[29]

In 1835, Andrew Reed calculated that the proportion of ministers who were "fairly educated" had fallen to around 55 percent, but he reassured his readers that the ministry still had as much "intelligence and cultivation as shall any where be found." By 1856, Robert Baird estimated that the number of "classically educated clergy" had sunk further to 37 percent. To Edwards Amasa Park at Andover Seminary, it looked as if Americans were more "will-

28. Reed and Matheson, *Narrative*, vol. 1, p. 66; Miller, *Letters*, p. 78; Anonymous, "Are There Too Many Ministers?" *The Princeton Review* 34 (1862): 133-46; Caswall, *America and the American Church*, p. 53; H. George Anderson, "Early National Period, 1790-1840," *The Lutherans in North America*, ed. E. Clifford Nelson (Philadelphia: Fortress, 1975), p. 102; Joseph M. White, *The Diocesan Seminary in the United States: A History from the 1780s to the Present* (Notre Dame: University of Notre Dame Press, 1989), p. 76.

29. Samuel Miller, *Brief Retrospect of the Eighteenth Century*, 2 vols. (New York: Swords, 1803), vol. 2, pp. 433-34; Lyman Beecher, *An Address of the Charitable Society for the Education of Indigent Pious Young Men for the Ministry of the Gospel* (n.p., 1814), p. 6.

ing to entrust the care of their souls, than of their bodies or estates, to incompetent pretenders."[30]

The call for an educated clergy harkened back to the sixteenth century, but it also reflected the steady growth of towns. In 1810, only 7 percent of Americans lived in towns larger than 2,500 people. By 1860, the number increased to 20 percent. The towns presented themselves as places of "mental culture," and they could make high demands on their ministers. As early as 1815, the Methodist bishop William McKendree kept private lists of clerical names, distinguishing preachers who were "qualified to fill any *station*" — which usually meant a town church — and others not sufficiently cultivated. Fledgling urban pastors were sometimes reminded that they were preaching to "town folks." Theodore Munger wrote his mother in 1854 that he had preached well at a country church. "But because I succeeded there it is no indication that I should succeed before a city congregation."[31]

When clerics spoke of an educated ministry, they were referring primarily to graduation from college. The proponents of clerical learning still expected the minister to know "all the sciences," not only a classical language but also logic, metaphysics, mental science, geology, history, geography, and rhetoric. They wanted this learning to manifest itself in "the highest grade of oratory in the pulpit," which implied, at a minimum, a mastery of English grammar and rhetoric. By 1860, Americans had erected more than 150 colleges, many sponsored by denominations seeking a steady supply of college-educated clergy. Most of the schools were financially weak and academically feeble, but they bespoke a desire for an educated public and an informed ministry.[32]

In the Congregationalist, Episcopalian, and Presbyterian churches, collegiate training became the norm, and by 1836 the majority of their ministers were college graduates even in Midwestern states like Ohio, where 68 percent of the Congregationalists and Presbyterians had graduated from college. A college education was rare in America. In the 1850s, when the population had grown to thirty-one million people, the Eastern colleges produced each year only 908

30. Reed and Matheson, *Narrative*, vol. 2, p. 140; Baird, *Religion in America* (New York: Harper and Brothers, 1856), p. 383; Edwards A. Park, *The Preacher and the Pastor* (Andover: Allenn, Morrell, Wardwell, 1845), p. 11.

31. William McKendree Papers, McKendree Collection, Vanderbilt University; E. Brooks Holifield, *The Gentlemen Theologians: American Theology in Southern Culture* (Durham: Duke University Press, 1978), pp. 16-17; Benjamin Bacon, *Theodore Thornton Munger: New England Minister* (New Haven: Yale University Press, 1913), p. 79.

32. Cannon, *Lectures*, pp. 21-25; Park, *Preacher and Pastor*, p. 14; William White, *Commentaries Suited to Occasions of Ordination* (New York: Swords, Stanford, 1833), p. 182; George P. Schmidt, "Colleges in Ferment," *The American Historical Review* 59 (1953): 19.

graduates. Only a tiny fraction of Americans went to college; the educated clergy stood out as members of an intellectual elite.[33]

It caused worry when the "proportionate numbers" of graduates who became ministers appeared to be "steadily lessening." Around 30 percent of graduates in the 1830s entered the ministry, and in some colleges more than half sought ministerial careers. But in thirty-seven Eastern colleges the number of graduates entering the ministry declined from 30 percent in 1820 to 25 percent in 1840 and 20 percent in 1860. Drawn by the "brilliant promise of other careers," graduates turned to law, medicine, and business.[34]

The losses intensified the desire of the churches to assist students who would enter the ministry. In 1815, Congregational and Presbyterian clergy in New England formed the American Education Society to provide fellowships for ministerial candidates to attend college; by 1830 the organization became a sophisticated bureaucracy annually supporting up to five hundred students. Old School Presbyterians and Episcopalians formed societies for the same purpose, as eventually did the Baptists, Dutch Reformed, Unitarians, and northern Methodists. In 1855, almost a thousand recipients of funding from the various education societies graduated from college. But by then college alone was not enough.[35]

The founding of Andover Seminary in 1808 began a concerted Protestant attempt to provide three years of theological learning beyond college. By 1850, eight denominations had formed forty-four seminaries in which students normally studied the Bible, theology, sacred rhetoric, church history, and pastoral care. Most of the schools were small — the average seminary in 1860 had three faculty members and twenty-five students — and more astute observers recognized their inadequacies. Presbyterians, Congregationalists, and Episcopalians tried to limit enrollments to college graduates, and Andover largely succeeded, but most schools accepted students without degrees, and in several of them college graduates were in the minority. Park complained in 1844 that even good

33. Mark A. May, *The Profession of the Ministry: Its Status and Problems* (New York: Institute of Social and Religious Research, 1934), p. 22; Burton J. Bledstein, *The Culture of Professionalism* (New York: W. W. Norton, 1976), p. 241.

34. Charles Brooks, *A Statement of Facts from Each Religious Denomination in New England Respecting Ministers' Salaries* (Boston: Crocker and Brewster, 1854), p. 12; Bledstein, *Culture of Professionalism*, p. 198; Natalie A. Naylor, "The Theological Seminary in the Configuration of American Higher Education: The Antebellum Years," *History of Education Quarterly* 17 (1977): 25.

35. Donald M. Scott, *From Office to Profession: The New England Ministry 1750-1850* (Philadelphia: University of Pennsylvania Press, 1978), p. 59; Baird, *Religion in America* (1856), pp. 320-21.

seminaries admitted everyone who applied, and some students remained only one or two years.[36]

The seminaries were nonetheless the first American educational institutions designed for a graduate education, and the best ones provided a demanding course of study. John Todd, studying at Andover in the 1820s, wrote a friend that he was "buried up in theology" and "driven in study," having to recite three times a week in theology, once in Hebrew, and once in Greek, in addition to attending lectures and meeting with four societies for debate and edification. One British visitor thought that education in the seminaries was superior to what students received in England and Wales. Medical education at the time consisted merely of three to four months of lectures followed by apprenticeships, and few medical students had college degrees. The nation had only a dozen law schools by 1850, and most of them offered a one-year course followed by apprenticeship.[37]

Seminaries promoted the vision of ministry as the "noblest of professions." They aimed to elevate their students into a "learned profession" by providing a body of knowledge and the principles for applying it. A clerical professional was, according to the ideal, a person of "sound scholarship," a person "learned and accomplished," capable of scaling "heights of knowledge." Ministry was, of course, always more than a profession. It was a calling, not to be chosen for "worldly advantage." Francis Wayland, the president of Brown, reminded his readers that ministry required an inward conviction of a divine call. But the advocates of seminary education believed that without "professional" learning no minister could properly teach biblical truth or meet the expectations of the laity. By 1835, the term "professional education" designated the three years of seminary training as "distinct from the collegiate."[38]

Black preachers normally had to seek other routes to a learned ministry. A handful, like the Methodist Daniel Payne, went to a seminary, but few had this option. Congregationalist Lemuel Haynes received tutoring from Calvinist

36. Baird, *Religion in America* (1856), pp. 318, 329; James W. Fraser, *Schooling the Preachers: The Development of Protestant Theological Education in the United States 1740-1875* (Lanham, Md.: University Press of America, 1988), p. 38; Schaff, *America*, p. 62; A Society of Clergymen [E. A. Park], "Thoughts on the State of Theological Science and Education in Our Country," *Bibliotheca Sacra* 1 (1844): 756, 760; Caswall, *America and the American Church*, p. 217; Nayler, "Theological Seminary," p. 22.

37. Nayler, "Theological Seminary," p. 23; Fraser, *Schooling the Preachers*, p. 41; Reed and Matheson, *Narrative*, vol. 2, p. 140.

38. Anonymous, "The Ministry Favorable to the Highest Development of the Mind," *The New Englander and Yale Review* 3 (1845): 56; Cannon, *Lectures*, p. 16; Holifield, *Gentlemen Theologians*, p. 34; Francis Wayland, *The Apostolic Ministry* (Rochester: Sage, 1853), pp. 35-36; Pond, *Young Pastor's Guide*, p. 324; Reed and Matheson, *Narrative*, vol. 2, p. 140.

colleagues and preached in mostly white congregations in New England and New York, where he published essays in support of the New Divinity of Jonathan Edwards. Presbyterians ordained a company of talented black orators who learned their theology through mentoring from other clergy. James W. C. Pennington, who preached at the Shiloh Presbyterian Church in New York, went on to lecture in Europe and to receive an honorary doctorate from the University of Heidelberg. Henry Highland Garnet, ordained in 1842, served churches in New York and Washington, D.C., and joined Pennington as a foe of slavery. But when Alexander Crummell, a graduate of Oneida Institute, applied to the Episcopal General Seminary in New York, the school refused him admission, and he had to travel to England to secure higher education in a field other than theology.[39]

The educated clergy still provided intellectual and literary leadership. The best-known theologians had real cultural influence, addressing religious but also social, economic, and ethical issues. The best theological journals — such as the *Christian Spectator* (1819), the *Biblical Repertory and Princeton Review* (1829), and *The New Englander* (1843) — were among the most erudite quarterlies published in the nation. Clergy introduced Scottish Realist philosophy to American colleges and made it the dominant philosophical movement of the era, and clergy wrote most of the textbooks in mental philosophy that promoted this empirical approach to knowledge. Such authors as Francis Wayland and Jasper Adams produced the texts in moral philosophy that served as the capstone of a college education.[40]

Their accomplishments extended from the promotion of literature to the popularization of science. The Unitarian clergy who formed the Transcendentalist Club — along with other more orthodox ministers drawn to Romantic literature — introduced American readers to trends in European fiction, philosophy, and theology. Some ministers became accomplished naturalists. Lutheran John Bachman in Charleston, for example, collaborated with the naturalist J. J. Audubon, and Edward Hitchcock at Amherst attained eminence as a geologist. At the level of popular culture, the Presbyterian William Holmes McGuffey wrote the "Eclectic Readers" that taught millions of schoolchildren moral maxims as they learned to read.[41]

Among the educated clergy, the sermon itself could become a polished cultural artifact. They often gave close attention to form and style, and visitors from Europe sometimes described the results as "finished literary efforts." John G.

39. Holifield, *Theology in America*, pp. 306-18.

40. Holifield, *Theology in America*, pp. 174-75; Holifield, *Gentlemen Theologians*, pp. 127-54; Jasper Adams, *Elements of Moral Philosopohy* (Cambridge: Folsom, Wells, and Thurston, 1837).

41. Holifield, *Theology in America*, pp. 173-96; R. Laurence Moore, *Selling God: American Religion in the Marketplace of Culture* (New York: Oxford University Press, 1994), p. 63.

Palfrey wrote in the *North American Review* in 1820 that some of the best literary work in America could be found in "the sermons of some of our divines." Seminaries devoted most of the third year to sermon preparation and delivery, and preachers experimented with new styles. They preached topical sermons (focused on one doctrinal point), textual sermons (explicating the sense of a scriptural passage), and expository sermons (proceeding from verse to verse). At the same time, some preachers treated the sermon as an art form that alluded to biblical texts but explored non-biblical topics in science and history or moralized about the beauties of nature. Pulpit orators made use of storytelling and the "portrait method," retelling biblical narratives, reconstructing the inner life of biblical characters, and recounting stories from everyday life.[42]

Every educated preacher had to decide whether to preach from a manuscript, employ sermon notes, or follow a trend toward more extemporaneous preaching. Some considered the reading of sermons to be "an evil," little more than a "mechanical exercise," while others thought that sermons preached without notes or manuscript collapsed in repetition, awkwardness of language, and formlessness. Intellectually demanding sermons found appreciative hearers. One English visitor remarked on the tendency in urban America to "deify" the "intellectual giants of the pulpit" whose "literary" sermons constituted a species of fine arts.[43]

The learned clergy were preachers, but they were also educators. As disciplines multiplied, the percentage of clergy teaching college classes declined, but the clergy still founded most of the antebellum colleges, and in 1850 more than 90 percent of the college presidents were ministers. From the colonial era to the Civil War, 262 of the 288 college presidents were ordained ministers. They furnished five of the seven presidents of Harvard, three of the four at Princeton, all four at Brown, and all three at Yale. At some state schools — the University of Georgia, for instance, or the University of Alabama — the clergy had a lock on the president's office. Many of them were the graduates of the theological seminaries. Between 1809 and 1848, a single professor — Moses Stuart at Andover Seminary — taught seventy students who later became college professors and presidents. More than 11 percent of the graduates at Andover and 15 percent at Princeton entered the ranks of the professors. And the clergy also sat on the boards of the state schools; the feuds between Methodists and Presbyterians

42. Bishop, *Aspects of Religion*, p. 147; Matthews, *Toward a New Society*, p. 123; Humphrey, *Thirty-Four Letters*, pp. 129-33; Lawrence Buell, "The Unitarian Movement and the Art of Preaching in Nineteenth Century America," *American Quarterly* 24 (1972): 166-69.

43. Reed and Matheson, *Narrative*, vol. 2, p. 84; "The Inefficiency of the Pulpit," *Southern Literary Messenger* 24 (1857): 103; Humphrey, *Thirty-Four Letters*, p. 117; Bishop, *Aspects of Religion*, p. 147.

over the trusteeship of Indiana University helped shape the state's political alignments.[44]

Some worried that their cultural leadership was waning. "We are exposed," wrote one minister in 1825, "to the mortification and disadvantage of having it said of us . . . [that] we are no scholars." In 1844, Park thought that increasing clerical duties left "little time for unbroken study," and Pond discerned signs of a disinclination to devote "a reasonable amount of time" to "study — severe study." He feared that the omission would lead to "commonplace and uninteresting" sermons and a declining reputation. To Park it even seemed that some of the brightest young college graduates had turned away from ministry because it appeared to demand "a sacrifice of mental excellence." Some feared that other professions would surpass the ministry. The Presbyterian George Howe issued a warning: "All the professions are advancing. We must at least advance with them, and if possible keep before them, or be despised."[45]

The professional ideal depicted the minister not only as learned but also as genteel. Samuel Miller's *Letters on Clerical Manners and Habits* (1829) typified a new genre of writing that urged upon young ministers "those manners which become the *Christian Gentleman;* which naturally flow from the meekness, gentleness, purity, and benevolence of our holy Religion." Humphrey explained that refinement gave the minister access to the "higher classes" as well as the poor and uneducated: "Every clergyman," he said, "ought to be a gentleman; not a man of show and ceremony, but a real gentleman in his manners, in his conversation, in all his habits and feelings." The ideal precluded boorishness. The handbooks taught young ministers not to put their feet on the furniture, smoke their cigars in others' faces, or spit tobacco in polite company. At the same time, they advocated a demanding ethic of patience, honesty, and self-possession.[46]

On the one hand, the ethic called for "decision of character," a "manly spirit" and bold firmness that resisted "timidity, indolence, and irresolution." The clergy often used masculine stereotypes to describe certain of the virtues they wished to embody, calling for "boldness," "energy," rigorous self-control,

44. Nayler, "Theological Seminary," p. 25; Carwardine, *Evangelicals and Politics*, p. 114; James B. Sellers, *History of the University of Alabama* (Tuscaloosa: University of Alabama Press, 1953); George P. Schmidt, *The Old Time College President* (New York: Columbia University Press, 1930), p. 184.

45. N. Tolland, "Remarks Addressed to Ministers," *Christian Spectator* 7 (1825): 284; [Park], "Thoughts on the State," p. 765; Pond, *Young Pastor's Guide*, pp. 67, 340; Park, *Preacher and Pastor*, p. 12; Holifield, *Gentlemen Theologians*, p. 34.

46. Miller, *Letters*, pp. 19, 54-61; Humphrey, *Thirty-Four Letters*, pp. 344-45; Pond, *Young Pastor's Guide*, p. 20; Cannon, *Lectures*, pp. 602-07.

independence, and courage. On the other hand, the ethic called for a "delicacy" as "scrupulous and pure as that of the most refined lady." Some of the demand for gentility had its source in the awareness that the clergy had "constant occasion to be in the company of females." Women persisted as the majority of church members. An extreme example was the membership of Henry Ward Beecher's first church in Laurenceburg, Indiana, which consisted of nineteen women and one man. Miller warned that women in the churches exercised an invincible influence.[47]

The language about gender and the membership statistics have led some historians, drawing on comments from the educated ministers of the Northeast, to see a feminization of the clergy — a tendency to adopt standards of gentleness and domesticity that made them more at home in feminine company than among other males. In contrast, other historians have found tense and discordant relationships between ministers and women, with the clergy of every region assuming a domineering stance that women resisted and subverted. But the gentle virtues represented only part of the clerical ethic, and while some women resisted, others admired their ministers, who worked more in concert with women than did any other male professional group.[48]

Most clergy challenged any move to ordain women as ministers. The debate over women's ordination surfaced after women began speaking publicly against slavery. In reaction against the anti-slavery speeches of the Quaker abolitionists Sarah and Angelina Grimké, the General Association of Congregational clergy in Massachusetts issued in 1837 a pastoral letter describing the ideal woman as a clinging vine and decrying women as "public lecturers and teachers." Sarah Grimké replied in her *Letters on the Equality of the Sexes and the Condition of Women* (1837), in which she claimed that God had ordained both men and women "to preach the unsearchable riches of Christ." If male clergy expected women to remain silent in the churches, then they should permit women neither to teach in the Sabbath schools nor sing in worship. If they took seriously Paul's directions to women on "how they should appear when praying or preaching in the public assemblies" and noticed the actions of women prophets in both the Old and New Testament, they would accept women's "equality with them in the highest and most important trust ever committed to man, namely, the ministry of the word."[49]

47. Miller, *Letters*, pp. 19, 26, 40, 104, 290, 334, 339; Karin E. Gedge, *Without Benefit of Clergy: Women and the Pastoral Relationship in Nineteenth-Century American Culture* (New York: Oxford University Press, 2003), p. 119; Ann Douglas, *The Feminization of American Culture* (New York: Avon Books, 1978), p. 116.

48. Douglas, *Feminization*, pp. 107, 189; Gedge, *Without Benefit*, pp. 197-220.

49. "The General Association of Massachusetts (Orthodox) to the Churches Under Their

At the 1848 Seneca Falls Convention that initiated the nineteenth-century movement for women's rights, the delegates deplored the exclusion of women from the ministry and resolved that success in the struggle for human rights required "the overthrow of the monopoly of the pulpit" by men. Some abandoned the churches as implacable enemies of reform, but others hoped for change. In 1853, Antoinette Brown, a Congregationalist, received ordination at the hands of a Wesleyan Methodist minister in New York. She had studied theology at Oberlin College, and Luther Lee, who ordained her, argued that she stood in the tradition of the biblical women prophets and the women who served the New Testament churches. The Apostle Paul assumed, he insisted, that women could "labor in the gospel" in the same way as men. Her pastoral ministry lasted only a year before she became an activist for women's rights.[50]

The clerical professionals emphasized refinement and good manners in part because they recognized that many of the clergy came from the ranks of "persons not born to wealth, but poverty rather," the children of "parents in moderate worldly circumstances." The directors of the American Education Society felt on the defensive against critics who implied that the scholarship students — young men "from the hill towns of New England" who had not known "early wealth and ease" — were "heavy, coarse-featured, and coarse-minded" rustics "liable to disgrace their sacred profession . . . by their misconduct."[51]

During the 1840s, Southern Presbyterians debated the merits of various programs that had provided funds to educate "poor and pious youth" for the ministry. In the General Assembly of 1856, Peyton Harrison of Virginia condemned "the current notion that only indigent young men are to be expected to offer themselves to the Lord. . . . The sooner we get rid of a class ministry the better." Isabella Bishop, viewing the landscape from an English vantage, recognized that "the clergy, as a general rule," came "from a different class in society from that which furnishes the clergy of the Church of England." They were men

Care," in *The Feminist Papers from Adams to deBeauvoir*, ed. Alice S. Rossi (New York: Columbia University Press, 1973), p. 306. Sarah Grimké, "Letters on the Equality of the Sexes and the Condition of Women, 1837," in *Feminist Papers*, pp. 310, 317.

50. "Declaration of Sentiments and Resolutions, Seneca Falls Convention," in *Feminist Papers*, pp. 417, 420; Luther Lee, *Woman's Right to Preach the Gospel* (Syracuse: Luther Lee, 1853), pp. 7-18.

51. "The Church and its Ministry," *The New Englander and Yale Review* 11 (1853): 115; *Forty-Fourth Annual Report of the Directors of the American Education Society* (Boston: Marion and Son, 1861), p. 15; *Twenty-First Annual Report of the Directors of the American Education Society* (Boston: Perkins and Marvin, 1837), p. 43.

of "high attainments and education," but "not many of 'The Upper Ten Thousand'" could be found within their company.[52]

The advocates of gentility wanted urbane manners and refined taste. They also wanted unimpeachable ethical probity. But some ministers proved disappointing, and in an era of mass-market journalism, the lapses could receive sensational publicity. When the Methodist Ephraim Avery in Rhode Island stood accused of murdering a young factory worker whom he had seduced, newspapers carried the story throughout the nation, and Catharine Read Williams gave a fictional account in her popular novel *Fall River*. The *Police Gazette* ran a regular feature on clerical scandals in its "religious" section, and during the church trial of Episcopal bishop Benjamin T. Onderdonk, who had been accused of sexual indiscretion, the "Onderdonk Excitement" stayed on the front pages of the *New York Herald* for almost two months. One of his supporters complained that "the newspaper press" depicted the clergy "as the most depraved class of mortals on the face of the earth. Not a mail arrives, nor a newspaper do we open, but our eyes light upon some malefaction committed by a clergyman."[53]

Between 1810 and 1860, more than twenty clergymen stood accused of misdeeds that drew heavy newspaper coverage, and half of them were found guilty, so the case of the fallen cleric became a staple formula of tabloid journalism. The advocates of a respectable and professional ministry found such lapses — and the publicity surrounding them — acutely painful, and their support for gentility represented not only deference to the refined classes but also a solicitude for the moral integrity of the profession.[54]

Conscientious clergy sought, above all, a religious life that was deep and faithful. A classical education was a necessary but secondary qualification: the primary demand was for religious integrity. Pond called for a "love of Christ" that would express itself in prayer, devotion, sacramental practice, and spiritual conversation. The seminaries nurtured religious feeling and practices as much as they did theological learning. Students gathered in devotional societies and met regularly as a group with faculty members to form deeper levels of religious sensibility. In the revivalist traditions, this meant an insistence on a converted ministry. In the liturgical traditions, it meant a ministry willing to devote hours to prayer, self-examination, and meditation. It did not mean, pastoral writers explained, "sanctimoniousness" or an absence of spiritual struggle. Archibald Alexander at Princeton taught his students that ministers

---

52. Holifield, *Gentlemen Theologians*, p. 15; Bishop, *Aspects of Religion*, p. 29.
53. Moore, *Selling God*, p. 130; Gedge, *Without Benefit*, pp. 26-39.
54. Gedge, *Without Benefit*, p. 51.

would have to face their own "spiritual troubles." Ministry boards not only examined candidates on their theology but also probed their "experimental acquaintance" with the truths they professed.[55]

The Populist Revolt

By 1855, if Baird was right, 63 percent of the clergy might have lacked the learning that the professional party considered essential. Many of them also scorned it. Methodists and Baptists produced outspoken critics of clerical higher learning. The Methodist Peter Cartwright in Illinois ridiculed Eastern colleges and seminaries as places "where they manufacture young preachers like they do lettuce in hot-houses." Primitive Baptists formed an alliance in 1832 that combined Calvinist theology with an opposition to mission societies, colleges, and seminaries. One faction of Presbyterians formed a separate Cumberland Presbyterian Church in 1810 when the General Assembly insisted on Calvinist orthodoxy and a classical education for the ministry. The Universalists, who coalesced into a separate denomination by 1803, rejected the need for any "theological school of human establishment."[56]

Such populist leaders as Abner Jones and Elias Smith, who after 1801 organized the Christian Connection, condemned colleges and seminaries as unbiblical and unnecessary. Alexander Campbell, the patriarch of the Disciples of Christ movement in the South and Midwest, initially found no biblical warrant for either. The Mennonites, the Amish, the Brethren, the Brethren in Christ, the Evangelische Gemeinschaft, and other smaller German groups refused to require higher education for their ministers. The more outspoken populists not only repudiated the need for higher learning but also verged on making the educated clergy "objects of popular odium."[57]

Some believed that Christians could support no practice not mandated in scripture; since the New Testament set no educational standard for pastors, no nineteenth-century church could impose one. Ministers who believed this liked to point out that the apostles had no special education. Other populists rejected

55. "On the Temptations of Beneficiaries who are Preparing for the Ministry," *The Christian Spectator* 4 (1822): 451; Pond, *Young Pastor's Guide*, pp. v, 292; Archibald Alexander, *Thoughts on Religious Experience* (Philadelphia: Presbyterian Board of Education, 1844), p. 52; Reed and Matheson, *Narrative*, vol. 1, p. 309.

56. Baird, *Religion in America* (1856), p. 383; Peter Cartwright, *Autobiography of Peter Cartwright*, ed. W. P. Strickland (New York: Methodist Book Concern, 1856), p. 307; Holifield, *Theology in America*, p. 219.

57. Reed and Matheson, *Narrative*, vol. 2, p. 40.

seminaries because such schools countered the spirit of religious democracy, implying that the common people could not read and understand the Bible for themselves. They believed that theology was a subject that "ought to be leveled to the apprehension of all." The educated, in their eyes, were merely trying to monopolize religious power. Still other populists contended that the educated could not reach the common people. Cartwright boasted that Presbyterians and Congregationalists had produced an educated ministry while the Methodists had "universally" opposed such a requirement, with the result that "the illiterate Methodist preachers actually set the world on fire" while the clerical gentlemen "were still lighting their matches."[58]

Populist clergy made broad use of arguments like Cartwright's. When the Freewill Baptist Benjamin Putnam consulted his colleagues about the possibility of college study, they tried to convince him "that extensive literary acquirements" would "embarrass and lessen" his influence. Populist Methodists, who took pride that their preachers "never rubbed their backs against the walls of a college," contended that theological schools established "modes of thought without reference to the popular standard" and sent out preachers ill-adapted to common people. Populist numerical success produced occasional self-doubt among the educated: Francis Wayland concluded that "other things being equal, the preacher of the gospel will be most successful, whose habits of thought are but little elevated above those of his hearers."[59]

The populists did not champion ignorance, but they preferred something like the older "field school" method, with practicing clergy educating their successors as they worked alongside them. The Methodists, for example, often paired a younger with an older circuit rider, who would train him to preach and examine him on doctrine. Cartwright recalled that William McKendree instructed him in grammar, selected books for him to read, and examined his progress, and he thought this a better way "than all the colleges and Biblical institutes in the land" because it allowed him to learn and practice every day. Andrew Reid found it a common practice in several denominations for pastors to "receive and train" young men.[60]

---

58. Holifield, *Theology in America*, p. 293; Cartwright, *Autobiography*, p. 79.

59. Catherine A. Brekus, *Female Preaching in America: Strangers and Pilgrims, 1740-1845* (Chapel Hill: University of North Carolina Press, 1998), p. 143; Schaff, *America*, p. 138; W. J. Sassnet, "The Pulpit," *The Quarterly Review of the Methodist Episcopal Church, South* 4 (1852): 565; Wayland, *Apostolic Ministry*, p. 52.

60. Cartwright, *Autobiography*, p. 78; Frederick A. Norwood, "The Americanization of the Wesleyan Itinerant," *The Ministry in the Methodist Heritage*, ed. Gerald O. McCulloh (Nashville: Board of Education, 1960), p. 55; Reed and Matheson, *Narrative*, vol. 1, p. 138.

The Midwest was especially receptive to the populist message, and as immigrants poured into the region, educated ministers in the East worried. Lyman Beecher urged in "A Plea for the West" that Easterners educate "a learned and talented ministry" to fill the Midwestern regions with "schools, academies, libraries, colleges, and all the apparatus for the perpetuity of republican institutions." Eastern ministers did move into the area, and they did, as Beecher had hoped, found schools, colleges, seminaries, and libraries as well as churches. But twelve years after Beecher's plea, Horace Bushnell still worried about "barbarism," "Romanism," and the "coarseness" of religion in the Midwest. He found Western clergy "crude in the matter and rough in the form," and he wanted to send missionaries, but when they traveled westward they encountered resentment at Eastern condescension and the conviction that the mission agencies cloaked "greed," "corruption," and "tyranny."[61]

No singular style of ministry characterized the clergy who rejected the professional model. The quiet manner of the Mennonites, who selected their preachers from the members of their churches, had little in common with the more boisterous style of the frontier Methodist and Baptist preachers. Neither the elaborate lay priesthood of the Mormons nor the elders and eldresses and deacons and deaconesses of the Shakers had parallels in other groups. The Mormons said that they had reestablished the priesthood of Aaron, open to all twelve-year-old Mormon boys, who became deacons, teachers, and priests over a period of six years before ascending into the priesthood of Melchizedek as elders and bishops — and, in a few instances, as high priests. The Shaker ministry consisted of the overseers of the various "families" that formed communal "villages." Neither Shakers nor Mormons had a "clergy" in the conventional sense. The movements illustrated the fluidity of religious leadership produced by the populist impulse.[62]

One set of populist ideals can be discerned in the autobiography of Cartwright, the Methodist circuit rider who preached in Kentucky and Tennessee before moving to Illinois, where he traveled a three-hundred-mile circuit. He did not disdain good manners; he was embarrassed at dinner with a middle-class family when his colleague manhandled the fried chicken, whistled for the dog, and threw the bones on the carpet. But he ridiculed the "coldness and stiffness" of clerical gentility and espoused an ideal of physical valor, a readiness for

61. Lyman Beecher, "A Plea for the West," in *God's New Israel*, ed. Conrad Cherry (Englewood Cliffs, N.J.: Prentice-Hall, 1971), p. 123; Horace Bushnell, "Barbarism the First Danger," *Work and Play* (New York: Charles Scribner's Sons, 1883), pp. 229, 230, 232; John Taylor, *Thoughts on Missions* (Franklin County: n.p., 1820), pp. 23, 26-29.

62. Stephen J. Stein, *The Shaker Experience in America: A History of the United Society of Believers* (New Haven: Yale University Press, 1992), pp. 133-34.

conflict, and a preference for earthiness of speech. "I did not permit myself," he once said, "to believe any man could whip me till it was tried."[63]

Among the populists, sermons could range from biblical exposition to fanciful reveries. Most preferred to preach without notes, often to the accompaniment of shouts and exclamations. They shouted, threatened, cajoled, and entertained their audiences with homely analogies, colorful stories, doggerel poetry, and ridicule. "We could not, many of us," said Cartwright, "conjugate a verb or parse a sentence, and murdered the king's English almost every lick." Some of the least educated forgot about interpreting the biblical text and invented new genres, such as alphabet sermons that assigned a meaning to each letter in a biblical word. One Baptist preached for two hours on the word "salvation" by telling his listeners that salvation was saving, almighty, lasting, vast, almighty again, eternal, incomprehensible, and honorable.[64]

Popular revival preachers captivated audiences at tumultuous outdoor camp meetings. Spreading after 1800, the camp meetings lasted several days and attracted vast crowds, some of whom responded to revivalist preaching by crying out, shouting, dancing, and jerking in ecstatic abandon. Not all populists favored the revivalist route — followers of Alexander Campbell, for instance, thought the revivals irrational, Mennonites and Brethren ignored them, and Universalists questioned their premises — but a few of the populist preachers attained regional fame as stars of the camp meeting.

Populist zeal permitted innovation and improvisation — a democratization of preaching that opened the pulpit to groups once excluded. The heat of revivalist piety again burned away some of the barriers to women preachers. Between 1790 and 1845, the Universalists, Quakers, United Brethren, and Freewill Baptists allowed women to preach; Methodists had women exhorters, and the Christian Connection produced around twenty women preachers. Some of the followers of the Vermont Baptist William Miller, who expected an imminent return of Jesus, also encouraged women's preaching as a sign of the coming apocalypse. More than 120 women during this period achieved public recognition as preachers of the gospel. Harriet Livermore preached in 1827 to the U.S. Congress, much to the displeasure of President John Quincy Adams.[65]

The willingness to hear women preachers extended to African American denominations. The African Methodist Jarena Lee, inspired to preach in 1809 by both voices and visions, finally won Bishop Richard Allen's permission to travel

---

63. Cartwright, *Autobiography,* pp. 94, 133, 187, 298.

64. Cartwright, *Autobiography,* p. 4; Nathan O. Hatch, *The Democratization of American Christianity* (New Haven: Yale University Press, 1989), pp. 134-40.

65. Brekus, *Female Preaching,* pp. 1-4, 5, 138, 320, 343-45.

from church to church in Pennsylvania, proclaiming a Methodist view of conversion and holiness. She was one of several African Methodist Episcopal (AME) women preachers, and other evangelical women traveled in similar paths. The preacher known to us only as Elizabeth, a freed slave of Methodist background, felt called around 1799 to "exercise in the ministry," and she preached with such authority that one auditor once cried out that God must have "revealed these things to her." Sojourner Truth, who combined her preaching with antislavery speeches and activism, was said to have had "magnetic power over an audience." But even churches that acknowledged women as preachers resisted ordination. When the Methodist Phoebe Palmer argued in 1859 that women should be allowed to preach, she made no case for ordination.[66]

The populist impulse encouraged an African American preaching tradition. The Methodist circuit rider Harry Hosier impressed the Methodist bishop Thomas Coke as "one of the best preachers in the world," producing sermons with "amazing power" that drew both white and black listeners. In 1810, Daniel Coker, who helped found the AME church, knew of fourteen ordained black Methodist itinerant clergy and a number of local pastors. By 1861, black Methodists, supervised by whites, preached in many of the 329 Methodist missions to the slaves in the South, in addition to scores of northern Methodist black congregations.[67]

Baptists had as many black preachers as the Methodists. George Liele, who was baptized in 1774, for example, preached to slaves on a South Carolina plantation, recruiting additional preachers and encouraging them to gather congregations. Black Baptists created their own institutions and placed black preachers at the head of them. Slave preachers had long exhorted in the "invisible institution" — the network of gatherings in which the slaves conducted their own worship, free from the oversight of whites. But Baptists gathered at least ten independent congregations with black preachers before 1801, and in the next half century they formed at least 205 more. Self-taught preachers led most of them. Noah Davis purchased his freedom in Virginia and began a congregation shortly after 1847 in Baltimore despite his having "never had a day's schooling." He "improved" his mind by learning to read the Bible and "other good

66. Brekus, *Female Preaching*, pp. 343-45; Elizabeth, *A Colored Minister of the Gospel, Born in Slavery* (Philadelphia: The Tract Society of Friends, 1889), pp. 5-10; Sojourner Truth, *Narrative of Sojourner Truth* (Battle Creek: for the author, 1878), p. 146; Phoebe Palmer, *Promise of the Father, Or a Neglected Specialty of the Last Days* (Boston: Henry V. Degen, 1859), p. 1.

67. Russell E. Richey, Kenneth E. Rowe, and Jean Miller Schmidt, eds., *The Methodist Experience in America: A Sourcebook* (Nashville: Abingdon Press, 2000), pp. 79-80; Daniel Coker, *A Dialogue Between a Virginian and an African Minister* (Baltimore: Benjamin Eades, 1810), pp. 37-42.

books," and he poured himself into preaching. By 1855, his congregation was large enough to erect a sizable chapel.[68]

The black populist preachers developed a singular style of oratory, marked by the retelling of biblical narratives in a manner reminiscent of West African storytelling practices. They used colorful images and stirring delivery to produce, as one observer noted, "vivid reproductions of Scripture narrative." Their sermons employed repetition, parallelism, and phrases and stories memorized from the Bible, and their listeners punctuated their cadences with the pattern of call and response inherited from the African past. On occasion a particular sermon — such as "The Sun Do Move" by the Virginian John Jasper — became so popular that both whites and blacks repeatedly requested to hear it. Such sermons made the black preacher the most influential figure in the slave community.[69]

Friends tried to convince the African Methodist leader Richard Allen to leave the Methodists, but he refused for populist reasons: "the plain and simple gospel," he argued, "suits best for any people," and Methodist "spiritual preaching" would reach the uneducated more easily than "high-flown" sermons. When in 1837 Daniel Alexander Payne, who had attended Lutheran Theological Seminary in Gettysburg, and who would become an AME bishop, advocated a regimen of reading and examination for the preachers, he encountered "open conflict between the advocates of ministerial education and the defenders of an illiterate ministry." Payne was seeking only a list of required readings, but opponents accused him of "branding the ministry with infamy," and the issue "convulsed" the denomination "from center to circumference" for a decade.[70]

The tensions between populists and professionals occurred during a period when the ministry, in some parts of the country, was becoming a "career" in which ministers expected to advance upward through several pastorates, moving toward larger urban congregations. Pond explained that ministers found their level — serving in "higher or lower stations" — according to their merits. Others thought that ministers had become perpetual "candidates" seeking

68. James M. Washington, *Frustrated Fellowship: The Black Quest for Social Power* (Macon: Mercer University Press, 1986), pp. 8-22; Mechal Sobel, *Trabelin' On: The Slave Journey to an Afro-Baptist Faith* (Princeton: Princeton University Press, 1979), p. 222; Noah Davis, *A Narrative of the Life of the Rev. Noah Davis* (Baltimore: Weishempel, 1859), pp. 32, 36, 41, 42.

69. Albert J. Raboteau, *Slave Religion: The "Invisible Institution" in the Antebellum South* (New York: Oxford University Press, 1978), pp. 235, 237.

70. Richard Allen, *The Life Experience and Gospel Labours of the Rt. Rev. Richard Allen,* ed. George A. Singleton (New York: Abingdon Press, 1960), pp. 29-30; Daniel A. Payne, *History of the African Methodist Episcopal Church,* ed. C. S. Smith (Nashville: Publishing House of the A.M.E. Sunday School Union, 1891), pp. 115, 396.

higher salaries from wealthier congregations. They spoke of a clerical market in which the pulpit would, unfortunately, "have its market-price, like that of stocks and manufactures."[71]

One result of the market ethos was a striking variation in pay scales, with the populists usually occupying the bottom rungs of the ladder. In 1855, the average ministerial salary was around $400 a year, but the larger urban churches paid anywhere from $1,200 to $6,000. The lowest-paid were the rural farmer-preachers — especially Baptists — who received only an occasional offering. Baptist clergy in the towns received salaries that varied with the wealth of the community. In 1855, full-time Baptist ministers in the Northeast averaged from $300 to $500 a year. In 1849, however, First Baptist in Richmond paid its college-educated minister $1,500, and Baptists in Mobile offered $2,500.[72]

Not far above the unsalaried Baptist farmer-preachers were the Methodist itinerants. In 1800, their book of *Discipline* limited them to $80 a year — when they could collect it — with a small allowance for wives and children. The amount rose until it reached $400 into the 1840s, but in 1844 the Methodists removed the limits, so some urban preachers began to receive $1,200 to $1,500 while others slipped behind. The average for Methodists in New York in 1854 was said to be $250 a year, and in New England slightly under $500.[73]

Presbyterian salaries could range from an average of $400 in 1835 to the more than $5,000 paid in 1856 to Benjamin Palmer in New Orleans. Episcopalians earned from $400 to $3,500, though the average was "not far from $600." The bishop of New York received $6,000, though he had to pay the salaries of his suffragan and assistants. Irish Catholic priests managed on subsistence salaries in the Northeastern cities, but they could receive $900 plus voluntary offerings and fees in Charleston. The Lutheran Olaus Fredrik Duus accepted a call to Waupaca, Wisconsin, in 1857 for $300 a year plus firewood, parsonage, and the use of forty acres, but the Lutheran minister in Frederick, Maryland, received $700 a year. The market now ruled.[74]

71. Scott, *Office to Profession*, p. 72; Pond, *Young Pastor's Guide*, p. 343; Brooks, *Statement of Facts*, pp. 8, 13.

72. Belcher, *Religious Denominations*, pp. 982-84; Baird, *Religion in America* (1856), p. 277.

73. Frederick A. Norwood, "The Shaping of Methodist Ministry," *Religion in Life* 43 (1974): 338-39; Holifield, *Gentlemen Theologians*, p. 30; Brooks, *Statement of Facts*, p. 5.

74. Baird, *Religion in America*, p. 277; Caswall, *America and the American Church*, p. 306; Brooks, *Statement of Facts*, p. 5; England, *Diurnal*, p. 7; Olaus F. Duus, *Frontier Parsonage*, ed. Theodore C. Blegan (Northfield, Minn.: Norwegian-American Historical Association, 1947), p. 45; Julius Bodensieck, ed., *The Encyclopedia of the Lutheran Church* (Minneapolis: Augsburg, 1965), p. 1865; John Nicum, "Pastor's Salaries," *Lutheran Cyclopedia* (New York: Charles Scribner's Sons, 1899), p. 369.

By 1860, it cost $1,200 to $1,500 to have a comfortable middle-class existence. The laboring classes spent from $200 to $600 a year to maintain themselves. One New England minister with a wife and two children claimed that house rent, horse, food, clothing, and wood cost him $955 a year, with nothing left for books or luxuries. For the average minister, that would have been a bonanza. Baird found it embarrassing that Americans did not provide better support, though he insisted that most lived "comfortably and respectably," at least in the Atlantic states. But a study of salaries in the Northeast in 1853 concluded that the average was "too low to meet the reasonable necessities of a professional man." Catholic bishops had to plead for "decent support" for priests.[75]

The differences accented class distinctions that clergy could rarely cross. Everyone recognized that certain pastors — such as Irish Catholic priests, Methodists, Universalists, Disciples, Cumberland Presbyterians, Dunkers, Brethren, most Baptists, and preachers in the Christian Connection — labored mainly "among the lower classes of the people," though some moved toward the middle class by the 1840s. The ministers that Harriet Martineau had in mind when she described the clerical profession as one of "high honor" were generally Presbyterians, Congregationalists, Unitarians, and Episcopalians, and it was sometimes difficult for the clergy of the upper strata to speak of their humbler colleagues without condescension.[76]

By the 1840s, the white populist denominations were seeking respectability, and their attitudes toward clerical education began to change. A sizable number threw themselves into the building of colleges, the publishing of theological journals, and the pursuit of gentility. By the time of the Civil War, both Northern and Southern Methodists produced quarterly reviews that modeled themselves after Presbyterian and Congregationalist journals. Both Methodists and Baptists made early ventures into theological education, and their urban churches began to emulate the gothic and colonial architecture once monopolized by the middle-class denominations. As a result, the populist groups divided internally into factions, some pushing for a professional ministry, others espousing populist values. With the populist upsurge, authority became, once again, more personal, more charismatic, and less dependent on office and learning. The effect was lasting.

75. Chester W. Wright, *Economic History of the United States* (New York: McGraw Hill, 1941), p. 409; Brooks, *Statement of Facts*, pp. 20-21; Baird, *Religion in America* (1856), p. 277; Kenneth R. O'Brien, *The Nature and Support of Diocesan Priests in the United States of America* (Washington, D.C.: Catholic University of America Press, 1949), pp. 14-15.

76. Schaff, *America*, p. 138; Martineau, *Society in America*, p. 117.

The Immigrant Priest

Between 1790 and 1860, more than 5,299,000 immigrants entered the United States, and among them were ministers and priests from every large religious group in Europe. Heavy German immigration increased the Lutheran presence; immigrants from Northern Ireland brought Presbyterian sympathies; and English newcomers added to the ranks of multiple Protestant groups. The earliest Russian Orthodox clergy entered Alaska in 1794, and by 1824, under Father John Veniaminov, they established a mission to the Aleuts, laying the groundwork for the permanent presence of Orthodoxy in the region. Unlike the Western Catholic church, the Orthodox permitted a married clergy (though not married bishops), but like the Catholics they thought of the priesthood primarily as a group of men ordained to celebrate the Divine Liturgy, or Holy Eucharist, dispense the remaining sacraments, and offer pastoral care to their flocks.[77]

No religious tradition underwent a more profound transformation than the Roman Catholic Church, which grew from around 35,000 members in 1790 to around 2,500,000 — maybe even 3,000,000 — in 1860. By the Civil War, the Catholic Church had become the largest denomination, and most of its members — like most of its clergy — were first- or second-generation immigrants. The influx made the Catholic clergy shepherds of the poor (since the affluent rarely became immigrants), and it stimulated anti-Catholic backlash on the part of nativists, throwing priests and bishops on the defensive. It also threatened Protestant ministers, who still envisioned America as a Protestant nation. And it meant that Catholic priests would face issues unlike those of the Protestant clergy.[78]

The church worried about a shortage of good clergy. The first Provincial Council in Baltimore in 1829 complained of "the utmost want of a sufficient ministry." "In vain has the number of our churches doubled within the last eight years," wrote Bishop Francis P. Kenrick of Philadelphia in the 1830s, "if there be not a proportionate increase of priests to minister to them." Bishop John England in Charleston feared in 1838 that the church was losing members because of "the absence of a clergy sufficiently numerous and properly qualified." In centers of Catholic population, the problem was difficult but

---

77. Thomas F. Fitzgerald, *The Orthodox Church* (Westport, Conn.: Greenwood, 1995), pp. 18, 122.

78. Gerald Shaughnessy, *Has the Immigrant Kept the Faith?* (1st ed., 1925; New York: Arno Press, 1969), pp. 29-140, 145; Roger Finke and Rodney Stark, *The Churching of America: Winners and Losers in Our Religious Economy* (New Brunswick: Rutgers University Press, 1992), p. 112.

manageable. In other regions, the Catholic laity rarely saw a priest; the entire diocese of Ohio in 1823 had only seven. As settlers moved into Illinois, two-thirds of the region's Catholics lived beyond the reach of priestly guidance and comfort.[79]

In 1829, the Catholic Church had around 232 priests in America, roughly one for every 1,370 Catholics. In 1860, the number had risen to around 2,235, but the ratio showed little change. Most of the priests came from Ireland, Germany, and France. As late as 1861 in the diocese of St. Louis, 47 percent of the secular clergy were Irish, 31 percent German, 7 percent French, 4 percent Dutch, 3 percent British, and 3 percent Bohemian. Only 5 percent were native-born Americans.[80]

A good number of the priests who came to America were refugees from revolutionary and anti-clerical European states, and they brought a style of Catholicism that was more stringent, more devoted to Rome, and more attuned to Roman-approved devotions and liturgical practices than eighteenth-century American styles. Scarred by battles with European liberals, they called for a piety of obedience to the hierarchical church, a polemical stance against error, a fascination with the miraculous and with the suffering Jesus, and a suspicion of the surrounding environment. They were "ultramontane" — unreservedly devoted to the pope in Rome, "beyond the mountains" — and they created tension within American Catholicism.[81]

Even linguistic differences contributed to the tensions. The parishes wanted priests who spoke their language. "Where," asked John Martin Henni, the first bishop of Milwaukee, "shall I get a sufficient number of priests who will be obliged to speak both English and German, and in some cases, French also, for the ever increasing number of immigrants?" Bishop Frederic Baraga in Michigan solemnly blessed the church of Portage Lake and then preached in English, French, and German, but he assigned the church a priest who spoke only English: "The dissatisfaction of the Germans and French towards him

79. *Pastoral Letters of the Most Reverend the Archbishop of Baltimore and the other Right Reverend and Very Reverend Prelates of the Roman Catholic Church* (Baltimore: James Myers, 1829), p. 910; White, *Diocesan Seminary*, p. 59; Peter Guilday, *The Life and Times of John England, First Bishop of Charleston (1786-1842)*, 2 vols. (New York: American Press, 1927), vol. 2, p. 361; Martin J. Spalding, *Life, Times, and Character of the Right Reverend Benedict Joseph Flaget* (Louisville: Webb & Levering, 1852), p. 223; Shaughnessy, *Has the Immigrant*, p. 250.

80. John Gilmary Shea, *History of the Catholic Church in the United States*, 4 vols. (New York: John G. Shea, 1890), vol. 3, p. 419; Shaughnessy, *Has the Immigrant*, p. 117; James Hitchcock, "Secular Clergy in Nineteenth Century America: A Diocesan Profile," *Records of the American Catholic Historical Society of Philadelphia* 88 (1977): 33.

81. John T. McGreevy, *Catholicism and American Freedom: A History* (New York: W. W. Norton, 2003), pp. 19-37.

showed itself immediately," Baraga reported. "Priests who speak English, German, and French are not too easy to find."[82]

Catholics worried that they had too many priests of modest ability, and it became a settled conviction among some that Europe sent to America too many of its misfits. The 1829 Provincial Council declared that bishops were no longer disposed "to permit that priests who have been elsewhere held in disrepute, shall be received into our churches, to create schisms, to encourage strife, to perpetuate abuses, and to disseminate scandal." Bishop John Hughes in New York argued that the dependence on foreign priests forced him to populate the "vineyard of the Lord" with workers whom he did not know, with less than satisfactory results, and the problems seemed intractable. The Plenary Council of Baltimore, held in 1852, announced that the bishops did not want "priests coming from Europe to be received into the ranks of our clergy" without permission from the local prelate. Unfamiliar immigrant priests should not be "too easily admitted to the exercise of the ministry, to the danger of souls."[83]

In 1860, the New York priest Jeremiah W. Cummings issued a plea in *Brownson's Quarterly Review* for a native American priesthood, arguing that the Europeans held on to their men of ability: "They do for us the best they can, that is to say, in commercial parlance, they allow the cheaper brands to be exported and keep the prime article for home consumption." The article drew spirited rebuttals, but the suspicion remained that "first rate" European priests could and would "stay at home."[84]

It could not help matters that the immigrant clergy — as well as the American priests — harbored ethnic resentments. In 1792, Bishop Carroll had to ask Rome to allow changes in the ritual because Irish priests refused to celebrate English saints. That was only the beginning of a long period of ethnic tension. The Revolution in France brought an influx of French priests, including members of the Sulpician Order, noted for its work in education, especially of the priesthood. Learned and polished, the French clergy educated Protestant children, trained Catholic priests, and became bishops. By 1817, the Sulpician Ambrose Maréchal was the archbishop of Baltimore, and soon half of the

82. William S. Morris, *The Seminary Movement in the United States* (Washington, D.C.: The Catholic University of America, 1932), p. 57; Frederic Baraga, *The Diary of Bishop Frederic Baraga*, ed. Regis M. Walling and N. Daniel Rupp (Detroit: Wayne State University Press, 1990), p. 146.

83. *Pastoral Letters*, p. 10; White, *Diocesan Seminary*, p. 57; Anonymous, "Seminaries and Seminarians," *Brownson's Quarterly Review*, 3rd Series, 2 (1861): 101.

84. Jeremiah W. Cummings, "Our Future Clergy; an Inquiry into Vocations to the Priesthood in the United States," *Brownson's Quarterly Review*, 3rd Series, 1 (1860): 505; Anonymous, "Seminaries," pp. 113-14.

Western bishops were French. Before long, the French would have tense relations with the Irish.[85]

Maréchal complained that eight of the first ten Irish priests in his diocese proved to be failures, and he told Rome that "so many priests who have come hither from Ireland, are addicted to the vice of drunkenness" that he was reluctant to "place them in charge of souls" without close supervision. But John England, of Irish birth, believed that the French could never become American: "their dress, air, carriage, notions, and mode of speaking of their religion, all, all are foreign." When John McCaffrey, president of the mainly Irish seminary in Emmitsburg, Maryland, needed a theologian, he let it be known that he desired no "censorious Frenchman."[86]

The German priests eyed both the French and the Irish, but especially the Irish, with suspicion. Schaff observed that the Germans and the Irish simply could not "agree very well." The Germans found the Irish bishops so unsympathetic that they sent complaints back home, prompting the Leopoldine Foundation, which supported Germans in America, to send Canon Josef Salzbacher to investigate. Salzbacher toured the country in 1842 and reported that the Germans received too little respect, had too few priests, and desperately needed their own seminaries. It appeared to the Germans that the American bishops were making "no provision for an increase of German-speaking priests."[87]

The solution seemed to be the creation of a priesthood that was "accustomed from infancy to the institutions, manners, and feelings" of Americans. Catholic leaders recognized the difficulties of recruitment: the "mentality of the country, especially in the upper classes of society," reported one Sulpician educator, was "hardly favorable to the ecclesiastical estate." Bishop John Connolly, the second bishop of New York, agreed: "American youth have an almost invincible repugnance to the ecclesiastical estate." Nonetheless, a seminary system appeared to be a feasible first step.[88]

85. Michael V. Gannon, "Before and After Modernism: The Intellectual Isolation of the American Priest," in *The Catholic Priest in the United States: Historical Investigations*, ed. John Tracy Ellis (Collegeville, Minn.: Saint John's University Press, 1971), p. 299; John P. Marschall, "Diocesan and Religious Clergy: The History of a Relationship, 1789-1969," in *Catholic Priest*, p. 387; Jay Dolan, *The American Catholic Experience: A History from Colonial Times to the Present* (Garden City: Doubleday, 1985), p. 119.

86. Gannon, "Before and After," p. 304; John Tracy Ellis, ed., *Documents of American Catholic History* (Milwaukee: Bruce, 1956), p. 216; Guilday, *England*, vol. 1, p. 482; White, *Diocesan Seminary*, p. 45.

87. Schaff, *America*, p. 184; Joseph Salzbacher, *Meine Reise Nach Nord-Amerika im Jahre 1842* (Wien: Wimmer, Schmidt, Leo, 1845), pp. 366, 370-71; Ellis, ed., *Documents*, p. 289.

88. White, *Diocesan Seminary*, pp. 37, 52; Lloyd Paul McDonald, *The Seminary Movement in*

In 1791, the Sulpicians created St. Mary's in Baltimore, and in the next thirty-eight years the school produced fifty-two ordained priests. Some bishops wanted the church to invest in a national seminary into which it could pour its resources, but most preferred a small school in each diocese. Michael O'Connor of Pittsburgh explained that a central seminary would encourage a "roving spirit" in priests and hinder the bishop's effort to secure commitments to his own diocese. By 1842, Catholics had twenty-two small struggling seminaries with around thirteen students in each. To support this system, wrote the bishops in 1840, was the only way for the American church to "become independent of foreign churches for the perpetuation of her priesthood."[89]

The Catholic seminaries assumed a task slightly different from that of the Protestant schools. The bishops wanted the schools to form candidates spiritually and train them in the practical duties of preaching, sacramental celebration, and the hearing of confessions. Bishop Carroll thought it less important for them to have "studied all the treatises of Divinity" than to be "virtuous priests" and "know the obvious and general principles of moral theology" so that they could function competently in the confessional.[90]

In accord with the practices of the Sulpicians, the seminaries instituted a program of priestly formation. At. St. Mary's in Baltimore, students rose at 5:00 for communal prayer, practiced mental prayer for an hour, and then went to mass. After breakfast, they studied theology and scripture and tutored the college students. At noon, they ate quietly, listened to readings from the New Testament, and meditated on a specific virtue, and then they continued class. In the later afternoon, they recited the rosary together before sharing supper and going to evening prayers, with examination of conscience, followed by spiritual reading for half an hour. They confessed their sins once a week and they remained silent most of each day. Some seminary training occurred in the home of a bishop; most took place in a setting like St. Mary's. Religious orders — from the Sulpicians to the Vincentians and the Benedictines — organized several of the seminaries and gave them a monastic atmosphere. Even in the diocesan seminaries, the aim was to shape the religious dispositions.[91]

---

the United States: Projects, Foundations, and Early Development (1784-1833) (Washington, D.C.: The Catholic University of America, 1927), p. 23.

89. John Tracy Ellis, "The Formation of the American Priest: An Historical Perspective," in *Catholic Priest*, p. 5; White, *Diocesan Seminary*, p. 64; Peter Guilday, ed., *National Pastorals of the American Hierarchy (1792-1919)* (Westminster: Newman Press, 1954), p. 136.

90. White, *Diocesan Seminary*, p. 122; Thomas O'Brien Hanley, ed., *The John Carroll Papers*, 3 vols. (Notre Dame: University of Notre Dame Press, 1976), vol. 3, p. 244; John Tracy Ellis, *Essays in Seminary Education* (Notre Dame: Fides Publishers, 1967), p. 91.

91. White, *Diocesan Seminary*, pp. 128-29; McDonald, *Seminary Movement*, pp. 32-37.

The seminaries began to educate a native priesthood, but they could not alleviate the tensions among the clergy. The tensions were not simply ethnic; they included familiar rivalries between the regular and the secular clergy. Such rivalries went back to the eighteenth century, when the Jesuits in Maryland secured independent sources of revenue. Successive archbishops in Baltimore fought with them over financial and administrative matters, and similar battles occurred between bishops and the religious orders in New York, St. Louis, Pittsburgh, and other dioceses.[92]

The disputes were partly about episcopal control, but there were other issues. The orders felt cheated when Rome appointed their leaders to bishoprics, removing them from service to the order. The bishops were irritated when the orders recruited candidates who might have served in diocesan churches. They were angry when orders lured priests away from diocesan congregations. The Sixth Provincial Council in 1846 asked Rome to rule that no diocesan priest could enter an order without written permission from the bishop, and Rome complied, but some orders ignored the ruling. And diocesan priests often felt that the religious clergy conveyed a sense of superiority. Boniface Wimmer, president of the American congregation of Benedictines, let it be known, for example, that he thought "secular priests are not the best adapted for missionary labors," partly because they were "in great danger of becoming careless and worldly-minded." Such sentiments did not commend themselves to diocesan pastors.[93]

There was another tension. Some of the diocesan clergy felt aggrieved that bishops could exercise arbitrary authority over them. The Catholic Church in America was a mission outpost, and the canon law that gave European clergy certain rights of tenure and appeal did not apply here. By the 1820s, some clergy called for policies that granted them tenure unless they disobeyed canonical rules, along with a right to a trial before any suspension, but the bishops ruled in 1829 that priests must move or resign whenever the bishop wanted. Bishop Henry Conwell in Philadelphia said that bishops had "absolute power" to suspend or move any priest in their dioceses.[94]

Some bishops were prepared to accept a certain number of canonical parishes from which pastors could not be removed without proper cause, but most of them worried about insubordinate priests. Other bishops proposed cathedral chapters — councils of priests to provide advice — but Rome saw no need for them, and only in the mid-1850s did the Vatican's Congregation for the

92. Marschall, "Diocesan and Religious," pp. 393-400.
93. Ellis, ed., *Documents*, p. 288; Marschall, "Diocesan and Religious," pp. 393-400.
94. Robert Trisco, "Bishops and their Priests in the United States," in *Catholic Priest*, p. 120; Patrick W. Carey, *People, Priests, and Prelates: Ecclesiastical Democracy and the Tensions of Trusteeism* (Notre Dame: University of Notre Dame Press, 1987), p. 216.

Propagation of the Faith, which oversaw missions, allow the appointment of "consultors." For some priests, this was only a first step: they wanted a voice in the selection of bishops, believing, as one priest wrote, that "the episcopate is too high here and the clergy too low."[95]

During his 1853 tour, Archbishop Gaetano Bedini, the representative of Pope Pius IX, questioned "the clergy's great dependence on the Bishops," but some of the bishops, including the autocratic John Hughes in New York, forbade their priests to write or speak on the rights of the clergy. In the face of a steady centralization of power in the bishops, the movements for clerical rights and due process made almost no headway.[96]

The laity — or at least some of them — could also pose problems. No issue created greater stress than the assertiveness of lay trustees, who challenged both the authority of the bishops and the desire of the clergy for secure appointments. The trustee system grew up in the eighteenth century when laity often had to take the initiative in forming and funding new churches. The lay trustees of these churches claimed the right to administer the "temporal" affairs of the congregation, and they also wanted to exercise a veto over clerical appointments and hold the authority to dismiss incompetent priests. Appealing to European customs and traditions, but also drawing on American "republican" sentiments, they resisted bishops who thought otherwise.[97]

Most of the antebellum Catholic churches had some form of trustee system, and some bishops would have accepted a limited trusteeism. John England promoted a constitution in his diocese that gave trustees some real power. But the system led to notorious conflicts in New York, Philadelphia, Norfolk, Charleston, and New Orleans, producing not only cases in the civil courts but also sporadic outbreaks of violence. By 1829, the bishops declared that whenever the state law permitted, they should hold the title to every new Catholic church. Slowly priests assumed more power on trustee boards, and the bishops attained the power they sought.[98]

In fact, both the laity and the clergy had similar conceptions of clerical duties. Most priests could easily have agreed with the Norfolk, Virginia, trustees who laid out in 1804 the main duties they expected their priest to perform: "1st to celebrate the Mass, 2d to administer the sacraments, 3d to assist the dying, 4th to instruct children in the catechism and Christian Morals, 5th to inculcate a decent and devout behavior in his congregation during the times of divine

---

95. Trisco, "Bishops and their Priests," pp. 116, 122-23, 127, 133, 140.
96. Trisco, "Bishops and their Priests," p. 127.
97. Carey, *People, Priests, and Prelates,* pp. 8-58.
98. Carey, *People, Priests, and Prelates,* pp. 59, 60, 70, 72.

service." Maréchal added that the laity also wanted "sacred eloquence" in "good sermons," but the sacraments came first.[99]

In 1818, the Jesuit John Grassi described the duties of his itinerant priesthood in rural Maryland. In setting out on each weekend journey, he carried sacramental elements and chrism for anointing baptized infants, the sick, and the dying. All Sunday morning, he heard confessions and pronounced absolution; at noon he celebrated the mass; after lunch he preached a sermon and catechized the children, but he also baptized infants and performed funeral services for anyone buried in the churchyard during his absence. In the late afternoon he instructed new Catholics and officiated at Holy Matrimony. His ministry was, above all, sacramental.[100]

The Eucharist was the superlative sacrament. As celebrated by antebellum priests, it proceeded with a stateliness and ceremonial splendor utterly unlike the forms of worship to which most Americans were accustomed. The priest, clad in vestments, faced the altar and recited the readings and prayers in Latin while congregants prayed silently, often with the rosary, or followed the service in vernacular prayer books. At the moment of consecration, the sound of a bell alerted the faithful to the miracle by which the substance of the bread and wine became Christ's body and blood. The faithful communed once or twice a year, some more often, but all viewed the uplifted elements, which only the priest could hold in his hands and which assumed their miraculous substance only by virtue of his words and actions. The large churches had three masses on Sundays and others during the week. In reenacting the sacrifice, the priest performed the principal action for which the church had set him apart.[101]

In a sermon-drenched American religious culture, Catholics recognized that the oratory of the priests sometimes failed to impress. Maréchal complained in 1826 that newly ordained priests often preached "abominably," and in 1858 Hughes pointed out that pastoral burdens made it difficult for priests to prepare first-rate sermons: "If one looks for extraordinary eloquence in the pulpit, or immense erudition, or able writers among the clergy of New York, he may be prepared for much disappointment." When Bedini toured the United States, he commented that "not many [of the priests] are good preachers." Catholics had other priorities; few antebellum Catholic seminaries had courses in preaching.[102]

99. Carey, *People, Priests, and Prelates*, p. 61; Ellis, "Formation," p. 19.

100. John Grassi, "The Catholic Religion in the United States in 1818," *Documentary Reports on Early American Catholicism*, ed. Philip Gleason (New York: Arno Press, 1978), pp. 238-39.

101. Jay Dolan, *The Immigrant Church* (Baltimore: Johns Hopkins University Press, 1975), pp. 55, 59.

102. Gannon, "Before and After Modernism," p. 302; Dolan, *Immigrant Church*, pp. 144-45.

Priests sought improvement as preachers by reading European handbooks, and the church did have some pulpit giants who could captivate an audience. Students at the University of North Carolina requested in 1860 that Bishop Hughes deliver the baccalaureate sermon, and they "listened with scarcely a stir for an hour and three quarters." Catholics cultivated their own form of revivalist preaching, importing from Europe the "parish mission," an eight- to fourteen-day campaign in a local parish with early morning and late evening services. During the 1850s, traveling priests in the Redemptorist and Jesuit orders became specialists in these services of renewal, which featured masses but also rousing songs and sermons designed to move the emotions with reminders of the dangers of hell and the rewards of heaven. The missions became a Catholic version of the evangelical revivals among Protestants, with the same themes of sin, hellfire, repentance, and conversion, though Catholics added the necessity of confession to a priest, which underscored his indispensability.[103]

Like Protestant ministers, the priests mostly oversaw the pious exercises of "devotional congregations." In Catholic churches in the Midwest between 1800 and 1860, more than 70 percent of all parish gatherings were for devotional groups like the Confraternity of the Immaculate Heart of Mary, which prayed for the conversion of sinners, or the Confraternity of the Sacred Heart, which meditated on the suffering of Christ. Priests organized confraternities, sodalities, rosary societies — all of which featured traditional practices of devotion and prayer.[104]

The heart of Catholic pastoral care was the sacrament of penance. Faithful Catholics confessed their sins to the priest at least once a year. By mid-century, many confessed more frequently, and priests in urban parishes sometimes spent four hours a day hearing confessions. One urban priest wrote that penitents lined up along the walls of his church part of each weekday and all day Saturday. The bishops therefore wanted their priests well schooled in moral theology, which guided priestly decisions about appropriate acts of penance. Archbishop Samuel Eccleston told one seminary president that he would not ordain a priest without "a good course in Moral Theology," which he saw as much more relevant than "Dogmatic Theology."[105]

---

103. Dolan, *Immigrant Church*, pp. 144-45, 149; Jay Dolan, *Catholic Revivalism: The American Experience, 1830-1900* (Notre Dame: University of Notre Dame Press, 1978), pp. 31-121.

104. Stephen J. Shaw, "The Cities and the Plains," *The American Catholic Parish*, 2 vols., ed. Jay Dolan (New York: Paulist Press, 1987), vol. 2, p. 304; Debra Campbell, "The Struggle to Serve: From the Lay Apostolate to the Ministry Explosion," in *Transforming Parish Ministry: The Changing Roles of Catholic Clergy, Laity, and Women Religious*, ed. Jay P. Dolan (New York: Crossroad, 1990), p. 210.

105. Dolan, *Immigrant Church*, p. 62; White, *Diocesan Seminary*, pp. 139-40.

Like Protestant ministers, Catholic priests visited the stricken, and they elicited admiration for their self-sacrificial willingness to enter the sickroom, even during periods of epidemic disease, in order to hear confessions, absolve sins, and administer the final rites. During the cholera epidemic in Philadelphia in 1832, one observer claimed, the priests "proved their character and their strong virtues, caring for the sick, in the exercise of the sacred ministry; while non-Catholic ministers generally fled from the city." During the yellow fever epidemic of 1854 in Savannah, most citizens left the town, but the priests and the Sisters of Mercy (along with some Protestant ministers) remained to attend the dying, until they too fell sick. Father Edward Quigley visited, as he wrote, "from eighty to one hundred sick persons a day, our deaths daily averaging from forty to forty-eight."[106]

Father Varela at the Church of Transfiguration in New York visited the sick and poor, climbed aboard quarantine ships, and "lived in the hospitals" during the cholera epidemic of 1832. He gave away his clothes and his bedding to the poor. He surrendered his watch, and when a friend replaced it, he gave the new one away as well. Admirers claimed that he "gave away everything that he owned." For the Catholics in his region of the city, he became a model of self-sacrifice.[107]

Catholic clergy produced their own version of the benevolent empire. They formed mutual aid societies, temperance organizations, hospitals, tract societies, orphanages, local libraries, societies to help the poor, shelters for the homeless, and schools. In the larger cities, St. Vincent de Paul societies and Women's Societies of Charity enabled lay men and women, under priestly oversight, to work with the poor. Redemptorist priests undertook special apostolates to the impoverished. In 1842, Salzbacher found scores of temperance societies, several orphanages in every diocese, and 207 schools. The aim was not so much social reform as it was individual acts of charity.[108]

Catholic schools educated both Catholics and Protestants, and in some areas they made formal education possible. In Lexington, Kentucky, three of the four schools in 1835 were Catholic, and one foreign observer wrote in 1847 that "the only really useful and corrective education" in America was "that of the Catholic schools." Catholics also maintained a steady missionary presence in the West. Spanish priests founded twenty-one missions in California, and some

---

106. Francis Patrick Kenrick, *Diary and Visitation Record of the Rt. Rev. Francis Patrick Kenrick,* ed. Francis E. Torscher (Lancaster: Wickersham, 1916), p. 78; T. Paul Thigpen, "Aristocracy of the Heart: Catholic Lay Leadership in Savannah 1820-1870" (Ph.D. dissertation, Emory University, 1995), pp. 125-26.

107. Dolan, *Immigrant Church,* pp. 121-40.

108. Dolan, *Immigrant Church,* pp. 121-40; Salzbacher, *Meine Reise,* pp. 316, 388-89.

of the missionaries to Native Americans — Pierre Jean De Smet, Casimir Chirouse, John Baptist Lamy (immortalized in Willa Cather's *Death Comes for the Archbishop*) — earned adulation throughout the church.[109]

The Bishop of Quebec in 1816 visited the congregation in Detroit and recorded the accomplishments of Father Gabriel Richard, one of the founders of the University of Michigan and a delegate from the Michigan Territory to Congress:

> Provided with newspapers well informed on all political questions, ever ready to argue on religion . . . , and thoroughly learned in theology, he reaps his hay, gathers the fruit of his garden, manages a fishery fronting his lot, teaches mathematics to one young man, reading to another, devotes time to mental prayer, establishes a printing press, confesses all his people, imports carding and spinning wheels and looms to teach the women of his parish how to work, leaves not a single act of his parochial register unwritten, invents an electric machine, writes letters to and receives others from all parts, preaches on every Sunday and holy-day both lengthily and learnedly, enriches his library, spends whole nights without sleep, walks for entire days, loves to converse, receives company, teaches catechism to his young parishioners, supports a girls' school under the management of a few female teachers of his own choosing . . . , whilst he gives lessons in plain-song to young boys assembled in a school he has founded, leads a most frugal life, and is in good health, as fresh and able, at the age of fifty, as one usually is at thirty.[110]

Richard was exceptional, but his round of activities included many of the typical duties of a nineteenth-century priest.

*　　　*　　　*

Three important trends dominated the early and mid-eighteenth century: the stunning expansion of the clerical populists in the large evangelical denominations, the unsure but steady countermove toward a professional clergy, and the growth of the immigrant priesthood. All three trends altered the shape of ministry in America, though their implications for clerical authority pointed in op-

109. Sarah Mytton Maury, *The Progress and Influence of the Catholic Church in the United States of America* (London: Thomas Richardson, 1847), pp. 9-10; Reed and Matheson, *Narrative*, vol. 1, p. 132.

110. Ellis, ed., *Documents*, p. 206.

posite directions. Catholics accentuated the authority of office — the sense that ordination conferred a status that set the priest apart as an authoritative mediator between God and humanity. The call for more clerical education emphasized a personal, rational form of authority that would gain increasing acceptance in the larger cities. The populists flourished through a different kind of personal charisma, claiming that the divine call was all-sufficient and displaying the power of forceful personalities to touch the emotions of common people. Their impassioned appeals for souls even provided, arguably, a model for the Democratic politicians in the age of Andrew Jackson who surged into office by adapting the rhetoric of the revival meeting. And the populists also left a permanent imprint on the American ministry by generating an anti-intellectual ethos that has never entirely disappeared. The clergy of the old colonial establishments could not have imagined the scope of the change. And after the Civil War, the pace of the transitions would accelerate even more.

CHAPTER 5

Protestant Alternatives

1861-1929

In 1871, the Episcopal rector of Trinity Church in New York City, Morgan Dix, expressed his satisfaction that he directed a parish that had become "a centre of life, activity, and far-extended influence" in the city. A graduate of Columbia College and the General Theological Seminary in New York City, Dix was the son of a U.S. senator, ambassador, and eminently successful businessman and politician. The younger Dix was one of the princes of the pulpit who made the large downtown urban church an attraction to locals and tourists alike. Elegant sermons and a "voice like that of a trained actor" gave him a reputation as "a master of the English tongue" who could hold his hearers in "rapt attention." By 1887, the church had 5,535 communicant members; the crowds of worshipers were sometimes so large that they could not all find a seat.[1]

Dix oversaw an ecclesiastical corporation, a congregation fast becoming a "vast machinery of service," with a parish school, an industrial school, a music school, a parish hospital, a retirement home, a medical dispensary, and classes in drawing, manual labor, and laundry work. It had dozens of girls' guilds, boys' clubs, women's auxiliaries, and men's groups. It was one of the city's centers of musical and artistic performance. By the time he died in 1908, Dix had supervised the work of eighteen other ministers. In a single year, he and his assistants

---

1. Morgan Dix, "Address at Trinity Church, New York, Ascension Day, 1871," in *The Church and the City*, ed. Robert D. Cross (Indianapolis: Bobbs-Merrill, 1967), p. 58; John A. Dix, ed., *A History of the Parish of Trinity Church in the City of New York* (New York: Columbia University Press, 1950), pp. 14, 143, 168, 270.

officiated at 1,158 baptisms, 268 marriages, 100 burials, and daily Eucharistic services.[2]

The New York pastor stood among the nation's clerical elite. He published books for children, biblical commentaries, and a four-volume history of the congregation. He attended to the church's Mission House, a social-service agency with programs for immigrants and the poor, and he sat on the boards of numerous social welfare groups. He was a trustee of Columbia College, and elite universities — Columbia, Princeton, Harvard, and Oxford — conferred honorary degrees on him. At his death, Trinity had become known as "the richest church in America." Its admirers saw it as a model of outreach to the whole city, rich and poor. Its critics derided it as an entrenched corporate power deriving its wealth from slum and tenement property and lavishly supporting its rector with "the largest salary of any clergyman in America, $15,000 a year." Admirers and critics alike recognized Dix as a man who eminently personified clerical authority.[3]

He was a pulpit celebrity in an era when such ministers attracted nationwide attention, a conservative Anglo-Catholic voice in a period marked by the rise of liberal theology, and an advocate of the professional ideal at a time when clerical populism still pervaded the churches. His ministry illustrated the stark alternatives that faced Protestant clergy in the six decades between 1865 and 1929: tensions between liberals and conservatives, conflicts between the social gospel and an otherworldly faith, continuing clashes between professionals and populists, and the differences between country and city churches. Any analyst who counted clergy in the mid-1920s would have found ministry still a rural vocation, but by then there were two distinct styles of Protestant ministry, one shaped by the pressures of urbanization and modern thought, the other more isolated from those pressures and more continuous with the Protestant past in a rural society. The urban pastors — some favoring and some opposing theological adaptation to modernity — became the leaders of the profession.

Civil War and Clerical Transitions

At the outset of the era, it was the Civil War that created the most serious divide in clerical ranks. The clergy had helped form the cultural climate for the war, and now they joined the troops. Ministers had served as military chaplains in colonial

2. Ray Stannard Baker, *The Spiritual Unrest* (1910), in *The Church and the City*, p. 72; Dix, ed., *History of the Parish*, pp. 142, 168, 269.

3. Baker, *Spiritual Unrest*, p. 72; Dix, ed., *History of the Parish*, p. 268.

militias, and the Continental Congress had formed a chaplaincy for the army and the navy in 1775, but no previous war had directly engaged the numbers of chaplains who went to the battlefields between 1861 and 1865. About 10 percent of the nation's ministers — more than 1,300 in the South and 2,500 in the North — received commissions as military chaplains. Several thousand other Northern ministers made forays into the battlefields on behalf of the interdenominational United States Christian Commission, bringing spiritual support and humane assistance to the soldiers. By 1862, the chaplains were reporting massive revivals in both armies. The message to the troops, on both sides, was that "God is with us."[4]

After the war, somber voices among the white Southern clergy valorized what historians call the Religion of the Lost Cause, arguing that the South had fought, in the words of Episcopal Bishop Richard Wilmer, "to maintain the supremacy of the Word of God, and the teachings of universal tradition." Clerics like Wilmer helped cobble together the pervasive myth of Southern honor that compensated for the fall of the Confederacy by exalting an idealized Southern past. Some tried to mitigate the harshness of the reaction against the former slaves, but white preachers defended white supremacy, some prayed at meetings of the Ku Klux Klan, and a few continued to depict slavery as a divinely ordained institution. The Baptist Thomas Dixon Jr. popularized racist ideology in novels that inspired the controversial 1915 blockbuster film *The Birth of a Nation.*[5]

Among the Northern clergy, the war animated religious nationalism and suggested new means of evangelism. Some placed flags in their churches, and others proposed in 1863 to amend the federal constitution to affirm the supremacy of God and the Bible. After the war ended, veterans of battlefield ministry drew on their new knowledge of organizations to create an American Christian Commission that would conduct social-scientific studies of the cities as a prelude to revivalist crusades. In the larger cities, some ministers began to refer to themselves as leaders of a "grand army of beneficent forces," setting their churches to work like a "commander-in-chief" or like "Grant directing an army." The church was to be "an army of occupation" rather than an "Ark of Safety," and the pastor was the leader of the troops.[6]

---

4. John W. Brinsfield, "Soldiers of God in Gray: The Churches, Clergy, and Chaplains of the Confederate States of America, 1861-1865," unpub. essay, p. 46; John William Jones, *Christ in the Camp, or Religion in Lee's Army* (Richmond: B. F. Johnson, 1887), pp. 232, 235.

5. Charles Reagan Wilson, *Baptized in Blood: The Religion of the Lost Cause, 1865-1920* (Athens: University of Georgia Press, 1980), pp. 42, 43-57, 100-118.

6. Franklin W. Fisk, "The Unity of the Professions," *The New Englander and Yale Review* 35 (1876): 542; Aaron Abell, *The Urban Impact on American Protestantism, 1865-1900* (Hamden: Archon, 1962), p. 12; William M. Taylor, *The Ministry of the Word* (New York: Randolph, 1876), p. 265; G. B. Willcox, *The Pastor Amidst His Flock* (New York: American Tract Society, 1890),

The biggest change occurred within the black churches. The freed slaves, subordinated in white-controlled congregations, migrated into the all-black denominations. By 1895, African American ministers — mostly Methodists and Baptists — led the worship of two million Christians in nearly 24,000 black congregations. It was the largest religious secession Americans had ever seen, and it created a pressing demand for preachers. Less than 10 percent of black Baptist churches in the South in 1895 had preaching every Sunday. The preachers who offered themselves for service became the leaders of the African American community.[7]

In most other ways, the Civil War changed little about ministry. In 1870, federal census takers discovered 43,874 clergy serving in 72,459 congregations and other institutions. Thirty-five percent of the congregations were Methodist, of one variety or another, and 20 percent belonged to various Baptist denominations. The nineteenth-century historian Daniel Dorchester, working from church records for 1870, found 51,575 ministers and priests and 70,148 congregations in fifty-four denominations. Thirty percent of the clergy in his count served in Methodist denominations and 36 percent in Baptist communions. Everyone agreed that Baptists and Methodists in 1870 still produced more than half the nation's clergy.[8]

In the next half century, the number of clergy more than doubled, and they led a proliferating array of new and old denominations. In 1910, the census found 118,018 ministers, priests, and rabbis, a number that grew to 127,720 in the next ten years. More than 80 percent were Protestants. In 1916, probably 25 percent of the ministers in America were Baptists, and 24 percent Methodists. In Protestant circles, the old populist churches retained their numerical superiority.[9]

By 1890, the number of congregations rose to 165,297, and membership steadily climbed — it might have reached 33 percent of the population. The number of adherents (members, attenders, and their children) could have been around 60 percent. But the meaning of membership was changing as the large

---

p. 77; Henry F. May, *Protestant Churches and Industrial America* (New York: Harper and Brothers, 1949), pp. 40-45.

7. Edward L. Wheeler, *Uplifting the Race: The Black Minister in the New South, 1865-1902* (Lanham: University Press of America, 1986), pp. 8, 16; Daniel Dorchester, *Christianity in the United States* (New York: Hunt and Eaton, 1890), pp. 739, 741.

8. Joseph C. G. Kennedy, ed., *Population in the United States in 1860: Eighth Census of the United States, 1860* (Washington, D.C.: Government Printing Office, 1864), pp. 506-8; Dorchester, *Christianity*, pp. 736-37.

9. Mark A. May, *The Profession of the Ministry: Its Status and Problems* (New York: Institute of Social and Religious Research, 1934), p. 36; Samuel L. Rogers, ed., *Religious Bodies, 1916*, 2 vols. (Washington, D.C.: Government Printing Office, 1919), vol. 1, p. 67.

denominations relaxed their membership standards, and many churches now had more members than regular attenders. In 1887, Josiah Strong surveyed thirty city congregations and found that 56 percent of the members faithfully attended worship. It is plausible to conjecture that even though the number of members had increased, roughly the same 40 percent of the population regularly attended as had always been present. They were the core constituency of the clergy.[10]

A Rural Calling

Most of the clergy were, as they had always been, country preachers. In 1865, 80 percent of Americans lived in rural areas with fewer than 2,500 inhabitants, and most ministers preached in country churches. By 1920, more than half of Americans lived in towns and cities, but more than 65 percent of the clergy still preached in the country. The majority of these rural ministers served two or more small congregations with an average membership of forty-six. Only 35 percent of the white Protestant country churches had a full-time, or even part-time, resident pastor, and many of the preachers supported themselves through other occupations. In the 1920s, the cities created a culture formed by big business, cars, sports, movies, jazz, and new and shocking styles of dress and consumption. Most of the clergy dwelt elsewhere.[11]

The country clergy lived within a landscape that urban America was beginning to view with patronizing nostalgia. The countryside was becoming a national problem — or sometimes a national joke. By 1909, when President Theodore Roosevelt's Country Life Commission submitted its first report to Congress, the president emphasized that rural America was failing to satisfy "the higher social and intellectual aspirations" of its people, and the country life movement that issued from these worries fretted that "rural depopulation,

10. Roger Finke and Rodney Stark, "Turning Pews into People: Estimating 19th-Century Church Membership," *Journal for the Scientific Study of Religion* 25 (1986): 187; Washington Gladden, ed., *Parish Problems* (New York: Century, 1887), p. 346.

11. C. Luther Fry, *The U.S. Looks at Its Churches* (New York: Institute of Social and Religious Research, 1930), p. 152. My figure of 65 percent is an extrapolation from a study of the twenty largest denominations, reported in Fry, which I take to be "roughly" representative, though they did not include several smaller denominations, including the fast-growing Pentecostal churches, which had large numbers of rural congregations. If those denominations had been included, the percentage of rural ministers would probably be higher than 65 percent. See also H. N. Morse and Edmund deS. Brunner, *The Town and Country Church in the United States* (New York: George H. Doran, 1923), p. 52.

social stagnation, and cultural decline" weakened American society. To urban sophisticates of the 1920s, the noble country yeomen had turned into "hicks" and "rubes." And the rural pastors felt the condescension.[12]

For most rural pastors, clerical duties consisted of preaching, visiting whenever possible, and presiding at baptisms, communion, marriage, and burial. Normally, the churches were one- and two-room buildings with bare floors, wooden seats, and a pine pulpit. By 1925, about 80 percent of the congregations had Sunday schools, but barely half the rural ministers had the time to attend, let alone teach, and more than a third of the preachers, rushing from one congregation to another on Sunday mornings, had almost nothing to do with the Sunday school programs. Rural reformers regretted that they spent little time with children and young people.[13]

The reformers lamented also the low salaries. Between 1890 and 1900, the average salary for all American ministers was about $574, though rural clergy received less than city pastors, and they often had to take much of their salary "in kind," through offerings of food and clothing. By the late 1920s, salaries in the countryside averaged only $1,063, considerably less than the national average for ministers, which was about $1,407. Urban factory workers made around $1,600 a year, textile workers $1,151, and farm laborers $587. In real dollars, clerical salaries between 1890 and 1928 declined slightly, and the rural clergy were the main losers. More than a third of them earned extra money by taking a second job.[14]

No single style of rural ministry prevailed throughout the nation. The immigrant farming areas of the Midwest and Northwest had a good number of pastors from Germany, Scandinavia, and Eastern Europe who resided near their churches and presided over community life; the Southern and Southwestern rural areas depended heavily on itinerants and uneducated part-time preachers; the Mountain West and Pacific regions attracted substantial numbers of home missionaries from the East. George Gilbert, the Episcopal rector of Emmanuel Church in the village of Killingworth, Connecticut, exemplified the cultural ideal of rural ministry in New England. A graduate of Trinity College and Berkeley Divinity School, Gilbert accepted his first parish in 1899 in

12. Jack Larkin, "Rural Life in the North," in *Encyclopedia of American Society History*, 3 vols., ed. Mary Kupiec Cayton, Elliott J. Gorn, Peter W. Williams (New York: Charles Scribner's Sons, 1993), vol. 2, p. 1219; "Rural Development," in *Concise Dictionary of American History* (New York: Charles Scribner's Sons, 1983), p. 911.

13. Morse and Brunner, *Town and Country Church*, pp. 129, 137.

14. Morse and Brunner, *Town and Country Church*, pp. 143, 147; Edmund deS. Brunner and J. H. Kolb, *Rural Social Trends* (New York: McGraw Hill, 1933), pp. 228, 363; May, *Profession of the Ministry*, pp. 106, 109.

the South Farms community on the outskirts of Middletown. There he preached twice every Sunday and once each Wednesday in a public building, fished with the local farmers, and pitched hay in their fields. He formed a church baseball team, took the boys on hunting trips, taught the Sunday school, and assembled a youth choir, prompting several members of the adult choir to leave the church. He moved in 1909 to nearby Killingworth, where he rode a bicycle and a horse on a forty-mile circuit, preaching at two school-houses until he had a congregation large enough to remodel the old Emmanuel building.[15]

At Emmanuel, he was the "jack of all trades," the janitor, bell ringer, and floor sweeper. He preached, administered sacraments, married the young, and buried young and old, sometimes making the coffins and digging the graves. He carried around several sermons in his head: "I just talk to people — the more informally the better — trying to fit the subject to my congregation." He found jobs for people, distributed food and furniture to the poor, and took troubled youth and ex-convicts into his home. A socialist in politics, he fought for public ownership of the utilities and ran successfully for local political office. He also bought a farm and became a director of the Farm Bureau, providing market reports to his members. "The farmers and I," he said, "had everything in common."[16]

The decline of population in the rural Northeast after 1890 meant that few preachers in that region could share Gilbert's sense of accomplishment. Most of them watched their churches stagnate or become smaller and their ministries became more difficult. In 1913, for example, the rural Protestant churches in Windsor County, Vermont, and Tompkins County, New York, had ministers who "engaged in a solitary struggle with small, discouraging, and unessential problems," with pews emptier each year. Several of them viewed the country parish as a "temporary stopping point on the road to a larger church."[17]

The two counties offered few enticements and attracted few educated ministers. About 25 percent of the clergy in Windsor — and 15 percent in Tompkins — had attended both college and seminary. Windsor had a handful of resident ministers who served single churches, but in Tompkins each minister preached, on average, in two small congregations. Salaries lost purchasing power; the mean salary of $814 in Windsor meant that the pastors had to absorb a 7 percent loss

15. George B. Gilbert, *Forty Years a Country Preacher* (New York: Harper and Brothers, 1939), pp. 73-111.

16. Gilbert, *Forty Years*, pp. 115, 117, 135, 141, 179, 182, 280, 284, 305.

17. G. O. Gill and Gifford Pinchot, *The Country Church* (New York: Macmillan, 1913), p. 50. In 1889, the churches in Windsor had an average attendance of 143; by 1909, the number fell to ninety-nine. In Tompkins, the fall was from sixty-two to forty-two, a decline of a third.

over two decades. Most lacked resources to buy books and journals. They poured their energies into preaching and annual revival services, but gains proved temporary.[18]

In the German and Scandinavian communities of the Midwest, the situation was better. Many of the immigrants — especially among the Germans and Swedes — honored ministers as both religious and community leaders. The typical pastor owned a farm and had no wish to move to a city parish, so pastorates of two to three decades were common. A 1920 study concluded that 35 percent of the foreign-language Lutheran churches in its sample had pastors responsible for only a single congregation; the majority normally served two churches. But 80 percent of the congregations had ministers. Their salaries — around $1,200 a year — were higher than the rural average, and the ministers had relatively high levels of education. In one assemblage of German-speaking rural Lutheran ministers, 73 percent had graduated from college and seminary. Only 22 percent of the rural clergy in America had that much education. In Swedish Lutheran villages, farmers removed their caps in the presence of their pastors.[19]

Many of the native rural churches of the Midwest displayed some of the features of the immigrant congregations. The pastorate of Matthew McNutt in the countryside six miles outside Naperville, Illinois, represented the apex of success in a Midwestern rural Presbyterian parish. He became the pastor in 1900 after graduating from seminary, replacing a lay preacher who had held the modest congregation together for three bleak years. On a salary of $250 a year, McNutt fixed up two rooms in the dilapidated manse near the church and began preaching every Sunday. He found it "hard to change the old ways of doing things," but within two years he made the church the social and religious center of the county. He began a singing school, formed a chorus and a quartet, organized a baseball team, trained his members — including the children — in public speaking, and directed plays that drew crowds of four hundred people. McNutt organized a group for young men, which had Bible study and social events, and a similar group for young women, which also sewed clothes for the urban poor. His adult discussion groups studied topics ranging from Christian missions to cattle farming. In a decade, the membership doubled to 163, and the Sunday school grew from one hundred to three hundred. By 1910, the congregation erected a new church building seating five

---

18. Gill and Pinchot, *Country Church*, pp. 15, 47, 133.

19. Morse and Brunner, *Town and Country Church*, p. 144; Edmund deS. Brunner, *Immigrant Farmers and their Children* (Garden City: Doubleday, Doran, 1929), pp. 123, 128; George M. Stephenson, *The Religious Aspects of Swedish Immigration* (Minneapolis: The University of Minnesota Press, 1932), p. 389.

hundred. In a region where many had "grown indifferent to the church," he was a star in the emerging rural church reforming movement.[20]

Still, not every Midwestern rural preacher could enjoy McNutt's sense of accomplishment. In six counties of southeast Ohio in 1913, for example, only 22 percent of the people held membership in mainline congregations, though holiness and Pentecostal preachers were beginning to make progress. More than half the churches had fifty or fewer members, and 81 percent of the clergy served from two to six churches each. They lived at a distance from most of their congregations, and most visited each church only once or twice a month. Only 16 percent of the preachers had both college and seminary training, and 56 percent of them had not gone beyond high school. More than half received salaries of less than $600 a year and most held part-time jobs. Their sermons tended to be revivalist in tenor, dwelling on the necessity for conversion, the threat of hell, and the joys of heaven.[21]

In the rural South, half the clergy in 1920 were part-time preachers, supporting themselves with outside jobs, and most of them served two to three churches. Only 20 percent of the churches had a resident pastor, and only 16 percent had a preaching service each Sunday. The typical Southern rural pastor preached in a one-room wooden church, lighted by oil lamps, administered baptism and communion, visited whatever members were reachable, and held a yearly revival. In some areas, the pastor preached funeral sermons at infrequent intervals for all who had died since the last pastoral visit. The average pastorate lasted only two years, so most had little opportunity to build long-term relationships. Sermons featured "an almost single-minded emphasis on individual regeneration."[22]

Few of the white country preachers in the South had much education. In 1886, a teacher at Wofford College in South Carolina complained that a man could become a Methodist itinerant "without giving to preparation for his great work as much time and pains as would be required to make him a journeyman carpenter!" Some Methodist preachers, he added, "cannot write a complex sentence or understand it when written." The denomination's leaders kept "a suspicious eye" on young educated pastors but seemed to think that "ignorance and weakness" could be "entirely trusted with the charge and oversight

20. Matthew B. McNutt, "Ten Years in a Country Church," *The Rural Community: Ancient and Modern*, ed. Newell Leroy Sims (New York: Charles Scribner's Sons, 1920), pp. 249-59.

21. "Ohio Rural Life Survey," *Rural Community*, pp. 429-48.

22. Edmund deS. Brunner, *Church Life in the Rural South* (New York: George H. Doran, 1923), pp. 59-60, 63. This was a study of seventy selected counties. See also Fry, *U.S. Looks at Its Churches*, p. 69; Kenneth W. Bailey, *Southern White Protestantism in the Twentieth Century* (New York: Harper and Row, 1964), p. 18.

of others." In 1926, the Methodists reported that only 4 percent of their clergy in the region — most of whom were rural pastors — had graduated from both a college and a seminary; 11 percent more had a college degree; 54 percent had a high-school education or less. Educational standards were equally minimal in the Southern Baptist churches: 11 percent had college and seminary degrees; 15 percent graduated from college alone; 70 percent had a high-school education or less.[23]

Regardless of denomination, the Southern white rural clergy in the 1920s lagged in education behind pastors in the rest of the country. In seventeen mainly white Protestant denominations, 64 percent of the rural Southern pastors had a high-school education or less; 15 percent graduated only from a college; 7 percent studied only in a seminary; 13 percent graduated from both a college and a seminary. Most occupied the same educational level and shared the same cultural assumptions as the people to whom they preached. The commonality enhanced their authority. Rural Southerners harbored a persistent suspicion of too much clerical education.[24]

In the black community, oppressed by poverty and violence, the black preacher emerged as "the leader of the race." After emancipation, the minister attained, in the words of W. E. B. DuBois, "preeminence" in the African American communities: "A leader, a politician, an orator, a 'boss,' an intriguer, an idealist — all these he is, and ever, too, the centre of a group . . . now twenty, now a thousand, in number." He was an authority on everything from moral living to teething infants. He had to be, as an observer remarked in 1893, "a horse doctor" and "weather prophet," someone who could "attend the living, bury the dead, [and] tell the farmers when to plant." During Reconstruction, black ministers ran for elected office, accepted governmental appointments, and organized voters for the Republican Party. They served as school board members, judges, and state legislators. The demise of Reconstruction put an end to the political side of such dual careers, but the leadership continued.[25]

By 1920, the black rural minister presided over a separate religious culture consisting of around thirty thousand churches, mostly Baptist and Methodist.

23. F. C. Woodward, "Methodism and Ministerial Education," *Methodist Quarterly Review*, n.s., 1 (1886): 212, 216; "An Episcopal Address: A Better Prepared Ministry," *Nashville Christian Advocate* 88 (24 June 1927): 774-75; Fry, *U.S. Looks at Its Churches*, p. 152.

24. Fry, *U.S. Looks at Its Churches*, p. 148.

25. W. E. B. DuBois, ed., *The Negro Church* (1st ed., 1903; Walnut Creek: Alta Mira, 2003), p. 61; W. E. B. DuBois, *The Souls of Black Folk* (1903), in *Three Negro Classics*, ed. John Hope Franklin (New York: Avon Books, 1965), p. 33; William E. Montgomery, *Under Their Own Vine and Fig Tree: The African-American Church in the South 1865-1900* (Baton Rouge: Louisiana State University Press, 1993), pp. 308, 322; Wheeler, *Uplifting the Race*, p. 71.

Talented African Americans sought the pulpit in disproportionate numbers. At a time when blacks constituted 10 percent of the population, 15 percent of the American clergy were black. In the Southern countryside, half the preachers farmed or had other secular work, and most served two to four churches, preaching in each once or twice a month, but they often lived in the communities where they preached, and they helped make the church "the center of public life." Their churches provided most of the organized social life of their communities, and they also administered social assistance. In some Southern counties, up to 75 percent of the black churches provided food, clothing, and money to help members and others in emergencies.[26]

Educated blacks worried about clerical competence. In 1890, the Tuskegee educator Booker T. Washington published in the *Christian Union* a bleak analysis of the black rural pastorate. The black clergy in the Congregational, Presbyterian, and Episcopal churches, he wrote, were "intelligent and earnest," but too many of the rural Baptist and Methodist preachers were "unfit." The educated ministers, he argued, migrated to the cities and towns, where they "uplifted" their congregations and exemplified "what a church should be." Washington believed that most rural clergy provided little "moral and intellectual training." He called for schools that would teach them how to read the Bible, prepare sermons, and help people in their everyday lives. But his essay drew a storm of condemnation, including a drive to boycott Tuskegee. In a segregated rural society, educational progress came hard. In 1926, 80 percent of the rural clergy in the African Methodist Episcopal churches, 84 percent in the black Baptist churches, and 85 percent in the Colored Methodist Episcopal churches had only a high-school education — or less.[27]

Between 1890 and 1925, black leaders conducted a spirited debate about the rural clergy. A Baptist Home Mission study in 1895 criticized the "great number" of preachers whose "moral standards" were "not in accord with those of the New Testament for the ministry," and speakers at the 1903 conference on the black church at Atlanta University charged that they had not been a force for moral progress. But others asserted that some of the black churches were demanding — and finding — "able preachers" of "much native ability." The Presbyterian pastor I. D. Davis argued in 1902 that the critics were missing the point. The black clergy had done more for the "uplift" of a fragile community than "any other class of persons." They had taught their people to save money,

26. May, *The Profession of the Ministry,* p. 36; DuBois, ed., *The Negro Church,* p. 122; Brunner, *Life in the Rural South,* p. 88.

27. Booker T. Washington, "The Colored Ministry: Its Defects and Needs," *Christian Union* 42 (1890): 199-200; Fry, *U.S. Looks at Its Churches,* p. 73; Brunner, *Church Life in the Rural South,* p. 89; Booker T. Washington, *Up from Slavery,* in *Three Negro Classics,* p. 153.

buy homes and lands, and send their children to school. The researchers at the Atlanta conference found a good number of critics, but they found more who spoke highly of pastors.[28]

In the rural West, ministers — black and white — faced the challenge of vast distances and religious indifference. The pioneer Protestant ministers were full-time organizers who moved from place to place, establishing churches and then moving on. The busiest created multiple congregations — Methodist Tom Harwood established sixty-six in New Mexico and Episcopal Bishop John Spalding built over fifty in Colorado — by riding circuits on horses, buggies, stages, and the railroad. Beginning in 1869, the Presbyterian Sheldon Jackson traveled as many as 30,000 miles a year on the railroads and organized scores of churches. The Episcopal bishop in North Dakota secured a chapel car on the Northern Pacific railroad in the 1890s that he called The Cathedral Car. It seated eighty people and allowed him to cover a circuit of fifty-three rural towns.[29]

The clergy tried to attract indifferent settlers with revivals, tracts, and Sunday schools. They brought the camp meeting tradition with them, and by the 1870s they could attract up to four thousand worshipers to a single event. They circulated religious tracts in areas that offered little else to read, and some of them drove "colportage wagons" filled with books and Bibles. Baptist Thornton Tyson claimed to have "given away over a million pieces of literature." To build new churches, they first formed Sunday schools. In 1914, the Presbyterians claimed that 80 percent of their new congregations grew from Sunday schools, and pastors poured time and energy into them.[30]

The West attracted Episcopal, Presbyterian, and Congregational ministers who were well educated by the standards of the time, but some of the best-known clergy had little training. Many worked at other occupations — as carpenters, mail carriers, grocers, or farmers — and preached on the weekends. Nonetheless, the clergy took the lead in organizing primary and secondary schools, and only the schoolteachers did more to transmit a print culture into the West. Yet the organizers of schools remained a minority. More typical would have been a place like Travis County, Texas, where, in 1916, 60 percent of the laity reported that their pastors had only a high-school education or less; almost half said that the pastor never visited their homes; and

28. DuBois, *Negro Church*, pp. 61-62, 122, 154-64; I. D. Davis, "To What Extent Is the Negro Pulpit Uplifting the Race?" in *Twentieth Century Negro Literature*, ed. Daniel Culp (n.p.: Nichols, 1902), p. 124.

29. Ferenc Morton Szasz, *The Protestant Clergy in the Great Plains and Mountain West, 1865-1915* (Albuquerque: University of New Mexico Press, 1988), pp. 19, 20, 75.

30. Szasz, *Protestant Clergy*, pp. 77-78, 82.

more than half believed that their preachers had little interest in their ordinary problems.[31]

Some of the preachers who did have a compelling interest in ordinary problems joined in the social protest that fed into the Populist movement in the rural South and West. Richard M. Humphrey, a white minister to black Baptist congregations in East Texas, inveighed, as a leader of the Farmers' Alliance, against railroads and commercial monopolies. Walter Patillo, an African American Baptist preacher in North Carolina, organized the statewide black Alliance. With the formation of the People's Party in 1891, rural clergy prayed at political rallies, organized local alliances, ran for political office, and preached about economic injustice. The majority of clergy, especially in the towns, seem to have decided that "the powers that be," as Methodist E. A. Yates put it, were "ordained of God," and that the "business of the church" was to "save souls," not rectify economic suffering. But the activist preachers gave Populism the aura of a revival meeting.[32]

Rural and urban clergy could unite in support of the prohibition of alcohol, and they served as publicists for the Anti-Saloon League, founded by a Congregationalist minister in 1895, which used local churches as organizing agencies. The crusade was among the forces leading to the Eighteenth Amendment in 1919, and it elevated a few clerics to positions of high influence. Methodist James R. Cannon Jr., who organized the largely rural clergy of Virginia into a potent force, occupied a seat on the floor of the state legislature in 1916 and ascended to such heights that the journalist H. L. Mencken described him as "the most powerful ecclesiastic ever heard of in America," a man "whose merest wink can make a President of the United States leap like a bullfrog." During the campaign of Al Smith for the presidency in 1928, Protestant ministers also preached, campaigned, and voted to keep the New York Catholic governor out of the White House.[33]

In 1865, most ministers had no other expectation than to spend their lives in service to rural congregations. Within half a century, however, attitudes toward country parishes had changed. Rural reformers complained that young

---

31. Szasz, *Protestant Clergy,* pp. 55, 66; "Social and Economic Survey of Southern Travis County," in *Rural Community,* pp. 423-24.

32. Robert C. McMath Jr., *American Populism: A Social History 1898-1898* (New York: Hill and Wang, 1993), pp. 92-93; Robert C. McMath Jr., *Populist Vanguard: A History of the Southern Farmer's Alliance* (Chapel Hill: University of North Carolina Press, 1975), pp. 21, 26, 42, 45, 69-70, 125, 135.

33. James H. Timberlake, *Prohibition and the Progressive Movement 1900-1920* (Cambridge: Harvard University Press, 1963), ch. 5; Virginius Dabney, *Dry Messiah: The Life of Bishop Cannon* (New York: Alfred A. Knopf, 1949), pp, 100, 190, 306.

pastors were "staying out of the rural pastorate not because it is hard or un-promising, but because it is considered inferior." By 1900, efforts were under-way to improve the quality of ministry in the countryside. Reformers regretted that too few rural clergy tried "to serve their community" or had anything more than a "negligible impact" on rural society. They wanted ministers to use plan-ning and consolidate their small and inefficient churches so that they could support trained resident-pastors who remained in the communities and orga-nized lively programs. But for the most part the reform went nowhere.[34]

Urban Pastors

It was the urban clergy who set the pace. Some became local, regional, even national celebrities. Tourists came to hear them preach, newspapers covered their sermons, and young pastors emulated their innovations. They took the lead in the denominational initiatives of the era — from world missions to theological revision — and they oversaw the restructuring of some urban con-gregations into vast enterprises of outreach and social service. They shared no common theological perspective, but they furnished the prominent combat-ants in the theological conflicts. In the eyes of the Protestant public, they were the leaders, and their innovations remade the churches.

By 1890 the pastoral theologian G. B. Willcox could announce that the de-cades since the Civil War era had produced a "complete revolution" in the social life of congregations in the American cities. Its symbol was the "church parlor," the room set aside for social gatherings. In any large church, in some denomina-tions, he claimed, the parlor "has become almost as necessary as a pulpit." Willcox praised the transition. He wanted the church to become a "social home" for its members. And a multitude of congregations opened their doors not only for worship but also for Sunday school concerts, church socials, women's meet-ings, youth groups, girls' guilds, boys' brigades, sewing circles, benevolent societ-ies, day schools, temperance societies, athletic clubs, and scout troops.[35]

Willcox argued that the minister's task was to set the church to work. "Every member," he wrote, "ought to be as busy as a bee in a swarm." For this to happen, the members had to know one another and to work together. As a pastor, he felt a responsibility to press upon his members "the duty of mutual acquaintance,"

34. Victor I. Masters, *Country Church in the South* (Atlanta: Home Mission Board of the S.B.C., 1916), p. 110; James H. Madison, "Reformers and the Rural Church, 1900-1950," *Journal of American History* (1986): 645-68; Edmund deS. Brunner and J. H. Kolb, *Rural Social Trends* (New York: McGraw-Hill, 1933), p. 209.

35. Willcox, *Pastor*, pp. 107, 110.

luring them to social events, singings, concerts, poetry readings, and parties. In addition, he organized his church into committees to oversee women's work, missions, the young people's society, a church newspaper, various social causes, and the Sunday school. He urged his church to serve the community and interest itself in a new school building, a local park, and the planting of trees.[36]

When Henry Ward Beecher addressed the seminarians at Yale in 1891, he advised them to "multiply picnics," and he wanted more than picnics. "No church ought to be built after this, in city or country, that has not in connection with it either a place set apart as a parlor, or a room which by some little change of seats could be made into a parlor. There ought to be, from week to week, or every other week, during the largest part of the year, such little gatherings as shall mingle the people together and make them like one another." Congregations of every variety proceeded beyond picnics to gymnasiums, parish houses, camps, baseball teams, and military drill groups, with one church report in 1897 asserting that "uniforms, guns, and equipment are as essential as the Bible and the Hymnal in the advance of our work." These urban centers required new pastoral skills.[37]

The most striking innovation was the sudden discovery of "administration." The modern church, Willcox observed, demanded skills of "organization and administration for which of old there was no call." The modern urban pastor needed to find "a new skill, namely, a work for everyone" and steadily hold everyone to it. Bishop Gregory Bedell of Ohio, praising the "comparatively new" emphasis on "pastoral administration," claimed that the Episcopal priest needed now to be a "business leader," able to "make a bargain" and "do things." Albion Small spoke of the pastor as "the operator of a vast social dynamo," and the *Princeton Review* announced that "the larger and more important work" of the minister was now that of "presiding and governing in the bending of the energies of the church to the work of the world's salvation." The journal quoted theologian Horace Bushnell on the virtues of church administration: "No matter what seeming talent there may be in the preaching, if there is no administrative talent," then the minister lacked the solidity of a true leader.[38]

---

36. Washington Gladden, *The Christian Pastor and the Working Church* (New York: Charles Scribner's Sons, 1907), pp. 9, 77, 108; Anonymous, "The Pastorate for the Times," *The Princeton Review* 40 (1868): 107; Willcox, *Pastor*, pp. 111-12, 130.

37. Henry Ward Beecher, *Yale Lectures in Preaching* (New York: Howard and Hulbert, 1892), pp. 155, 159; E. Brooks Holifield, "Toward a History of American Congregations," in *American Congregations*, ed. James P. Wind and James W. Lewis, 2 vols. (Chicago: University of Chicago Press, 1994), vol. 2, pp. 38-40.

38. Willcox, *Pastor*, pp. 7, 9, 10-11; Gregory Bedell, *Personal Character the Source of Ministerial Influence* (Cleveland: Annual Convention, 1878), p. 21; Albion W. Small, "The Value of Sociology to Working Pastors," *Outlook* 62 (1899): 389-92; Anonymous, "The Pastorate for the

The accent on administration coincided with a revamping of church bureaucracies. The missionary societies of the pre-Civil War era became large denominational organizations, and similar boards oversaw Sunday schools, colleges, ministerial relief, church extension, evangelism, urban ministries, work with immigrants, and temperance campaigns. In the 1880s the boards began to erect large buildings as national headquarters and to expand their staffs within a growing hierarchy of divisions and departments. They followed the example of business and government, urging that churches employ "scientific management" and "systematic planning." Especially after Frederick W. Taylor published *The Principles of Scientific Management* in 1911, ministers echoed the rhetoric of "efficiency," designating staff members as "efficiency experts" and arranging "efficiency conferences" to train executives in "systematic finance."[39]

The First World War — and the economic boom that followed — elevated the manager of massive organizations and the successful businessman to even greater cultural authority. In *The Man Nobody Knows* (1925), the advertiser Bruce Barton depicted Jesus as a strong, forceful, successful business executive, and the image of "the minister as executive" now permeated the pastoral literature, which praised clergy who had "the splendid executive facility of keeping an organization functioning." The minister with "an executive point of view" could formulate a plan, schedule regular meetings, and make them function like a "bank board." Every church could become a "General Efficiency Board for the Kingdom of God."[40]

Some found the new duties exhausting. Theodore Cuyler, who occupied the pulpit of Lafayette Avenue Presbyterian Church in New York City, remarked in 1890 that "the strain upon pastors grows heavier every year. The multiplication of societies (some of them without much effect); the tendency to overload churches with what does not belong to them; the encroachments and competition of the busy world, make the life of an earnest spiritual pastor no holiday business." By the 1920s, some pastors were complaining that the churches had "made efficiency, organization, and 'pep' our gods," and that the parish minister

---

Times," *The Princeton Review* 40 (1868): 100, 106; Gregory T. Bedell, *The Pastor: Pastoral Theology* (Philadelphia: Lippincott, 1880), p. 517.

39. Ben Primer, *Protestants and American Business Methods* (Ann Arbor: UMI Research Press, 1979), pp. 45, 52, 55, 74, 75, 94.

40. Theodore P. Greene, *America's Heroes: The Changing Model of Success in American Magazines* (New York: Oxford University Press, 1970), pp. 110-65, 310-34; William H. Leach, *How to Make a Church Go* (New York: George H. Doran, 1922), pp. 11-18; Cleland Boyd McAfee, *Ministerial Practices* (New York: Harper & Brothers, 1928), pp. 194-96; A. W. Beaver, *Putting the Church on a Full-Time Basis* (Garden City: Doubleday, Doran, 1928), p. xix. See also W. H. Leach, *Church Administration* (New York: Cokesbury, 1926).

had always to "hustle and devise something for his people to do," even at the cost of thoughtful ministry.[41]

The denominations required pastors to submit "more frequent and detailed reports." One pastor estimated that he spent a third of his time on the denomination's financial program: "I see myself becoming little more than the well-paid executive of a large business corporation." Even advocates of the "executive" image worried that it could promote "meetings, meetings, meetings."[42]

The Congregationalist Washington Gladden reminded readers, however, that preaching was still the "one great business" of the Protestant minister. And Protestants of the era seemed, in the midst of all the busyness, to have an unfailing desire for good preaching. At the most popular churches, crowds lined up before the doors opened to gain a good seat, and tourists flocked to hear celebrity preachers as part of their experience of the city. The pulpit was, as Gladden put it, "the minister's throne," and newspapers printed the sermons of the superstars. Some of these princely figures refashioned the sermon for an urban middle-class audience, while others retained older styles of biblical exposition or evangelical exhortation. But the urban pulpit encouraged innovation.[43]

Growing numbers of clergy no longer felt bound to "speak from a text of Scripture." They sought "the truth of God" in "the circumstances of daily life." Some of the most eminent preachers, from Henry Ward Beecher to Phillips Brooks, practiced a style of pulpit oratory that conveyed, in Brooks's phrase, "truth through personality." The preacher was to "be natural" and even "buoyant," to avoid the rigid forms of earlier doctrinal sermons, and to engage the audience through stories and illustrations. William Jewett Tucker, a Congregationalist in New England, noted in 1903 a fascination with "the personality of the preacher," and he shared the assumption that preachers grew in "preaching power" as they grew in "the use of their personality."[44]

Gladden recognized that the administrative work left little time for visits. He urged urban pastors to visit their members once a year, but he thought that the "variety of meetings" in the church gave pastors the best opportunity to "get to know" their people. Urban ministers could no longer agree about the

---

41. Theodore H. Cuyler, *How to Be a Pastor* (New York: Baker and Taylor, 1890), p. 117; Percy T. Fenn, "Lo, the Poor Cleric," *The North American Review* 224 (1927): 665.

42. Primer, *Protestants*, pp. 160, 168; James Brett Kenna, "Ministers or Business Executives," *Harpers Magazine* 157 (1928): 38-44; McAfee, *Ministerial Practices*, p. 206.

43. Gladden, *Christian Pastor*, pp. 107, 130.

44. Gladden, *Christian Pastor*, p. 130; Willcox, *Pastor*, pp. 65, 69; William Jewett Tucker, *My Generation: An Autobiographical Interpretation* (Boston: Houghton Mifflin, 1919), p. 162; Edwin S. Gaustad, "The Pulpit and the Pews," in *Between the Times: The Travail of the Protestant Establishment in America, 1900-1960* (Cambridge: Cambridge University Press, 1989), p. 25.

benefits of extensive visiting. Some found it increasingly "distasteful," complaining that the pastor was "apt to find only the ladies at home." Phillips Brooks convinced his congregation to allow him simply to preach, without calling from house to house. Beecher advised ministers to visit, but he left this "pastoral work" to assistants. To some ministers, pastoral visits seemed little more than occasions for "bell-pulls and card exchanges," an "effeminate" enterprise that was "a tragic waste of a strong man's time." By 1912, one pastoral writer complained of "widespread skepticism" among the clergy about the "utility" of visitation.[45]

Other ministers argued that pastoral visits provided the best occasion to "win souls." Theodore Cuyler thought that they produced "larger congregations and a far larger number of conversions to Christ" than polished sermons. Pastoral theology textbooks continued to offer guidance about conversations with the awakened, the anxious, the skeptical, and the suffering, and even a pastor like Charles Reynolds Brown, who disliked "the older, solemn calling, with catechizing," defended the pastoral visit as the most effective means of "Christian influence." Countering arguments that the practice was "obsolete," Brown depicted it in 1927 as an occasion for "friendly sympathy" rather than "pious exhortation" or "small talk." He claimed that Henry Sloan Coffin, pastor of the Madison Avenue Presbyterian Church, made a thousand visits a year.[46]

In some denominations, the pace of urban ministry altered the pastor's relationship with children and youth. The Episcopal, Lutheran, Dutch Reformed, and Presbyterian churches and some of the smaller immigrant groups continued to catechize, but elsewhere the catechism faded into the background. Especially in the big downtown churches, catechizing sometimes seemed out of the question, and some urban pastors confessed that they now had "other interests and labors." At the same time, they sought new ways to appeal to the child. Some strove to revamp the Sunday schools, while others organized children's choirs and included brief sermons for children as part of the Sunday worship. By 1890,

45. Gladden, *Christian Pastor,* p. 197; Willcox, *Pastor,* 145; Charles Edward Jefferson, *The Minister as Shepherd* (New York: Thomas Y. Crowell, 1912), p. 44; David Spence, *The Education and Problems of the Protestant Ministry* (Worcester: Clark University Press, 1908), p. 36; Alexander V. G. Allen, *Life and Letters of Phillips Brooks,* 2 vols. (New York: E. P. Dutton, 1900), vol. 2, p. 104; Beecher, *Yale Lectures,* p. 100; Raymond J. Cunningham, "From Preachers of the Word to Physicians of the Soul: The Protestant Pastor in Nineteenth Century America," *Journal of Religious History* 3 (1965): 327-46.

46. Cuyler, *How to Be a Pastor,* p. 9; T. Harwood Pattison, *For the Work of the Ministry* (Philadelphia: American Baptist Publication Society, 1907), p. 404; Stephen H. Tyng, *The Office and Duty of a Christian Pastor* (New York: Harper and Brothers, 1874), p. 77; Charles Reynolds Brown, *The Making of a Minister* (New York: Century, 1927), pp. 124, 168-70, 173-75, 182, 186.

these "sermonettes," delivered in a "vivacious style" with "abundant illustration," became a familiar Sunday morning feature. Handbooks assured young pastors that "a winsome way with the children" would attract parents into the church.[47]

The downtown churches competed with mass entertainment to hold young people. As early as the 1850s, some of the largest churches had assistant ministers who spent most of their time working with youth, and by the 1870s pastors were busily organizing youth groups. They led young people in worship and Bible study, but they also believed that the churches had exaggerated the dangers of "amusements," and they encouraged parties and picnics. Curmudgeons protested against "the notion that young people need to be amused in order to be retained in the church," but churches could not ignore the demand. The push for youth ministries accelerated after the forming in 1881 of the Young People's Society of Christian Endeavor, a Congregationalist innovation that spread to thirty denominations. By 1922, more than 80 percent of urban churches — and 25 percent of rural churches — had "young people's societies."[48]

Gladden captured the new style of ministry when he called for pastors with a "genius for friendship." The route to success was not preaching, wrote one minister, but rather "the attraction of the man as a whole." His "enthusiasm" would "charm" the youth, and his "popularity" would draw new members. Gladden intended his ideal of "the pastor as Friend" to suggest the qualities that could inspire "confidence and affection" in the urban parish. In place of the "reserve" of the antebellum cleric, the "social gifts" of the modern pastor would ensure influence. One clerical writer after another mocked the image of the "sanctimonious" preacher with a "professional piety." The "merely professional qualities" needed to give way to the power of "personal" influence.[49]

To critics, the new image appeared to be a compromise with secular formulas for success. They had little sympathy with "the clerical man of the world" who sought popularity by attending afternoon teas and football games. In 1899 *The Ladies' Home Journal* caricatured the "modern" pastor who might be "great fun" but who lacked the gravity of "the Old-Time Clergyman." Instead of a "study lined with books of grave divinity," the modern cleric had "an office with

47. Willcox, *Pastor*, pp. 11, 118-19, 144; Gladden, *Christian Pastor*, p. 33; Pattison, *Work*, pp. 355, 366; Bedell, *The Pastor*, pp. 68, 74, 97, 501.

48. Dix, ed., *History of the Parish*, p. 103; Willcox, *Pastor*, p. 110; Pattison, *Work*, p. 372; H. Paul Douglass, *1000 City Churches* (New York: George H. Doran, 1926), p. 79; Gladden, *Christian Pastor*, 316.

49. Gladden, *Christian Pastor*, pp. 73, 172; Willcox, *Pastor*, p. 111; Cuyler, *How to Be a Pastor*, p. 18; Noah Porter, "The Christian Ministry as a Profession and a Sacred Calling," *Andover Review* 1 (1884): 353; Taylor, *Ministry of the Word*, p. 261; A. J. Lyman, "Opportunities for Culture in the Christian Ministry," *The New Englander and Yale Review* 34 (1875): 644.

pigeonholes for his programs and endless correspondence," a "telephone ever tingling," and a "set of handbooks" filled with anecdotes and canned sermon ideas. One critic remarked that "the clerical after-dinner speakers" ranked among "the most popular entertainers of the day," but he saw their popularity as a sign of decline.[50]

A small nationwide poll in 1908 found that at least some of the laity applauded the new image. When asked to describe their ideal pastor, 38 percent expressed a desire for a "good man," honest, reliable, and conscientious; 34 percent wanted a manly, strong, courageous, broadminded executive; 23 percent wanted a friendly pastor with social skills; and 5 percent preferred a "modest gentleman." In 1878, Bishop Bedell had observed that "practically nothing remains to be a source of clerical influence in this age, except individual clerical character." The poll suggested that Bedell's promotion of character still resonated with churchgoers, but admiration for executive facility and friendliness now complicated the clerical role.[51]

By 1925, 35 percent of American ministers served in urban congregations, but only a small number led the large churches that enthroned celebrity princes of the pulpit. The Presbyterian reformer Charles L. Stelzle complained in 1907 that most city churches merely provided an elaborated version of "a country church programme." A study in 1922 discovered that only 30 percent of 1,044 urban Protestant congregations maintained the expanded programs recommended in the pastoral theology texts; 35 percent limited themselves to worship, Sunday school, a choir, four or five groups, and assorted social events; and 35 percent gathered only for worship, women's groups, choir practice, and young people's societies. The report omitted the growing number of small storefront churches that restricted themselves to worship and Bible study. Few of the urban pastors held a princely post, but the princes of the pulpit created the images that later generations would remember.[52]

Social Gospels

For the "lonely prophets" who welcomed a "social gospel," the job of the minister was to assist in God's creation of "a redeemed society on earth." Working

50. Robert Drail, "The Passing of the Clerical Man of the World," *New England Magazine* 19 (1895): 496; John Watson, "The Candy-Pull System in the Church," *The Ladies' Home Journal* 16 (1899): 19; "Pastorate for the Times," pp. 90-91.

51. Hill, *Education and Problems*, p. 16; Bedell, *Personal Character*, p. 14.

52. Charles Stelzle, *The Institutional Church*, in *Church and the City*, p. 331; Douglass, *1000 City Churches*, pp. 154, 171.

mainly in urban parishes in the North and Midwest, the social gospel ministers stood in the tradition of the antebellum clergy who staffed the voluntary societies. The Bible, they argued, proclaimed the kingdom of God, a community of peace, justice, and righteousness. By the 1870s they were beginning to preach about justice, support labor unions, agitate for child labor laws, investigate labor disputes, and found settlement houses. Charles Sheldon, a Congregationalist in Topeka, reached millions with the novel *In His Steps* (1883), which instructed Christians to ask: What would Jesus do? The social gospel remained a minority voice, but its advocates convinced several of the larger denominations to establish offices for social ministries and to adopt progressive social principles. It presented itself as a more biblical alternative than a merely otherworldly view of pastoral duty.[53]

Washington Gladden (1836-1918) preached every Sunday morning on traditional themes, but he filled his church on Sunday evenings by preaching sermons about the kingdom of God and social sinfulness. He taught that the heart of the gospel was "the fatherhood of God and the brotherhood of man." As a social critic, he defended labor unions, criticized monopolies, and advocated government intervention to ensure a just peace between labor and capital. He built a settlement house to shelter the poor and homeless, and he served two years on the Columbus, Ohio, city council, where he introduced a successful ordinance mandating municipal ownership of the electric company. His progressive stance brought more than one death threat.[54]

For such ministers, the ideal parish became the new "institutional church," a congregation organized to provide social services to the poor. William Rainsford convinced St. George's Episcopal Church in New York City to offer ethnic missions, industrial schools, kindergartens, employment bureaus, a medical clinic, visiting nurses, a legal service bureau, workers' clubs, girls' boarding houses, a circulating library, and a gymnasium for the tenement dwellers in the surrounding neighborhoods. By 1906, New York City had at least 112 institutional churches; Chicago about twenty-five; and every other major city at least one. Most were Northern, though several black congregations followed the model in the larger Southern cities. Their success depended on "the gift of organization, and the power of enlisting others in the work of the church."[55]

53. Gladden, *Christian Pastor*, p. 108.

54. Jacob Henry Dorn, *Washington Gladden: Prophet of the Social Gospel* (Columbus: Ohio State University Press, 1966), pp. 78, 170-93, 232, 244, 312, 412, 417-31.

55. Ferenc M. Scasz, *The Divided Mind of Protestant America, 1880-1930* (Tuscaloosa: University of Alabama Press, 1982), pp. 48-55; Ralph E. Luker, "Missions, Institutional Churches, and Settlement Houses: The Black Experience, 1885-1910," *Journal of Negro History* 69 (1984): 108; Gladden, *Christian Pastor*, p. 74.

African American clergy put racial justice on the social gospel agenda. They helped resurrect the Convention Movement, which protested against racist legislation, and they were active in the Niagara Movement (1905) and the National Association for the Advancement of Colored People (1910). The "conservatives" among them supported Booker T. Washington's plan for training skilled workers while making a temporary accommodation to a segregated society. The "radicals" worked for civil rights and racial integration. Urban black clerics initially favored conservatism, but by 1912 they were shifting toward a civil rights platform.[56]

No African American minister better illustrated the social gospel impulse than Reverdy Ransom, the pastor of Bethel AME Church in Chicago. In 1900, he founded the Institutional Church and Social Settlement to make the church "exist for the people rather than the people for the church." He convinced the black elite of Chicago to sponsor kindergartens, classes, clubs, manual training, a gymnasium, and an employment bureau, and the church taught people to sew, cook, sing, play the piano, and run a print shop. Ransom drew opposition from AME conservatives who claimed that the social gospel perverted "the essential mission of the church," which was to convert individuals to Christ. Weary of fighting the opposition, he departed for New England in 1904, and his successor tried "to cut out the social foolishness and bring religion back."[57]

Like Ransom's clerical opponents, most Protestant ministers rejected or ignored the social gospel. For the most part, Southern white clergy defended racial segregation and the economic status quo and Northern conservatives applauded an unrestricted capitalism. Henry Ward Beecher denounced labor unions and remarked in 1877, during an economic depression, that any worker unable to live on bread and water was unfit to live. Phillips Brooks joined Beecher in teaching that social inequality was necessary and good. Proclaiming a "gospel of wealth," the Baptist Russell H. Conwell in Philadelphia baptized the pursuit of riches and told other ministers that they were failures unless their members could "get larger salaries, obtain larger aggregate profits, and occupy more comfortable homes." Conwell's *Acres of Diamonds*, which taught how to "become rich," outsold any social gospel treatise.[58]

---

56. August Meier, *Negro Thought in America 1880-1915* (Ann Arbor: University of Michigan Press, 1963), pp. 180, 220-22; Ralph E. Luker, *The Social Gospel in Black and White: American Racial Reform, 1885-1912* (Chapel Hill: University of North Carolina Press, 1991), pp. 265-67.

57. Calvin S. Morris, "Reverdy C. Ransom: A Pioneer Black Social Gospeler" (Ph.D. dissertation, Boston University, 1982), pp. 134, 139, 141, 142.

58. William G. McLoughlin, *The Meaning of Henry Ward Beecher* (New York: Alfred A. Knopf, 1970), p. 99; May, *Protestant Churches*, p. 65; Russell H. Conwell, *Acres of Diamonds: How Men and Women May Become Rich* (Philadelphia: Harper and Brothers, 1890), p. 203.

During the wars of the era, the clergy furnished prophetic critics but also militant nationalists. E. L. Godkin, editor of *The Nation,* claimed that preachers stood among "the most powerful propagandists" for imperial ventures in Cuba and the Philippines in 1898. A few resisted American entry into World War I, but one poll in New York showed that as early as 1916, while the public remained wary of war, 90 percent of ministers in the region were willing to see America send troops to Europe. When Americans began to fight, some well-known ministers called for the punishment of conscientious objectors, the execution of "traitors," and the obliteration of German society. The War Department convinced some of the clergy to recruit soldiers and sell Liberty Bonds.[59]

For a while, the social gospel ministers had real influence in the upper reaches of several denominations, and at the founding of the Federal Council of Churches in 1908, a statement of social principles committed the new organization to a program of social reform. During the 1920s, however, religious conservatives pulled away from a progressive social agenda because they associated it with liberal theology, and the social gospel became the object of their scorn. By then, clergy were encountering new alternatives.

Liberals and Conservatives

In 1900, Arthur Tappan Pierson, a Presbyterian minister in Philadelphia, described the "more conspicuous spiritual movements" of the previous fifty years. In his *Forward Movements of the Last Half Century,* he drew attention to missions, women's work, student movements, urban evangelism, and charitable enterprises, and he praised the theological trends. He found a growing interest in the Bible as the infallible and inspired word of God. He noted a stronger conviction that the Spirit enabled the Christian to attain "victory over sin." He praised the burgeoning attention to "the doctrine of divine healing, in answer to prayer." And he devoted a chapter to "the increasing study" of "the approaching 'end of the age.'" Protestant theology, as Pierson saw it, had rediscovered biblical inspiration, holiness, healing, and the "numerical system" within Scripture that revealed the chronology of the end of the world.[60]

In 1916, Arthur Cushman McGiffert, a Presbyterian professor at Union

59. Kenneth H. Mackenzie, *The Robe and the Sword: The Methodist Church and the Rise of American Imperialism* (Washington, D.C.: Public Affairs Press, 1961), p. 66; Ray Abrams, *Preachers Present Arms: The Role of the American Churches and Clergy in World Wars I and II* (Scottdale: Herald Press, 1969), pp. 35, 83, 109, 122, 136, 194-95.

60. Arthur T. Pierson, *Forward Movements of the Last Half Century* (1st ed., 1900; New York: Funk and Wagnalls, 1905), pp. 1, 9-10, 17, 24, 44, 152, 389, 409-10.

Theological Seminary in New York, presented an alternative version of "the progress of theological thought." McGiffert emphasized the "growing control of theology by the concept of evolution." He saw a turn toward "naturalism" and a move away from the supernatural and the miraculous. He thought that the best Protestant theologians had learned from painstaking historical study that the Bible was no "infallible authority." They had discovered that "experience" provided "the only legitimate basis of theology." They had also departed from individualism — an undue emphasis on conversion experiences — and recovered a "social" emphasis on ethics, community, and the immanence of God.[61]

McGiffert and Pierson lived in the same era, but they lived in two different worlds.

The theologians McGiffert admired had decided that theological formulations needed to change in accord with the spirit of the age. They were confident that they could retain the "substance" of the gospel while freeing it from "past forms which were never of its essence." The Congregationalist Newman Smyth at Center Church in New Haven summarized the guiding principle: "Every doctrine," he wrote, "is to be thought out afresh and taught in methods better suited to the temper of the times."[62]

The theologians in Pierson's camp deplored the suggestion that theology should adapt itself to changing circumstances. Convinced that "the sure Word of Truth" was "the same yesterday, today, and forever," they feared that a theology subject to "the wisdom of this world" would find itself "driven hither and thither, according to the course of the popular tide." The Princeton Presbyterian Charles Hodge believed it possible to show that "the true people of God in every age" agreed about "the true meaning of Scripture in all things necessary either in faith or practice." And since he could see no legitimate distinction between "the thoughts" in Scripture and "the words" that expressed them, he believed that theologians who sought new formulations strayed from the faith.[63]

When in the 1870s theologians began to discuss Charles Darwin's theories of

61. Arthur Cushman McGiffert, "The Progress of Theological Thought During the Past Fifty Years," *The American Journal of Theology* 20 (1916): 291, 323, 324, 327, 329, 331-32.

62. Theodore Munger, *The Freedom of Faith* (Boston: Houghton Mifflin, 1883), p. 67; Henry C. King, *Reconstruction in Theology* (1st ed., 1901; New York: Macmillan, 1909), p. v; Newman Smyth, "Orthodox Rationalism," *The Princeton Review* 58 (1882): 312; William R. Hutchinson, *The Modernist Impulse in American Protestantism* (Cambridge: Harvard University Press, 1976), pp. 1-12.

63. A. W. Pitzer, "The Wisdom of this World," *The Fundamentals*, 10 vols. (Chicago: Testimony, 1910), vol. 9, p. 22; Charles Hodge, *Systematic Theology*, 3 vols. (New York: Scribner, Armstrong, 1874), vol. 1, pp. 164, 188.

evolution, the liberals — and a few conservatives — found it possible to accept evolutionary science by reinterpreting Genesis. Some shared Newman Smyth's desire for a "theistic conception of evolution" as "God's way of doing things." In 1885, Henry Ward Beecher's *Evolution and Religion* inaugurated a trend among the liberal theologians to accept evolution as "the method of the universe" and to interpret not only Genesis but also all Christian doctrine in evolutionary terms. But when Hodge published *What is Darwinism?* he concluded that the absence of teleology in Darwinian biology made the theory inevitably atheistic.[64]

The divide widened when the liberals abandoned theories of biblical infallibility, questioned traditional assumptions about biblical authorship, and described the Bible as the product of a "prolonged historical process." They affirmed the Bible because it conveyed authoritative truths; conservatives affirmed the truths because they came from an infallibly authoritative book. For the liberals, the Bible was "a continually unfolding revelation of God" that recorded a progression from the primitive conceptions of the patriarchal era to the higher insights of Jesus. For the conservatives, the Bible provided "a supernaturally revealed knowledge of the plan of salvation," an errorless revelation, displaying the miraculous powers of God.[65]

For liberals, history was a movement toward God's kingdom, and they found God's presence wherever they discovered the good, the true, and the beautiful. For many conservatives, the world was a "wrecked vessel," and they saw history as a steady decline that would be arrested only by the return of Jesus. In the 1870s, one faction among the conservatives organized a series of conferences to study biblical prophecies that revealed the imminence of Christ's second coming. By the 1880s some of them began adopting a theory known as premillennial dispensationalism, which charted the periods of history and taught that the imminent return of Christ would inaugurate violent and apocalyptic events in Israel as a prelude to the millennial kingdom.[66]

---

64. Newman Smyth, *Old Faiths Cast in a New Light* (New York: Charles Scribner's Sons, 1879), p. 24; William Newton Clarke, *An Outline of Christian Theology* (1st ed., 1894; New York: Charles Scribner's Sons, 1919), p. 115; Lyman Abbott, "The Need of a New Theology," *The American Journal of Theology* 1 (1897): 462; E. Brooks Holifield, *Theology in America: From the Age of the Puritans to the Civil War* (New Haven: Yale University Press, 2003), p. 380; R. A. Torrey, *Revival Addresses* (Chicago: Fleming H. Revell, 1903), p. 8.

65. Smyth, *Old Faiths*, p. 33; Munger, *Freedom*, p. 19; Washington Gladden, *Who Wrote the Bible?* (Boston: Houghton Mifflin, 1892), p. 363; J. J. Reeve, "My Personal Experience with the Higher Criticism," *The Fundamentals*, vol. 3, p. 103.

66. George A. Gordon, "The Contrast and Agreement Between the New Orthodoxy and the Old," *The Andover Review* 19 (1893): 7; W. E. Blackstone, *Jesus is Coming* (1st ed., 1878; New York: Revell, 1908), pp. 18-19, 37; C. Norman Kraus, *Dispensationalism in America* (Richmond: John Knox, 1958), chs. 5-6.

The liberals stressed the historical Jesus of Nazareth, who proclaimed the kingdom of God as a community of love and justice and revealed through his life and death God's love. His character and his consciousness of God were as redemptive as his death. When they talked about his miracles, they explained them as natural events with religious meaning or "illustrations of a wider law." The conservatives thought that liberals merely wanted to "eliminate the supernatural" from the life and death of Christ, who was, for them, the savior whose death had reconciled God to humanity, whose physical resurrection was "an absolutely certain fact of history," and whose return to "judge the world" was imminent. To minimize Jesus' miracles, they thought, was to reject faith in a personal God.[67]

The two groups disagreed about the meaning of salvation. In 1877, liberal ministers began to question the idea that the sinful would suffer eternally in hell. Nine years later the faculty at Andover Seminary published *Progressive Orthodoxy*, which suggested that perhaps the sinful, along with all who had never heard of Christ, would have a second chance after death, when Christ would reveal himself to everyone. Some liberals demurred, but they deemphasized hell and damnation and taught that salvation was not merely the continuation of existence but also a quality of life in this world. To the conservatives, such inclinations undercut Christian missions and the call for conversion. Reuben A. Torrey of the Moody Bible Institute in Chicago insisted that Christ, sitting on his heavenly throne, "his eyes like flames of fire," would pronounce eternal judgment, and that all who had rejected him would suffer "eternal death, darkness, despair, and shame." He scorned the "false hopes" held out by the "liberal preachers."[68]

The divisions produced widely publicized heresy trials, which continued into the twentieth century, and they generated struggles for control of church agencies. By 1920 some Northern Baptists began to describe themselves as "fundamentalists," and the creation in 1919 of a World's Christian Fundamentals Association suggested that the movement extended beyond denominational boundaries. But the fundamentalists constituted only one segment of the antiliberal Protestants. Lutheran and Anglican traditionalists opposed liberal theology more by appeal to the centrality of sacraments and honored creeds than by

---

67. Smyth, *Old Faiths*, p. 185; George Harris, "Ethical Christianity and Biblical Christianity," *Andover Review* 15 (1891): 461-70; Newman Smyth, *The Religious Feeling* (New York: Scribner and Armstrong, 1877), pp. 61-80; Torrey, *Revival Addresses*, pp. 9, 49, 51; J. Gresham Machen, "History and Faith," *The Princeton Review* 13 (1915): 342, 349; J. Gresham Machen, "The Relation of Religion to Science and Philosophy," *Princeton Theological Review* 24 (1926):39.

68. Munger, *Freedom*, p. 38; Torrey, *Revival Addresses*, pp. 51, 53-55, 69; R. A. Torrey, *The Baptism with the Holy Spirit* (New York: Fleming H. Revell, 1895), pp. 37-50.

assertions of biblical infallibility. Other Protestants, intent on personal holiness, formed more than two hundred small holiness denominations, often designating themselves as Churches of God. After 1901, the Pentecostal movement, which featured speaking in tongues as evidence of the indwelling Spirit, began a gradual ascent to public recognition.[69]

The split altered the self-understanding of the Protestant clergy. While many remained distant from the battles, the new alignments compelled them to locate themselves in relation to the conflict. Denominational identities remained strong through the 1920s, but they grew less prominent as markers of theological identity. William Adams Brown at Union Seminary pointed out as early as 1906 that "the present generation has witnessed a growing disposition to break down denominational lines." Clergy could now feel more affinity with like-minded colleagues in other denominations than with theological opponents in their own.[70]

A study of seven hundred ministers and seminary students from twenty denominations in the Midwest, published in 1929, revealed that 55 percent of the ministers viewed the Bible as supernaturally inspired; two-thirds thought that inspiration enabled the prophets to predict future events; and 77 percent considered the New Testament an "infallible standard." Only 47 percent believed that creation occurred "in the manner and time recorded in Genesis," and 61 percent thought that evolution was acceptable, but 68 percent also believed that God could set aside natural laws to perform miracles. More than three out of four — 76 percent — thought that Jesus was "equal in power, knowledge, and authority with God," 82 percent that he restored the dead to life, 71 percent that he was born of a virgin, and 84 percent that he was physically raised from the dead. A majority — around 61 percent — thought that all who rejected Christ would suffer eternal punishment; 53 percent believed that hell existed as an actual location; two-thirds thought that Jesus would come again to judge humanity.[71]

Denominational affiliation made a difference. Lutherans and Baptists stood on the conservative side; Methodists, Episcopalians, and Presbyterians in the middle; Congregationalists leaned toward the liberal end. The survey's bias

69. Norman Furniss, *The Fundamentalist Controversy, 1918-1931* (New Haven: Yale University Press, 1954), p. 120; George M. Marsden, *Fundamentalism and American Culture* (New York: Oxford University Press, 1980), pp. 141-64; Vinson Synan, *The Holiness-Pentecostal Movement* (Grand Rapids: Eerdmans, 1971), pp. 13-76; Grant Wacker, *Heaven Below: Early Pentecostals and American Culture* (Cambridge: Harvard University Press, 2001), pp. 1-17.

70. William Adams Brown, "Changes in the Theology of American Presbyterianism," *American Journal of Theology* 10 (1906): 405.

71. George Herbert Betts, *The Beliefs of 700 Ministers* (New York: The Abingdon Press, 1929), pp. 26-28, 38.

toward mainline denominations minimized the full extent of conservative be-lief among ministers. It was clear, however, that Protestant clergy were divided in 1929 in ways they had not been in 1865. Theology had created new fault lines, and they would not disappear.

Professionals and Populists

The clergy also disagreed still about professionalism, and even the advocates of clerical education were no longer sure exactly what the seminaries should teach or what authority professional education conferred. The antebellum founders of the schools had emphasized theological learning, assuming that theology would guide the minister and the congregation. By the late nineteenth century, it was not uncommon to hear even the defenders of a professional clergy mini-mize the importance of scholarly attainment. Many a "scholarly pastor," Willcox observed, was unsuccessful. Bishop Bedell said much the same thing: "A minister who is merely a theologian stands little chance."[72]

For Bedell the ministry was no mere profession but "a divinely appointed" order, "perpetuated by divine regulation." He favored an educated and full-time ministry, but he denied that a distinctive "knowledge" defined the minister in the way that legal knowledge defined the lawyer or medical knowledge the physician. What defined the minister was the status conferred through a divine vocation and the ordination that brought it to fulfillment as an act of the church. To the Baptist Harwood Pattison, writing in 1907, it was clear that the ministry "must be a calling rather than a profession." It should certainly never become "merely a profession." Detached from a theology of the divine call, he thought, the profes-sional ideal became little more than a quest for "status, affluence, and position."[73]

Clerical populists still thrived, and they feared that seminaries made clerical "success" depend on "proficiency in the several departments of human science" rather than faithful proclamation of the gospel. They still thought that the schools educated students "away from the masses." The revivalist Sam Jones boasted that he had "never attended a theological 'cemetery.'" He knew nothing, he said, of sys-tematic theology, and he had never "studied 'hermaletics' or 'exegetics,'" but he claimed that he had "seen 700,000 people turned from the error of their ways" un-der his ministry, and theological education would have merely stood in the way.[74]

72. Willcox, *Pastor*, p. 10; Bedell, *The Pastor*, p. 19.

73. Bedell, *The Pastor*, p. 10; Pattison, *Work*, pp. 47, 57; Murphy, *Pastoral Theology*, p. 27; James William Kimball, *The Christian Ministry* (Boston: J. A. Whipple, 1884), pp. 133-35.

74. Kimball, *Christian Ministry*, pp. 34-35; Walt Holcomb, *Sam Jones* (Nashville: Methodist Publishing House, 1947), p. 108.

George Park Fisher argued in 1866 that the church had suffered more from the "dullness and ignorance" of its clergy than from their "excess of knowledge." He saw "far more danger that ranters will abound, than that the clergy will suffer from excessive erudition." Neither Fisher nor the authors of the pastoral handbooks ever defined the ministry merely as one profession among others, but they took for granted the "professional character" of the clergy, and some still identified it with the notion that the minister was an "instructor in theology." For all who agreed, it was troubling that the spread of education had "brought the congregation up to the intellectual level of the clergy" and that some of the laity were fully "as scholarly" as the minister. By the 1920s some feared that "most clergymen today could not qualify before adequate judges as learned men."[75]

The educated clergy gravitated toward the urban pulpits. By 1926, in the twenty largest Protestant denominations, 46 percent of the urban clergy had both a college and a seminary degree, 14 percent graduated from college alone, 12 percent graduated from a seminary without having earned a college degree, and 28 percent had a high-school education or less. In the ministry as a whole, the educational levels were lower. In the largest denominations, only 27 percent, maybe only 24 percent, had a college and seminary education, and only 41 percent had graduated from college. Fully 50 percent had only a high-school education or less.[76]

The ministry remained open to anyone who felt called, and even the churches that wanted seminary-educated ministers did not necessarily want scholars with distinctive biblical and theological learning. They wanted good preachers, but they wanted much more, and clergy were adapting to the new expectations. Almost half the clergy still thought of the ministry as an educated profession — requiring at least a college education — but the meaning of professionalism was changing.

Between 1850 and 1900, the churches founded 119 new seminaries, and by the turn of the century 159 schools offered ministerial training. The number of students increased more than threefold. But criticism of the schools also intensified. Some argued that too many schools provided a "cloistered system of training" that isolated students from "grimy contact" with the problems of society. Francis Greenwood Peabody at Harvard said that they trained ministers

75. G. P. Fisher, "Systematic Training for the Ministry," *The New Englander and Yale Review* 25 (1866): 213; W. G. T. Shedd, *Homiletics and Pastoral Theology* (New York: Scribner, 1869), p. 371; Bedell, *Personal Character*, p. 15; Edwards A. Park, *Theological Education* (Boston: T. R. Marvin, 1865), pp. 4-27; Anonymous, "Ministerial Problems I. Pastoral Work," *Outlook* 56 (1897): 979; Slattery, *The Ministry*, p. 22.

76. Fry, *U.S. Looks at Its Churches*, p. 152; May, *Profession of the Ministry*, p. 14.

in "subjects which they cannot use" and left them "ignorant of much which they need to know."[77]

In response to such criticisms, William Rainey Harper of the University of Chicago argued in 1899 that the older professional ideal was focused overmuch on producing "scholars." Harper wanted future ministers to learn not primarily by mastering a theological system but by developing special skills in preaching, teaching, pastoral duties, music, and church administration. He would link this academic work to "the clinical or laboratory method," with students working in churches under a pastor, or participating in "theological clinics" in urban settings, like the slums of Chicago. He wanted to redefine the meaning of clerical professionalism. The professional minister would have specialized knowledge linked to practical skills, not necessarily theological learning in the older manner but a theologically informed capacity to carry out the functions associated with ministry to a congregation.[78]

Harper's model would eventually help reshape Protestant training for ministry; it drew attention because it seemed to represent the way in which the ministry as a profession was moving. The older professional ideal had assumed that learning conveyed authority, but it was not clear that American Protestants really wanted a ministry steeped in theological erudition. By the end of the twenties it should have been clear that ministry in America would be a vocation. It would have a professional contingent, but the sources of ministerial authority — and even the meaning of ministerial "professionalism" — would be far more complicated than the gentlemen preachers of the nineteenth century could ever have imagined.

Decline?

For the authors of late-nineteenth-century clerical handbooks, the minister was to be a living example, exceeding others in "spiritual attainments," "holiness," and a "Christ-like" life. The spiritual requirements were demanding: zeal, love, and self-sacrifice nurtured by "constant" prayer and the unremitting effort to follow "the example of Christ." A minister, wrote the Methodist Daniel Kidder, should be "the highest style of Christian." "A clergyman's character,"

77. Hill, *Education and Problems*, p. 61; Francis Greenwood Peabody, "The Call to Theology," *Harvard Theological Review* 1 (1908): 2; May, *Profession of the Ministry*, p. 27.

78. William Rainey Harper, "Shall the Theological Curriculum Be Modified, and How?" *The American Journal of Theology* 3 (1899): 56-59, 61-63; Conrad Cherry, *Hurrying Toward Zion: Universities, Divinity Schools, and American Protestantism* (Bloomington: Indiana University Press, 1995), pp. 4-13.

wrote one Episcopal bishop, "will not bear a taint or even a reasonable suspicion of fault." "It is not entirely unjust," wrote another pastor, that "the world demands a higher standard of the Christian minister than it requires of itself."[79]

Realists recognized that "unworthy" pastors had "disgraced and dishonored" the ministry. One anti-clerical critic estimated, after collecting stories in eleven newspapers for eight years, that at least 2 to 3 percent of the nation's clergy were malefactors of greater or lesser degree. Clerical immorality remained a staple of popular journalism, and when Henry Ward Beecher incurred charges of adultery in 1874, the nation's newspapers gave the trial front-page coverage for six months. The jury failed to convict, but the journalists concluded that Beecher was a fraud. Washington Gladden, writing in 1909, urged churches to screen carefully against "scoundrels" and "plausible villains, with smooth tongues." But nothing suggested that ministers were any more — or less — prone to malfeasance than they had been in earlier eras.[80]

The ideal was still gentility, but now it complemented a new admiration for a muscular clergy. "A minister should be, wherever he is, a true gentleman," the Presbyterian theologian James Hoppin had written in 1869. It was an "exceptional qualification for the ministry," wrote Charles Lewis Slattery in 1921, to be a "genuine gentleman." After all, Jesus had been a "true gentleman." But now writings about ministry often accentuated the minister's "masculinity." After the Civil War, American writers popularized a vocabulary of toughness as part of a backlash against "soft," "sentimental," and "unmanly" virtues, and a rhetoric of "manliness" echoed in the nation's colleges and universities. Americans gravitated toward "muscular Christianity" — an import from nineteenth-century England — that depicted an athletic, decisive, courageous Jesus as the model for "ministerial manliness."[81]

Beecher exemplified the ethos when he advised Yale seminarians in 1891 to

79. Thomas Murphy, *Pastoral Theology: The Pastor in the Various Duties of His Office* (Philadelphia: Presbyterian Board of Publication, 1877), pp. 37-40; Daniel Kidder, *The Christian Pastorate* (Cincinnati: Hitchcock and Walden, 1871), pp. 225, 241; Bedell, *Pastor,* p. 36; Pattison, *Work,* p. 449.

80. Pattison, *Work,* p. 34; M. E. Billings, *Crimes of Preachers in the United States and Canada, From May 1876 to May 1883* (New York: Truth Seeker, 1883), p. 245; Clifford E. Clark Jr., *Henry Ward Beecher: Spokesman for a Middle-Class America* (Urbana: University of Illinois Press, 1978), pp. 197-229; Gladden, *Christian Pastor,* p. 81.

81. James M. Hoppin, *The Office and Work of the Christian Ministry* (New York: Sheldon, 1869), p. 467; Charles Lewis Slattery, *The Ministry* (New York: Charles Scribner's Sons, 1921), p. 34; Pattison, *Work,* pp. 25, 27, 443; Burton J. Bledstein, *The Culture of Professionalism* (New York: W. W. Norton, 1976), p. 153; George M. Fredrickson, *The Inner Civil War: Northern Intellectuals and the Crisis of the Union* (New York: Harper and Row, 1968), p. 87.

"be manly" in their preaching — to "thrust" and "lunge" with vigor and vitality. "It takes a *man*," he said, "to refashion men." The handbooks advised ministers to look to their health, practicing "gymnastics" and exercising each day. They were to exhibit manliness both as a mark of physical prowess and as an ethical ideal that uplifted the virtues of self-denial, courage, energy, and simplicity of character. Respondents to the 1908 survey said that they wanted their ministers to have an "imposing physique" and to be "tall, stately, six feet, strong to look at, and well proportioned." By the 1920s, when revivalist Billy Sunday was advertising the idea that the Christian was a "red-blooded he-man" and "Jesus was the greatest scrapper that ever lived," some ministers could take comfort that the impression of the clergy as "anaemic and wan" had disappeared.[82]

Because women still constituted the great majority of church members, some of the manuals expressed worries that ministers had to spend too much time working with women rather than with the men, who held real power in the society. In such an atmosphere, calls for the ordination of women generated intense debate. Frances Willard, a Methodist reformer, felt called to the ministry but met resistance from her denomination. Her *Woman in the Pulpit* (1888) charged that men played "fast and loose" with the Bible by highlighting a few passages but ignoring others. But the 1890s brought a surge in the number of denominations willing to ordain women, from 7 percent of them in 1890 to 25 percent ten years later. The main rationale was the new demand for gender equality that accompanied the campaign to enfranchise women politically. But although the churches responded to the pressure of transitions in the culture, their growing openness produced modest results. In 1910, the census found 685 women clergy; 99 percent of the ministers were male.[83]

The Holiness and Pentecostal revivals after 1906 opened the pulpit to such charismatic women preachers as Alma Bridwell White, founder and bishop of the Pillar of Fire holiness church. The Pentecostal evangelist Aimee Semple McPherson conducted large tent crusades until she opened in 1923 her Angelus

---

82. Beecher, *Yale Lectures,* pp. 120, 192; Kidder, *Christian Pastorate,* p. 245; William S. Plumer, *Hints and Helps in Pastoral Theology* (New York: Harper and Brothers, 1874), pp. 75, 118; Pattison, *Work,* pp. 36, 40; Hill, *Education and Problems,* p. 18; Slattery, *Ministry,* pp. 40-41; William G. McLoughlin, *Billy Sunday Was His Real Name* (Chicago: University of Chicago Press, 1955), pp. 141, 179.

83. Pattison, *Work,* p. 31; Willcox, *Pastor,* p. 22; Plumer, *Hints,* p. 109; Frances Willard, *Woman in the Pulpit* (Chicago: Women's Temperance Publication Association, 1889), pp. 17-18; Mark Chaves, *Ordaining Women: Culture and Conflict in Religious Organizations* (Cambridge: Harvard University Press, 1997), pp. 48, 70, 77; Robert J. Kelly, *Theological Education in America* (New York: George H. Doran, 1924), p. 181; May, *Profession of the Ministry,* p. 36.

Temple in Los Angeles, the mother congregation for her International Church of the Foursquare Gospel, which welcomed women as pastors and made her a national radio celebrity. Their success had little effect on sentiments in the older denominations, which tended to view the new groups as an unpleasant rabble. In 1920, only 1.4 percent of American ministers were women, and at the end of the decade the number had risen to only 2.2 percent.[84]

Women were resuming their quest for the pulpit at the moment that the mainline clergy were worrying about the decline of clerical status. In 1870, Hoppin bewailed the diminution of clerical authority. "It is growing quite the fashion," he wrote, "not only in familiar speech, but in the various forms of literature . . . to decry the vocation of the preacher, and to set forth in more or less direct terms his general inutility and insufficiency." Novelist and poet Oliver Wendell Holmes concluded in 1881 that ministers had "lost to a considerable extent the positions of leaders," and in the following year, the Yale church historian George Park Fisher wrote that "the decline of the authority of the clergy" was one of "the characteristic features of modern society." In 1899, E. L. Godkin asserted in *The Nation* that "among educated people, none of the so-called learned professions is held in so slight esteem or made the target for so hot a fire of criticism."[85]

The critiques continued into the twentieth century. In 1922, the Congregational theologian Henry Hallam Tweedy noticed that too many Americans viewed the minister as "unreceptive" to science and philosophy and derided the clergy as "impractical and visionary." He claimed that novels and stage plays lampooned the pastorate "mercilessly." The publication of Harold Frederic's *Damnation of Theron Ware* (1896) — a gentle but skeptical depiction of a naïve young Methodist — foreshadowed the sarcasm of Sinclair Lewis's *Elmer Gantry* (1927), a skewering of a hypocritical revivalist preacher. "The authority of the pulpit," wrote author Fred Perry Powers in *The North American Review,* "has entirely evaporated." When Robert Kelly published in 1924 a study of Protestant seminaries, he observed that critics dismissed ministers as "second-rate" functionaries serving an institution no longer "representative of modern life." He claimed to have found widespread worries that "the number and the quality of ministerial candidates" had declined and that the churches faced a "prospective dearth of leaders."[86]

84. Edith Blumhofer, *Aimee Semple McPherson: Everybody's Sister* (Grand Rapids: Eerdmans, 1993), pp. 232-80; May, *Profession of the Ministry,* p. 36.

85. Willcox, *Pastor,* p. 266; Oliver Wendell Holmes, "The Pulpit and the Pew," *The North American Review* 132 (1881): 119; G. P. Fisher, "The Decline of Clerical Authority," *The North American Review* 135 (1882): 564; F. L. Godkin, "The Clergyman of Today," *The Nation* 69 (1899): 310.

86. Henry Hallam Tweedy, et al., *Christian Work as a Vocation* (New York: Macmillan,

Such laments were ancient, but the assertions of decline now came primarily from four different groups: secular writers who were unsympathetic to the churches, church leaders troubled by such criticisms, ministers calling for change in the profession, and clergy located in elite colleges and universities. Were they accurate? By 1890 the higher intellectual culture of America had become strikingly more secular than it had been fifty years earlier, and the resistance of some clergy to evolutionary theory and their hostility to certain realistic trends in literature meant that they began to feel like outsiders. Theology still had a hearing in philosophy departments in 1890, but thirty years later academic disciplines and scientific fields were becoming so specialized that the talented clerical amateur, so familiar before the Civil War, no longer had a voice. And some philosophers, scientists, novelists, and playwrights regarded "the men of the cloth" with skepticism. By the twenties, publishing companies were printing more books hostile to traditional Christianity than they had in the nineteenth century.

Ministers also lost their place as presidents and trustees of the elite colleges and universities. Between 1884 and 1926, the number of clerical trustees "declined by 50% at Amherst, 60% at Yale, and 67% at Princeton; at fifteen other private colleges, clergy trustees declined from 39% in 1860 to 23% in 1900." Ordained ministers rarely served as presidents of the best-known universities. Harvard appointed its last ordained president in 1862, Yale in 1886, Princeton in 1888. It seemed that the colleges and universities founded so largely by the clergy were "passing slowly into other hands."[87]

By 1890, Americans were flooding into new professions that claimed scientific expertise and specialized knowledge. Beginning in 1874, social workers, lawyers, architects, pharmacists, schoolteachers, accountants, librarians, veterinarians, and specialists in ten branches of medicine formed professional associations alongside at least 200 learned societies in fields ranging from chemistry and physics to modern language and folklore. The emergence of scientific psychology in the 1870s led to new forms of psychotherapy that competed with older forms of pastoral counsel, prompting such innovations as the Emmanuel Movement (1905) in which clergy tried to appropriate the new psychology, though with only mixed success. The "culture of professionalism" meant that more people turned to physicians and therapists for services once reserved largely for ministers. The awareness of talented competitors accounted for some of the

1922), p. 5; Fred Perry Powers, "The Crisis in the Church," *The North American Review* 224 (1927): 269; Kelly, *Theological Education*, pp. vii, 154.

87. Dorothy Bass, "Ministry on the Margin: Protestants and Education," *Between the Times*, p. 57; Charles J. Little, "The American Pulpit," *The Chautauquan: A Weekly Newsmagazine* 22 (1896): 653.

rhetoric of decline, and the professionalizing of the culture did represent a challenge to clerical influence in education, counseling, and social welfare.[88]

The complaints about ministerial losses also appeared to find confirmation
in the economics of the calling, though low salaries were ambiguous markers of
decline. Superstars like Dix and Beecher drew more than $15,000 a year, and
other pastors in the urban pulpits earned $3,000, but most earned under $1,000
a year, and the average salary of $574 in 1890 left most ministers at the lower end
of the scale. One clergyman complained in 1894 that "many an able, well-
educated minister must content himself with a salary of $500 a year, barely
sufficient for the most pressing necessities of his family with no margin for the
education of his children." An Episcopalian reported that some of his peers
survived on $300, a stipend "that a mechanic would have scorned." Salaries for
Lutherans in the East varied from $400 to $3,000, while the average Lutheran
salary in the West was closer to $800. It was common for merchants and rail-
roads to give ministerial discounts, but many ministers considered it a matter
of honor not to ask for them.[89]

Some believed that ministers lived as well as "the average of their parishioners, and [that] they ought to live no better," but for the minority of ministers
with seven years of higher education, the disparities with other professions
served as a reminder, as G. B. Willcox said, that religion was "a thing which the
average man fails to rate at its full worth."[90]

The twentieth century brought further slippage in purchasing power. In
1923, the *Literary Digest* claimed that the average minister in the Northeast, who
made around $1,500 a year, earned less than plumbers, masons, plasterers, and
bricklayers, who took home $2,500 or more. In the cities, salaries in 1925 ranged
from $500 to $8,000, but most earned from $1,000 to $2,000. In New England
cities, the better-paid Congregationalists made $3,250 while the highest-
earning Baptists drew $1,800. The average salary of $1,407 in 1928 placed ministers below postal employees, factory workers, and railway conductors. The average for surgeons was $9,255; for law school faculty, $5,197; for physicians, $4,188;
for elementary school teachers, $1,788. Yet clerical salaries had never been high,
so it was hard to say that the low pay evidenced decline.[91]

---

88. Bledstein, *Culture of Professionalism,* pp. 85-88; E. Brooks Holifield, *A History of Pastoral
Care in America: From Salvation to Self-Realization* (Nashville: Abingdon Press, 1983), pp. 184-209.

89. H. K. Carroll, "The Pay of Preachers," *The Forum* 17 (1894): 751; Henry C. Potter, "Ministerial Support," *American Church Review* 43 (1884): 197; John Nicum, "Pastor's Salaries," *Lutheran Cyclopedia* (New York: Charles Scribner's Sons, 1899), p. 370; Willcox, *Pastor,* p. 62.

90. "The Calling of a Christian Minister," *The Century* 30 (1885): 491; Willcox, *Pastor,* p. 19.

91. Gaustad, "Pulpit and the Pews," p. 131; Tweedy, *Christian Work,* p. 34; May, *Profession of
the Ministry,* pp. 103, 106.

The denominations did introduce pension plans that made it possible for retired clergy to live with a measure of dignity. Lutherans in the Swedish Augustana Synod established a pension fund in 1865, ten years before industry created its first plan. In 1876 the Presbyterian Church (USA) established a relief board, which in 1906 created a pension program. Within a few years, Episcopalians and Northern and Southern Baptists moved in the same direction. Pension plans were not easy to establish. The Northern Baptists needed a pledge of $40,000 from John D. Rockefeller Sr. in 1911. The Northern Methodists began debating strategies in 1888 and put a program into place only in 1928. Some denominations resisted for decades, either for practical or for religious reasons. Opponents argued that pensions had no biblical precedent, or that they required too much bureaucracy, or that God would provide sufficient care.[92]

The ministry found it difficult to draw candidates from the upper economic levels, but this was nothing new. The directors of the American Education Society pled for support in 1892 by asserting that "more and more" of its students came from "our smaller and less thriving towns" and lacked "means of their own to pursue a regular course of education." In 1907, Charles Stelzle also concluded that most Protestant clergy came from rural areas: "the country supplies the Church with practically all her ministers." In the 1920s, Kelly found that more than half the students in 160 seminaries were the sons of ministers or farmers, that most required financial aid, and that the great majority came from rural areas. But similar reports had been heard in antebellum America.[93]

Alongside the laments were countless affirmations of reassurance that the clergy continued to occupy a position "of power, of prominence, and of trust." Ministers retained, wrote the optimists, "a high place in the best society" and even "a certain authority in matters of learning." Some claimed that they ranked "with the leaders of opinion and action" in almost every community, and that no other profession offered a better opportunity of becoming "widely and honorably known." Several believed that the ministry was more respected in America than in Europe, and there were reminders that their access to "all

92. ECLA Board of Pensions, http://www.elcabop.org/about us/history.asp; *The Christian Century* (1924): 718; http://www.materialreligion.org/documents/jan97doc.html; T. A. Stafford, *Pension Administration in the Methodist Episcopal Church* (New York: The Methodist Book Concern, 1937), pp. 12, 18; http://www.mmbb/org/engine?s=who&c=who.html; H. Leon McBeth, *The Baptist Heritage* (Nashville: Boardman, 1987), p. 655; R. Douglas Breckinridge and Lois A. Boyd, *Presbyterians and Pensions, 1717-1988* (Atlanta: John Knox, 1988).

93. *Eighteenth Annual Report of the American College and Education Society, 1892* (Boston: Rapid Printing, 1892), p. 9; Stelzle, *Institutional Church*, p. 339; Kelly, *Theological Education*, pp. 152, 154, 157.

classes of society" gave them "a large and important part in the social, industrial, and civic life."[94]

By 1890 the clerical sphere of influence was narrowing — and it is fair to see this as a sign of decline in the profession — but the great majority of clergy had never claimed to be specialists in higher education or social work. All but a few of them had defined their task as the leadership of Christian communities. And when one considers them in that role, it is hard to find evidence that the vocation suffered any decline whatsoever. Compared to the preachers of antebellum America, ministers after 1860 led churches that were more internally complex, expanded home and foreign missions, organized more innovative ministries for children and youth, and reached out more to each other in ecumenical cooperation. They continued to proclaim the gospel, administer the sacraments, and encourage the laity to serve other people. Despite the gaps in clerical education, more of them went to both college and seminary for training.

The theological paradox — the gospel of the immanent-transcendent God — complicated the criteria for making assessments. Everyone agreed that Christians — and therefore Christian ministers — were to be in the world but not of the world. So did larger churches with more extensive programs signal success, or did they represent a capitulation to worldly standards? Were the new array of social activities in the churches, the youth organizations, the softball games and gymnasiums, and the denominational bureaucracy signs of achievement, or were they dangerous marks of compromise? Was the adaptation of theology to science a sign of doctrinal laxity, or was it an appropriate response to God's immanence in the world? The paradox made it difficult to agree on a singular standard. The sense of crisis — the question of decline — continued to intrude itself. In the 1930s, the mainline churches would employ all the complex instruments of social science in order to find an answer.

94. Carroll, "Pay of Preachers," p. 741; "Calling of a Christian Minister," p. 491; Pattison, *Work,* p. 58; Tweedy, *Christian Work,* p. 39.

CHAPTER 6

Catholic Order

1861-1929

The career of James Cardinal Gibbons, the Roman Catholic Archbishop of Baltimore, exemplified the growing presence of Catholicism in American public life after the Civil War. The son of Irish immigrants, Gibbons spent his first three years in Baltimore before the family returned to Ireland, where he lived until he was eighteen. When his widowed and impoverished mother led the family back to America, he learned Latin from a local priest and in 1855 entered St. Charles College in Baltimore to study for the priesthood. Ordained in 1861, he served tiny St. Bridget's church, a congregation of mill workers on the outskirts of the city. His appointment as secretary to Archbishop Martin Spalding led to his being named in 1868 to the see of North Carolina, making him, at age thirty-four, the youngest bishop in the Catholic Church. His participation in the Vatican Council in Rome in 1870 brought him to the attention of Roman authorities. In 1872 he moved up to the see of Richmond, where he published *The Faith of Our Fathers* (1876), a book on Catholic doctrine that sold 65,000 copies in three years. In 1877, Rome made him an archbishop.[1]

His oversight of the Third Plenary Council in Baltimore in 1884 led to his being honored as the second cardinal in the American episcopate, an honor that made him a papal counselor, envoy, and elector. He traveled in the highest circles of American political life. Gibbons regularly called at the White House during Grover Cleveland's presidency, advised William McKinley on policy in the Philippines, served as a confidant for Theodore Roosevelt, and had a close

---

1. John Tracy Ellis, *The Life of James Cardinal Gibbons, Archbishop of Baltimore 1834-1921*, 2 vols. (Milwaukee: Bruce, 1951), vol. 1, pp. 3-29, 67-154.

relationship with Woodrow Wilson. The State Department sought his help with the League of Nations and his advice on international diplomacy, and the secretary of state praised him for his "patriotic service" to the nation. In 1911, on the fiftieth anniversary of his ordination, a chartered train traveled to Baltimore carrying President Taft, the vice president, the speaker of the house, members of the cabinet, justices of the Supreme Court, and members of Congress to pay tribute. He maintained his high office almost until the year of his death in 1921.[2]

Gibbons held office during a period in which the priesthood expanded from fewer than 3,000 priests in 1865 to more than 21,000 in 1920. To all outward appearances, they displayed the order and discipline of a well-trained army. The ranking prelate was the apostolic delegate, who as the representative of the pope assumed "precedence at all ecclesiastical functions." By 1908, the American church also had fifteen archbishops, each of whom oversaw a province consisting of several dioceses. They met annually to discuss church policy, but their meetings had only advisory authority. The church also had ninety-one bishops, each having supreme power within his diocese, responsible only to the pope, who had appointed them.[3]

Priests and laity were expected to receive their bishops as they would "receive the Lord Himself." Priests reminded their people of the bishop's "sublime authority" as the "representative of their Holy Father." They were to hearken to the words of the bishop "as to the words of God," and when the bishop visited their parish they were to accord him a "princely welcome." One priest encouraged marching bands, the ringing of bells, and the firing of cannons. In the largest dioceses, joyous parades with tens of thousands of cheering Catholics inaugurated a new episcopal appointment.[4]

In 1908, the ninety-one bishops supervised the work of 15,655 priests. Most of the priests — 12,513 of them — served as pastors or curates in local parishes. Each of them had a "power of order," received through ordination, enabling him to celebrate the mass and forgive sins. In these two functions the priesthood was "complete," and all other priestly activity flowed from them. The par-

---

2. John T. McGreevy, *Catholicism and American Freedom: A History* (New York: W. W. Norton, 2003), p. 123; Ellis, *Life of Gibbons,* vol. 2, pp. 110, 217, 246, 248, 285-86, 509.

3. Gerald Shaughnessy, *Has the Immigrant Kept the Faith?* (1st ed., 1925; New York: Arno Press, 1969), p. 262; Thomas F. Meehan, "The Organization of the Catholic Church in the United States," *The North American Review* 188 (1908): 691; Frederick Schulze, *A Manual of Pastoral Theology* (St. Louis: B. Herder, 1923), p. 295.

4. William Stang, *Pastoral Theology* (New York: Benziger Brothers, 1897), p. 92; Charles R. Morris, *American Catholic: The Saints and Sinners Who Built America's Most Powerful Church* (New York: Random House, 1997), pp. 165-95.

ish priests included 8,408 secular clergy, bound in obedience to the bishop, and 4,105 regular clergy, who had taken a vow not only of chastity and obedience, like the secular priests, but also of poverty. The regular priests were subject to the superiors of their orders, not to the bishops, though they could locate in a diocese only with the bishop's permission. Catholic priests constituted roughly 11 percent of the nation's clergy.[5]

Despite the appearance of order, the Catholic Church struggled with conflicting crosscurrents that swept over bishops and priests alike. In the background of the turbulence was a massive inflowing of immigrants, first from Western and then, after 1870, from Eastern and Southern Europe. This immigration shaped the course of American Catholic history for more than a century, and it created two countervailing trends. The first was an impulse toward decentralized authority, which expressed itself in affirmations of ethnic pride, conflicts between priests and bishops, tensions between regular and secular clergy, and rivalries among the bishops. The second was a push toward homogeneity, which found expression in a drive for "Americanization," an opposing push for "Romanization," an emphasis on uniform priestly formation, and an attempt to regulate and standardize even the minute details of pastoral work.

Ethnicity

Ethnic diversity created unending problems. As the immigrants arrived, the bishops continually heard requests — or demands — for priests from the homelands. Both the "territorial" parishes, which in theory embraced everyone in the neighborhoods surrounding a church, and the "national" parishes, which served Catholics of a single linguistic and cultural background, depended on clerical leadership from abroad. Between 1860 and 1880, almost 90 percent of the priests in St. Louis came from Europe or Ireland. In the diocese of Detroit in 1870, only six of eighty-nine priests were native-born Americans. In the diocese of St. Paul, Minnesota, 70 percent of the clergy between 1880 and 1930 came from Ireland or Germany. Each wave of immigrants brought its own priests, and it was no easy matter for them to work together.[6]

5. Meehan, "Organization," p. 690; Schulze, *Manual*, p. 294; Samuel L. Rogers, ed., *Religious Bodies*, 2 vols. (Washington, D.C.: Government Printing Office, 1919), vol. 1, p. 67.

6. Daniel P. O'Neill, "The Development of an American Priesthood: Archbishop John Ireland and the Saint Paul Diocesan Clergy," in *The American Catholic Religious Life: Selected Historical Essays*, ed. Joseph M. White (New York: Garland Publishing, 1988), p. 236; John Tracy Ellis, "The Formation of the American Priest: An Historical Perspective," in *The Catholic Priest in the United States: Historical Investigations*, ed. John Tracy Ellis (Collegeville: Saint John's University

By 1865, the Irish were in control. More than a third of the American priests traced their ancestry to Ireland, and in some dioceses Irish-born priests constituted more than half the Catholic clergy. In a few regions the Irish still encountered suspicion from older Catholic groups — Archbishop John J. Williams in Boston from 1866 to 1907 kept his distance from Irish priests — but the magnitude of Irish immigration elevated the Irish clergy. By 1900, 62 percent of the American bishops claimed Irish descent, and more than half of them came directly from Ireland.[7]

The Irish priests had a reputation for being ascetic and authoritarian, but they earned respect and affection for their closeness to their people. In Ireland, the church relied on voluntary support, which meant that the Irish adapted easily to the American voluntary system. This meant that the clergy shared the poverty of the Irish laity, and no great social distance separated priest and parishioner. In America, therefore, the Irish priests functioned not only as religious guides but also as advisers in ordinary matters, mediators between immigrant families and employers, local politicians, and labor bosses. They helped assimilate two generations into American society, and many of them wanted an English-speaking church, patriotic, reforming, and attuned to American values.

These ambitions brought them into conflict with the Germans, who formed the second largest immigrant group. German Catholics wanted to preserve their national language and culture, and they felt that the Irish, above all, stood in their way. In 1878, Archbishop Martin Henni in Milwaukee petitioned Rome for a German successor. The request led to a public quarrel when Irish priests lobbied unsuccessfully against the appointment of the German bishop Michael Heiss. Six years later, German priests serving national parishes in St. Louis demanded equal rights with English-speaking pastors in territorial parishes, and the issue created intense behind-the-scenes debates at the Plenary Council. Non-German bishops complained to Rome that the Germans wanted priests of their own nationality even when they were a minority in the parish.[8]

In 1886 a Milwaukee priest, Peter M. Abbelen, traveled to the Vatican to pro-

Press, 1971), p. 17; Edward Kantowicz, "Church and Neighborhood," in *Building the American Catholic Church: Parishes and Institutions*, ed. Brian C. Mitchell (New York: Garland Publishing, 1988), p. 65.

7. William L. Smith, *Irish Priests in the United States: A Vanishing Subculture* (Lanham: University Press of America, 2004), pp. 44-45; Donna Merwick, *Boston Priests, 1848-1910: A Study of Social and Intellectual Change* (Cambridge: Harvard University Press, 1973), p. x; Jay P. Dolan, *The American Catholic Experience: A History from Colonial Times to the Present* (Garden City: Doubleday, 1985), p. 143.

8. Colman J. Barry, *The Catholic Church and German Americans* (Milwaukee: Bruce, 1953), pp. 50, 59, 60.

test against the Irish bishops. He asked for German priests in German parishes and a German vicar-general in every diocese with a large German population. Two Irish-American bishops promptly went to Rome to oppose "special rights" for the Germans. The next year, German priests in America organized an association to lobby for more German bishops and protect the rights of German-speaking parishes, and within a year nine hundred priests and bishops joined.[9]

In 1891, the St. Raphael's Association — a European group formed by the German layman Simon Peter Paul Cahensly — presented Pope Leo XIII with the Lucerne Memorial, which urged that each national group in America be allowed to have its own priests and bishops. Cahensly also wanted separate parochial schools, more German bishops, and equal rights for all priests. He claimed that neglect of immigrants who did not speak English had resulted in the loss of ten million souls to the Protestants. English-speaking bishops, led by the Irish, decried such "impudence" and foreign interference, which they attributed to the "plots and intrigues" of a German-American "clique." They worried that permanent ethnic parishes would cast Catholics as members of a "foreign church."[10]

By that time, the arrival of Polish priests had further complicated matters. They had begun to arrive before the Civil War, but it was the Polish influx after 1880 — which created a Polish-American community of three million by 1920 — that brought the Polish clergy into the conflict. In the early Polish-American neighborhoods, the priest embodied religion, language, and national culture: "He told us what a Pole is and who the Polish people are," wrote one layman. Polish immigrants wanted their own priests. They fretted about shortages and worried that "we will have no one to turn to." Such fears led in 1886 to the founding of an ethnic seminary in Detroit devoted solely to the formation of priests for Polish-American congregations.[11]

By 1900, Poles established 517 national churches in America, some of them massive in size and complexity. The parish of St. Stanislaus Kostka in Chicago had 45,000 members and an array of institutions that provided cradle-to-grave care. These churches required Polish priests, and the priests — or at least many of them — wanted Polish bishops. Both the Irish and the Germans resisted those desires.[12]

---

9. Barry, *German Americans*, pp. 80, 101; Ellis, *Gibbons*, p. 347; John Tracy Ellis, *Essays in Seminary Education* (Notre Dame: Fides, 1967), p. 142.

10. John Tracy Ellis, ed., *Documents of American Catholic History* (Milwaukee: Bruce, 1956), pp. 497-98; Barry, *German Americans*, pp. 136, 138, 160.

11. Anthony J. Kuzniewski, S.J., "The Catholic Church in the Life of the Polish Americans," in *A Church of Many Cultures: Selected Historical Essays on Ethnic American Catholicism* (New York: Garland Publishing, 1988), pp. 279, 282.

12. Kuzniewski, "Polish Americans," p. 403.

The crusade for "equality" divided the Polish clergy. The Association of Polish Roman Catholic priests, founded in 1875, called for a bishop who could be a national leader for American Polish Catholics. By 1890, priests were sending petitions and delegations to Rome. Even the government of Poland tried to intervene, prompting Irish and German bishops to decry foreign interference. But the founders of the association, especially the leaders of the largest Polish religious order, the Resurrectionists, then decided not to antagonize the largely German and Irish hierarchy. In reaction, diocesan priests created in 1902 the Secular Priests Society, which excluded the Resurrectionists.[13]

By 1907, frustration with the leadership of the American church produced a separatist Polish National Catholic Church, which attracted about 5 percent of the Polish laity. By then the archbishop in Chicago recognized the need for a Polish auxiliary bishop, and he asked the city's Polish priests for nominations. In 1908 Paul Rhode became the first Polish-American bishop. His appointment did not end the tensions. Cardinal Archbishop George Mundelein in Chicago, who soon became the dominant voice in American Catholicism, let it be known in the years following World War I that he did not approve of Polish American bishops.[14]

Like the Poles, the Italian clergy had to contend with both cultural condescension and immigrant dissatisfaction with territorial parishes. At the urging of Rome, the 1884 Third Plenary Council sought a solution to the "Italian Problem," but some of the bishops took offense at the implication that they had been neglectful, and the council did little more than urge zealous, moral, and educated Italian clergy to come to America. Learned Italian priests were not eager to come.[15]

In America the Italian priests endured virulent, sometimes violent, anticlericalism from Italian nationalists, who despised the pope's resistance to a unified Italy. They suffered, in addition, disdain from other American Catholics, who scorned the processions, prostrations, and festivals of southern Italian immigrants and looked askance at their propensity for amulets, potions, and spells to ward off evil spirits. And the mostly southern Italian immigrant peasants had little use for northern Italian clergy. Italian bishop Giovanni

13. Gerald P. Fogarty, "The Parish and Community in American Catholic History," in *Building the American Catholic City*, pp. 21-22; William Galush, "Both Polish and Catholic: Immigrant Clergy in the American Church," in *Church of Many Cultures*, pp. 266-67.

14. Galush, "Polish and Catholic," p. 275; Kuzniewski, "Polish Americans," p. 286; Earl Boyea, "Father Kalasinski and the Church of Detroit," *Catholic Historical Review* 74 (1988): 420-21.

15. Rudolf J. Vecoli, "Prelates and Peasants: Italian Immigrants and the Catholic Church," *Journal of Social History* 2 (1969): 243.

Scalabrini formed in 1888 an order of immigrant priests, but few ventured to America. "Above all we have need of Italian priests," wrote one pastor in 1913; "this is the general lament." In 1918, only 710 Italian priests were available to serve over three million Italian Americans, who mostly stayed out of the churches.[16]

The demands of Italians for their own priests and bishops alienated the hierarchy, and it became a frequent refrain that Italy sent its clerical misfits to America. The more established immigrant clergy complained that Italian laity disrespected priests and failed to support financially even their own Italian American pastors. In turn, Italian priests resented the local pastor's relegating their worship services to the basement of the parish church, and the laity felt aggrieved when bishops assigned them non-Italian priests. They also resented the patronizing air of German and Irish priests and bishops.[17]

The tiny company of African American priests struggled against familiar forms of discrimination. In 1902 only six black priests served the church in the United States, and the Superior General of the Josephite Order — an English Order with a mission to African Americans — condemned the resistance of the clergy to the ordination of blacks. To serve as a black priest was no easy path. John Henry Dorsey, for instance, was ordained in 1902 as a priest of the order. Assigned to Arkansas, he met with hostility from the rector of his parish, the bishop, and the Sisters of the Holy Family, who did not want to receive communion from him. The Josephites tried to send him to San Antonio, but the bishop there refused, as did the bishop in Montgomery. For eight years, Dorsey conducted preaching missions, mainly to black congregations in the South, but he ended up in a bedraggled parish in Baltimore that could pay him only three dollars a week.[18]

By 1880 the church was trying to absorb Catholics from Austria-Hungary, Switzerland, Poland, Italy, Bohemia, Slovakia, Lithuania, Portugal, Ruthenia, Slovenia, Syria, Belgium, Croatia, Holland, Mexico, Romania, and South America. Most of them wanted to form homogeneous national parishes with priests who spoke their language, and by 1916 the church had 2,230 parishes that worshipped only in languages other than English and 6,076 that used English alongside other languages. This left 11,411 predominantly English-speaking parishes, but the size of some of the ethnic parishes meant that almost half of

16. Vecoli, "Prelates and Peasants," pp. 217-68, 247.

17. Vecoli, "Priests and Peasants," pp. 238, 240; Fogarty, "Parish and Community," p. 251; Robert Orsi, *The Madonna of 115th Street: Faith and Community in Italian Harlem, 1880-1950* (New Haven: Yale University Press, 1985), pp. 83-85.

18. Stephen J. Ochs, "The Ordeal of the Black Priest," in *American Catholic Religious Life*, pp. 255-73.

American Catholics worshiped with a language other than English. Catholics conducted services in at least twenty-seven languages. In the long run, the Catholic priests helped assimilate the immigrants, but in the short term the tensions kept the clergy divided.[19]

Every impasse led to an appeal to Rome, and both the Congregation of Propaganda and the papacy felt obliged — and often eager — to intervene. The Holy See convoked the 1884 plenary council, despite the reluctance of some American bishops, partly to compel the Americans to resolve the ethnic issues. Leo XIII let it be known that he did not like the contention every time he appointed a new bishop. In 1892 he sent to America, despite the opposition of most bishops, a permanent apostolic delegate, Francesco Satolli, partly to put an end to ethnic and other controversies, but within two years Satolli was embroiled in tensions between the Irish and the Germans. Because the ethnic strife continually pulled the Vatican into American struggles, it contributed to impulses toward Romanization in the American church.[20]

The Rights of Priests

The Vatican had other reasons to worry. It worried about tensions between bishops and priests in America. Strife about priests' rights after the Civil War caused some priests to complain of "slavery" and one prelate to lament that "the last thing a sensible man ought to desire is to be a bishop, at least in the United States." Even before the war ended, the lay theologian Orestes Brownson complained that in America — which was a mission field, not yet subject to canon law — each bishop was "well-nigh absolute in his own diocese." The freedom and welfare of the priests, he said, had "no security but in the will and conscience of the bishop."[21]

In New York, a group of priests calling themselves the Accademia illustrated the dissatisfaction. The group lasted less than a year after its formation in 1865, but they continued to meet informally and to raise dangerous questions. They took political positions, defended public schools, opposed the temporal power of the pope, and entertained cautious doubts about scriptural inerrancy,

19. Shaughnessy, *Has the Immigrant Kept the Faith?* p. 220; Roger Finke and Rodney Stark, *The Churching of America 1776-1990* (New Brunswick: Rutgers University Press, 1992), p. 127.

20. Barry, *German Americans*, p. 207.

21. Gerald P. Fogarty, S.J., *The Vatican and the American Hierarchy from 1870 to 1965* (Wilmington: Michael Glazier, 1985), p. 29; Ellis, *Gibbons*, vol. 2, p. 153; Orestes Brownson, "The Church Not a Despotism," in *The Works of Orestes Brownson*, 20 vols. (Detroit: T. Nourse, 1882-87), vol. 20, p. 240.

papal infallibility, and clerical celibacy. They disliked the fact that that bishops could prohibit their wearing beards or compel them to wear Roman collars, and they objected to all the other arbitrary powers of bishops as well. Such questioning was not limited to New York. In 1862, priests in Cleveland protested against arbitrary episcopal power, and they received signs of support from across the nation.[22]

In response to such complaints, Bishop Francis Patrick Kenrick of Philadelphia proposed that the American church grant some priests "immovability." After a priest served ten years in a parish, a bishop would not move him against his consent or remove him without a canonical cause and procedure. The Second Plenary Council in 1866 decided instead that when priests protested a move, bishops should consult with advisers. But the bishops would choose the advisers. An unhappy priest could still appeal to the archbishop and then to Rome, but so could the bishop. The decision did not produce universal happiness.[23]

In 1868 the editor of the *New York Freeman's Journal,* James McMaster, began publishing rabble-rousing stories about the misuse of episcopal authority. He also printed letters from priests urging their colleagues to unite against the arbitrary decisions of bishops and pleading with bishops to follow canon law, even though it did not apply in America. When local priests began to call meetings to seek due process in clerical trials and to secure immovability for some pastors, McMaster claimed that at least a thousand priests, a third of the nation's Catholic clergy, supported the cause. It was at least true that a thousand of them subscribed to his paper and even more read it.[24]

The canonist Sebastian B. Smith, a priest in Newark, heightened tensions when he published his *Notes on the Second Plenary Council of Baltimore* (1874), in which he argued that the bishops failed even to follow the council's injunction to consult. Priestly councils existed "merely in name." Four years later, when the Vatican asked the Irish bishop George Conroy to assess the matter, he reported "ever increasing discord between the bishops and the priests." The bishops insisted that they needed authority to move priests at will in order to deal with priestly misbehavior. The Vatican agreed, but its 1878 *Instructio* on clerical discipline stipulated that in disputes over removals, bishops had to

---

22. Robert Emmett Curran, "Prelude to 'Americanism': The New York Accademia and Clerical Radicalism in the Late-Nineteenth Century City," in *American Catholic Religious Life,* pp. 164, 165, 170.

23. Sebastian Bach Smith, *Notes on the Second Plenary Council of Baltimore* (New York: O'Shea, 1874), pp. 367-70, 384; Robert Trisco, "Bishops and their Priests in the United States," in *Catholic Priest in the United States,* p. 141; Fogarty, *Vatican and American Hierarchy,* p. 15.

24. Trisco, "Bishops and their Priests," pp. 157-58, 175-76.

appoint an investigating commission. The requirement displeased the bishops, so Rome conceded that the commission would merely consult.[25]

By that time, some of the bishops were warning priests not to publicize their "real or imaginary grievances" against bishops. Bishop Joseph Baltes in Illinois reminded his priests that he had "the power, and the will, and the determination" to punish anyone who disobeyed. As for rights, priests had the right to do "the work of the ministry for the salvation of souls, entirely according to the direction and under the jurisdiction of the Bishop," whom they had promised "forever [to] serve and obey." Baltes added that the bishops had "not sinned near as much by permanently removing clergymen from missions, as they have by closing their eyes to the faults of unworthy priests, and leaving them in charge of souls."[26]

The priests' rights movement continued to press for American adherence to canon law, which made provision for immovable priests. In *The Rights of Priests Vindicated; or a Plea for Canon Law in the United States* (1883), William Mahoney, a priest in Wisconsin, claimed that a bishop was obliged to support even "an erring priest" if the offender expressed true penitence. The bishops reacted angrily to the book, and the Catholic historian John Gilmary Shea supported them. Since America had no canonical parishes, a bishop could appoint or remove priests "at his discretion." He "must have the power to remove a priest who is not able to manage affairs for the good of the parish."[27]

The bishops who gathered, somewhat reluctantly, for the Third Plenary Council in 1884 agreed, under pressure, to grant tenure to a limited number of priests who had served ten years in a parish, passed a competitive examination, and had the support of their bishop. Ten percent of the pastors in a diocese would be irremovable without due process. The bishops also agreed to accept "consultors" to provide advice in conflicted decisions. They concluded the council with a carefully worded recognition of "the rights and interests" of "all ranks of the clergy in this country."[28]

The decisions represented a compromise, and the activist priests soon found it lacking. In 1887, Richard Burtsell, a New York priest who was respected

25. Smith, *Notes on the Second Plenary Council*, p. 66; Trisco, "Bishops and Their Priests," pp. 193, 198, 201, 204.

26. Peter Joseph Baltes, *Pastoral Instruction of the Bishop of Alton to the Clergy, Secular and Regular* (Alton: Perrin and Smith, 1879), pp. 19, 21, 48.

27. Trisco, "Bishops and their Priests," pp. 208, 224; John Gilmary Shea, "The Coming Plenary Council of Baltimore," *The American Catholic Quarterly Review* 9 (1884): 352.

28. *Pastoral Letter of the Archbishops and Bishops of the United States Assembled in the Third Plenary Council of Baltimore* (Baltimore: Baltimore Publishing, 1884), p. 12; Trisco, "Bishops and their Priests," p. 250.

for his knowledge of canon law, published *The Canonical Status of Priests in the United States*. He argued that canon law applied to America, that it forbade bishops to remove priests without a reasonable cause and a just process, and that all priests had a right of appeal to Rome. The archbishop of New York, Michael Corrigan, tried to stop circulation of the book and transferred its author to a rural mission.[29]

By that time, Corrigan stood in the middle of the most contentious dispute over priests' rights in nineteenth-century America. Father Edward McGlynn, pastor of the largest church in New York City, St. Stephen's, had disturbed Corrigan by criticizing parochial schools, commending the labor movement, and campaigning for Henry George as mayor of New York on a platform that Corrigan considered socialist. McGlynn even contended that priests received their power not through the bishop but through the people. In 1887, Corrigan forbade him to speak at political rallies, and when McGlynn disobeyed, the archbishop suspended him, prompting 75,000 people to march through the New York streets in protest.[30]

After McGlynn refused to obey a papal summons to Rome, Corrigan excommunicated him. Because the case became entangled in the rivalries of the hierarchy, the apostolic delegate eventually restored him to the church, but Corrigan displayed his irritation by assigning McGlynn to a small town in upstate New York. In the midst of such turmoil, the more conservative bishops were in no mood to expand the rights of parish priests.[31]

Twenty years later, most diocesan priests remained entirely subject to the will of the bishop. About 10 percent had "irremovable" tenure. They had passed an examination, served as priests for ten years and as pastors for five, and shown "special ability as executives, besides moral and sacerdotal zeal and worth." A bishop could expel them from their parish only for grave offenses and after due trial. Other priests could only appeal to the apostolic delegate or through him to Rome. Sometimes the appellant won, though by 1908 it was clear to everyone that "Rome is usually very slow to decide against episcopal authority."[32]

In 1908, the Vatican transferred the oversight of the American church from the Propaganda to the Sacred Consistorial Congregation. America was no longer

---

29. Richard L. Burtsell, *The Canonical Status of Priests in the United States* (New York: n.p., 1889), pp. 11, 13, 37, 45-53; Trisco, "Bishops and Their Priests," pp. 252-53, 257-58.

30. Robert Emmett Curran, S.J., "The McGlynn Affair and the Shaping of the New Conservatism in Ameican Catholicism," in *American Catholic Religious Life*, pp. 183-184; Curran, "Prelude," p. 175.

31. Curran, "Prelude," p. 188; Curran, "McGlynn Affair," p. 201.

32. Meehan, "Organization," pp. 91, 94.

a mission field. But the Congregation's new stipulations diminished the security of immovable priests and left the status of movable ones unchanged. When the Americans finally came under the Code of Canon Law in 1918, every priest gained the right to due process, and bishops could transfer irremovable pastors only with Rome's approval, but 90 percent of the priests — the movable ones — could be transferred rather easily.[33]

The activists wanted more than due process. They wanted priests to have a stronger voice in the selection of bishops. The current practice was for bishops to nominate new prelates, with the final decision made in Rome. Conroy reported that many of the priests saw the process as secretive and partisan, and he added that it produced a mediocre episcopate. Nominees, he said, sometimes looked more like bankers than pastors. The clergy had begun "to lose the respect due the episcopacy."[34]

Some priests wanted to elect their own bishops; a larger number wanted the right to submit nominations. In 1883, Patrick Corrigan, a pastor in New Jersey, published a provocative book on *Episcopal Nominations*, arguing that the current system failed to give the church "the best men" and that pastors should be able to submit the names of nominees to Rome. He was confident that they would select bishops "with piety and learning, prudence and tact." His bishop ordered him to halt publication and suspended him when he refused, but the suspension aroused widespread protest, and the topic appeared on the agenda of the 1884 Third Plenary Council.[35]

The council sought a compromise. It determined that a select group of priests — those with ten years of experience at the head of a parish — could submit names to Rome alongside the names submitted by the bishops. Bishop John Spalding feared that the laity would demand similar rights, but for three decades the practice seemed to work. Priests felt that they had a voice. Yet by 1916 critics were complaining that the process took too long and that the names of nominees too frequently became public, so the Vatican returned the privilege of nomination to the bishops, insisting only that they consult trusted clergy. Canon law confirmed this procedure, while it also gave bishops alone the right to choose their "consulters."[36]

The bishops had to contend not only with rebellious diocesan priests but also with clerics in the orders. By 1908, forty-three orders of men and 109 orders of women lived in the United States, and they sometimes coexisted uneasily

33. Trisco, "Bishops and Their Priests," pp. 269-70.

34. Trisco, "Bishops and Their Priests," pp. 269-70.

35. Patrick Corrigan, *Episcopal Nominations* (New York: Sullivan and Schaefer, 1883), pp. 33, 34; Trisco, "Bishops and Their Priests," pp. 214-16, 222.

36. Trisco, "Bishops and Their Priests," pp. 245, 268; Mehan, "Organization," p. 691.

with diocesan authorities. The disputes were mainly administrative and financial. Who had jurisdiction within a diocesan area? In whom should the title to church property be vested? When Richard Gilmour, the bishop in Cleveland, urged Cardinal Gibbons to "defend the Bishops against the Religious," he was trying to protect the authority of bishops over the funds contributed in their dioceses. But bishops also worried when churches established by the orders seemed to compete with diocesan churches. And lines of jurisdiction were unclear. When a regular priest served in a diocesan parish — as many did — he was subject to the bishop in parochial matters but also subject to the superior of the order.[37]

Bishops disliked it when orders claimed sole authority over schools, monasteries, and churches in a diocese. As a result, some bishops tried to avoid appointing regular priests to parishes. Bishop John Ireland in St. Paul intentionally reduced the proportion of regular priests in his diocese from 25 percent to 16 percent by 1918, though in some dioceses 40 to 50 percent of the parish clergy came from religious orders.[38]

The secular priests often sympathized with the bishops. They sometimes complained that regulars saw themselves as superior — a resentment fed by occasional lapses in diplomacy. The Jesuit Provincial of New York allegedly said, during a dispute over the Catholic University of America, that the diocesan clergy "were not intended to be an educated Clergy or at least a learned and erudite body" with the ability to run a university. One diocesan priest, on the other hand, wrote that in America the secular priest had risen to power while the religious orders showed that they belonged to "the aristocratic Old World." In addition, the more liberal secular clergy looked upon conservative orders like the Jesuits as people of "cramped minds" who wanted to "fossilize us with the habits of the middle ages."[39]

---

37. Mehan, "Organization," p. 696; Gerald P. Fogarty, "The Bishops versus the Religious Orders: The Suppressed Decrees of the Third Plenary Council of Baltimore," in *American Catholic Religious Life*, p. 157; John P. Marschall, "Diocesan and Religious Clergy: The History of a Relationship, 1789-1969," in *Catholic Priest in the United States*, p. 392.

38. Marschall, "Diocesan and Religious Clergy," p. 392; O'Neill, "Development," pp. 250-51.

39. Ellis, *Seminary Education*, p. 239; John Talbot Smith, *The Training of a Priest: An Essay on Clerical Education* (New York: Longmans Gree, 1908), p. 9; Richard L. Burtsell, *The Diary of Richard L. Burtsell, Priest of New York: The Early Years, 1865-1868*, ed. Nelson J. Callahan (New York: Arno Press, 1978), p. 100.

Liberals, Conservatives, and Rome

After 1884, all of these debates over clerical authority occurred in the shadow of the great struggle between liberals and conservatives. The distinction between the two groups emerged in the course of disputes over ethnicity, education, the state, ecumenical relations, and social reform. Their conflicts created turmoil for fifteen years, and the clergy sometimes defined themselves by their allegiance to one party or the other. The division resulted from a drive for the "Americanization" of the church; it had the ironic result of accelerating the impulse toward "Romanization."

The liberals were no doctrinal innovators; their chief aim was to adapt the church to American institutions and ideals, shedding its aura of "foreignness." The "Americanist" bishops, led by John Ireland in St. Paul, wanted immigrant Catholics to learn English and integrate themselves into American culture. They were unsympathetic to ethnic groups that wanted to remain in linguistic enclaves. Even while supporting parochial schools, they defended the public school system and agreed that the state had an obligation to educate its citizens, including Catholics unable to attend a parish school. Ireland tried to negotiate innovative forms of cooperation between public and parochial schools. The liberals also organized the Catholic University of America for the graduate education of priests who could make a difference in the nation's higher culture.

The Americanists were never fully of one mind, but they shared a conviction that democratic American culture would prove to be hospitable to the Catholic Church. At a time when Catholic teaching dictated that Catholics avoid religious activities with non-Catholics, they shared speaking platforms with Protestants, lectured at places like Harvard, and interpreted Catholic faith at the 1893 World Parliament of Religions. At a time when the Vatican forbade Catholics to join secret societies, they defended Catholic membership in labor unions like the Knights of Labor despite their penchant for secrecy. Some of them sympathized with McGlynn in his battle with Corrigan. They praised the separation of church and state. In the eyes of their conservative opponents, they accommodated Catholic truth to American ideals.[40]

The conflicts drew the Vatican more deeply into American Catholic culture. Pope Leo XIII sometimes favored the liberals: he supported the Catholic University of America, agreed to tolerate the Knights of Labor, and accepted the liberal openness to public schooling. Sometimes he favored the conservatives: he condemned several secret societies, removed the liberal Denis O'Connell from his position as rector of the American College in Rome, and asked for the

40. Fogarty, *Vatican and the American Hierarchy*, pp. 27-194.

resignation of the liberal John Keane from the presidency of Catholic University. In 1895, he declared it an error to teach that "in America is to be sought the type of the most desirable status of the Church" or that the state had no responsibility to support the church. In 1899, he condemned what he saw as certain dangerous features of "Americanism," and he later forbade Catholic clerics to participate in interfaith events.[41]

Leo XIII was acting in accord with a trend toward Roman centralization, and he took more initiative than earlier popes in the appointment of American bishops. In 1901, he rejected all the American nominees and named William O'Connell as the Bishop of Portland. Five years later, Pius X (1903-1910) appointed O'Connell to Boston, again ignoring both the bishops and the priests in order to elevate a prelate who said that he "stood for Rome, for Roman views, and for Roman sympathies." By 1908 it was a truism to say that each bishop was "responsible only to Rome," and Pope Benedict XV (1914-22) expanded the authority of the apostolic delegate in the naming of American bishops. Benedict tended to appoint bishops who had been trained in Rome.[42]

Papal initiatives extended into local parishes. Pius IX encouraged a vernacular piety that popularized devotion to the Immaculate Conception of Mary, the Sacred Heart of Jesus, the Forty Hours Devotion to the body and blood of Jesus, and the benediction of the Blessed Sacrament. The bishops praised these devotions and supported the formation of local societies — confraternities or sodalities — that nurtured a piety responsive to Roman preferences. Rome also kept watch over local priests. In 1907 Pius X condemned "modernism" — calling a halt to a trend in Catholic theology to recognize biblical criticism, historical development, and an anti-dogmatic view of belief — and by 1910 all candidates for ordination had to sign an oath against modernism. The condemnation redirected the creative energies of the clergy toward social and political problems, for theological and philosophical innovation was now off-limits.[43]

41. Fogarty, *Vatican and the American Hierarchy,* p. 137; Pope Leo XIII, *Longinqua Oceani,* in *The Papal Encyclicals,* ed. Claudia Carlen, 5 vols. (Raleigh: McGrath, 1981), vol. 2, pp. 363-69; Pope Leo XIII, *Testem Benevolentiae,* in *Documents,* p. 542; Ellis, "Formation of the American Priest," p. 57.

42. Fogarty, *Vatican and the American Hierarchy,* pp. 196, 201, 220; Mehan, "Organization," p. 692; James Gaffey, "The Changing of the Guard: The Rise of Cardinal O'Connell in Boston," *Catholic Historical Review* 59 (1973): 226, 237.

43. Ann Taves, *The Household of Faith: Roman Catholic Devotions in Mid-Nineteenth Century America* (Notre Dame: University of Notre Dame Press, 1986), pp. 21-45; Dolan, *American Catholic Experience,* pp. 209-14; S. B. Smith, *Notes on the Second Plenary Council,* pp. 302-7; *Pastoral Letter of the Archbishops and Bishops,* p. 26; Michael V. Gannon, "Before and After Modernism: The Intellectual Isolation of the Catholic Priest," in *Catholic Priest in the United States,* p. 337.

The best and brightest candidates for priesthood increasingly received some of their training in Rome. The term "magisterium," referring to the teaching office of the church, had typically included bishops and theological faculties. It now began more often to designate the views of the Vatican's administrative departments or the words of the pope. The directives of the Vatican established daily devotional routines for the priesthood and governed the details of clerical dress. Rome would play a large role in the effort to standardize the work of the parish priest.[44]

Forming a Priesthood

The educators who sought to form the American priesthood did not share the same strategy. Some wanted to preserve national traditions, even at the sacrifice of uniform expectations. The Americanist party wanted priests who were attuned to the wider culture, able to speak its language, participate in its intellectual life, and attract its citizens. Their opponents included not only the ethnics but also conservatives who favored a program of Romanization. All three groups placed their hopes in clerical education and priestly formation, but they had different understandings of what priestly training should be.

Most saw priestly formation as beginning in the parochial school. In 1866, the bishops called for a school near every parish, and in 1884 they mandated a school in every parish within two years. The goal was too ambitious, but by 1900 more than 3,800 parishes — close to 37 percent of the total — had schools, a figure that remained stable for the next twenty years. Their aim was to provide secular and religious education for every Catholic child, but their advocates also saw them as the first step in the education of future priests.[45]

The pastor was supposed to assume "immediate supervision" of the school, and most pastors complied, but more often the *de facto* principals were women — members of such religious orders as the Sisters of Mercy, the Sisters of Charity, and the Visitation Sisters. During the nineteenth century, more than 250 communities of sisters established themselves in the United States, and by the

44. Clyde F. Crews, "American Catholic Authoritarianism: The Episcopacy of William George McCloskey, 1868-1909," *Catholic Historical Review* 70 (1984): 561-62; Joseph M. White, *The Diocesan Seminary in the United States: A History from the 1780s to the Present* (Notre Dame: University of Notre Dame Press, 1989), p. 161.

45. Patricia Byrne, "In the Parish But Not Of It: Sisters," in *Transforming Parish Ministry: The Changing Roles of Catholic Clergy, Laity, and Women Religious,* ed. Jay P. Dolan (New York: Crossroad, 1990), p. 116; Daniel Murphy, *A History of Irish Emigrant and Missionary Education* (Portland: Four Courts Press, 2000), p. 236.

end of the era they outnumbered priests by a ratio of four to one. The manuals for priests recognized that their "indefatigable labors" accounted for the church's success in maintaining hospitals, colleges, asylums, and academies, but their chief service came in the schools, which survived only because sisters staffed them at minimal expense. This meant that women religious were often the people who identified and nurtured the boys who showed promise as future priests.[46]

For other young men, the men's college was the first serious experience of formation in a religious setting. By 1896 the church had 120 colleges, most of them under the control of the religious orders. The Jesuits administered twenty-five, the Christian Brothers fifteen, and the Benedictines ten, with other orders and secular clergy in charge of the rest. The colleges conveyed "the outlines of Latin, Greek, and English literature," and the bishops supported them in part because they prepared future priests. They believed that the discipline of the colleges made them superior settings for inculcating moral and religious culture.[47]

The most intense formation came in the seminary. In 1868 Catholics had fifty institutions, enrolling 913 students. By 1900 they had 109 seminaries; the thirty schools that trained secular priests had 2,630 students, while the seventy-nine houses of study for the regular clergy had 1,998. By that time, some Catholic educators disliked the proliferation of small seminaries in almost every diocese and called for a few well-financed and well-staffed schools, but bishops were intent on maintaining the local character of the oversight and training. Only St. Mary's in Baltimore could make a credible claim as a national seminary.[48]

The Third Plenary Council decided that the optimal sequence of training required attendance at both a minor and a major seminary. They first took boys of around the age of twelve and kept them five or six years, teaching them some of the subjects normally taught in the men's colleges, especially Latin, while also exposing them to spiritual disciplines and giving them duties in nearby churches. The major, or higher, seminary — which included the final years of training known as the "theologate" — provided six more years of study, exposing students to courses in scripture, moral theology, dogmatic theology, and history, as well as forming them in the spiritual life. In some dioceses, half or more of the priests had attended both a minor and a major seminary.[49]

The teachers had at least two visions of seminary education, and the students

---

46. Mary Ewens, "The Leadership of Nuns in Immigrant Catholicism," in *American Catholic Religious Life*, p. 14; Stang, *Pastoral Theology*, p. 239; Schulze, *Manual*, p. 406.

47. Smith, *Training of a Priest*, pp. 26, 32-33.

48. Ellis, *Seminary Education*, p. 86; Smith, *Training of a Priest*, p. 51; S. B. Smith, *Notes on the Second Plenary Council*, p. 138.

49. Smith, *Training of a Priest*, pp. xxvi, xxvii; Ellis, "Formation," p. 46.

sometimes had their own aims. A visiting committee at St. Mary's in Baltimore in 1874 noticed that the students "attached importance to what they thought to be immediately useful in the ministry" and lacked a love for knowledge. Thirty years later, a similar committee reported that students there applied themselves to matters "practically useful for the needs of the ministry" but lacked intellectual curiosity. The faculties had broader goals. The majority favored a program of formation through the regulation of the daily schedule from morning to bedtime, mandating daily worship, prayer, and silence, supplemented by the learning of doctrinal and moral truths through the use of authorized manuals. Reformers promoted a more "professional" model, envisioning priests with a liberal arts education, a discerning appreciation of theological tradition, and competence in professional skills as well as spiritual disciplines.[50]

At St. Joseph's in New York, students could leave the seminary grounds only with permission. They rose around 5:00 A.M. and gathered for morning prayer, followed by meditation. It was customary to attend mass before breakfast, listen to sacred readings during the noon meal, and gather for evening prayers before supper. Six or seven times a day the advanced students read the prayers and texts of the *Breviary,* a discipline they would be expected to follow for the rest of their lives. Once a week they went to confession. In most seminaries, visiting the Blessed Sacrament, periods of silence, recitation of the rosary, and spiritual reading punctuated each day. Students normally wore the cassock wherever they went. In Sulpician seminaries especially, the watchword was the virtue of "docility."[51]

By 1884 reformers were intent on requiring wider reading and emphasizing professional skills. They wanted to expose students to new ideas in natural science and history, broaden their views of philosophy, expand scriptural studies, and attend more to preaching. Adopting a theme that had resonated for decades in Protestant circles, John Talbot Smith, a teacher in New York, explained in *The Training of a Priest* (1896) that the cleric of the future needed to be a "gentleman to his finger-ends," learned in scripture and philosophy, adept in singing, public speaking, and preaching, and knowledgeable about fundraising and the laws of church incorporation. Others suggested that seminaries link up with parishes in which students could preach, instruct children, visit, and learn other skills of ministry.[52]

50. White, *Diocesan Seminary,* pp. 143, 145-64, 254.

51. White, *Diocesan Seminary,* pp. 122-30; Robert E. Sullivan, "Beneficial Relations: Toward a Social History of the Diocesan Priests of Boston, 1875-1944," in *American Catholic Religious Life,* pp. 221-22.

52. M. Heiss, *A Plan of Studies for the Direction of Those Institutions Which Educate Youth for the Priesthood* (Baltimore: s.n., 1886), pp. 14-21; Bernard Feeney, "The Seminarist Instructed

When James Cardinal Gibbons published *The Ambassador of Christ* (1896), he explained that the "essential office" of the priest was, as always, sacramental, but that the priesthood was also "pre-eminently one of the learned professions." He assumed that any good priest would recite the *Breviary,* visit the Blessed Sacrament, and engage in spiritual reading and meditation every day, but he also cautioned that piety, "though indispensable, can never be an adequate substitute for learning." Piety without knowledge made a priest an "unprofitable servant." The book wove competing strands of thought about priesthood and clerical education, but no one could have missed the emphasis on priestly learning and skill.[53]

The advocates of a more professional priesthood founded journals intended to deepen the work of the clergy. The *American Catholic Quarterly Review* published theology; the *American Ecclesiastical Review* (1889) addressed itself to "working priests." The *Catholic University Bulletin* (1895) reached mainly college and university educators, while the *Homiletic Monthly and Catechist* (1900) offered advice about preaching and catechesis. The Jesuit journal *America* (1909) treated both theological and social topics, while the *Catholic Historical Review* (1915) disseminated knowledge of church history. The governing assumption was that the clergy wanted and needed a more sophisticated understanding of their duties and their traditions.

The seminary alone could not carry the full weight of the change that the reformers wanted. John Lancaster Spalding acknowledged in 1884 that the seminary was "not a school of intellectual culture": "Its methods are not such as one would choose who desires to open the mind, to give it breadth, flexibility, strength, refinement, and grace." But Spalding wanted a priestly elite who could help Catholic theology "come forth from its isolation in the modern world." He agreed with others who wanted priests more aware of "the questions of the day," with knowledge of politics, science, history, and literature that would make them leaders "in the modern parish."[54]

Spalding wanted to supplement seminary education — for a select few — with advanced study at a Catholic university, a graduate school for priests. His proposal created controversy, partly because some of the religious orders

---

in Preaching, Catechizing, and Pastoral Visitation," *The Ecclesiastical Review* 45 (1871): 154, 115-64; John Hogan, *Clerical Studies* (Boston: Marler, Callanan, 1898), pp. 2, 15, 21, 139, 197; Smith, *Training of a Priest,* pp. 86, 184-94, 240-41.

53. James Cardinal Gibbons, *The Ambassador of Christ* (Baltimore: John Murphy, 1896), pp. 2, 12, 169, 171.

54. John L. Spalding, "University Education," in *A History of the Third Plenary Council of Baltimore* (Baltimore: Baltimore Publishing, 1885), pp. 92-94; Smith, *Training of a Priest,* pp. 250-52.

assumed that only they could create a strong institution and partly because Bishop Corrigan in New York had plans for a Jesuit university in his diocese. But in 1889 a determined group of bishops, mainly Americanists, succeeded in founding the Catholic University of America as a graduate school of theology.[55]

Papal directives, however, elevated the ideal of spiritual formation over the ambition for professional attainment. The *Testem Benevolentiae* (1899) of Pope Leo XIII called for greater reverence for the "supernatural," and his encyclicals on Marian piety encouraged greater use of the rosary by priests and laity. When Pius X launched the Eucharistic movement in 1902, he endorsed frequent communion, and the seminaries made daily communion part of formation. After condemning theological modernism, Pius X told seminary directors to ensure that students had the "appropriate degree of sanctity," adding that "enthusiasm for learning should be kept under control." His emphasis on daily mass, meditation, and mortification left a mark on seminary training. He also forbade seminarians to read newspapers and journals. By the end of the nineteenth century the accent in the seminaries was not on professional skills, but rather on the supernatural virtues.[56]

The Parish Priest

At the beginning of the twentieth century, the lines of authority in Catholic ministry were fixed and visible. The Polish American priest Vincent Barzynski offered a familiar description of clerical authority: "If you desire to work in the name of God, pay heed to the words of Christ, because God the Father gave us only one Christ; if you wish to labor for Christ, then listen to Peter, for Christ gave us only one Peter; if you want to work in Peter's name, obey the Pope, because he is the only true successor to the first Pope; if you wish to work in the Pope's name, obey the bishop, because only the bishop rules the diocese; if you wish to obey the bishop, then you must obey your pastor, for the bishop gave you only one pastor."[57]

Within the parish, the pastor ruled. In a few dioceses — the Diocese of Detroit, for example — the majority of pastors assumed the office immediately upon ordination, but in the large Eastern parishes, priests spent ten to fifteen years as curates, or assistants, before they received an appointment as pastors;

---

55. Gannon, "Before and After Modernism," p. 322.

56. Pope Pius X, *Haerent Animo*, in *Clergy and Laity*, ed. Odile M. Liebard (Wilmington: McGrath, 1978), pp. 23, 25; White, *Diocesan Seminary*, pp. 224, 225, 235, 263, 267.

57. Joseph John Parot, *Polish Catholics in Chicago 1850-1920* (DeKalb: Northern Illinois University Press, 1981), p. 124.

many had to wait more than twenty years. As curates, they were entirely subject to the demands of the pastors, who reported to the bishop on their conduct. The desire of almost every curate was to receive an assignment as pastor. Once in place, most pastors remained in a parish around ten years. Some spent their careers in one church. Larger parishes kept their pastors longer than smaller and poorer ones, which some priests looked upon as "hardship duty" while they awaited a larger church.[58]

Whether pastor or curate, the priest occupied a position above the laity. Leo XIII had spoken of two orders — the shepherds and the flock — with the first obliged to "teach and govern" and the second required "to obey, to carry out its orders, and to pay it honor." Pius X declared in 1906 that the church was "essentially an unequal society . . . comprising two categories of persons, the Pastors and the flock." The "one duty" of the laity was to "allow themselves to be led, and like a docile flock, to follow the Pastors." Priests and parishioners were no spiritual equals. "The priest is a father," wrote one American cleric. "The spiritual child has a right to be guided and instructed by its parent." Bishop John Ireland gave the metaphor a military cast: "Priests are officers, lay-men are soldiers." Gibbons described the priest as the "ambassador of Christ" who "personated" Christ to such a degree that "his official acts are Christ's acts." Pastoral guidebooks advised priests to maintain the appropriate social distance implied in such a role. It was "not advisable" for a priest to "move much in the society of lay people simply for the sake of pastime."[59]

Conscientious priests found in this elevation a demanding responsibility. They were "obliged" to live among their flocks and to be available "at any time in case of necessity." When summoned, they were to respond "without delay or hesitation." A priest was obligated to provide the sacraments "even at the risk of his life." (Occasional journal articles advised them how to preserve their health when ministering to members with contagious diseases.) And they were to perform these labors without ceasing. Some manuals insisted that they sacrifice any summer vacations. For such dedication, parishioners often felt extraordinary affection for their priests, and local histories record stirring tributes and elaborate gifts to priests who retired or moved to another parish.[60]

58. Leslie Woodcock Tentler, *Seasons of Grace: A History of the Catholic Archdiocese of Detroit* (Detroit: Wayne State University Press, 1990), p. 34; Sullivan, "Beneficial Relations," pp. 209, 225, 234; Smith, *Training of a Priest*, pp. xxix-xxx; Kantowicz, "Priest and Neighborhood," p. 72.

59. Pope Leo XIII, *Est Sane Nolestum*, in *Clergy and Laity*, p. 1; Pope Pius X, *Vehementer Nos*, in *Papal Encyclicals*, vol. 3, pp. 47-48; John Ireland, *The Church and Modern Society* (Chicago: D. H. McBride, 1897), p. 81; Dolan, *American Catholic Experience*, p. 222; Gannon, "Before and After Modernism," p. 307; Gibbons, *Ambassador of Christ*, p. 15; Schulze, *Manual*, p. 499.

60. Stang, *Pastoral Theology*, pp. 69-70; Austin O'Malley, "The Priest on Sick-Calls in Con-

The diary of Father James Anthony Walsh at St. Patrick's Church in Roxbury, Massachusetts, reveals a pastor who surrendered his control over his own time. Sharing a rectory with other priests, he rose in the middle of the night to help parishioners in distress. He was supposed to have one night a week to himself, but he spent it at home and could not avoid entreaties. He had a steady stream of callers — people burdened by poverty, alcoholism, family strife, or other distress. The confessional required up to five hours at a sitting. During one two-month period, he heard more than twenty-eight confessions a day. He oversaw the devotions of sodalities and confraternities, often speaking to gatherings of more than 300 members. He taught, administered the church, and visited. Visits to the sick sometimes meant arranging for hospitalization or the care of physicians. He normally had two to three hours a week to prepare his Sunday sermons, which lasted between ten and twenty-five minutes.[61]

By 1884 powerful forces within the church were exerting pressure for standardizing parish ministry. The foreign-language churches sometimes resisted, and bishops could direct their dioceses in divergent paths, but the push toward uniformity was pronounced. Pastoral theologians published manuals designed to regularize the routines. William Stang, a German who served fifteen years as a parish priest in Rhode Island, wrote his *Pastoral Theology* (1896) after he began to teach at the American College at Louvain. Many American seminaries adopted it as a standard text. Frederick Schulze, a German who served nine years as a parish priest in Illinois, wrote his *Manual of Pastoral Theology* (1899) while teaching at St. Francis Seminary in Milwaukee, and it also became popular in American classrooms.[62]

The priest was the envoy of Jesus Christ, "identical" with Christ in his ministerial functions. Because Jesus was "the divine Model," the priest was to strive for "the practice of perfection," a life of humility, obedience, purity of heart, virtue, and "a supernatural zeal for the glory of God and the salvation of souls." The aim was "perfect union" with Christ. When Robert Howard Lord, a Harvard graduate and the American expert on Russia at the Versailles Conference after World War I, entered the priesthood, he wrote that this "noblest and most sacred of callings" demanded total commitment: God must have "my whole heart, mind, and soul."[63]

---

tagious Diseases," *American Ecclesiastical Review* 20 (1899): 341-62; Schulze, *Manual*, p. 351; Kantowicz, "Church and Neighborhood," p. 66.

61. Sullivan, "Beneficial Relations," pp. 235-37.

62. Fogarty, *Vatican and the American Hierarchy*, pp. 195-206; White, *Diocesan Seminary*, pp. 215-16; Anonymous, "Twenty Clerical Don't's," *American Ecclesiastical Review* 20 (1899): 153-62.

63. Gibbons, *Ambassador of Christ*, p. 15; Stang, *Pastoral Theology*, pp. 122, 212, 217; Smith, *Training of a Priest*, p. 171; Sullivan, "Beneficial Relations," p. 206.

At the same time, the "perfect Christian" was also to be the "perfect gentleman." The priest was to master "all the rules and details of social etiquette." In both respects, the priest was "the model" for the faithful: "By his virtuous example chiefly the priest directs souls committed to him unto salvation." Edward McSweeney, rector of St. Mary's Seminary in Maryland, considered it a wonderful and "appalling" thought that "our every slightest act may be noted and treasured up, and produce an everlasting effect on those who observe it." In 1918 canon law decreed that the priest was obliged to lead "a more saintly interior and exterior life than the laity."[64]

The external symbol of the priest's distinctiveness was his mode of dress. In the early nineteenth century, it was not unusual (despite the decrees of the Council of Trent) for priests on the streets to dress like the laity. In 1829, church councils began to enforce a distinctive dress, and by the 1880s the church had precise regulations, both for worship and for daily wear. At the mass, the priest wore the long robe known as the alb along with the shawl-like amice covering the neck and shoulders. Both had to be made of fine white linen. He also wore a long stole, which could be white or colored but which had to be made "of some material not inferior to silk." Its colors had to correspond to the seasons of the Christian year. As a Eucharistic outer garment, he wore the elaborate chasuble, a semi-circular cape, usually of silk, often with colorful ornamentation. At non-Eucharistic functions, the cope, equally colorful, replaced the chasuble. The vestments varied according to rank and office. In the rectory or its vicinity priests were to wear the cassock, a robe reaching to the ankles, which could be black for priests, purple for bishops, and red for cardinals, though color could vary in the orders. The three-cornered cap, the biretta, was to match the cassock in color. When away from the residence and traveling, priests were always to wear the Roman collar and a black or dark suit of clothes. As McSweeney observed, the dress identified the priest and conveyed authority.[65]

The seminaries and manuals urged uniform priestly activity. They specified not only the vestments but also the actions and dispositions requisite for the mass. The priest would say the mass once every day, preparing by meditation and standard prayers as he vested himself. He was to observe the rubrics — the ceremonial directions — "to minutest detail." The position of the hands, the movement of the head, and the genuflections and crosses were to conform "exactly" to uniform rules. He was, for example, to bow down directly to kiss

64. Stang, *Pastoral Theology*, pp. 217, 218; Edward McSweeney, "The Priest and the Public," *Catholic World* 47 (1888): 746; White, *Diocesan Seminary*, p. 269.

65. Tentler, *Seasons of Grace*, p. 36; Stang, *Pastoral Theology*, p. 219; Meehan, "Organization," p. 675; McSweeney, "Priest and Public," p. 747.

the altar, not leaning to one side or the other. He was to begin the *Kyrie* only when standing at the middle point of the altar. When he extended his hands, his palms were to face each other and the fingers touch without rising higher than the shoulders.[66]

Priests learned how to wash the fingers, cover the chalice, and consume the wine. They learned that the bread had to be unleavened, baked of wheat flour, and round in shape, and that the wine had to be unadulterated and fermented from grapes alone. They were to purchase the wine from practicing Catholics, and there were rules for conveying and storing it. They were to teach communicants "the exact position of the tongue" for receiving the bread. If they neglected the rubrics, they incurred divine punishment. If they observed them, they acquired "merits and eternal recompense."[67]

Second in dignity to the sacrament of the altar was the sacrament of penance, through which the priest continued "the work of Christ's redemption." To administer it, the confessor had to know "the generic distinction between mortal and venial sins, the circumstances which cause a specific distinction of sin, the impediments of marriage, the laws of natural justice, their violation and reparation, and the occasions and remedies of sin." Most of this he derived from moral theology texts, but he also learned how to question the penitent "to get a more accurate knowledge of the sins committed," how to find the balance between laxity and severity in assigning penances, and how to teach parishioners to avoid "occasions of sin" — an array of activities from joining secret societies to attending dances and theaters, reading bad books, or sitting up late alone with someone of the opposite sex. Hearing confessions in the cramped, narrow box, always too hot or too cold, was a "sore trial," and the flow of "rude and ignorant people" could be repulsive, but faithful duty ensured the priest's "advance in perfection."[68]

Manuals offered detailed instructions. They taught priests how to ensure a proper blessing for the water, oils, and salt for baptism and how to sprinkle the water, apply the chrism (or consecrated oil) to the crown of the head, and place the salt in the infant's mouth. They taught how to prepare children for confirmation, what to do when the bishop arrived, what to ask and teach in premarital consultations, and how to conduct the marriage service. Priests received detailed instructions for performing the last rites: how to carry the Blessed Sacrament, or *viaticum,* to the room in a consecrated pyxis (a container worn around the neck and reposing on the breast), how to sprinkle the room and the

---

66. Stang, *Pastoral Theology,* pp. 94, 120, 124, 135; Schulze, *Manual,* pp. 92, 100-102.

67. Stang, *Pastoral Theology,* pp. 94, 110, 120, 124, 135; Schulze, *Manual,* pp. 92, 100-102, 126.

68. Stang, *Pastoral Theology,* pp. 139, 140, 147; Schulze, *Manual,* pp. 155, 173-85, 288.

person with holy water, how to administer the holy oil, and how to invite confession. With the seriously ill and dying, the priest was always to wear the cassock, the surplice, and the stole, to make the sign of the cross frequently, and to recite three standard prayers. At the moment of death, he could bestow the Apostolic Benediction, which conveyed a plenary indulgence that destroyed the remnants of sin and remitted its temporal punishments. He needed to know exactly how the church wanted all of this to be done.[69]

Priests learned to administer a wide variety of "sacramentals." While sacraments were instituted by Christ and operated through their own efficacy, the sacramentals were instituted by the church and produced their effects through its prayers and blessings. They included blessings for church buildings, church bells, altars, crosses, statues, chalices, candles, water, pictures, medals, and rosaries. A consecrated cross placed at the door of a new church could protect it against "the wicked attacks of the devil." The priest was to see that every Catholic family would have a supply of blessed water "to chase away evil spirits, to banish bodily diseases, and to preserve peace and comfort in the Christian home."[70]

Sacramentals could also provide blessings for persons. They included exorcisms that cast out demons and destroyed their influence; the ritual churching of women following childbirth; the tonsuring of young candidates for priesthood; and rites for the sick. The priest needed to know the precise formulas: "Do not omit words, or change and mutilate them, because you might run the risk of destroying the effect and thus commit a fraud on the people."[71]

The church formulated uniform standards for ministry with children. The First Plenary Council in Baltimore in 1852 issued *A General Catechism of the Christian Doctrine,* which sufficed until 1884, but the Third Plenary Council issued the book that would form the religious life of Catholic children for the next eight decades. *A Catechism of Christian Doctrine* (1885) — the Baltimore Catechism — became the most widely used handbook of its kind in America, though not every pastor used it. While much of the catechesis occurred in the parochial schools under the sisters, priests were to catechize every Sunday and holy day. The priest was "the duly authorized catechist" even if the bishop could authorize others to assist. Stang considered catechetical teaching "more important than preaching."[72]

Educators called for boys' clubs and girls' groups and insisted that the priests "show up at every meeting." They wanted "special attention" to training

69. Stang, *Pastoral Theology,* pp. 79-81, 91; Schulze, *Manual,* p. 285.

70. Stang, *Pastoral Theology,* pp. 198, 202-4, 207, 206; Schulze, *Manual,* 329, 332.

71. Stang, *Pastoral Theology,* pp. 200, 208; Schulze, *Manual,* p. 332.

72. Stang, *Pastoral Theology,* pp. 46, 52; Schulze, *Manual,* pp. 373, 376, 388.

children to confess their sins. Upon reaching the age of seven, they were to come to confession at least four times a year, and the priest taught them how to confess. They also trained altar boys to assist at the mass, conducted first communion classes for eleven- and twelve-year-olds, and held children's retreats. Some considered ministry with children "the important work" of the priesthood.[73]

It was easier to standardize catechetical teaching than to bring order and unity to preaching. For centuries the church had used a lectionary designating the biblical texts to be read each Sunday, and Stang suggested that priests preach on the Sunday Gospel texts, but he implied that many were following no pattern. John Talbot Smith said that the seminaries were simply not producing good preachers: "The American Catholics are a humorous people, and take their pulpit medicine with sly resignation, but the professors of our seminaries ought to hear their merciless criticisms on the preachers sent out from these seats of learning." The interesting preacher, he conceded, was the exception rather than the rule.[74]

Pastoral theologians tried to get priests to preach simple sermons grounded in a scriptural text and not to rely on "witty stories or amusing anecdotes." They suggested thirty-minute sermons that interpreted scripture and conveyed the church's moral teaching, as well as doctrinal sermons on the Trinity, the Incarnation, grace, and the sacraments. A sermon might communicate "a tender devotion to Mary immaculate" or use the saints as illustrations of gospel truths. Both Stang and Schulze shared the view, popular in Protestant circles, that "the personality of the preacher" needed to shine through the words.[75]

The preaching missions prevalent in antebellum America — the Catholic revival meetings — continued into the twentieth century. Stang suggested that they occur, for maximal effect, only once every six or seven years, but traveling missionaries abounded, and many parishes had missions every two years. Descriptions of "the thronging mass of men and women, the pale faces of terrified sinners, [and] the ecstatic thanks" of the pardoned suggest that early nineteenth-century practices remained intact. Priests measured the success of the missions by their "long hours in the confessional."[76]

In addition, the priest ensured that his church observed the standard devotions: the Forty Hours' Devotion at the altar, the Thirteen Hours' devotion, the nine-day Novenas, the Apostleship of Prayer, and the recitation of the rosary. Sacred Heart and Marian devotions drew special interest. And priests had to or-

---

73. Stang, *Pastoral Theology*, pp. 44, 156, 268; Schulze, *Manual*, pp. 71-84, 119.

74. Schulze, *Manual*, p. 361; Smith, *Training of a Priest*, pp. 120, 122, 149.

75. Stang, *Pastoral Theology*, pp. 20, 22, 33; Schulze, *Manual*, 354, 360-61; Smith, *Training of a Priest*, pp. 120, 122, 149.

76. Stang, *Pastoral Theology*, pp. 25, 234; Fogarty, "Parish and Community," p. 23.

ganize a choir and know what music the church approved. For all these activities, wrote Schulze, "ecclesiastical authority" had "minutely determined the rites and ceremonies to be followed."[77]

Ministry in the large urban parishes required administrative skill. Urban parishes were large, sometimes encompassing thousands, and internally complex. Stang expected that a lively parish would have a Society of the Infant Jesus for children, a Sodality of St. Aloysius for boys who had made their first communion, a Rosary and Scapular Society for women, a Young Ladies' Sodality for teenage girls, an Altar Society to provide vestments, a Holy Name Society for men, and a Young Men's Society for teenage boys. The priest was to attend weekly meetings of all these groups in order to form the church into "one solid army for the defense of faith and virtue."[78]

Salaries, Status, and Society

Most priests performed these tasks for minimal pay. The Plenary Council of 1866 called for better financial support, but regular priests turned their earnings over to the orders, and diocesan priests — who had not joined the regulars in a vow of poverty — lived on modest stipends. Churches found various ways to pay their priests: some asked members to make voluntary contributions; others rented pews; still others made assessments on property owners. In some dioceses, the pastors had the use of freewill offerings, which they could apply to their own income or to the pay of their assistant priests. The bishops determined the salaries, and during the 1860s they often decided that priests could live on $300 a year in addition to room and board. By 1884, the fixed salary, or *congrua*, was about $600 a year. The diocese of Boston, for example, set that amount in 1886, and it remained unchanged into the 1920s. By 1908, the diocese of New York paid pastors $800 and assistant pastors $600 in addition to housing and food.[79]

Clerical salaries could be supplemented by perquisites, or stole fees, which consisted of voluntary gifts given to priests in connection with — though not in payment for — priestly services ranging from special masses to blessings, baptisms, last rites, and benedictions. The amounts varied from place to place: large and wealthy parishes could mean hefty perquisites. In the larger New York

---

77. Schulze, *Manual*, pp. 3, 55-60, 141.

78. Stang, *Pastoral Theology*, pp. 258, 270-67; Schulze, *Manual*, pp. 434-60.

79. Sullivan, "Beneficial Relations," p. 227; Kenneth R. O'Brien, *The Nature of Support of Diocesan Priests in the United States of America* (Washington, D.C.: Catholic University of America Press, 1949), p. 16; Burtsell, *Diary*, p. 91; Meehan, "Organization," p. 693.

parishes, Richard Burtsell claimed, parish priests received $1,000 a year in stole fees and donations, more than doubling the set salaries. So while no priest could receive a salary higher than the amount set by the bishop, popular priests in large parishes could live comfortably, and some accumulated wealth. A priest in Lowell, Massachusetts, left $500,000 to his sister when he died in 1885 after a thirty-eight-year ministry.[80]

Some priests worried about the perquisites. Burtsell, troubled by the Irish custom of donations to the priest, resolved not to accept offerings for sick calls. He thought that the members of religious orders, who had taken a vow of absolute poverty, would ultimately do "the most good" in America because they never profited from pastoral duties. It was considered unethical for a priest to require the payment of these stole fees, and in a few dioceses the bishops required that all perquisites go into the common fund for clerical salaries.[81]

Bishops received more than ordinary priests. Their income came from a tax, known as the "cathedricum," laid on each parish according to its size and wealth. The income of the bishop, however, was intended to maintain the diocese. After beating back the trustee movement, the bishops held the diocesan property, which passed to succeeding bishops when they died. The civil law of Massachusetts, for example, began in 1897 to recognize the archdiocese of Boston as a corporation, administered by the archbishop, owning the greatest part of the church's property. Bishops could live in comfort, and they could oversee large amounts of money, but they did not accumulate personal fortunes.[82]

The church expected priests to donate unneeded income to works of charity, and one pastoral guidebook urged them not even to keep funds in savings accounts but to trust in providence. Canon law in 1918 reaffirmed a prohibition against engaging in any moneymaking occupations outside the ministry. Nothing resembling a pension program appeared until the Third Plenary Council in 1884 mandated the use of diocesan funds for sick and aged priests. But the young men who became Catholic priests had not been accustomed to wealth or ease. Stang may have exaggerated slightly when he claimed in 1897 that "the majority of our zealous and hard-working priests have come from the homes of the poor and lowly," but through the 1920s most of Boston's clergy, for instance, came from the homes of families headed by blue-collar workers.[83]

---

80. O'Brien, *Nature of Support*, pp. 102, 107; Burtsell, *Diary*, pp. 55-56; Sullivan, "Beneficial Relations," p. 228.

81. Burtsell, *Diary*, pp. 4, 91.

82. Meehan, "Organization," pp. 693-94; Sullivan, "Beneficial Relations," p. 232.

83. Edward N. Peters, *The 1917 or Pio-Benedictine Code of Canon Law* (San Francisco: Ignatius Press, 2001), p. 71; Stang, *Pastoral Theology*, pp. 188-89, 220; Sullivan, "Beneficial Relations," p. 205.

Despite the burdens, the church made steady progress in attracting candidates to the priesthood. Every national pastoral letter in the nineteenth century called for more vocations, and priests felt an obligation to recruit "the promising lads of the Diocese." By 1906 Schulze claimed that the problem of supply had improved: although vocations in the United States had long been "comparatively rare," he saw a "change for the better." Many dioceses no longer faced a shortage. Although recent immigrants complained that they lacked priests who knew their language, the ratio of priests to the Catholic population rose steadily: in the early nineteenth century, it stood at roughly one priest for every 1,350 Catholics; between 1890 and 1920, it was closer to one priest for every 975 Catholics.[84]

To have a son enter the priesthood was to rise in community honor and social standing. John Ireland was not merely appealing for vocations when he told the faithful of his diocese that "the crowning honor of a Christian family is to have a representative in the temple praying and offering sacrifice for them." The effects of family encouragement were visible in Boston in the frequency with which siblings became priests together. Cardinal Gibbons even worried occasionally that candidates for priesthood might too frequently enter the seminary "in obedience to parental wishes," but he also expressed gratitude to "the host of Christian mothers" to whom the church was indebted for many of its "most zealous and devoted priests."[85]

By the late nineteenth century, Catholics had good reason for a sense of accomplishment in providing leaders, but they also worried about persistent problems. They expressed concern about occasional ethical lapses. The English cleric Peter Benoit observed in 1875 that American Catholics "suffered much from discarded European priests, coming and causing scandal." Priests complained about colleagues given to "excessive drink," sexual indiscretion, and "wayward" behavior. Archbishop Gibbons founded "houses of refuge" for Catholic priests in need of discipline, and the Third Plenary Council instructed bishops to assign fallen priests to places of asylum and support them financially during a reasonable period of rehabilitation.[86]

Reformers complained also about clerical competence and learning. In

---

84. Stang, *Pastoral Theology*, p. 188; David J. O'Brien, "The American Priest and Social Action," in *Catholic Priest in the United States*, p. 431; Schulze, *Manual*, p. 298; Shaughnessy, *Has the Immigrant*, p. 262.

85. O'Neill, "Development of an American Priesthood," p. 39; Sullivan, "Beneficial Relations," p. 208; Gibbons, *Ambassador of Christ*, p. 27.

86. Ellis, *Seminary Education*, p. 121; Burtsell, *Diary*, pp. 26, 41; Ellis, *Gibbons*, p. 237; Anselm Kroll, *The Support of Sick, Old, and Delinquent Clergymen* (Washington, D.C.: American Ecclesiastical Review, 1900), pp. 15-16.

1868 the *Catholic World* noted that most priests had "no time to write, very little time to read," and three years later the *Catholic Advocate* in Louisville wondered about the "deplorable dearth of intellectual men" in the priesthood. Bishop Thomas Andrew Becker in Wilmington commented on the "utter superficiality" of some of the younger clergy. But in 1868 the *Catholic World* pointed out that priests in America had to be as familiar with "bricks and mortar" as with "books of theology," and Conroy's 1878 report to Rome observed that the bishops placed priority on fundraising and church building. Even the pastoral manuals recognized that Americans had to be brick-and-mortar priests: "We are in the building period of the Church in America," wrote Stang. "Almost every priest on the mission will find himself in the situation to build a church, school, or rectory."[87]

Apart from the brick-and-mortar work and the continual fundraising, priests organized charitable and temperance societies and sometimes created vast "institutional churches" that had industrial schools, free lunch programs, clothing distribution, poor relief, soup kitchens, libraries, and gymnasiums. It became a truism in the late nineteenth century that most Catholic clergy — apart from a celebrated few — stayed away from political and social questions beyond the local parish, and Father John A. Ryan, who would eventually help transform Catholic involvement in social problems, noted in 1908 that "the great majority of our clergy" had not "begun to study systematically or take more than superficial interest in the important social problems of the age and country." With the creation of the National Conference of Catholic Charities in 1910, priests began for the first time in significant numbers to seek specialized training in social work and to develop ministries removed from direct pastoral work.[88]

The formation in 1917 of the National Catholic War Council, which attended to the needs of Catholic soldiers and chaplains in World War I, marked a further change. Reorganizing in 1919 as the National Catholic Welfare Council, the organization represented the first serious concerted effort to address social problems, and its "Bishops' Program on Social Reconstruction," which Ryan wrote, placed the church decidedly on the side of working people and the poor. By that time the church was developing administrative structures that drew priests into fulltime work with specialized agencies. The centralization of

87. "Family, Parish, and Sunday School Libraries," *Catholic World* 6 (1868): 550; White, *Diocesan Seminary*, p. 148; Gannon, "Before and After Modernism," p. 321; Trisco, "Bishops and their Priests," p. 197; Stang, *Pastoral Theology*, p. 251.

88. Fogarty, "Parish and Community," p. 9; "Religion in New York," *Catholic World* 3 (1866): 389; John A. Ryan, "The Study of Social Problems in the Seminary," *American Ecclesiastical Review* 39 (1908): 117; O'Brien, "American Priest and Social Action," pp. 439-40.

dioceses required administrators at multiple levels, from examiners of the clergy to diocesan attorneys, and priests began to fulfill a variety of offices in ways reminiscent of the multilayered priesthood of the late medieval church.[89]

Most priests continued to labor in the parishes, which were becoming complex institutions that embodied residues of ancient Christian traditions, ethnic customs, American ideals, and Roman imperatives. With the growing standardization those priests repeated, from parish to parish, the same words, gestures, and rituals. They organized the same parish groups, encouraged the same devotions, and offered the same sacraments and sacramentals. Of course, the movement toward uniformity was never total; distinctive ethnic and linguistic traditions maintained a hold, different saints graced the sanctuaries, and different devotions mirrored the mosaic of Catholic life.

The irony was that the reaction against the more innovative forms of Americanism by the Vatican and by the next generation of prelates helped to propel the American church toward Romanization — not the direction the early Americanists had in mind. Yet the priesthood was moving toward greater uniformity, and the transitions laid a foundation for what would become, in the three decades after 1930, the "golden age of the American priest."[90]

89. O'Brien, "American Priest and Social Action," pp. 423-69.

90. Jay P. Dolan, "Patterns of Leadership in the Congregation," in *American Congregations*, vol. 2, ed. James P. Wind and James W. Lewis (Chicago: University of Chicago Press, 1994), p. 248.

CHAPTER 7

The Protestant Ministry Examined

1930-1940

Descriptions of Protestant ministry in the 1930s could sound as if they came straight from eighteenth-century ordination sermons. Ministers were "ambassadors" from "the Ruler of the Universe." They followed "the highest" path open to human beings and devoted themselves to the "supreme calling" of life, the "most sacred" of all enterprises. Divinely called to "save human beings damaged by sin" and to reconcile them to God, ministers guided the faithful into eternal salvation. But they did even more. They also prepared men and women for "their rightful place in society" and helped them through "the great crises of life." They were guides, inspirations, and models for a life in accord with the way God wanted people to live. Protestant clergy regarded their calling as "high, holy, and unique." Most never regretted their decision to enter the ministry. "The Christian minister," observed one pastor, "has more influence today than ever before."[1]

Yet the decade brought worries about decline. While some lauded clerical authority, others saw marginality. They believed that ministers could no longer count on a consensus about "conventions and standards" and that other professional groups were gaining more influence. In learning and knowledge, they thought, ministers lagged behind physicians and lawyers. They noted that ministers no longer took the lead in higher education and that they no longer

---

1. H. A. Boaz, *The Essentials of an Effective Ministry* (Nashville: Cokesbury, 1937), pp. 12-13; H. Paul Douglass and Edmund deS. Brunner, *The Protestant Church as a Social Institution* (New York: Harper and Brothers, 1935), p. 131; Edwin H. Byington, *The Minister's Week-Day Challenge* (New York: Richard A. Smith, 1931), p. 10.

provided the culture's intellectual leaders. It was not unusual to hear ministers describe the thirties as a "period of decline in the prestige of the ministry."[2]

The 1930s brought a new determination to gauge the standing of the profession — and new money to do it. In 1921 the Rockefeller Foundation funded an Institute for Social and Religious Research, which sponsored at least fifty surveys and published ninety volumes on the Protestant church in rural and urban America. In 1929 the Conference of Theological Seminaries and Colleges — a group that had originated in 1918 when deans at the largest seminaries began to plan the future of Protestant schools — asked it to produce a study of ministerial education and the ministry.[3]

In the early twenties, the group had authorized a study of the theology schools by Robert Kelly, who shocked them with his findings. Kelly found theological education largely in disarray, partly because few seminaries enforced "the highest scholastic qualifications for admission." Many admitted all candidates; they did not normally require a college degree, even when their catalogues upheld the standard; and they had too many students who were "not intellectually mature," who lacked either scholastic preparation or native ability. The schools tolerated an ethos of mediocrity, and Kelly suggested that their failings implied a weakness in the profession.[4]

Some of the administrators believed that Kelly had criticized the schools without sufficient information, and they wanted a more thorough report. The result was the most detailed study of the American Protestant clergy ever published, a four-volume compilation on *The Education of American Ministers*. The authors, educational psychologist Mark A. May from Yale and theologian William Adams Brown of Union Seminary in New York, wanted to accomplish for the ministry what the Carnegie Foundation reports on medical education in 1910, legal training in 1914, and engineering in 1918 had achieved for those professions: elevated standards and enhanced effectiveness.

Brown and May concentrated on the churches of the white mainline denominations, but the institute commissioned Benjamin E. Mays and Joseph

2. William Adams Brown, *Ministerial Education in America: The Education of American Ministers* (New York: Institute of Social and Religious Research, 1934), pp. 6, 8; Edwin McNeill Poteat, *Reverend John Doe, D. D.: A Study of the Place of the Minister in the Modern World* (New York: Harper and Brothers, 1935), pp. 23, 30; William H. Leach, *The Making of a Minister* (Nashville: Cokesbury, 1938), p. 4.

3. R. Laurence Moore, "Secularization: Religion and the Social Sciences," in *Between the Times: The Travail of the Protestant Establishment in America, 1900-1960*, ed. William R. Hutchison (Cambridge: Cambridge University Press, 1989), p. 238.

4. Robert L. Kelly, *Theological Education in America: A Study of One Hundred Sixty-One Theological Schools in the United States and Canada* (New York: George H. Doran, 1924), pp. 51, 55.

Nicholson to examine the black church and its ministry. Mays was a Baptist minister with a Ph.D. in sociology from the University of Chicago who taught at Morehouse College in Atlanta. In 1934 he would become the dean of the Howard University School of Religion and later the president of Morehouse. Nicholson had earned a Ph.D. from Northwestern University and taught religious education at Talladega College. Convinced that the black church had the potential to become "the greatest spiritual force in the United States," they spent two years studying black congregations and their ministers.[5]

Set alongside other studies, the volumes provide a snapshot of Protestant ministry in the era of the Great Depression. They found an abundant number of impressive ministers — people who faithfully represented the "principles of the Christian message and the Christian way of life" while finding inventive ways to connect with their people. Energetic ministers had built strong institutions and developed intimate relationships with their congregations, and "no business or professional men in the community were more respected." The best black clergy oversaw a veritable "training school" — in religion, morality, music, and leadership — for a subjugated people. They exercised a "dominant influence" on their members, and the laity accorded them respect and affection.[6]

Most of the studies looked at parish ministers, but not every minister worked in a parish. Thirteen percent of the clergy worked as chaplains, denominational officials, and directors of philanthropic agencies. Though they no longer presided over the large universities, they remained active in higher education. The churches appointed campus ministers, and they also owned almost a third of American universities and colleges. Ministers were usually the presidents of the smaller church schools. The clergy raised roughly a third of their endowment, and they also raised funds for about three hundred Protestant hospitals, four hundred children's homes, and three hundred group homes for the elderly. More than 40 percent of the retirement homes in America depended on money raised by ministers. The Protestant churches ran more than 630 community-welfare agencies, from health clinics to homeless centers, and clergy raised funds and provided personnel.[7]

When the researchers looked at the parish clergy, however, they came away with sobering conclusions. From their perspective, the ministry was a troubled profession, mainly because it was insufficiently professional. It lacked uniform

5. Benjamin E. Mays and Joseph William Nicholson, *The Negro's Church* (New York: Negro Universities Press, 1933), p. 292.

6. Mark A. May, *The Profession of the Ministry: Its Status and Problems* (New York: Institute of Social and Religious Research, 1934), pp. 140, 283, 338, 374; Mays and Nicholson, *Negro's Church*, p. 58.

7. Douglass and deS. Brunner, *Protestant Church*, pp. 132, 166, 192, 196.

standards, tolerated mediocrity, suffered from internal disarray, and opened its doors to uneducated and untrained practitioners. The churches needed urgently to "elevate the standards of the profession as a whole." By pressing the point relentlessly, these studies laid a foundation for the "professional era" of Protestant ministry after the Second World War.[8]

A Sociological Vantage Point

Some of the difficulties that worried the researchers in the 1930s came from cultural changes that altered the way Americans spent their time. One minister remarked that the newspapers, radio, and movies, combined with professional sports, gave the preacher "more competition than ever before in history." For some ministers, radio provided a regional pulpit, but it also sponsored competing voices. By 1939, about 86 percent of the population had radios. Advice programs that dispensed financial tips, astrological predictions, and solutions to personal problems proved to be stunningly popular.[9]

The movies reigned supreme in the image-making business, and they depicted standards far different from the virtues the ministry represented. In an era when Clark Gable's on-screen shirts or Jean Harlow's hairstyle could shift consumption patterns overnight, Hollywood formed American attitudes, and the industry brought both competition and condescension. As one pastor noted, moviemakers liked to make fun of "preachers prattling and pretending." In 1930, the Hollywood Production Code declared that films should not depict ministers as "comic characters or as villains," but enforcement was spotty. Rare was the film with realistic and sympathetic images of the Protestant minister.[10]

The ethos of the marketplace constantly exerted pressure on clerical self-understanding. Despite the stock market crash, the language and ideals of a capitalist economy pervaded religious life in the 1930s. As one Methodist bishop observed, the "captains of industry" looked for "efficient" leaders, and the church had the duty to emulate them: "Every true minister feels that he must be the most efficient man it is possible for him to be." May and Brown

---

8. Brown, *Ministerial Education*, p. 5.

9. Albert W. Palmer, *The Minister's Job* (Chicago: Willett and Clarke, 1937), p. 4; Terry A. Cooney, *Balancing Acts: American Thought and Culture in the 1930s* (New York: Twayne, 1995), p. 91; Brown, *Ministerial Education*, p. 10.

10. Brown, *Ministerial Education*, p. 10; Hampton Adams, *The Pastoral Ministry* (Nashville: Cokesbury, 1932), p. 51; "Hollywood Motion Picture Product Code (1930)," in *The Dame in the Kimono: Hollywood, Censorship, and the Production Code from the 1920s to the 1960s*, ed. Leonard Leff and Jerold Simmons (New York: Weidenfeld, 1990), p. 285; Cooney, *Balancing Acts*, p. 83.

worried about the degree to which "the modern psychology of business success" guided lay expectations of ministers. The churches wanted "a winner, not only of souls, but of dollars and prestige." Even in rural churches, they wanted a man who knew how to organize, advertise, sell, and mix easily with others. "The qualities," May noted, "are more or less the same sort one would seek in a salesman."[11]

Above all, the image of the ministry changed because of the increase in the number of professions. The 1930 census counted 148,838 clergy in America — a respectable growth from previous decades — but it also showed that ministers now worked alongside about thirty other callings classified as "professions." Each of them offered opportunities for "lives of service and usefulness," attracting young people who once might have chosen the ministry. Some of those vocations — especially psychiatry and social work — had successfully "invaded" clerical territory by using specialized techniques and knowledge that ministers did not have. The increasing differentiation of the professions meant that the ministry began to seem unlike other professions at precisely the moment when professionals were striving to become more specialized, scientific, state-certified, and monopolistic over delimited domains of expertise.[12]

In facing such problems, the ministry presented no united front. In addition to the denominational distinctions, the fissures of social class, the racial divide, and differing regional patterns, theological differences cut through denominational boundaries, and liberals, conservatives, and fundamentalists differed about both doctrine and the aims of ministry.

William Adams Brown wrote the best-known theology of ministry from a liberal perspective. In *The Minister: His World and His Work* (1937), Brown depicted ministers, in terms derived from the German theologian Albrecht Ritschl, as citizens of "two countries," the natural and the eternal, whose "distinctive function" was to lead worship that invited their fellow citizens to live in the presence of God and to honor "eternal verities which outlast the changes of the years." Through preaching, pastoral care, and worship, ministers were to evoke a "vivid consciousness" of God as the "supreme object of our devotion." This was not a "wonder-worker" God who intervened here and there to solve mundane problems, but the God of "all life," who called his creatures to "loyalty to that universal society of which Jesus the Christ is Lord."[13]

Convinced that men and women found God — and salvation — whenever

11. Boaz, *Essentials*, pp. 14-15; May, *Profession of the Ministry*, pp. 130, 137, 141.

12. Mark A. May, *The Education of American Ministers: The Institutions That Train Ministers* (New York: Institute of Social and Religious Research, 1934), p. 222.

13. William Adams Brown, *The Minister: His World and His Work* (Nashville: Cokesbury, 1937), pp. 52, 109, 120.

such a loyalty brought their lives "into a meaningful and valuable whole," Brown described the minister as a priest who nurtured loyalty in worship, an evangelist who announced the good news of God's universal presence, a teacher who conveyed the Christian story, and a pastor whose counseling helped people move toward lives of service to God and the neighbor. Such a ministry would, he thought, constitute a step in the gradual march toward the kingdom of God.[14]

Fundamentalists — and many other religious conservatives — viewed matters differently. For many of them, the minister was, above all, an evangelist who proclaimed the message and called for conversion. Ministers were chiefly in "the business of saving souls" by eliciting assent of heart and mind to the work of Christ on the cross and guiding their converts in accord with biblical mandates. Some Reformed denominations emphasized right belief more than an experience of rebirth; traditional Lutherans viewed the minister as the preacher of an orthodox message rather than a pleader for conversions; conservative Episcopalians saw the priest as the bearer of a sacramental ethos. These groups had little in common with fundamentalists, Pentecostals, or holiness preachers. But conservatives of every stripe shared a wariness of liberal innovation.[15]

Fundamentalists created their own institutions to compete with the mainline churches. By the end of the decade, they had established at least fifty Bible schools to train laity — and then clergy — in evangelistic work. Such older schools as the Bible Institute of Los Angeles and Moody Bible Institute in Chicago provided not only education but also centers for publishing and broadcasting that linked together clerical networks. Fundamentalists organized summer Bible conferences and the beginnings of what would become a publishing empire. They proved adept at using radio. By the end of the decade, they sponsored twenty-five broadcasts a week in Chicago alone, and by 1939 Charles Fuller's "Old Fashioned Revival Hour" reached an estimated audience of fifteen to twenty million on 152 stations. As mainline Protestants, beset by budgetary problems, reduced their foreign missions, the fundamentalists filled the gap, and by 1935 they furnished about 1,700 of the 12,000 American missionaries to foreign countries.[16]

Both the liberal clergy and the old-line conservatives shied away from fundamentalists, Pentecostals, and holiness preachers. In Muncie, Indiana, Robert and Helen Merrell Lynd found that "marginal" holiness and Pentecostal

14. Brown, *The Minister*, pp. 58, 161, 166, 189.

15. Ambrose Moody Bailey, *The Pastor in Action: Tested Ways to Ministerial Success* (New York: Roundtable Press, 1939), p. 6.

16. Joel A. Carpenter, *Revive Us Again: The Reawakening of American Fundamentalism* (New York: Oxford University Press, 1997), pp. 24, 25, 58.

preachers and the clergy of the "older denominations" divided along lines of both religion and social class, rarely talked to each other, and never cooperated. When the sociologist Liston Pope studied the churches of Gastonia, North Carolina, he found also that entrepreneurial and self-educated holiness and Pentecostal preachers ridiculed the "exclusive, proud, 'stuck-up' character of the older religious institutions." Combative fundamentalist preachers in the large cities — such colorful figures as J. Frank Norris in Fort Worth, "Fighting Bob" Ketcham in Gary, and "Fighting Bob" Schuler in Los Angeles — made headlines with attacks on liberal ministers.[17]

The theological "Realists" — Americans influenced by European neo-orthodoxy — tried to provide an alternative to both liberalism and fundamentalism. In his *Moral Man and Immoral Society* (1932), Reinhold Niebuhr at Union Seminary in New York contended that the efforts of "modern religious idealists" to realize the kingdom of God through an ethic of love would always collapse in the face of human selfishness and pride. He accused liberals of failing to grasp the depth of sinfulness and fundamentalists of trying to enclose the divine mystery in simplistic formulas. In *Beyond Fundamentalism and Modernism* (1934), the Reformed theologian George W. Richards, drawing inspiration from the Germans Karl Barth and Emil Brunner, claimed that the "Gospel of God" stood in judgment over every cultural value, every program of ethics, every economic system, and every theology. H. Richard Niebuhr at Yale Divinity School accused the liberals of turning God into a means to human ends and the fundamentalists of practicing a form of bibliolatry.[18]

The Realists wanted the minister to be the prophet who saw and announced the conflict between the gospel and an individualistic, materialist, capitalist culture that rested on "faith in the self-sufficiency of the human and finite world." In the first few years of the Realist movement, its ideas took root mainly among a small number of educated ministers — often located in seminaries and ecumenical agencies — and an even smaller group of clerical social activists. Its broader influence would come after World War II.[19]

---

17. Robert S. Lynd and Helen Merrell Lynd, *Middletown in Transition: A Study of Cultural Conflicts* (New York: Harcourt, Brace, 1937), p. 297; Liston Pope, *Millhands and Preachers: A Study of Gastonia* (New Haven: Yale University Press, 1942), p. 128; Carpenter, *Revive Us Again*, p. 65.

18. Reinhold Niebuhr, *Moral Man and Immoral Society* (New York: Charles Scribner's Sons, 1932), pp. xix, 73; H. Richard Niebuhr, "Value Theory and Theology," *The Nature of Religious Experience*, ed. Julius Seelye Bixler, Douglas Clyde Macintosh, and H. Richard Niebuhr (New York: Harper and Brothers, 1937), pp. 93-108; George W. Richards, *Beyond Fundamentalism and Modernism: The Gospel of God* (New York: Charles Scribner's Sons, 1934), pp. 93, 135, 161, 203.

19. Niebuhr, "Value Theory," p. 10.

The average Protestant minister in the 1930s stood with the conservatives. One survey of 1,000 urban congregations in 1932 discovered that 16 percent defined themselves as fundamentalist, 48 percent as conservative, and 34 percent as liberal. Their clergy probably shared these orientations, but if the survey had included small towns and the countryside, conservative domination would have been overwhelming. In the denominational offices and the seminaries of the mainline churches, liberal ministers held the reins of power — and in decisive votes, the moderate conservatives often joined them — but the conservative voice held forth in most Protestant pulpits.[20]

Ministry

What the May-Brown study revealed was that the ministers in this fragmented profession faced heavy and conflicting demands. Congregations wanted clergy who could meet an "endless variety" of expectations. Some wanted good pastors, others good preachers, and still others money raisers, builders, or promoters. Laypeople wanted ministers with "personality," clerics who were poised, tactful, and socially at ease, filled with self-assurance and enthusiasm, and able to get along with people. They sought "spirituality" in their pastors — devotion to the Christian "way of life" and "evangelistic zeal" — but they also favored "executive ability." A recurring assumption was that they could find such qualities especially in young male pastors. May was struck by "the young-man obsession."[21]

Ministerial functions had "multiplied into a perfect maze," but preaching continued to hold priority. Protestant clergy still spoke of preaching as "the supreme business" of the minister, and strong preachers were "in great demand." The style of preaching had changed. Forty-minute sermons were still acceptable, but the norm in the mainline churches was now closer to thirty. "The old-fashioned oratory of forty years ago," noted one preacher, was "gone forever." Sermons were "less ornate and more direct." Yet the preachers of the large downtown churches still attracted large crowds and attained regional celebrity.[22]

It was more difficult for "ordinary preachers." Interviews with church members revealed that "a considerable group" of college-trained laypeople did

20. Douglass and deS. Brunner, *Protestant Church*, p. 290.

21. May, *Profession of the Ministry*, pp. 13-32, 129, 132.

22. Byington, *Minister's Week-Day Challenge*, p. 1; Boaz, *Essentials*, pp. 73, 77, 108; Douglass and deS. Brunner, *Protestant Church*, p. 50.

not consider the minister "as an educational peer" and found the sermons less than challenging. Even in rural areas, with different kinds of expectations, three-fourths of the laity wanted "a more effective preacher." Denominational leaders voiced an "urgent need" for "better preachers."[23]

The teaching office of ministry presented new challenges. Brown and May believed that the ministers, as teachers, were finding it harder to "meet the intellectual problems" of young people and thoughtful laity. Proponents of the religious education movement urged the clergy to revamp the Sunday schools and create institutes for education, summer schools, vacation Bible schools for children, and weekday release-time programs with local schools, but a survey published in 1935 concluded that ministers gave only about 5 percent of their time to educating children or adults, even though three-fourths of them supervised Sunday school and youth programs.[24]

Ministers experimented with different ways of reaching children. The liturgical churches — Lutherans, Episcopalians, and Catholics — still used the catechism, but in other denominations, pastors sought alternatives. Some continued the children's sermons; others sponsored "children's church," an innovation of the previous decade that gathered the young into a separate service during the regular worship hour; even more formed children's choirs, another earlier innovation that became widely popular in the 1930s. Clerical guidebooks urged ministers to know the children, learn their names, visit their classes, and form special classes to teach them. But time studies revealed that most ministers spent little time with them.[25]

Clergy outside the liturgical traditions complained that it was hard to teach people to worship. Their congregations considered prayer and singing to be merely "preliminary exercises" before the sermon rather than "the practice of the presence of God." A "considerable minority" of ministers — especially in the large downtown churches — instituted processionals, donned robes, and introduced service books. Episcopalians approved a revised *Book of Common Prayer* in 1928, Presbyterians revised their *Book of Common Worship* in 1932, and Methodists published an unofficial *Book of Common Worship* in 1932. Advocates of "public worship as an art" recovered ancient traditions in order to

23. Byington, *Minister's Week-Day Challenge*, p. 4; Brown, *Ministerial Education*, p. 201; May, *Profession of the Ministry*, pp. 139-40; Boaz, *Essentials*, p. 108; Douglass and deS. Brunner, *Protestant Church*, p. 149.

24. Brown, *Ministerial Education*, p. 202; May, *Profession of the Minister*, p. 175; Douglass and deS. Brunner, *Protestant Church*, p. 175. See Hugh Hartshorne, *Standards and Trends in Religious Education* (New Haven: Yale University Press, 1933).

25. Bailey, *Pastor in Action*, p. 89; Adams, *Pastoral Ministry*, pp. 100-104; May, *Profession of the Ministry*, p. 156.

dignify the liturgy and move away from "folksy" services, but the changes often created tensions.[26]

By the end of the decade, the educated clergy were reading a new literature in "pastoral psychology." In 1936, the Presbyterian minister Russell Dicks and the Boston physician Richard Cabot published *The Art of Ministering to the Sick,* which tried to teach the minister how to discern a parishioner's "growing edge" through "good listening." They encouraged pastors to cultivate "directed listening" and "quietness" that would help people grow by discovering their inner resources. Rollo May, a teacher at Garrett Biblical Institute who combined psychoanalytic ideas with the theology of Reinhold Niebuhr and Paul Tillich, advocated a similar style of counseling that could promote self-understanding and insight. Amateurish advice-giving was out. By the time May published *The Art of Counseling* in 1939, Protestant seminaries were inserting psychology into the curriculum and some ministers were announcing that serious pastoral work was "coming back." Seventy-five percent of the clergy in the Brown-May study did individual counseling.[27]

Ninety percent of the ministers surveyed said that they found their greatest satisfaction in preaching and pastoral work. Teaching and administration fell near the bottom on their ideal agendas. In the larger churches, however, administrative work absorbed more and more of their time. They spent from nine to twelve hours a week on the "church machinery," with constant attention to finance and budget. Some supervised a "subordinate ministry" of parish assistants, directors of education, deaconesses, youth leaders, Sunday school teachers, parish nurses, music directors, and secretaries. When asked to name their most persistent difficulties, they talked about administration.[28]

The ministers claimed to work, on average, seventy-nine hours a week, spending more than twenty on their sermons, twenty on pastoral duties, and nine on administration. The figures were not entirely credible. Studies using time sheets revealed that some of them, at least, spent closer to an hour or two a

26. Brown, *Ministerial Education,* p. 198; Douglass and deS. Brunner, *Protestant Church,* pp. 147-48; James F. White, *Protestant Worship: Traditions in Transition* (Louisville: Westminster/John Knox, 1989), pp. 73, 111, 166, 167.

27. Adams, *Pastoral Ministry,* p. 64; Richard Cabot and Russell Dicks, *The Art of Ministering to the Sick* (New York: Macmillan, 1936), pp. 16, 74, 96, 117-18, 130; Rollo May, *The Art of Counseling* (1st ed., 1939; Nashville: Abingdon Press, 1978), foreword, pp. 154-57, 220-21; Leach, *Making of a Minister,* p. 122; May, *Profession of the Ministry,* p. 156; E. Brooks Holifield, *A History of Pastoral Care in America: From Salvation to Self-Realization* (Nashville: Abingdon Press, 1983), pp. 237, 252.

28. May, *Profession of the Ministry,* pp. 161-63, 170-71; Douglass and deS. Brunner, *Protestant Church,* pp. 94, 125; Byington, *Minister's Week-Day Challenge,* p. 41.

week on sermon preparation, which other activities often pushed to the last moment. But conscientious ministers stayed busy. All of them preached on Sundays, and three-quarters still had midweek services; 90 percent attended meetings and social gatherings; about half taught a weekly class. Most still counseled and visited. "They feel continuously in a hurry," wrote one observer. "They have an uneasy consciousness of always being subject to call."[29]

A chastened social gospel still drew the allegiance of a "genuine minority." In the Depression years, 25 percent of the clergy in the North favored some variety of a socialist economy. Reinhold Niebuhr ran as a socialist candidate for the U.S. Senate, and the Fellowship of Socialist Christians, which he helped to form in the winter of 1930-31, mobilized left-wing clergy. Howard "Buck" Kester organized cotton pickers and sharecroppers in the South and helped create the Southern Tenant Farmers' Union. James Dombrowski worked with miners in Pennsylvania. In 1934, the Disciple activist Kirby Page surveyed 21,000 clergy: 60 percent of them said that the churches should not support any future war, and only 5 percent favored laissez-faire capitalism. Some six thousand described themselves as socialists. Two years later, Jerome Davis at Yale Divinity School surveyed 4,700 ministers and learned that 79 percent favored restrictions on child labor, 75 percent were willing to preach against lynching, 47 percent would affirm publicly the right of labor to picket and strike, and 53 percent supported public ownership of utilities and basic industries.[30]

The polls overlooked the Pentecostals, holiness preachers, and fundamentalists; they reflected the views mainly of ministers from the mainline churches. Community studies suggested that most ministers shared the political and social attitudes of their parishioners or restricted their social concern to conventional vices. Liston Pope found that ministers in Gastonia opposed labor unions, avoided the issue of child labor, and devoted their reformist energies to Sabbath desecration, drinking, gambling, dancing, and suggestive movies. The Lynds concluded that the clergy in Muncie, Indiana, largely affirmed "the causes and symbols of the local business control groups."[31]

Clerics could be drawn to right-wing extremism. The rabble-rousing Disciples minister Gerald L. K. Smith — editor of *The Cross and the Flag* —

---

29. May, *Profession of the Ministry,* pp. 144, 155, 156, 167; Douglass and deS. Brunner, *Protestant Church,* p. 132.

30. Donald B. Meyer, *The Protestant Search for Political Realism, 1919-1941* (Berkeley: University of California Press, 1961), pp. 174, 175; Richard Fox, *Reinhold Niebuhr: A Biography* (New York: Pantheon Books, 1985), pp. 128, 157; "Ministers on the March," *Christian Century,* 9 May 1934, pp. 624-25; Jerome Davis, "The Social Action Pattern of the Protestant Religious Leader," *American Sociological Review* 1 (1936): 105-7.

31. Pope, *Millhands and Preachers,* p. 127; Lynd and Lynd, *Middletown in Transition,* p. 312.

combined anti-communism, anti-Semitism, and racist sentiments with opposition to the New Deal. The fundamentalist preacher Gerald B. Winrod, who founded the Defenders of the Christian Faith in Salina, Kansas, attracted sixty thousand subscribers to *The Defender,* which promoted anti-Catholicism, anti-Semitic ideology, and the regime of Adolf Hitler. In the South and Midwest, a clerical fringe group joined the Ku Klux Klan in opposing blacks, Jews, and Catholics.[32]

Every survey and community study, however, revealed that most ministers had neither the time nor the inclination for social causes or social welfare ministries. In the rural areas, such ministries were "almost non-existent." In the cities, only about 4 percent of the churches had social programs. Both liberal and conservative ministers were "skeptical of too much emphasis on social problems." Pastors helped people find jobs, food, and shelter, and their churches distributed food, cared for shut-ins, and visited prisons and hospitals. But less than 25 percent of the ministers in the Brown-May survey spent any time in the community on health care, labor troubles, homelessness, literacy, or unemployment. The "general attitude of the minister" toward social agencies, May wrote, "is one not of hostility but rather of indifference due to absorption with his own work."[33]

A few African American ministers in the cities presided over expansive institutions with community houses, parlors, gyms, athletic teams, drama and art classes, and social services, but they were the exceptions. Urban black clergy took a prominent part in movements against lynching and discrimination. In Harlem, for example, Adam Clayton Powell Jr. built his eleven-thousand-member Abyssinian Baptist Church into a base for a career in the U.S. House of Representatives. But the social activists were not the majority in the African American churches of the 1930s. Most black ministers preached, led worship, visited, and organized the church.[34]

The Bronzeville area of Chicago in 1938 had five hundred black churches. Five of them had over 2,500 members, and their ministers presided over small empires that had recreational and welfare programs, socials, plays, and concerts. But close to a quarter of the churches met only for worship and Sunday school, and the majority were "storefront churches" with fewer than twenty-five members who met in vacant stores or abandoned theaters for ecstatic celebration. Their pastors were untrained entrepreneurs who faced incessant competition —

32. Leo P. Ribuffo, *The Old Christian Right: The Protestant Far Right from the Great Depression to the Cold War* (Philadelphia: Temple University Press, 1983), pp. 80-127, 128-78.

33. Douglass and deS. Brunner, *Protestant Church,* p. 190; May, *Profession of the Ministry,* pp. 157-58, 165; Davis, "Social Action Pattern," p. 114; Poteat, *Reverend John Doe,* p. 43.

34. Mays and Nicholson, *The Negro's Church,* pp. 120-22; Charles V. Hamilton, *The Black Preacher in America* (New York: William Morrow, 1972), p. 111.

the area had seven hundred preachers — and held their position through oratorical agility and force of personality. They left the social services up to the aldermen and precinct captains. In the rural areas, most black churches offered only Sunday preaching, a Sunday school, and a yearly revival. In the South, Mays and Nicholson found an "atmosphere of deterioration," with one-room churches in ill repair and absentee pastors who preached only once a month.[35]

Most churches in America were still located in the countryside and small towns; only 71,205 of the nation's 195,574 Christian congregations were in areas with a population of more than ten thousand people. Most churches gathered for worship, preaching, baptism, the Lord's Supper, and Sunday school — and little more. Even in the cities, a mere 18 percent of the churches had "intensely elaborated" programs, with multiple subgroups and expanded ministries. Reformers wanted the churches to do more, and they thought that the clergy were the only people with the authority to change direction.[36]

A Social Portrait

The reformers believed that they heard the clergy saying they were in trouble and needed help. In a nation with roughly 150,000 clergy for about 195,574 churches — most of which were small and poor — many preachers still served multiple congregations. The average Protestant church had 191 adult members: rural churches averaged 98, small city churches 274, larger city churches 596. Most churches were in the countryside and small towns, and they often struggled. More than 60 percent of the open-country churches and at least 13 percent of the village churches had only occasional preaching. Two-thirds of the open-country churches — and half the village churches — had non-resident ministers.[37]

Many a church during the Depression, however, could no longer afford a full-time pastor, and some of the denominations began to worry about an over-supply of clergy. Some estimated that the nation had thirty thousand unemployed ministers. By the end of the 1930s, students who might have chosen ministry had gotten the message, and then the seminaries complained about

35. St. Claire Drake and Horace R. Cayton, *Black Metropolis: A Study of Negro Life in a Northern City*, 2 vols. (1st ed., 1945; New York: Harper and Row, 1962), vol. 2, pp. 412, 416, 420, 617; Mays and Nicholson, *Negro's Church*, p. 252.

36. Bureau of the Census, *Religious Bodies: 1936*, 2 vols. (Washington, D.C.: United States Government Printing Office, 1941), vol. 1, p. 19; Douglass and deS. Brunner, *Protestant Church*, p. 142.

37. Douglass and deS. Brunner, *Protestant Church*, pp. 83, 85, 104.

declining enrollments. The economic malaise affected even ministers lucky enough to have a secure position. In the cities, for example, only 20 to 25 percent of the churches had additional paid religious workers to help the minister, and researchers reported frustration and low morale from ministers asked to do more with less.[38]

A bleak picture emerged also from studies of clerical salaries. By the beginning of the 1930s, the average salary for a minister was $1,407, though many also received a rent-free parsonage. Rural pastors averaged $1,062. Between 1926 and 1936, the mainline denominations cut their expenditures by 36 percent, and in 1939 the median income for clergy was $1,264. Ministers received less than postal workers, kindergarten teachers, skilled craftsmen, and railroad workers. The disparities were still vast: the pay of Congregationalist clergy in New York in 1934 ranged from $400 to $12,000. Black clergy made less than whites, and in the country churches, African American preachers earned, on average, only $266 from each church, prompting them to serve more than one church at a time. The twenties had brought economic slippage for the clergy, and the thirties brought even more of it.[39]

Brown and May worried that too many of these pastors had not enjoyed the cultural advantages of the American middle class. They found that only 4 percent came from affluent homes and almost a third came from families that were poor or "very poor." Sixty-seven percent had fathers who were farmers, small tradesmen, or workers. Seminarians came from the same social location. Only 20 percent came from cities of 100,000 or more people; 45 percent came from rural areas. Their fathers were mainly farmers (29 percent), workers or tradesmen (24 percent), or ministers (15 percent). This was not surprising, since 43 percent of Americans lived in rural areas throughout the decade, so they simply provided their proportionate share of pastors. But Brown and May lived and worked in the urban Northeast, and upper-middle-class urban norms lurked behind their assessments.[40]

It troubled them, for example, that many seminarians lacked "the culture made possible by ampler economic resources." Brown wanted the schools to of-

38. Jackson W. Carroll and Robert L. Wilson, *Too Many Pastors? The Clergy Job Market* (New York: Pilgrim Press, 1980), p. 54; Douglass and deS. Brunner, *Protestant Church,* p. 104.

39. Robert Wuthnow, *The Restructuring of American Religion: Society and Faith Since World War II* (Princeton: Princeton University Press, 1988), p. 25; Edwin S. Gaustad, "The Pulpit and the Pews," in *Between the Times,* p. 31; Leach, *Making of the Minister,* p. 55; Mays and Nicholson, *Negro's Church,* pp. 186, 266-67; Douglass and deS. Brunner, *Protestant Church,* p. 130.

40. May, *Professsion of the Ministry,* p. 41; Brown, *Ministerial Education,* p. 111; Leon E. Truesdell, ed., *Sixteenth Census of the United States: 1940, Population, Volume II, Characteristics of the Population* (Washington, D.C.: United States Government Printing Office, 1943), p. 18.

fer more counsel on "personal decorum" in which students with "faulty social background" were deficient. They worried, as well, that so few of the students were widely read. More than half read only religious publications, about a tenth read news magazines, and about the same number read literary magazines. The ministry seemed not to attract the academic elite from the colleges: only 3.2 percent of the college graduates in seminary had been members of Phi Beta Kappa and only 11 percent had graduated with honors. A considerable number had never been to college.[41]

Mays and Nicholson shared similar concerns that the black churches failed to attract the best and brightest into the pulpit. While blacks formed less than 10 percent of the population in 1930, the black clergy constituted 17 percent of American ministers. But many of the ablest African American college students had other vocational aims. Only 5 percent planned to become pastors, while 25 percent hoped for careers in medicine, 21 percent in teaching, and 7 percent in law. It appeared that fewer than fifty college graduates would enter the ministry each year — hardly a leaven among the more than 25,000 black preachers in the 1930 census. Mays and Nicholson saw education as a route of upward mobility for African Americans. They wanted ministers to travel the same path.[42]

For a good many ministers, black and white, educated and uneducated, the ministry was a second career, even for the seminary-educated pastors. Thirty-four percent of seminarians had decided to enter the ministry after they were thirty-five years old, and ministers as a group were older than doctors, lawyers, architects, and other professionals. The finding bothered May, who noted that in 1910 around 48 percent of active ministers were forty-five or older. In 1920, slightly more than 53 percent of the clergy were that old. He worried that the trend was continuing into the thirties. Was the ministry not attracting the younger generation?[43]

Brown and May found much to like about the era's seminarians. Most had serious religious convictions, nurtured in devout homes with parents active in the church. Almost half reported an experience of conversion. On average, their parents had nine or ten years of education, including two years of high school, which placed them above the national norm. Most of the college graduates in the seminaries had studied at denominational colleges that helped them maintain their ties to the church. The average student had also been active as a leader in local churches, and most had made relatively early decisions to enter the

41. Brown, *Ministerial Education*, pp. 111, 116, 118, 150; May, *Profession of the Ministry*, p. 304; May, *Education of American Ministers*, p. 301.

42. Mays and Nicholson, *Negro's Church*, pp. 39, 54, 390.

43. May, *Profession of the Ministry*, pp. 44-45; Douglass and deS. Brunner, *Protestant Church*, p. 116.

ministry, 40 percent between the ages of seventeen and twenty-four, 26 percent between twenty and thirty-four. Their pastors, their parents, and their friends had encouraged the decision, and a network of church agencies, from student conferences to volunteer programs, had helped confirm it. The students knew from the inside the culture of the church and the local congregation.[44]

Nonetheless, the "most single significant fact" was that such a small proportion of white Protestant ministers had "a standard theological education." The finding that in 1926 probably only a fourth of the white Protestant ministers had graduated from both college and seminary startled them. They concluded that "the general educational level of the Protestant ministry" had declined, and they laid the blame on the lax standards of the denominations. "How can the ministry of today be the learned and respected profession it once was when fully half its members are not even college graduates: when, in some denominations, any farmer, blacksmith, or merchant may become ordained by the simple process of convincing a group of ministers that he has heard the 'call' to preach?"[45]

When they examined denominational requirements, they found disarray. Episcopalians, Presbyterians, and Lutherans had high standards on paper, but they allowed too many exceptions. Among Congregationalists, Methodists, Baptists, and Disciples, the exceptions were so numerous that the standards lost their meaning. Brown thought that "so long as the churches are willing to ordain men who have had only a high-school education or less," no large improvement was possible; Mays and Nicholson reached the same conclusion. The poorly educated minister could no longer count on automatic respect, yet 80 percent of the urban black clergy lacked a college degree, and only 11 percent of them had both a college and a seminary education. In the rural churches, more than 90 percent of the preachers had only high-school training or less; only 2 percent were college graduates; and almost none had seminary training. For the researchers, this was a problem. The answer was more and better education.[46]

The proponents of professionalism were swimming upstream. Seminary graduates were furnishing only 21 percent of the replacements for ministers who were retiring. And large numbers of laity even in the mainline denominations seemed not to care. The laity had little formal education. At the end of the thirties, only 5.4 percent of native whites, 2.3 percent of foreign-born whites, and 1.2 percent of African Americans had graduated from college. Only 29 per-

44. Brown, *Ministerial Education*, pp. 112-14.
45. May, *Profession of the Ministry*, p. 375; May, *Education of American Ministers*, p. 322.
46. Brown, *Ministerial Education*, pp. 34-37, 222; Mays and Nicholson, *Negro's Church*, pp. 41, 249.

cent of native-born whites, 5 percent of foreign-born whites, and 7 percent of African Americans had even graduated from high school. This was not a generation inclined to demand a seminary-educated clergy; they were more likely to be suspicious of too much education. They valued the minister's "practical ability to make religious enterprises successful." The reformers of the profession, however, saw an educated clergy as the wave of the future.[47]

The Professional Solution

Brown and May argued that seminary-trained ministers — the clerical professionals — were more successful than untrained preachers. Educated clergy attracted more members, raised higher budgets, constructed more buildings, and stimulated more benevolent giving. They took more initiative in denominational and community activities, established more extensive programs of fellowship and social service, and adapted their work more successfully to the communities in which they served, helping others "live gracefully and purposefully." Better and more widespread education could create more ministers in the same mold.[48]

To accomplish this aim, the seminaries needed to be better. First, the schools had low admission standards. More than three-fourths of the 198 divinity schools admitted students who lacked a college degree. In the African American seminaries, 88 percent of the students had no college degree, and a third of them had not graduated from high school. Brown and May found it problematic that even in some of the better divinity schools, 25 percent of the students had not completed college, which meant that the schools had to relax standards in the classroom. Brown believed that "many students" graduated with only "the most superficial mastery" of theology and the Bible, and the schools had failed to create good programs of "field work" in which students could benefit from supervision in the practice of ministry.[49]

The Education of American Ministers concluded with a plea for an agency that could raise the standards. It produced almost immediate action. In 1934, the Conference of Theological Seminaries and Colleges assumed an accrediting function for the schools it represented, and in 1936 its members reorganized themselves into the American Association of Theological Schools (AATS) in

47. Douglass and deS. Brunner, *Protestant Church,* pp. 105, 108; Truesdell, ed., *Sixteenth Census,* p. 41.

48. May, *Profession of the Ministry,* pp. 248-49.

49. May, *Education of American Ministers,* pp. 63, 66, 68, 97, 148, 192-251; Brown, *Ministerial Education,* p. 123; Mays and Nicholson, *Negro's Church,* p. 54.

the United States and Canada. The group decided that it would accredit only seminaries that required a three-year course of study and restricted admission to graduates of accredited colleges. They were determined that the requirements for the "professional degree" in ministry should equal those "usually required in any other field of graduate professional study."[50]

The organization gradually elevated the standards of the schools. In 1931, about 25 percent of the seminary students had not graduated from college. In 1936, the number fell to 18 percent, and it would continue to fall. By 1938, sixty-four Protestant schools had joined the association.[51]

The professional model attracted support among groups that had once disdained it. Since 1882, Bible institutes had provided practical training to prepare men and women for work as evangelists, missionaries, music leaders, and Christian educators. Most of the early students had no plans for ordained ministry. The schools admitted students without a high-school diploma, and they operated without full-time faculties, granted no degrees, and nurtured piety and practical skills more than historical and theological learning. Their founders accused the seminaries of favoring the "academic" rather than the practical and of "impoverishing" students through an "excess of learning."[52]

By the 1920s, Bible institutes added programs in pastoral preparation, and aspiring clergy enrolled in them, especially fundamentalists alienated from mainline seminaries. In 1930, more than fifty Bible schools trained both lay workers and pastors. They extended their course work to three or four years, taught liberal arts subjects, and granted degrees. In their pastoral training tracks they incorporated much of the curriculum of the Protestant seminaries, including courses in Greek and Hebrew. They trained students from any denomination, though they became especially popular for aspiring pastors from the Churches of Christ and certain Baptist, Wesleyan, Mennonite, and Pentecostal churches.[53]

Within the mainstream denominations, the quest for a more professional ministry prompted experiments beyond the walls of the seminaries. None was more influential than clinical pastoral education. In 1925, a chaplain at Worcester State Hospital in Massachusetts, Anton T. Boisen, brought theological stu-

50. AATS, *First Report of the Commission on Accrediting of the American Association of Theological Schools* (Louisville: AATS, 1938), pp. 5-9.

51. Conrad Cherry, *Hurrying Toward Zion: Universities, Divinity Schools, and American Protestantism* (Bloomington: Indiana University Press, 1995), pp. 135-36; AATS, *First Report*, p. 9.

52. Virginia Lieson Brereton, *Training God's Army: The American Bible Schools, 1880-1940* (Bloomington: Indiana University Press, 1990), p. 67.

53. Brereton, *Training God's Army*, pp. 70-76; S. A. Witmer, *The Bible College Story: Education with Dimension* (Manhasset, N.Y.: Channel Press, 1962), p. 44.

dents into psychiatric wards to explore the religious dimensions of mental illness. In the same year, the Boston physician Richard Cabot of the Harvard Medical School issued "A Plea for a Clinical Year in the Course of Theological Study." Cabot had less interest in the psychology of religion than in the deepening of clerical competence. He wanted ministerial students to receive supervision in pastoral work within hospitals and other institutions where people suffered. He wanted them to learn how to listen, to hear unspoken words, to write things down, to question themselves, and to fail and admit failure in an effort to discern the "growing edge" of the soul, whether their own or that of the suffering patient, and to respond appropriately.[54]

In 1930, Cabot and Boisen joined others in forming the Council for the Clinical Training of Theological Students. They wanted to expose students to "the real problems" of men and women, to teach them the "art" of helping people in trouble, and to promote "a greater degree of mutual understanding among the professional groups" that dealt with human problems. The clinical movement soon divided into two factions, a New York group emphasizing themes from psychiatry and psychoanalysis and favoring mental hospitals as training sites, and a New England group accenting social ethics and pastoral skills and preferring general hospitals, but the differences were mostly matters of emphasis. In 1936, the AATS recommended that every ministerial student undergo clinical training, and both groups formed alliances with seminaries.[55]

In the late 1920s, clergy from several denominations began to formulate ethical codes. They stipulated that ministers give "full service" to their parishes, declining to pursue other paid work unless their church encouraged it. They should honor contracts made with their churches and fulfill the obligations. They should cooperate with other ministers, neither criticizing them nor interfering with their work nor luring their members away. They should undertake "serious study," keep abreast of "current thought," and refrain from using sermon material from another preacher without acknowledging the source. As a "professional," the minister should make "service primary and the remuneration secondary."[56]

The reformers hoped that the studies of the 1930s would lead the way toward a more educated clergy, with more ministers who understood the history and theology of the church, possessed the judgment and skills to lead faithful congregations, extended their ministry into the larger community,

54. Holifield, *History of Pastoral Care*, pp. 234-35.

55. Edward E. Thornton, *Professional Education for Ministry: A History of Clinical Pastoral Education* (Nashville: Abingdon Press, 1970), p. 62.

56. Printed in Nolan B. Harmon, *Ministerial Ethics and Etiquette* (Nashville: Abingdon-Cokesbury, 1928), pp. 175-76.

and conducted themselves with ethical integrity and religious depth. The sociological studies of the thirties had their biases and blind spots. They ignored a large portion of the clerical population, reflected the preoccupations of urban liberal Protestantism, and underestimated the continuing strength of the populist impulse. But they sensed the currents that would alter the ministry after the Second World War, and they provided the impetus for the postwar move toward a more professional ministerial office.

CHAPTER 8

Ministry: From Revival to Crisis

1940-1970

In 1950, sixty thousand Protestant ministers preached in the churches of the Protestant "establishment." They constituted — depending on who was doing the counting — from a fourth to a half of the Protestant clergy in America. The establishment was informal, even inchoate, but its ministers enjoyed a social standing and a position of community leadership that set them apart. It consisted of nine mainly white denominations: the Congregationalists, Episcopalians, Methodists, Disciples of Christ, United Lutherans, Evangelical Lutherans, and American Baptists, along with the two largest Northern and Southern branches of the Presbyterians. It did not include some of the largest Protestant churches. The Southern Baptist Convention, with 22,300 pastors, maintained a wary distance from other denominations and built its own informal establishment in its region of the country. In 1950 the more than 25,000 preachers claimed by black Baptists, along with roughly eleven thousand black Methodist clergy, still stood on the margins of a segregated society. The ministers of the "mainline" churches exercised a cultural influence that was disproportionate to their numbers.[1]

Mainline ministers served as the pastors of most of the largest congregations, the leaders of the ecumenical agencies, the confidants of the nation's rulers, and the trustees of the country's Protestant colleges, hospitals, and humanitarian enterprises. Their denominations held almost half the members of the

---

1. The figure of 60,000, which comes from church reports, represents a fourth of the clergy if one accepts the numbers given by the churches in George Ketcham, ed., *Yearbook of the American Churches* (New York: National Council of Churches, 1951), p. 243, or half the clergy if one relies on the numbers in the federal census.

mainly white churches. They taught religion in the colleges, filled the college chaplaincies, oversaw the most prestigious seminaries, wrote the books that attracted public attention, and set the agenda for public discussion of religious life. They were the best educated among the Protestant clergy, and they propounded the professional ideal. But by 1970 many of them were deeply anxious about "crisis in the ministry."[2]

During the Second World War and afterward, these ministers — along with the others — had basked in public esteem. In 1942, Roper opinion polls ranked the clergy third among the groups "doing the most good." In 1947, ministers ranked first, with almost a third of adults saying that they did more good than any other group, and by 1953 about 40 percent of the population reached the same judgment. Roper said that no other group came close to matching the "prestige and pulling power" of ministers.[3]

Various rating scales placed the ministry among the most desirable and respected occupations. In a national poll in 1947 that asked people to rank the "prestige" of eighty-eight occupations, ministry ranked thirteenth, well below physicians (2.5) and scientists (8), but above lawyers (18). A 1958 survey ranked them seventh, and a poll of college students that year placed them fourth among eight professions judged according to their "usefulness to society." Some ministers worried about their "reduced importance" in American culture, but the public seemed to hold them in high esteem.[4]

By the end of the 1960s, however, the ministers in the mainline were beset by "turmoil and uncertainty," recruitment rates were declining, and some of the ablest young ministers had left the profession. National opinion polls showed that ministers had fallen in "public esteem and confidence." A 1967 Lou Harris poll showed that only 45 percent of the public expressed "confidence in the clergy," as opposed to the 74 percent who felt good about physicians or the 62 percent who spoke well of educators. Critics now spoke of "the pretensions of

2. William R. Hutchison, "Protestantism as Establishment," in *Between the Times: The Travail of the Protestant Establishment in America, 1900-1960*, ed. William R. Hutchison (Cambridge: Cambridge University Press, 1989), pp. 3-16.

3. W. Seward Salisbury, *Religion in American Culture: A Sociological Interpretation* (Homewood: Dorsey Press, 1964), p. 235; Stanley H. Chapman, "The Minister: Professional Man of the Church," *Social Forces* 23 (1944): 202-6.

4. Robert W. Hodge, Paul M. Siegel, and Peter H. Rossi, "Occupational Prestige in the United States, 1925-1963," *American Journal of Sociology* 70 (1964): 290; James D. Glasse, *Profession: Minister* (Nashville: Abingdon, 1968), pp. 109, 329-39; Salisbury, *Religion in American Culture*, p. 235; Theodore Caplow, *The Sociology of Work* (Minneapolis: University of Minnesota Press, 1954), p. 53; Bernard Barber, *Social Stratification* (New York: Harcourt, Brace, and World, 1957), pp. 100-111; Chapman, "The Minister," p. 203; Robert S. Ellwood, *1950: Crossroads of American Religious Life* (Louisville: Westminster John Knox, 2000), p. 213.

the white Anglo-Saxon Protestant establishment," announcing that "its past supremacy" was "everywhere threatened and tumbled" and that seminarians were "generally busy extricating themselves from its shameful tentacles." The rhetoric was hyperbolic, but everyone recognized that something was changing.[5]

Postwar Revival

On February 3, 1943, four military chaplains were sailing aboard the *Dorchester* when German submarines sank it with torpedoes. The four men — two Protestant ministers, one Catholic priest, and one Jewish rabbi — gave their life preservers to soldiers, locked their arms, and prayed as the waters swallowed them. For Americans, they became symbols of sacrifice and devotion to duty. One town after another honored them with monuments and attached their names to chapels and parks, and in 1948 the postal service printed 115 million stamps with their images in order to carry "their message" into "every home in the country." President Truman said that their sacrifice was "the greatest sermon that ever was preached." In honoring them, the nation honored the profession they represented.[6]

More than six thousand Protestant, three thousand Catholic, and three hundred Jewish clergy volunteered as military chaplains during World War II. They charted new paths. In the First World War, chaplains had chafed under a hodgepodge of duties, from overseeing dining halls to acting as defense counsel in courts martial. The military gradually upgraded standards, and during World War II it limited the secular duties. It also required most chaplains to have a college and seminary education. More than eight thousand received additional training in the Chaplain's School at Harvard. In each year of the war, more than one-fourth of the soldiers serving overseas consulted a chaplain. The chaplains spent so much time on the front lines that only the infantry and the Air Force exceeded their casualty rate. Their sacrifices impressed the public.[7]

---

5. Murray H. Leiffer, *Changing Expectations and Ethics in the Professional Ministry: A Research Report on the Attitudes of Ministers in Five Protestant Denominations* (Evanston: Garrett, 1969), p. 19; Charles R. Fielding, ed., *Education for Ministry* (Dayton: AATS, 1966), pp. 6, 23; Donald G. Bloesch, "Why People Are Leaving the Churches," *Religion in Life* (1969): 92; Jeffrey K. Hadden, *The Gathering Storm in the Churches: A Sociologist Looks at the Widening Gap Between Clergy and Laity* (1st ed., 1969; New York: Doubleday, 1970), p. 29.

6. "Post Office Rally Thanks 4 Chaplains," *New York Times,* June 27, 1948, p. 21; "Truman Says Deaths of 4 Chaplains at Sea Was the Greatest Sermon Ever Preached," *New York Times,* May 29, 1948, p. 17.

7. Roy J. Honeywell, *Chaplains of the United States Army* (Washington, D.C.: Department

Mainline theologians interpreted the war for the Christian public. Most of the clergy had supported the decision to enter the conflict, and in 1942 nearly four hundred Protestant leaders addressed the churches and the nation on the topic of "a just and endurable peace," warning against nationalism but projecting the hope for a "new world order" of human rights and international cooperation. The following year, twenty-six theologians wrote "The Relation of the Church to the War in the Light of the Christian Faith" — a subtle and nuanced application of Christian thought to an international tragedy. Some of the same theologians attracted national attention in 1945 by condemning the use of the atomic bombs. In short, the clergy claimed a voice in debates over national policy, and they had an audience. When Reinhold Niebuhr analyzed Soviet aggressiveness in Europe, his views circulated in *Time, Life,* and *Reader's Digest.*[8]

By 1948 leaders among the mainline mingled with the nation's policymakers, who wanted the churches to generate support for the European recovery plan and the creation of the United Nations. Throughout the next decade, the Protestant "reform establishment" — people like Niebuhr, John Bennett of Union Seminary, and the Methodist bishop G. Bromley Oxnam — had the ear, even though not always the assent, of presidents and the State Department. After the founding of the National Council of Churches in 1950, they issued, often under its auspices, statements on topics ranging from atomic weapons and foreign policy to economic justice and social welfare. It was imaginable, at least in church circles, that a small company of Protestant clergy might help shape the postwar world.[9]

Closer to home, the clergy were leading what appeared to be a religious revival. During the late 1940s, church membership surpassed 50 percent of the population for the first time, and by the mid-1950s it rose to more than 60 percent. The increase coincided with a demographic bubble as the postwar baby-boom generation reached the age at which parents wanted children to have religious instruction. But membership growth was only part of the story. In the ten years after 1945, the churches launched the largest building program in the history of American religion, spending more than three billion dollars on construction. Bible sales more than doubled, as did financial contributions, which reached two and a half billion dollars a year by the end of the 1950s. Whether all

---

of the Army, 1958), pp. 226-28, 272; Richard M. Budd, *Serving Two Masters: The Development of the American Military Chaplaincy, 1860-1920* (Lincoln: University of Nebraska Press, 2002), pp. 121-23; Dale R. Herspring, *Soldiers, Commissioners, and Chaplains* (Lanham: Rowman and Littlefield, 2001), pp. 39, 42.

8. Richard Fox, *Reinhold Niebuhr: A Biography* (New York: Pantheon, 1985), pp. 224, 229.

9. William M. King, "The Reform Establishment and the Ambiguities of Influence," *Between the Times*, pp. 125-29.

this constituted a "revival" remains a matter of definition, but many believed that it did.[10]

The sense of awakening came partly from the spread of Protestant churches into the suburbs. Right after the war, most Protestant church buildings — as many as 80 percent — still remained in small towns and the countryside, but as the population shifted, the suburban churches grew. The editor of the *Christian Century* remarked in 1951 that "the 'strong' Protestant churches" were now "typically in the suburbs." A ten-year study of fourteen denominations showed that 19 percent of their new church buildings stood in cities, 17.5 percent in small towns and the country, and 63.5 percent in suburban towns and neighborhoods. The suburban churches seemed to point the way to the future.[11]

The large churches — urban and suburban — were busy, and in the largest congregations, the norm became the diversified staff ministry. A senior pastor assumed the pulpit duties and coordinated the work of a staff that could include an assistant pastor, a minister of music, an education director, a minister of counseling, a minister of evangelism, a minister to youth, and a church administrator. By 1966, about a third of mainline congregations had multiple-staff ministries, and a third of all seminary graduates started out as staff members. They assumed specialized duties, and senior pastors oversaw their work.[12]

The majority of ministers served alone in single congregations, but they found, like the senior pastors, that administration consumed their time. The sociologist Nathan Hare thought that black pastors with large congregations were becoming executives instead of pastors and shepherds. In 1954, Samuel W. Blizzard examined the weekly schedules of seminary-educated pastors and found a marked change over twenty years. While Thomas May and William Adams Brown had concluded in their landmark 1934 study that ministers spent about 20 percent of their week as administrators, Blizzard found that adminis-

---

10. Ellwood, *1950*, p. 213; James Hudnut-Beumler, *Looking for God in the Suburbs: The Religion of the American Dream and Its Critics, 1945-1965* (New Brunswick: Rutgers University Press, 1994), p. 37; "Church Building Boom Reaches New High," *Christian Century* 48 (Nov. 30, 1955): 1390.

11. Robert Wuthnow, *The Restructuring of American Religion: Society and Faith Since World War II* (Princeton: Princeton University Press, 1988), p. 27; Martin E. Marty, *The New Shape of American Religion* (New York: Harper and Brothers, 1958), pp. 95, 103; Paul Hutchinson, "American Protestantism at the Mid-Century Mark," *Religion in Life* 20 (1951): 192.

12. David O. Moberg, *The Church as a Social Institution* (1st ed., 1962; Grand Rapids: Baker Book House, 1984), p. 499; Glasse, *Profession: Minister*, p. 120; Ross P. Scherer and Theodore O. Wedel, eds., *The Church and Its Manpower Management* (New York: National Council of Churches, 1966), pp. 45-57; Robert Clyde Johnson, ed., *The Church and Its Changing Ministry* (Philadelphia: General Assembly, 1961), pp. iv, 142.

tration and organization required about half their time. Most ministers did not enjoy it.[13]

Clergy told him that they relished their pastoral and preaching roles; they disliked administration. They saw preaching and pastoral care as their most important duties, administration as the least important. They thought they did their best work as preachers and pastors, their worst as organizers. But they spent most of their time administering and organizing. Some country pastors spent almost half their time the same way. Ministry was no profession for studious introverts. Blizzard found that the pastors he interviewed spent about 23 percent of their time on "idea-oriented" roles, like preaching and teaching, and 77 percent on "people-oriented" tasks.[14]

In the midst of this busy schedule, pastors heard demands from the laity for "more meaningful worship." The response of at least some pastors was to spend more time trying to make their sermons "interesting and exciting," even though the press of other duties pushed preparation time to Friday nights and Saturdays. The laity thought of the minister as "paid to preach," but they had little desire for long sermons, which often shrank, in the mainline churches, to twenty minutes. Sermons also became more "topical," making points only loosely related to biblical texts. "Many ministers are convinced," wrote one critic, "that this is the only kind of sermon to which modern American congregations will listen." Congregations were not as eager for sermons as they had once been. Sunday evening services were fading away.[15]

What did more meaningful worship mean? Many tried merely to enliven the familiar threefold revivalist order of worship: preliminaries, sermon, and invitation. But urban and suburban pastors — at least some of them — continued the trend, already underway in the 1930s, of introducing older liturgical forms. *Christian Century* editor Paul Hutchinson remarked in 1951 that "a stately liturgy" had become "commonplace." Liturgical reformers moved the pulpit to the side and the communion table to the front and center, and A. B. Dick's stencil

13. Nathan Hare, "Have Negro Ministers Failed Their Roles?" *Negro Digest* (1963): 11-19; Samuel W. Blizzard, *The Protestant Parish Minister: A Behavioral Science Interpretation* (Storrs: Society for the Scientific Study of Religion, 1985), pp. 100-101, 102; Moberg, *Church as a Social Institution*, p. 497.

14. Blizzard, *Protestant Parish Minister*, p. 101; Robert A. Lee, "The Organizational Dilemma in American Protestantism," in *Ethics and Bigness*, ed. Harlan Cleveland and Harold D. Lasswell (New York: Harper and Brothers, 1962), p. 201.

15. Blizzard, *Protestant Parish Minister*, p. 112; Kenneth Wilson Underwood, *Protestant and Catholic: Religious and Social Interaction in an Industrial Community* (Boston: Beacon Press, 1957), p. 72; Moberg, *Church as a Social Institution*, p. 488; James D. Smart, *The Rebirth of Ministry* (Philadelphia: Westminster Press, 1960), pp. 60-70; Lefferts A. Loetscher and George L. Hunt, *A Brief History of the Presbyterians* (Philadelphia: Westminster Press, 1978), p. 119.

duplicator allowed them to distribute printed orders of worship on Sunday mornings. The Methodists prepared their first official *Book of Worship* (1945), Presbyterians issued a new edition of their *Book of Common Worship* (1946), Congregationalists printed *A Book of Worship for Free Churches* (1948), and several Lutheran communions joined in publishing a *Service Book and Hymnal* (1958).[16]

Ministers recognized soon enough that the suburban churches also had other distinctive demands. For one thing, they had to be child-centered. The baby boom filled the churches with children, and parents wanted programs for them. It became a cliché that church growth required attention to children, so ministers continued with children's sermons, "junior church" during the Sunday worship hour, and recreation programs. The Presbyterian James Smart argued that ministry with children and young people offered the best chance to mold a congregation, but by the early 1960s Yale theologian James Gustafson found a restiveness among ministers weary of "running the new children's crusade in the child-centered program of the suburban church."[17]

Urban and suburban sprawl made it more difficult to visit, but house calls remained a staple of clerical work. During the 1940s, the large denominations touted "visitation evangelism" by pastors and laity — one enthusiast called it "the most important development" in Protestantism in two decades — and some pastors spent a part of every weekday in pastoral calling. Two decades later, proponents still argued for visits with "content and purpose." Sixty-one percent of Methodists ranked preaching and visiting as their "most important pastoral responsibilities." No minister could neglect the hospital call and the visit to the bereaved. Yet some now spoke of general visiting as the "older way," less meaningful than the counseling session in the pastor's office.[18]

No topic created more interest after the war than pastoral counseling. In 1939 seminaries offered few courses, but by the 1950s almost every seminary had at least one counseling course and more than 80 percent provided courses in

16. Hutchinson, "American Protestantism," p. 193; Peter H. Pleune, *Some to Be Pastors* (Nashville: Abingdon-Cokesbury, 1943), p. 13; James F. White, *Protestant Worship: Traditions in Transition* (Louisville: Westminster John Knox, 1989), pp. 5, 13, 167; James F. White, "Public Worship in Protestantism," in *Altered Landscapes: Christianity in America, 1935-1985*, ed. David W. Lotz, Donald W. Shriver Jr., and John F. Wilson (Grand Rapids: Eerdmans, 1989), pp. 107-12.

17. Pleune, *Some to Be Pastors*, pp. 157-65, 169; James Gustafson, "The Clergy in the United States," *Daedalus: Journal of the American Academy of Arts and Sciences* 92 (1963): 737; Smart, *Rebirth of Ministry*, p. 91.

18. William C. Martin, *To Fulfill This Ministry* (Nashville: Abingdon, 1949), p. 70; C. Stanley Lowell, "Visitation Evangelism? Yes," *Christian Century* 63 (April 14, 1946): 988-89; Leiffer, *Changing Expectations*, p. 134; Blizzard, *Protestant Parish Minister*, pp. 84-85.

psychology. Observers of the schools concluded that the "new emphases in psychology and pastoral counseling" had produced a momentous "turn in the education of the ministry." Countless theology students and ministers learned the techniques of the therapist Carl Rogers, whose theory of "client-centered therapy" urged counselors to avoid advice-giving. For some clergy, the proper style of counseling was now a non-directive listening that enabled parishioners to discern their own path.[19]

"A good minister cannot now escape personal counseling," wrote Harry Emerson Fosdick at New York's Riverside Church. "It is in the air." A survey conducted during the 1950s by the National Institute of Mental Health showed that 42 percent of all people who sought help for emotional problems turned first to their ministers. Ethicist Gibson Winter at the University of Chicago worried that pastors were coming to think of counseling as "*the* pastoral care of the Church," even though they lacked the time to do much of it.[20]

Everyone agreed that ministers stayed busy. Assessing the state of the profession in 1963, theologian James Gustafson highlighted one theme: the activities of the clergy were "increasing in number and variety." They were preachers, scholars, teachers, priests at the altar, and counselors, but they also conducted financial campaigns, managed public relations, devoted time to extra-parochial church boards and councils, assumed denominational tasks, mediated community conflicts, prayed and spoke in civic groups, cooperated with social agencies, engaged in social reform, directed recreation, and administered "multiple organizations" within the congregation. Commentators marveled at the "multitude of ever more diversified functions" that ministers had to perform. "The list of things that occupy the average pastor's time," wrote one, was "prodigious."[21]

Was the minister being asked to do too much? In 1956 Wesley Shrader of Yale Divinity School published in *Life* magazine an article that tried to explain why ministers were "breaking down." Shrader contended that the "multiple roles" assigned to ministers and the "impossible tasks" expected of them by congregations had led to a surfeit of emotional distress. The article ignited a de-

19. E. Brooks Holifield, *A History of Pastoral Care in America: From Salvation to Self-Realization* (Nashville: Abingdon, 1983), pp. 270, 300; H. Richard Niebuhr, Daniel Day Williams, and James M. Gustafson, *The Advancement of Theological Education* (New York: Harper and Brothers, 1957), p. 128; Seward Hiltner, "Why Pastoral Psychology?" *Pastoral Psychology* 1 (1950): 8, 43.

20. Harry Emerson Fosdick, "The Minister and Psychotheraphy," *Pastoral Psychology* 11 (1960): 13; Holifield, *History of Pastoral Care*, p. 274; Gibson Winter, "Pastoral Counseling or Pastoral Care," *Pastoral Psychology* 8 (1957): 16.

21. Gustafson, "The Clergy," pp. 724-27; Johnson, ed., *Church and Its Changing Ministry*, pp. vi, 154.

bate. The dean of Andover-Newton Theological School, Roy Pearson, thought the problem was that churches and seminaries accepted candidates without a clear vision of ministry. William Hudnut replied in the *Christian Century* that Shrader's premise was a myth. The evidence for pastoral "breakdown" was merely anecdotal: "Most of the ministers I know are so fascinated by their jobs that they would not consider anything else; the ministry is too exciting."[22]

Theologian Daniel Day Williams believed that Shrader had identified real tensions. The problem was that the clergy lacked "an integrating conception of ministry." Lutheran Joseph Sittler cast the blame on an "instrumentalist" mentality in the churches, which turned ministers into "executive officers" absorbed by "promotions" and "programs": "A minister has been ordained to an Office; he too often ends up running an office." Samuel Southard agreed that the problem was "the tyranny of expectations" from both congregations and officials, and ex-minister James B. Moore, writing in *Harper's Magazine,* took a similar line: young ministers were leaving the church, he argued, because the demands of the institution subverted their sense of integrity.[23]

Worries about the loss of "an integrated conception of ministry" surfaced often in the 1950s and 1960s. Too often, Gustafson claimed in 1954, ministers lacked a "central focus" for the "integration" of their various activities. Seminaries had failed to provide them with a theoretical foundation that united a "theological doctrine" of ministry with a "sociological definition" of clerical tasks. Ministers lacking such a foundation felt obliged to spend their time "in activity that is useful in the eyes of the laity" even if they saw it as peripheral to the mission of the church. He thought that too many of them fell back on the cultivation of a genial personality and a feverish busyness. Gustafson wanted seminaries to do a better job of providing principles to guide the minister's work.[24]

22. Wesley Shrader, "Why Ministers Are Breaking Down," *Life* (August 20, 1956): 95-104; Roy Pearson, "Why Ministers Break Down," *Christianity and Crisis* 16 (1956): 144-45; William H. Hudnut, "Are Ministers Cracking Up?" *Christian Century* 73 (Nov. 7, 1956): 1289.

23. Daniel Day Williams, "Ministry Under Tension," *Christianity and Crisis* 16 (Dec. 10, 1956): 169-70; Joseph Sittler, "The Maceration of the Minister," *Christian Century* 76 (June, 1959): 698, 700; Samuel Southard, "The Tyranny of Expectations," *Pastoral Psychology* 8 (1957): 9-11, 16; James B. Moore, "Why Young Ministers Are Leaving the Church," *Harper's Magazine* 215 (July, 1957): 65-69.

24. Williams, "Ministry Under Tension," p. 169; James M. Gustafson, "An Analysis of the Problem of the Role of the Minister," *The Journal of Religion* 34 (1954): 187, 190; Gustafson, "The Clergy," p. 732.

The Professional Era

By the 1950s, the professional ideal — the goal of a highly educated ministry — had gained broad support, and theological educators were again turning their attention to the performance of the schools. With the aid of the Carnegie Corporation, the seminaries undertook yet another study of clerical training, assigning oversight to Gustafson, Williams, and ethicist H. Richard Niebuhr of Yale Divinity School. As director of the study, Niebuhr wrote the volume — *The Purpose of the Church and Its Ministry* (1956) — that interpreted its findings for the schools and the clergy. Describing the ministry as a "perplexed profession," he emphasized the "over-busyness" of clergy who lacked a "set of principles" that could give them a "standard" for "the exercise of a profession."[25]

Niebuhr claimed that the interviews and surveys of his research teams had identified an "emerging new conception of the ministry." Unlike the medieval governor of souls, the Reformation preacher, the eighteenth-century evangelist, or the liturgical priest, ministers in the mid-twentieth century were moving toward a conception of themselves as "pastoral directors," responsible for training the laity to carry on the mission of the church. Niebuhr identified that mission as the increase among men and women of "the love of God and neighbor."[26]

He assumed that the seminaries educated "a large proportion" of the clergy. It was not clear how large the proportion was. In 1940, the census counted 133,449 ministers, priests, and rabbis, a figure that increased to 160,694 in 1950, though the churches themselves claimed by then to have 285,014. Most of the Protestant clergy had no exposure to a theological seminary. A decade before the publication of Niebuhr's volume, one study found that fewer than half of them had graduated even from a college. Even fewer were seminary graduates.[27]

Comprehensive figures are not available, but in the American Baptist Convention, the largest northern Baptist denomination, only 22 percent of the ministers in 1945 had both college and theological training; 32 percent had not attended college. In the state of Missouri, only a third of the rural clergy in the mainline denominations — and only 1 percent in the "sectarian" churches — had a seminary education in 1952. In the Methodist Church, the largest

---

25. H. Richard Niebuhr, *The Purpose of the Church and Its Ministry* (New York: Harper and Row, 1956), pp. 48, 52.

26. Niebuhr, *Purpose of the Church*, pp. 59, 82, 83, 110,116.

27. Niebuhr, *Purpose of the Church*, p. vii; Truesdell, ed., *Sixteenth Census*, p. 75; Robert W. Burgess, *Census of Population: 1950 Part I: United States Summary* (Washington, D.C.: Government Printing Office, 1953), p. 276; Ketcham, ed., *Yearbook of the American Churches*, p. 243; Wuthnow, *Restructuring*, p. 29; Niebuhr, et al., *Advancement*, p. 9.

Protestant denomination in the 1950s, 52 percent of the fully ordained clergy throughout the nation had seminary degrees in 1959, but when the Methodist figures included the non-ordained "approved supply pastors," who occupied 43 percent of Methodist pulpits, the number of seminary-educated Methodist clergy dropped to 22 percent, even though the Methodists had fully embraced theological education and created twelve seminaries.[28]

Some of the smaller denominations — such as the Church of the Nazarene, the Churches of Christ, and the Seventh-day Adventists — were only beginning to encourage young pastors to study at seminaries, and many of their congregations remained suspicious. The African American churches in the 1950s sent only a few hundred students to seminaries. In some regions, seminary-trained black pastors were as rare as they had been half a century earlier; only 1 percent of the more than twenty thousand black Baptist preachers in the South had a college degree, and only 2 percent had taken any theological courses. The Niebuhr study lamented the "appalling shortage" of seminary graduates in the black pastorate.[29]

Twelve years after Niebuhr published his observations, the seminary-educated were still in the minority. In 1968, 59 percent of the Congregationalists, 52 percent of the fully ordained United Methodists, 51 percent of northern Presbyterians, 49 percent of southern Presbyterians, and 36 percent of Southern Baptists had seminary degrees. But by then America had at least 238 denominations, and only around 12 percent of them expected their clergy to have college and seminary training. Most of them, including the rapidly growing Pentecostal churches, refused to require a college education, and the largest Protestant denominations did not always insist on it. In the late 1960s, more than half the 37,000 Southern Baptist clergy had not graduated from college. One survey in 1965 produced an estimate that the state of Tennessee alone had more than five thousand ministers without college or seminary training. The sentiment was still strong in some circles that too much education tended to "alienate the minister" from the congregation.[30]

Yet congregations were becoming more educated and demanding better-educated ministers. In 1940 only 15 percent of American Protestants graduated

28. Robert G. Torbet, *The Baptist Ministry Then and Now* (Philadelphia: Judson, 1953), p. 65; Moberg, *Church as a Social Institution*, p. 487; Paul N. Garber, *The Methodist Ministry 1959* (Nashville: Department of Ministerial Education, 1959), p. 39.

29. Niebuhr, et al., *Advancement*, pp. 5, 226; Charles Hamilton, *The Black Preacher in America* (New York: William Morrow, 1972), p. 213.

30. Leiffer, *Changing Expectations*, p. 173; W. A. Criswell, *Standing on the Promises* (Dallas: Word Publishing, 1990), pp. 135, 235; Fielding, ed., *Education for Ministry*, p. 7; T. Valentine Parker, *American Protestantism: An Appraisal* (New York: Philosophical Library, 1956), p. 98.

from college and only 34 percent had a high-school education. In the subsequent ten years, with the aid of the G.I. Bill, the colleges doubled their enrollment. As a result, the numbers of college-educated laity in some denominations rose steadily. By the mid-1950s, about 33 percent of Presbyterian laity, 20 percent of Methodists, and 14 percent of Baptists and Lutherans had college degrees. The expansion of higher education in the 1960s meant that by 1970 around 25 percent of the laity in the larger denominations — and more than half in a few of the mainline churches — had a college education. As early as the 1940s, denominational leaders were insisting that these rising educational levels required "a well-educated ministry." The lay members of Protestant churches echoed the call. Sixty-seven percent of Methodist laity in 1947 said they wanted pastors with a seminary education.[31]

The result was a steady upward trend in applications to theological schools and a determined effort to improve the quality of seminary education. By 1950, the number of students was about double the prewar enrollment, and the American Association of Theological Schools was having some success in its drive to raise standards. Theological education was finally becoming a graduate-professional enterprise. The seminaries in the AATS could report by the mid-1950s that 80 percent of their students had graduated from college. By 1962, the figure rose to 89 percent, and the better schools would admit no student without a degree and acceptable grades from an accredited college.[32]

Niebuhr's team reported steady advance in the quality of seminary faculties. The seminaries were the American centers for the scholarly study of religion, and some of the best schools — Yale, Harvard, Union, Chicago, and others — generated scholarship that attracted attention among scholars throughout the world. The seminaries still had difficulty attracting the most academically gifted college graduates, but "on the whole" the students were of "good average intelligence and achievement" and included a respectable number of "first-rate minds." Academic expectations were not high enough: the schools routinely granted higher grades than other comparable graduate-level programs. But for the most part the study found progress in ministerial education.[33]

In 1957, Charles L. Taylor, the former dean of the Episcopal Divinity School

31. Theodore Caplow, et al., *All Faithful People: Change and Continuity in Middletown's Religion* (Minneapolis: University of Minnesota Press, 1983), p. 172; Muray H. Leiffer, *The Methodist Ministry in 1948* (Evanston: Garrett Biblical Institute, 1948), p. 5; Wuthnow, *Restructuring*, p. 160; Murray H. Leiffer, *The Layman Looks at the Minister* (Nashville: Abingdon, 1947), p. 139.

32. Wuthnow, *Restructuring*, p. 36; Niebuhr, et al., *Advancement*, p. 8; Keith R. Bridston and Dwight W. Culver, *Pre-Seminary Education: Report of the Lilly Endowment Study* (Minneapolis: Augsburg, 1965), p. 100.

33. Niebuhr, et al., *Advancement*, pp. 70, 208.

in Massachusetts, became the first full-time executive director of the American Association of Theological Schools, and he set himself to promoting the professional ideal. The church required leaders who could "do that which no others do so clearly or so well" and were able to "do it with a competence derived from special education." Whatever one might call it, he said, this was a professional model of ministry, and the seminaries offered the best means to nurture it. By the end of the 1960s, membership in the AATS grew to 182 seminaries.[34]

The desire for a more professional clergy also left its mark on the Bible schools. In 1947, they formed an Accrediting Association of Bible Institutes and Bible Colleges, and many began to expect high-school graduation as a prerequisite for admission. They set a lower mark than the seminaries, but by 1960 most were raising standards for students aiming at ordained ministry. In that year, 248 Bible institutes and colleges were training 25,000 students, many of whom were destined for a clerical vocation. In 1969, about 31 percent of Southern Baptist clergy, 15 percent of the Methodists, and a much higher percentage of ministers in smaller conservative and fundamentalist denominations had received most of their training in the Bible schools.[35]

The clinical pastoral education movement also expanded its style of professional education. By 1955, CPE centers had trained four thousand Protestant clergy, and in 1967, when the New England and the New York clinical training organizations merged into the Association for Clinical Pastoral Education, eighty-one seminaries applied for affiliation. CPE supervisors trained students in 217 hospitals, medical centers, prisons, reformatories, and community service agencies. By then, the Lutherans and Southern Baptists had formed their own clinical associations, and clinical training was becoming a familiar option for seminary students.[36]

The clinical educators contrasted their methods of professional formation with the more "academic" emphasis of the seminaries. The popularity of CPE meant that increasing numbers of theological students spent several months — sometimes a year — working in unfamiliar institutions, usually as chaplains, and meeting in small groups in which they presented case studies or verbatim accounts of pastoral conversations. The supervisors introduced them to themes from psychology, sociology, and theology, but they also required the students to

34. Walter D. Wagoner, *Bachelor of Divinity* (New York: Association Press, 1963), p. 50; Jesse H. Ziegler, *ATS Through Two Decades: Reflections on Theological Education 1960-1980* (Vandalia, Ohio: Jesse H. Ziegler, 1984), p. 210.

35. S. A. Witmer, *The Bible College Story: Education with Dimension* (Manhasset, N.Y.: Channel Press, 1962), pp. 44, 54, 107; Leiffer, *Changing Expectations*, p. 173.

36. Edward E. Thornton, *Professional Education for Ministry* (Nashville: Abingdon Press, 1970), pp. 116, 151, 153, 191; Holifield, *History of Pastoral Care*, p. 271.

explore their interactions within the group, to recognize and assess their assumptions about ministry, and to discern their styles of relating to other people. For many students, the sessions functioned as a form of group therapy, softening rigidities, fostering a capacity for self-criticism, and nurturing strengths. The aim was to produce self-aware and skillful pastors.

The push toward professionalization brought new attempts at organization and new degree programs. In 1965, a chaplain at the Texas Medical Center in Houston proposed an Academy of Parish Clergy, and four years later the Lilly Endowment provided the initial funding for an association that would offer clinical training, encourage continuing education, and recognize "professional excellence." The hope was to attract a substantial portion of the nation's clergy, though the organization never drew large numbers of adherents. The more popular move came in the formation of graduate programs offering a doctor of ministry degree in the seminaries. In 1961, San Francisco Theological Seminary advertised an in-service doctoral program, and Claremont and the Divinity School of the University of Chicago also proposed professional doctorates. By 1976, ninety schools would be involved in D.Min. programs training almost four hundred students.[37]

Even the ecumenical passions of the Protestant mainline included a nod toward a more professional ministry. Directed at overcoming the divisions within the church, the mergers and federations of the era also aimed at a ministry united in a common enterprise with uniform standards. In 1960, several mainline churches began a Consultation On Church Union (COCU), which eventually included nine denominations, white and black. In discussing the ministry, they emphasized the relatively new theme of the ministry of "the whole people of God," lay and clerical. But they also insisted that the "ordained ministries" — the bishops, presbyters, and deacons — had a distinctive "representative" character as guardians of "Gospel, Scripture, and Tradition" who were charged with "equipping" the laity for their witness.[38]

Tracing the origins of the ministry to "Christ's action through his apostles," the COCU documents assigned ordained clergy responsibility for proclaiming the Word and celebrating the sacraments as expressions of the "redemptive work of Christ through his church." The documents accented "three immediate

37. Granger E. Westberg, "An American Academy of Parish Clergy," *Christian Century* 82 (April 28, 1965): 557; "Academy of Parish Clergy Founded," *Christian Century* 86 (May 21, 1969): 704; "The D.Min Degree After Ten Years: A Symposium," *Christian Century* 93 (Feb. 4-11, 1976): 96-104; Harry B. Adams, "Doctoral Studies for Pastors," *Christian Century* 82 (April 28, 1965): 560.

38. *A Plan of Union for the Church of Christ Uniting* (Princeton: Consultation on Church Union, 1970), p. 44.

necessities": ministers would need an ecumenical vision, a passion for social justice, and a first-rate education. The uniting denominations would have to make "massive provision" of educational resources "for every ordained person." Educational disparities in the denominations called for "intensive programs" to "prepare the clergy to minister in the united church." The need was for a more professional ministry.[39]

Specialization

The drive for a more professional clergy paralleled a desire for "specialized ministries." The churches needed experts. They needed them, for example, to staff the growing national boards and agencies. By 1963, as Gustafson noted, a denominational social action agency could have experts on "race relations, international affairs, labor relations, economic polity, and politics." National and regional offices had "specialists in social welfare, in urban and rural church problems, in social research, in fund-raising, in planning church buildings, in financial affairs, [and] in public relations and mass communications." Foreign mission boards needed experts who could oversee work in particular countries or regions. The churches sought experts in youth work, aging, and families; they also required specialists in parish, collegiate, and seminary education. In a single denomination, the Disciples of Christ, the central staff of the national offices increased tenfold between 1900 and 1968. The national boards of other large denominations saw similar rates of growth.[40]

The most recognizable specialist was the foreign missionary. By 1940 American Protestants sponsored about ten thousand full-time "career" missionaries throughout the world, and twenty years later they provided two-thirds of the world's foreign mission personnel. No stereotype can capture the diversity within this company of foreign missionary clergy. Some identified themselves with their new cultures and broke free from homegrown ideologies. Missionaries to Vietnam were among the earliest critics of American military policy there.[41]

39. *Plan of Union*, pp. 44-45.

40. *Plan of Union*, p. 40; Gustafson, "The Clergy," p. 727; Gibson Winter, *Religious Identity: A Study of Religious Organization* (New York: Macmillan, 1968), p. 21. Carr-Saunders (1955) claimed that ministry was "less influenced by specialization than any other profession" and that priests and ministers remained uniformly "general practitioners." The claim seems less than plausible.

41. William R. Hutchison, "Americans in World Mission: Revision and Realignment," in *Altered Landscapes*, p. 155; David M. Stowe, "Heritage and Horizon in Missions," *Christian Cen-*

Some spent their lives in isolated mission posts, but others launched enterprises with far-reaching effects. The Presbyterians Frank and Effa Seely Laubach, for example, promoted the spread of literacy, publishing primers in 239 languages and instituting an initiative called "Each One Teach One" that taught, according to one estimate, sixty million people to read and write. Apart from their various forms of work abroad — ranging from evangelism and pastoral care to college teaching, health care, social work, agricultural assistance, and community development — missionaries continued to be vital sources of information about the world for Americans.[42]

As a result of budgetary pressures, changing theological views, and demands abroad for indigenous leadership in the mission churches, the mainline denominations began during the 1950s to reduce their foreign presence. In 1951, Paul Hutchinson spoke of a reassessment on the part of missionaries who felt troubled by the colonial excesses of Western nations and responsive to the desires for an "indigenous Christian church and culture" in the regions where they had served. But evangelical and fundamentalist churches redoubled their efforts, and by 1960 they sponsored 65 percent of the more than 29,000 missionaries serving overseas. Even before the Second World War, the missionaries had divided into two camps, the first pushing above all for conversions to Christianity, the second emphasizing a Christian presence alongside others who worked for the common good. But both sides shared knowledge of foreign languages and cultures that marked them as specialists.[43]

The ecumenical impulse in the mainline churches offered additional sites of specialization. In 1928, the Federal Council of Churches, the largest cooperative Protestant organization, employed fifty-two staff members, clerical and lay. Its successor, the National Council of Churches, began work in 1951 with four divisions, each with twelve to twenty departments and commissions, and by the end of the 1960s it had a staff of 187, most of them clerics, all of them specialists in some field of ecumenical activity. The National Association of Evangelicals, founded in 1943, provided a smaller conservative Protestant counterpoint. Clergy staffed national councils for home and foreign missions, stewardship, and education. They ran a Protestant Film Commission, a Protestant Radio Commission, and an Inter-Seminary Movement. As early as 1949, there were

tury 77 (Nov. 9, 1960): 1311; Scott Flipse, "To Save 'Free Vietnam' and Lose Our Souls," in *The Foreign Missionary Enterprise at Home*, ed. Daniel H. Bays and Grant Wacker (Tuscaloosa: University of Alabama Press, 2003), pp. 206-22.

42. Hartzell Spence, *The Clergy and What They Do* (New York: Franklin Watts, 1961), p. 9.

43. Hutchinson, "American Protestantism," p. 197; Hutchison, "Americans in World Mission," pp. 155-70; Stowe, "Heritage," pp. 1311-13; Wuthnow, *Restructuring*, p. 182.

forty state councils of churches and nearly 850 local councils, and for the next decade the number of such agencies grew steadily.[44]

Some ministers gravitated toward the college campus. Clergy had always been active at colleges, but as late as 1900 only a dozen ministers devoted all their time to campus work. As the religious ethos of the schools dimmed, agencies like the YMCA-sponsored campus ministers, and such groups as the Presbyterian Westminster Foundation began to function as campus churches. By the 1930s, two-thirds of the campus pastors considered student ministry their life work, and they saw themselves as set apart from parish clergy. Beginning in 1948, they formed their own national associations for "professional fellowship" and organized workshops and conventions for professional training.[45]

The campus ministers were better educated than the average parish pastor, and they enjoyed more freedom, which some expressed by promoting peace movements, economic cooperatives, racial justice, and women's rights. They were also more theologically liberal and more devoted to ecumenical cooperation. An upsurge of financial support after the war brought their number to more than three thousand by 1963, and during the 1960s they often took the lead in campus activism and social reform.[46]

Still other clergy took up specialized ministries in counseling centers. The establishment in 1937 of the American Foundation for Religion and Psychiatry in New York, which created a counseling center connected to the Marble Collegiate Church, began a national trend. By 1960, at least eighty-four Protestant centers, staffed by ministers, psychiatrists, and social workers, offered counseling services. A single center at Boston University conducted eleven thousand counseling sessions in one year. Soon clergy were debating the merits of private practice by full-time pastoral counselors. The counselors created their own professional associations, notably the American Association of Pastoral Counselors, formed in 1963 to set accrediting standards for centers and determine procedures for certifying counseling specialists.[47]

44. Robert A. Schneider, "Voice of Many Waters: Church Federation in the Twentieth Century," in *Between the Times*, p. 109; H. George Anderson, "Ecumenical Movements," in *Altered Landscapes*, pp. 94-95, 97; Lee, "Organizational Dilemma," p. 193.

45. Donald G. Shockley, *Campus Ministry: The Church Beyond Itself* (Louisville: Westminster John Knox, 1989), pp. 27, 34-35; Kenneth Underwood, ed., *The Church, the University, and Social Policy: The Danforth Study of Campus Ministries* (Middletown: Wesleyan University Press, 1969), p. 75; Clarence P. Shedd, *The Church Follows Its Students* (New Haven: Yale University Press, 1938), pp. 145-47, 246, 272.

46. Underwood, ed., *Church, University, Social Policy*, pp. 334, 347.

47. Holifield, *History of Pastoral Care*, pp. 273, 345.

Ministers who received training in the clinical centers found openings as chaplains in hospitals and other institutions. In 1940, only a handful of Protestant hospitals employed full-time chaplains; the Veterans Administration had no regular chaplaincy; and no state mental hospital had a plan for including chaplains on its staff. By the 1950s, almost five hundred full-time chaplains were serving in general hospitals, at least two hundred more worked in mental hospitals, and the Veterans Administration alone employed 241 chaplains. Ministers interested in chaplaincy crowded into a host of institutions — prisons, reform schools, nursing homes, drug and alcohol rehabilitation centers, and other agencies — which required distinctive skill and knowledge. Like the counselors, they created their own forms of professional association — such groups as the Chaplain's Section of the American Protestant Hospital Association (1946) and the Association of Mental Hospital Chaplains (1948). For more than a few, the specialized guild became the source of professional identity.[48]

In seminaries and colleges — and sometimes in the religious studies departments founded in state universities during the 1960s — clergy practiced yet another form of specialized ministry. By 1946, two-thirds of all accredited colleges — including all the church-related schools and 30 percent of the state colleges — had religion departments. Prior to the 1970s, most of the teachers in college and university religion departments were ordained ministers, and they produced scholarship that interpreted religion to the broader public. The minister in the academy often became a highly specialized expert in one carefully delimited field of religious studies.[49]

By the 1960s, Protestant observers were noting an "accelerating movement of clergy toward preference for work in 'experimental' and 'specialized' ministries rather than the parish church." The majority of students in some of the best-known seminaries indicated that they hoped to "enter some field other than 'leadership of a local parish.'" A study of mainline divinity schools in 1961 found that no more than a third of the students said that they wanted to go into parish churches. In 1967, only about 18 percent of the entering class at Yale Divinity School expressed a desire for ministry in a local church. The specialized ministries proved to be so numerous and so inviting that they seemed, to some, to threaten the stability of traditional parish ministry. And students also veered away from parish ministry because many of them — Catholics as well as Protestants — saw local congregations as bastions of conventionality, resistant to

48. Holifield, *History of Pastoral Care*, p. 273; Thornton, *Professional Education*, p. 115.
49. Dorothy C. Bass, "Ministry on the Margin: Protestants and Education," in *Between the Times*, p. 59.

change and indifferent to social justice. Quite apart from the lure of specialization, parish ministry appeared to face a crisis.[50]

Conflicts

In 1949, Paul Moore entered the Episcopal priesthood. The privileged son of an industrialist, he had studied at the elite St. Paul's School and Yale University before enlisting in the Marines in World War II. Almost fatally wounded in hand-to-hand combat in the Solomon Islands, he returned to the United States as a decorated war hero. Influenced by conversion as a schoolboy — and by school and military chaplains — he attended General Theological Seminary in New York before moving into an inner-city parish in Jersey City. He involved himself in the cause of civil rights, helping to form a human relations council that tried to convince the mayor and city council to provide services to ghetto neighborhoods. He helped organize the Urban Mission Priests, who sponsored work with children, social action cells, and Bible classes in public housing projects. When he moved to Christ Church Cathedral in Indianapolis in 1958, he again worked on a human relations council that lobbied city hall even as "the brunt of McCarthyism" raised barriers to social ministry.[51]

Moore recited the Office of Morning and Evening Prayer every day, and he nurtured a worshipping congregation while also nudging its members to involve themselves in the suffering of the streets. In 1963, he became suffragan bishop of the Diocese of Washington, D.C., where he mixed with the power-brokers of the nation, helping organize the Coalition of Conscience to lobby Congress on behalf of the poor. He spent much of the summer of 1964 working for civil rights in the Delta Ministry in Mississippi, and he joined the march in Selma that helped maintain the momentum for civil rights legislation. With the outbreak of war in Vietnam, he worked for the antiwar movement. He later became the bishop of New York, where he dealt with student demonstrators in Episcopal churches, opposed and then supported demands for women's ordination, and encouraged an Anglo-Catholic piety. To many who entered the ministry in the 1960s, Moore would have been a model for prophetic service.[52]

For many others, the model would have been someone like Willie Amos Criswell Jr. The son of an impoverished Texas farmer, Criswell, like Moore, had

50. Underwood, ed., *Church, University, Social Policy,* p. 5.

51. Paul Moore, *Presences: A Bishop's Life in the City* (New York: Farrar, Straus, and Giroux, 1997), pp. 37, 46, 106, 118, 131, 157.

52. Moore, *Presences,* pp. 174, 183, 219.

a boyhood conversion experience that set him on an early path to a pastoral career. As a student at Baylor University, he preached in the slums on the Brazos River and held student pastorates in villages like Marlow, White Mound, and Pecan Grove. Admitted to Yale Divinity School, he decided that he risked his faith if he entered, and he chose instead to attend Southern Seminary in Louisville, where he earned a doctoral degree. His first call came from a small congregation in Oklahoma, where he spent five or six hours a day studying the Bible while preparing sermons calling for his hearers to be "born again."[53]

By 1944 Criswell was the pastor at the First Baptist Church in Dallas, Texas, where he set out to "mobilize a great army" in the heart of the city with the pastor as the "commander-in-chief." After a four-month world tour in 1950, he called for "a strong America," with universal military training to ensure that "the communists will not triumph." He built his congregation into the largest white Baptist church in the nation, erecting a vast Activities Building with chapels, classrooms, a family life center, a skating rink, and a bowling alley. In the early civil rights movement, he urged the South Carolina legislature to maintain segregation in schools and churches, and he criticized the federal courts for "stirring up our people." Years later he convinced his congregation to accept racial integration, and he apologized for his South Carolina address.[54]

During the 1960 presidential election, Criswell opposed the election of John Kennedy, arguing that a "committed Catholic" should not be elected president. He criticized preachers who lost hold of "God's infallible Word" and rode their "hobby horses" on issues like war and peace, civil rights, ecology, hunger, or nuclear arms. He would later pray at the convention that nominated Ronald Reagan as the Republican candidate for the presidency. While serving as president of the Southern Baptist Convention, he wrote *Why I Preach That the Bible Is Literally True* as part of what he saw as a "full-fledged war between Baptists who held to the fundamentals of Southern Baptist belief and those who did not." When Baptists faced the question of the ordination of women, Criswell opposed it as unbiblical. Like Paul Moore, he took on the big issues of his time, but he stood on the other side of the battle lines.[55]

Thousands of ministers found that the social turmoil between 1940 and 1970 altered their ministries. No period since the era of the American Revolution brought a greater sense of baffling change. Ministers who had begun their work in 1940 discovered, thirty years later, that they seemed to be living in an-

---

53. Criswell, *Standing*, pp. 113, 133, 153.
54. Criswell, *Standing*, pp. 180, 184, 200, 202, 203.
55. Criswell, *Standing*, pp. 204, 222, 227.

other world. The changes undermined assumptions that almost everyone had taken for granted and generated the sense of crisis that beset mainline Protestants in the 1960s.

Protestant and Catholic clergy reevaluated their relationship. In the forties, Protestant pastors viewed Catholic priests with wariness, disdain, and incomprehension. In 1945, the New York minister Ralph Sockman declared that the "ecclesiastical air" was "electric with tension." The two groups battled over freedom of expression, funding for parochial schools, gambling, birth control, and theology. They almost never conversed, and each saw the other as the advocate of damnable error. Protestant clergy led "demonstrations of Protestant unity" — some attracting as many as nineteen thousand participants — that condemned Catholic positions on church and state, religious freedom, diplomatic relations with the Vatican, support for fascist Spain, and "clericalism."[56]

By 1954, a few Protestants began to notice that Catholic theologians seemed to be rethinking older positions on religious liberty and church-state relations. When Cardinal Roncalli of Venice became Pope John XXIII in 1958, his views and personality drew favorable Protestant notice, as did the fruitfulness of the Catholic liturgical movement. In 1958 Harvard Divinity School created an endowed chair in Roman Catholic studies. The following year Protestant ministers and Catholic priests in Massachusetts joined to protest against illegal gambling and racial segregation in public housing.[57]

In 1959, Father Gustave Weigel, S.J., one of the pioneers in "the Dialogue," praised the "great change" in Protestant-Catholic relations, and the *Christian Century* rejoiced at the "thaw" in the "cold war among Christians." Ecumenical gatherings of clergy became commonplace. For a few months, John Kennedy's presidential candidacy stirred old fears, and Norman Vincent Peale, proponent of positive thinking and minister at the Marble Collegiate Church on Fifth Avenue, made headlines when he and other Protestant ministers questioned whether a Catholic could support religious freedom, but the candidate met with Baptist pastors in Texas to reassure them of his independence from Rome. The conciliatory tone of the Second Vatican Council (1962-65) encouraged openness across confessional boundaries. In 1964 Catholic and Episcopal clergy

56. Ralph Sockman, "Catholics and Protestants," *Christian Century* 62 (May 2, 1945): 545; Underwood, *Protestant and Catholic,* pp. 3, 27; Hampton Adams, "Protestant Rally Held in St. Louis Church," *Christian Century* 46 (Nov. 14, 1945): 1267-68.

57. "Catholic Demands Apology," *Christian Century* 67 (Nov. 29, 1950): 1431; "The Widening Gulf," *Christian Century* 71 (Apr. 7, 1954): 421; "New Pope May Present Some Surprises," *Christian Century* 75 (Nov. 12, 1958): 1293; "Catholic Theology at Harvard," *Commonweal* 5 (May 2, 1958): 117; Myron W. Fowell, "Catholic Protestant Cooperation," *Christian Century* 76 (Jan. 21, 1959): 76-77.

joined in an unprecedented common worship service at Christ Church (Episcopal) in Cambridge, Massachusetts.[58]

As early as 1951, alert Protestants acknowledged that their branch of Christendom had "lost its former domination" in the United States. By 1960 both Catholic and Protestant leaders welcomed the harmony, but some of them must have recognized that it signified a transition in the status of the mainline Protestant clergy. Accustomed to speaking for American Christianity, mainline ministers now had to share the stage, and they could no longer assume that they would have the lead role.[59]

While some tensions abated, others intensified, as politically liberal pastors in the mainline churches came under attack from political forces acting in the name of free enterprise and the American way of life. During the 1940s, Protestant reformers carried on the traditions of the social gospel by calling for economic justice, human rights, racial reconciliation, and international peace. Their efforts evoked, as always, strong reactions. Before the decade ended, the head of the Federal Bureau of Investigation, J. Edgar Hoover, was publicly announcing his "apprehension" that the international communist conspiracy had "secured" these "ministers of the Gospel" to promote its "evil work" and "espouse a cause that is alien to the religion of Christ and of Judaism."[60]

In 1949 the publicist John T. Flynn charged, in *The Road Ahead*, that well-known clergy who were associated with the Federal Council of Churches — including Bishop Oxnam, the ethicist John Bennett, and the popular missionary leader E. Stanley Jones — shared a "peculiar affinity for the godless and brutal system of Russia" and sought to bring about the overthrow of American freedom. Such charges hardly affected most parish ministers, but Flynn's book sold over a million copies, and newspaper publicity expanded its reach. After Senator Joseph McCarthy charged in 1950 that communists had infiltrated the State Department, his allies asserted that the Red Menace had also infiltrated the clergy.[61]

In 1953 Joseph B. Matthews, a former liberal minister who was working for the House Committee Investigating Un-American Activities, claimed in the *American Mercury* that "the largest group supporting the Communist appara-

---

58. "Protestant-Catholic Tensions," *Commonweal* 68 (June 27, 1958): 315-16; *Christian Century* 76 (Nov. 4, 1959): 1267-68; John Cogley, "A Small News Item," *Commonweal* 72 (May 20, 1960): 208; "When Is Brotherhood More Than a Word?" *Christian Century* 77 (Feb. 10, 1960): 157; "Hold Unprecedented Ecumenical Service," *Christian Century* 81 (Dec. 16, 1964): 1548; "Noted Briefs," *Christian Century* 81 (May 20, 1964): 662.

59. Hutchinson, "American Protestantism," p. 192.

60. Hudnut-Beumler, *Looking for God*, p. 192.

61. John T. Flynn, *The Road Ahead: America's Creeping Revolution* (New York: Devin-Adair, 1949), p. 109.

tus in the United States today is composed of Protestant clergymen." He contended that the Communist Party had enlisted the support of "at least 7,000" Protestant ministers, and he included many of the most distinguished leaders of the era, who had offended him by signing appeals for peace or supporting liberal causes. McCarthy hired him as executive director of his Senate committee, and even though he resigned after President Eisenhower shamed him for his censure of the clergy, his charges continued to echo in right-wing circles. In 1961, the founder of the John Birch Society, who considered Eisenhower a communist agent, was still proclaiming that "the largest single bloc of Communists in America is in the Protestant clergy." Clergy who advocated civil rights or supported peace movements could expect to be labeled communist.[62]

Politically right-wing clergy were eager to repeat the charges. Carl McIntire, for example, was the pastor of a 1,600-member separatist Presbyterian church in New Jersey who had organized in 1941 a small fundamentalist American Council of Christian Churches to oppose the National Council. Serving as a resource for Flynn, he and his allies called for the House Committee to investigate the liberal clergy. They charged, among other things, that ministers who supported the "One Great Hour of Sharing" — an ecumenical offering for humanitarian relief — were engaged in a plot to undermine free enterprise and promote socialism. For three decades, the clerical leaders of the "old religious right" condemned the clergy of the mainline Protestant churches as heretics, "Moscow-loving" communists, and "pro-Kremlin" subversives.[63]

The mainline clergy — joined by the Catholics — decried the reign of "irresponsible accusation." "We resent," said the Methodist bishops, "unproved assertions that the Protestant ministry is honeycombed with disloyalty." But the drumbeat of aggression continued through the 1960s. The Air Force apologized after one of its officers reprinted, in a training manual, attacks from the Tulsa evangelist Billy James Hargis, who charged ministers in the denominations of the National Council of Churches with subversion and treason. By the end of the 1960s, the *Christian Century* voiced fears that the relentless attacks were damaging to the churches and the clergy.[64]

62. J. B. Matthews, "Reds and Our Churches," *American Mercury* 77 (July, 1953): 3; "Go Climb a Birch Tree Dept." *Commonweal* 75 (Oct. 27, 1961): 110.

63. "Noted Briefs," *Christian Century* 67 (Jan. 4, 1949): 6; Ralph L. Roy, "Ministry of Disruption," *Christian Century* 70 (Apr. 18, 1953): 410-11; Ralph L. Roy, "Attacks on the Churches," *Christian Century* 70 (Apr. 15, 1953): 443; Robert G. Kemper, "Reformation or Deformation," *Christian Century* 80 (Apr. 10, 1963): 465; "The Counter-Counter Ecumaniac," *Christian Century* 86 (Nov. 19, 1969): 1475; Leo P. Ribuffo, *The Old Christian Right: The Protestant Far Right from the Great Depression to the Cold War* (Philadelphia: Temple University Press, 1983), pp. 246-48.

64. "Methodist Bishops Speak for Freedom," *Christian Century* 70 (Dec. 30, 1953): 515;

The right-wing critics especially deplored clerical activism on behalf of civil rights. The clergy were never of one mind about the civil rights movement, but for a decade after the war, clerical gatherings, even in the South, passed a stream of resolutions against racial segregation. Southern black pastors provided most of the local leadership for the NAACP, the best-known civil rights organization. After the Supreme Court ruled against legally segregated schools in 1954, the large denominations, black and white — including the Southern Baptist Convention — affirmed the decision. By the end of the year, however, white Christian opponents of black civil rights organized to preserve segregation. The reactions to the Montgomery bus boycott in 1955-56 signaled a growing polarization.[65]

The organizers of the boycott against segregated seating on buses appealed for help to the city's black clergy, and most of them signed on, thrusting the young Baptist pastor Martin Luther King Jr. into the leadership. When black ministers organized similar boycotts in other Southern cities, the clergy divided. Many black ministers disliked the activism; many whites disliked its goals. Polls consistently showed that the majority of ministers, black and white, favored an end to racial segregation, but a vocal minority of white conservative clergy decried civil rights activists as "infidels" opposed to "the great spiritual aims of our churches."[66]

Little Rock put clerical disagreements on the front pages. When Governor Orval Faubus resisted school integration in Arkansas in 1957, seven clergymen helped escort the black children through the mobs outside Central High School, and forty of the city's two hundred pastors organized a "ministry of reconciliation." But twenty-four independent fundamentalist Baptist pastors, who did not want "everyone thinking that all of Little Rock's ministers were against segregation," launched a countermovement. The conflict displayed the severe limits that congregations could impose on their clergy. Even though a majority of the white ministers privately favored integration, they could offer little public leadership. Some worked behind the scenes, but most stayed out of the fray, and at least nine who were more outspoken had to leave their pulpits.[67]

Wayne M. Cowan, "Air Force Red Alert," *Commonweal* 71 (Mar. 11, 1960): 651-53; Aubrey B. Haimes, "Polarization Within the Churches," *Christian Century* 87 (Sept. 2, 1970): 1039.

65. Aldon D. Morris, *The Origins of the Civil Rights Movement: Black Communities Organizing for Change* (New York: Free Press, 1984), pp. 15, 37; "Southern Baptists Approve Decision," *Christian Century* 71 (June 9, 1954): 691; Hadden, *Gathering Storm*, p. 210; "Find Laity Ready for Desegregation," *Christian Century* 52 (Dec. 29, 1954): 1573.

66. Morris, *Origins*, pp. 51-56; "Criswell Not the Pope of Southern Baptists," *Christian Century* 73 (Mar. 11, 1956): 325.

67. Hadden, *Gathering Storm*, pp. 202, 214; *Christian Century* 42 (Oct. 16, 1957): 1219; Er-

During the 1960s, the black clergy furnished much of the leadership for the movement. In 1960, King and his clerical allies formed the Southern Christian Leadership Conference, which built part of the campaign's infrastructure. Seminarian James Lawson in Nashville taught students to "sit in" as a protest against segregated lunch counters — when Vanderbilt University expelled him, most of the divinity school faculty resigned — and black clergy in five states helped organize sit-in demonstrations. In Philadelphia, Leon Sullivan led four hundred ministers in "selective patronage" campaigns to gain equality in hiring practices. In the South, the Congregationalist pastor Andrew Young organized Citizenship Schools. In Birmingham, King addressed two hundred black ministers in 1963 and persuaded most of them to open their churches as centers for an economic boycott and mass demonstrations that drew national attention when police chief T. E. "Bull" Connor tried to suppress them with dogs and fire hoses.[68]

By 1961 white clergy began to share that attention when they joined black protesters in the freedom rides that integrated the bus stations, and the clerical collar became part of the imagery of civil rights protest. When King spoke at the March on Washington in 1963, black and white clergy were working together for civil rights legislation. In both Northern and Southern cities, police carted ministers and bishops off to jail for marching and demonstrating, and in the South dissenting white pastors faced the wrath of congregations. Thirteen Southern Baptist pastors in Virginia had to leave their parishes after they signed a statement in support of integration. Twenty-eight young white native-born Mississippi Methodist pastors signed a manifesto against racial discrimination; two years later only two remained in their pulpits.[69]

During the 1964 debates over a proposed civil rights law, the National Council of Churches brought hundreds of clergy to Washington as advocates, and senators testified to their influence. Joseph Clark of Pennsylvania described the churches as the "single most potent force" behind the bill. Richard Russell of Georgia was heard to say that the bill passed because "those damned preachers got the idea it was a moral issue." This overstated the case (and civil rights

---

nest Q. Campbell and Thomas F. Pettigrew, "Men of God in Racial Crisis," *Christian Century* 75 (June 4, 1958): 663-65; *Christian Century* 40 (Oct. 1, 1958): 1102; Ernest Q. Campbell and Thomas F. Pettigrew, *Christians in Racial Crisis: A Study of Little Rock's Ministry* (Washington, D.C.: Public Affairs Press, 1959).

68. Morris, *Origins*, pp. 77, 201, 250-67; Charles V. Hamilton, *The Black Preacher in America* (New York: William Morrow, 1972), p. 135.

69. Robert McAfee Brown, "The Race Race," *Commonweal* 79 (Oct. 11, 1963): 73; "Not Words but Acts," *Commonweal* 78 (July, 1963): 444; Larry A. Witham, *Who Shall Lead Them? The Future of Ministry in America* (New York: Oxford University Press, 2005), p. 85; *Christian Century* 80 (Feb. 20, 1963): 229.

workers in Mississippi in the 1960s discovered that Southern white clergy were usually hostile), but in one 1965 poll more than 90 percent of the ministers in six large denominations approved of the civil rights movement and almost three-fourths believed that the white churches had failed to do what they should. Polls in the later sixties showed that the laity had reservations about clergy who joined in "direct action" — marches, picketing, and sit-ins — on behalf of civil rights; only 37 percent of the laity supported the ministers and seminarians who went South to work for the movement. Fully 44 percent of them expressed disapproval of the civil rights movement altogether. The *Christian Century* began to write about "backlash."[70]

By then the movement was producing renewed tension among the clergy. In the summer of 1966, during a march in Mississippi, activists in the Student Nonviolent Coordinating Committee defied King by demanding a rallying cry of "black power," disdaining integration, and repudiating nonviolence. Black power initially divided the African American clergy, especially after one of its advocates denounced "Uncle Toms" and "black preachers." It also divided their white allies. Some saw it as a necessary assertion of autonomy; others heard it as a dismissal of them and their dream of racial reconciliation. The National Commission of Black Churchmen tried to explain that black power did not mean "separatism" or "anti-whiteism," but the label did suggest that the agenda was changing, a shift exemplified in the publication of James Cone's *Black Theology and Black Power* in 1968 and James Forman's Black Manifesto demanding $500 million in reparations from the white churches the following year.[71]

Black critics took aim at institutions that had seen themselves in the vanguard of change. The mainline seminaries had encouraged their students to embrace the cause of civil rights. By the mid-1960s, African American seminarians in those white-dominated schools pointed out that when they looked around in the classroom they saw too few black students and teachers. In 1969, C. Shelby Rooks, director of the Fund for Theological Education, observed that no "white" seminary in the nation had more than twenty or twenty-five black students. Of the three hundred black students in ninety-five accredited semi-

70. "A.C.P. Meets in Washington," *Christian Century* 81 (May 6, 1964): 597; James F. Findlay Jr., *Church People in the Struggle: The National Council of Churches and the Black Freedom Movement 1950-1970* (New York: Oxford University Press, 1993), pp. 140-60; Hadden, *Gathering Storm*, pp. 65, 116, 141, 155 220; Wuthnow, *Restructuring*, p. 148; "Backlash," *Christian Century* 41 (Oct. 12, 1966): 1232-33.

71. "Too Many Cooks, Too Much Spice," *Christian Century* 28 (July 13, 1966): 880; "Black Power for Whom?" *Christian Century* 83 (July 20, 1966): 903-4; Hamilton, *Black Preacher*, p. 122; "A Fresh Look at Black America," *Christian Century* 84 (Oct. 25, 1967): 1340; Findlay, *Church People in the Struggle*, pp. 155, 200-201.

naries, half were enrolled at two historically black schools. Only about twelve of the "white" schools had any black faculty members. Institutions that had called for change now became the target of protest.[72]

One poll in the late sixties suggested that clergy in the mainline denominations still supported civil rights but that a significant number harbored doubt about the direction the movement had taken. Only a small minority questioned the ideal of equal civil rights for all Americans, but a larger minority — 22 percent of Presbyterians, 30 percent of American Baptists, 31 percent of Episcopalians, 33 percent of American Lutherans, 41 percent of Methodists, and 51 percent of Missouri Synod Lutherans — declined to express "sympathy with civil rights workers." The successes in the civil rights struggle defined a high moment for the liberal clergy — and a turning point for the black clergy — but disputes over the tactics of reform hardened lines of division within clerical ranks.[73]

The actions of clergy in the protest against the Vietnam War deepened those divisions. Some American religious groups had warned against an Indo-Chinese war as early as 1954, but only in 1963 — when twelve liberal ministers published in the *New York Times,* on behalf of 17,358 of their fellow clergy, a full-page denunciation of American policy — did the debate over the war begin to set ministers in opposition to each other. After the escalation of the war in 1964, most clergy still trusted the White House. When 2,500 ministers published an appeal against the war later in the year, other clergy accused them of lacking the competence to speak and disregarding the consequences of withdrawal. Teams of ministers who toured Vietnam reached conflicting conclusions.[74]

With the formation in 1966 of the National Emergency Committee of Clergy Concerned About Vietnam, politically liberal pastors once again placed themselves in public view as critics of American policy. They spoke at rallies, joined noisy marches, and opened their churches as sanctuaries to draft resisters. By 1969, large majorities of mainline pastors wanted the United States to withdraw, pull back into enclaves, or stop the bombing of Vietnam. To clerical

72. C. Shelby Rooks, "Theological Education and the Black Church," *Christian Century* 86 (Feb. 12, 1969): 212-16.

73. Eldon P. Jacobson, Hoyt P. Oliver, and Lorna J. Bergstrom, "The Parish and Campus Ministries," in *Church, University, and Social Policy,* ed. Underwood, p. 367. Six percent of Presbyterians and Episcopalians, 9 percent of American Lutherans, 10 percent of American Baptists, 12 percent of Methodists, and 14 percent of Missouri Synod Lutherans disapproved of equal civil rights.

74. "Urge Cease Fire in South Vietnam," *Christian Century* 82 (Jan. 13, 1965): 37; "Who Is Adequate, Monsignor?" *Christian Century* 82 (May 26, 1965): 688; "Johnson Ends Strike Threat," *Christian Century* 82 (Sept. 22, 1965): 1150.

supporters of the war, such views were nothing more than "a cause of rapture to the men in the Kremlin and to all who wish the cause of freedom ill." When pollsters asked Southern Baptist pastors how they felt about the war, 82 percent wanted to increase military efforts and 44 percent sanctioned the use of nuclear weapons if they were needed. Seventy percent of Missouri Synod Lutherans and 65 percent of American Baptists wanted to continue the bombing.[75]

The divisions corresponded to theological alignments. Ninety-one percent of fundamentalists and 73 percent of conservatives wanted to escalate the war or continue bombing, while only 31 percent of neo-orthodox and 24 percent of liberal clergy preferred one of those options. The chief of military chaplains lamented the "divisions growing among American churchmen over our defense of South Vietnam."[76]

War and race were not the only discordant topics, and one additional struggle was destined to have a profound effect on the ministry. In 1947, Inez Cavert, working with the Federal Council of Churches and several women's organizations, directed a worldwide study of women and the church in preparation for the imminent meeting of the World Council of Churches in Amsterdam. Cavert was a leader in the ecumenical United Church Women, and her findings received a serious hearing. After long debate, the delegates appointed a study commission, and its preliminary report in 1952 made it clear that the subject of women's rights in the church was "becoming a hot one" that required "immediate attention."[77]

In 1947, 43 percent of Americans approved the idea of ordaining women and 47 percent opposed it. In some mainline denominations, the opposition was even stronger, with as many as 72 percent of the laity opposing. Mildred Horton, a prominent Congregational advocate of women's rights, concluded that up to that point, the opposition had largely won. In 1950, the census reported 6,744 women clergy, about 4 percent of the total number. (Women at

---

75. "Clergy Concerned about Vietnam," *Christian Century* 83 (Jan. 26, 1966): 99; Harold Quinley, "The Protestant Clergy and the War in Vietnam," *Public Opinion Quarterly* 34 (1970): 45; "Brotherhood Where Are You?" *Christian Century* 85 (Feb. 14, 1968): 188; "Belligerent Baptists," *Christian Century* 85 (Sept. 4, 1968): 1096. According to Quinley, the opponents of the war included 75 percent of United Methodist ministers, 77 percent of ministers in the United Church of Christ, 58 percent of Presbyterians, and 59 percent of the clergy in the two largest Lutheran denominations.

76. Quinley, "Protestant Clergy," p. 46; "Admiral Kelly and (in)credibility," *Christian Century* 85 (May 8, 1968): 609.

77. "Consider Role of Women in Church," *Christian Century* 64 (Apr. 23, 1947): 532; *Christian Century* 66 (Nov. 30, 1949): 1411; "Women in the Churches," *Christian Century* 69 (May 21, 1952): 606-7; Margaret Frakes, "Women's Status in the Churches," *Christian Century* 70 (Oct. 14, 1953): 1164-66.

this time constituted about 4 percent of lawyers, 6 percent of physicians, and 23 percent of college faculties.) Few of the ordained women served as parish ministers. Most of those who did oversaw small congregations in the smaller denominations.[78]

No more than one-tenth of the women pastors served in denominations affiliated with the National Council of Churches. More than 60 percent of ordained women were in the Church of God, the International Church of the Foursquare Gospel, and Christian Unity Science — Pentecostal or independent churches. But during the 1950s, women in the mainline denominations pushed for full ordination, and they won some victories. In 1953 the Disciples of Christ called for the equal standing of men and women in ministry. In 1956, after years of debate, the Methodists ordained Maud Keister Jensen, and the Presbyterian Church, U.S.A., after rejecting proposals for women's ordination in 1930 and 1947, ordained Margaret Towner. Some of the divinity schools began to educate women for ordained ministry.[79]

The women who moved into pulpits in the 1950s were breaking with centuries of tradition. In 1959 Martha Kriebel accepted, along with her husband, a call from a Pennsylvania congregation of the United Church of Christ. When her husband became a full-time teacher, she remained as the congregation's sole pastor. She had attended Lancaster Theological Seminary because she felt "God's call to service," but one woman in her congregation told her that she was "going against the Bible," and some members left. She won her way into leadership partly by listening. "As they told their stories, I saw acceptance happening. Their community became mine, and by their choice, they welcomed me as a neighbor because I valued their neighborhood's history." She also decided to "be a pastor according to the congregation's previous experience of the parish ministry." "When people saw me doing the things a pastor does, making calls, attending meetings, preparing sermons, they seemed pleased. I was directing my time to serving them."[80]

By every conventional standard, her ministry in the congregation was a

---

78. Leiffer, *The Layman Looks at His Minister,* p. 133; *Christian Century* 64 (July 16, 1947): 869; Salisbury, *Religion in American Culture,* p. 286; "Breakthrough for the Woman Minister," *Christian Century* 74 (Jan. 23, 1957): 100; Frakes, "Women's Status," p. 1165.

79. Frakes, "Women's Status," p. 1164; Salisbury, *Religion in American Culture,* p. 285; "Breakthrough," p. 100; Virginia Lieson Brereton and Christa Ressmeyer Klein, "American Women in Ministry: A History of Protestant Beginning Points," in *Women of Spirit: Female Leadership in the Jewish and Christian Traditions,* ed. Rosemary Ruether and Eleanor McLaughlin (New York: Simon and Schuster, 1979), p. 319.

80. Martha B. Kriebel, *A Stole Is a Towel* (New York: The Pilgrim Press, 1988), pp. 3, 22, 49, 56.

success. She expanded the church program, brought in new members, supervised a building program, involved herself in community activities, and assumed responsibilities in the denomination. She went on to work on the staff of the statewide conference, overseeing projects in evangelism, health and welfare ministries, and ecumenism. When she decided to reenter the parish ministry, however, in a congregation that had not known her face-to-face, 10 percent of the members voted against her appointment. She had to begin anew, slowly building confidence in her leadership, struggling with the ambivalence that some parishioners felt about women in the ministry.[81]

In 1965 one commentator remarked that "the problem of women's rights" now "loomed second only to that of civil rights." But the denominations that had refused to ordain women continued to resist, and the decade of the 1960s brought little further change. By 1961 the Presbyterians had ordained only thirty women, and most of them worked in Christian education. At the end of the decade, less than 1 percent of the United Methodist, American Baptist, Presbyterian, and Disciples clergy were women. The movement seemed to have stalled.[82]

It was becoming clear by the end of the 1960s that large numbers of the laity disliked the social action of the "new breed" of younger activist clergy. A survey in 1967 found 72 percent believing that clergy who marched and picketed did more harm than good and an equal number declaring that it would upset them if their priest or minister joined a demonstration. Less than a third of white church members saw Martin Luther King Jr. as an example of relevant Christian faith at work. About half of them said that the clergy should stay out of public reform. In the liberal United Church of Christ, only 20 percent of the laity thought that their clergy should spend much time "working for social justice." Some black congregations shared such sentiments. "The social-action interpretation of the ministry," said one African American pastor, "is not what my people want."[83]

In contrast, almost 90 percent of the clergy in some of the mainline churches — and 65 to 70 percent even among the Southern Baptists and Southern Presbyterians — believed that ministers should try to influence the "power structures of our society." Unlike their predecessors in the 1930s, the ministers of the 1960s, especially the younger ones, felt a sense of obligation to the community beyond their congregations. They believed that they should take public

81. Kriebel, *A Stole Is a Towel,* p. 2.
82. Anne Perkins, "Are Women People?" *Christian Century* 82 (July 21, 1965): 917; Salisbury, *Religion in American Culture,* p. 287; Brereton and Klein, "American Women," p. 322.
83. Hadden, *Gathering Storm,* pp. 30, 148, 150-52, 154; Hamilton, *Black Preacher,* pp. 171, 174.

positions on issues of human well-being, even on controversial topics. They were enthusiastic about such initiatives as providing seed money to bring federally funded housing for the poor. Many of the laity, however, looked to the church for comfort and reassurance, and they saw no connection between theology and social struggle.[84]

Despite the newspaper headlines, the profession tended toward political and social conservatism. One poll in the early sixties suggested that religious conservatives usually voted Republican and that even theologically liberal pastors were slightly inclined to do the same. According to another poll, 68 percent of fundamentalist clergy were Republican while only 13 percent were Democrats. Among "evangelicals," 62 percent favored the Republicans, 15 percent the Democrats. Thirty-nine percent of clergy calling themselves "neo-orthodox" went with the Republican Party, while 35 percent identified with the Democrats; and the theological liberals split right down the middle in political affiliation. About a fourth of all the ministers claimed to be "independents."[85]

In the forties and fifties, many of the clergy had appeared to move beyond the fundamentalist-modernist divide. Across all the denominations, the watchword was "evangelism," and by 1947 Protestants had launched at least thirty evangelistic drives for "the conversion of America." The popularity of neo-orthodoxy in the mainline seminaries signified the recovery of traditional language within mainly liberal institutions; ministers across the theological spectrum now appealed to the authority of the Word of God. Insiders knew, however, that definition was everything. Some ministers defined the Word of God as the Bible. Others defined the Word of God as the Christ who was manifest within the Bible. The distinction signaled an ineradicable disagreement about biblical interpretation, and by the 1960s the theological division among the clergy was as sharp as it had ever been.[86]

In the early 1960s, most ministers were theologically conservative. A survey in 1962 of 17,565 theology students revealed that only 5 percent thought of themselves as fundamentalist, but 37 percent labeled themselves as "conservative" and 18 percent as "neo-orthodox." Only 16 percent were "liberal," though 10 percent more described themselves as "ecumenical," and 2 percent held on to the "modernist" label. If the survey had included older ministers, clergy trained

---

84. Leiffer, *Changing Expectations*, pp. 80, 102, 104, 112; Hadden, *Gathering Storm*, pp. 107-10.

85. Leiffer, *Changing Expectations*, p. 155; Wuthnow, *Restructuring*, p. 148; Benton Johnson, "Theology and Party Preference Among Protestant Clergymen," *American Sociological Review* 13 (1966): 200-208; Hadden, *Gathering Storm*, p. 82; Wuthnow, *Restructuring*, p. 148.

86. C. Stanley Lowell, "The Conversion of America," *Christian Century* 66 (Sept 28, 1949): 1133-35; Wuthnow, *Restructuring*, p. 140.

in the Bible schools, and pastors without theological education, the percentage of fundamentalists and conservatives would have vastly increased.[87]

Ministers differed profoundly about Christian doctrines. Only 11 percent of Episcopal priests interpreted the Bible literally, but 76 percent of Missouri Synod Lutherans read it that way. Only 16 percent of Presbyterian clergy viewed the creation story in Genesis as literally true, but 45 percent of American Baptists accepted its depiction of a six-day creation. Only 40 percent of Methodists accepted the stories of the virgin birth of Jesus as depictions of a biological miracle, but 81 percent of American Lutherans held that belief. Ministers disagreed about the authority of scripture, the meaning of divine judgment and hell, and the physical resurrection of Christ. The laity had the same range of disagreements, but some pastors worried that the ministry had such "uncertainty about theological verities."[88]

The most popular minister in America — the evangelist Billy Graham — stood with the conservatives. He had begun his career preaching for Youth for Christ, but after the Hearst newspapers and *Life* magazine publicized his 1949 revival in Los Angeles, he attained nationwide recognition with a series of large meetings that filled baseball stadiums and drew vast radio and television audiences. Reinhold Niebuhr feared that he was arousing a "wave of fundamentalism," but Graham modulated the severity of his early hellfire sermons and allied himself with the "evangelical" movement that had surfaced during the war years. He spoke of Christian conversion as the way to give life meaning and America renewed moral purpose. He also proclaimed biblical infallibility, the need to repent of sin and make a "decision for Christ," and an imminent physical return of Jesus to pronounce the final sentence of damnation or eternal salvation, but he was willing to work alongside clergy with other views. He became the rallying point that drew together an otherwise diverse collection of conservative clergy.[89]

Already in the mid-1950s those evangelical clergy were leading a growing cultural movement with its own parachurch groups, publishing companies, student movements, summer camps, and mass rallies. Conservative denominations, especially Pentecostals, grew at faster rates than the older mainline churches. The healing evangelist Oral Roberts drew national attention on al-

87. Bridston and Culver, *Pre-Seminary Education*, p. 250.

88. Hadden, *Gathering Storm*, pp. 44, 48; Jacobson, Oliver, and Bergstrom, "Parish and Campus Ministries," pp. 348-50; Leiffer, *Changing Expectations*, pp. 146-47; Charles Y. Glock and Rodney Stark, *Religion and Society in Transition* (Chicago: Rand McNally, 1965).

89. Marshall Frady, *Billy Graham: A Parable of American Righteousness* (Boston: Little, Brown, 1979); Reinhold Niebuhr, "After Comment, the Deluge," *Christian Century* 74 (Sept. 4, 1957): 1035.

most a hundred television stations, and other evangelicals made equally adept use of television and radio. Students flocked into fundamentalist and evangelical seminaries — schools like Dallas Theological Seminary or Fuller Theological Seminary in Pasadena — and pastors subscribed to new nondenominational journals like *Moody Monthly* and *Christianity Today.* The momentum continued into the next decade. In 1967 the conservative Southern Baptist Convention surpassed the United Methodist Church as the largest Protestant denomination, and the national secular magazines were writing about the potency of evangelicalism as a cultural force.[90]

Crisis?

By 1969 mainline Protestants acknowledged that their ministry was "passing through a period of turmoil and uncertainty." Critics noted that recruitment rates had declined, that many seminarians did not want to "waste their time in a local church," and that the profession failed to attract the brightest and best. They spoke of ministers "bored with the trivia of local church life" and claimed that "many of them are opting out of the parish ministry." They noticed polls showing that clergy were "down in public esteem and confidence," and one study of five mainline denominations found that 80 to 90 percent of the ministers believed that the profession carried less prestige than it had earlier. "No period in the history of American Christianity," wrote sociologist Kenneth Underwood in 1969, "has been the occasion of so pervasive and anxious a reappraisal of the structures and functions of ministry."[91]

Accustomed since the 1940s to attacks from the political right, the mainline clergy came under scrutiny in the 1960s from critics of another kind. In 1961 sociologist Peter Berger argued in *The Noise of Solemn Assemblies* that the "most successful ministers" were not "prophets" but "regular guys" who directed a "leisure-time activity" with no influence on "public life." His fellow sociologist Gibson Winter added in *The Suburban Captivity of the Churches* (1961) that they spent their lives in "organizational drudgery" within homogenous churches, organized on the principle of "association by likeness," that contradicted the "inclusive message" of the Christian gospel. The Presbyterian theologian Robert Johnson observed that ministers were being widely caricatured as

90. Ellwood, *1950*, p. 188; Wuthnow, *Restructuring*, p. 179; "Demythologizing Neoevangelicalism," *Christian Century* 82 (Sept. 15, 1965): 1115.

91. Leiffer, *Changing Expectations*, pp. 19, 139, 141; Fielding, ed., *Education for Ministry*, pp. 23, 25; Bloesch, "Why People Are Leaving," p. 92; Underwood, *Church, University, Social Policy*, p. xv.

overseers of a religious ghetto, fussing about petty vices, leading saccharine worship, wasting money on pretty buildings, and "adding more busywork."[92]

In 1962 sociologists Keith Bridston and Dwight W. Culver set out to conduct one more study of the ministry and theological education. They found that ministers and seminarians were paying close attention to the "attacks on Christendom." Some seminary students disparaged parish ministry as a "functional service necessary to maintain outmoded ecclesiastical systems rather than the free service of Word and Sacraments to the world." They believed that the forms of ministry for which they were preparing were "in many cases irrelevant and obsolescent." The "unprecedented" scrutiny had shaken their confidence in ministry within the local church.[93]

Like the earlier May-Brown study, the Bridston-Culver project sketched a social portrait of the candidates who would soon stand behind American pulpits. The differences were marked. In 1962 only 39 percent — rather than 53 percent in the earlier study — came from families of farmers and workers. Twenty-three percent came from professional families, though only 9 percent — rather than the earlier 15 percent — came from the parsonage. Twenty-one percent had family backgrounds in business or sales. Slightly more than half viewed the ministry as having a higher "social standing" than the occupations of their fathers. Only 25 percent — rather than the earlier 45 percent — came from rural areas; the suburbs produced another 25 percent, with cities and smaller towns providing the remainder. They were younger than the seminarians of the 1930s. Less than 16 percent were older than thirty-five; 52 percent were twenty-five or younger. In many ways they were more attuned to the mores of an urban and suburban America.[94]

In other ways, the backgrounds of seminarians had changed little. They came — 73 percent of them — from homes that encouraged church attendance, and they said that their families and their ministers had most influenced their decision to enter the ministry. Most attended church-related colleges. These students were still formed by a religious culture in which the church was a "dominant institution," even though increasing numbers were attending state colleges and universities. Many chose religion majors and participated in religious organizations in college. For the most part, they had stayed in the denominations that had formed them. As college students, most had been "average." As in the 1920s, only 3 percent had been members of Phi Beta Kappa, and only

---

92. Peter Berger, *The Noise of Solemn Assemblies* (Garden City: Doubleday, 1961), pp. 38, 46; Gibson Winter, *The Suburban Captivity of the Churches* (New York: Macmillan, 1962), pp. 25, 33, 96; Johnson, ed., *Church and Its Changing Ministry*, p. 3.

93. Bridston and Culver, *Pre-Seminary Education*, pp. 5, 61, 159, 168-69.

94. Bridston and Culver, *Pre-Seminary Education*, pp. 216, 220, 223, 224.

13 percent had graduated from college with honors. They saw a sense of divine calling as more important than other qualifications.[95]

The denominations, meanwhile, worried about shortages. As early as 1948 the churches that required "a well-trained ministry" appeared to be suffering. One denomination reported that 45 percent of its parishes lacked "regularly installed pastors," another claimed that it had lay preachers in 26 percent of its churches, and two others each reported over a thousand vacant pulpits. The National Council of Churches pointed in 1952 to "a continuing shortage of pastors and a lag in efforts to fill thousands of vacant pulpits." The Rockefeller Foundation estimated that the nation had fifteen thousand unfilled Protestant and Orthodox pulpits.[96]

In the mid-1950s, several denominations launched recruitment campaigns, and they showed some success. During the sixties, in fact, the number of clergy remained almost stable. In 1960, clergy constituted .30 percent of the civilian labor force; at the end of the decade, they dipped only to .27 percent. But the difficulty in filling rural and inner-city pulpits created a sense that the decline was more pronounced than it had really been, and even a small dip was noticeable.[97]

Salaries were still a problem. They continued to slide below the national average income for all occupations. After World War II, the average lawyer made more than twice as much — and the average physician three times as much — as the average minister, and bus drivers and factory workers also had higher incomes. By 1950, the average income for full-time religious workers was $2,276, which was 25 percent below the national average. "No other occupational group," wrote the *New York Times*, "has suffered a similar loss of status." Schoolteachers now made 30 percent more than ministers.[98]

In the upper-status mainline denominations, the salaries were rising: Episcopalians in 1951 averaged $4,225, United Presbyterians $3,412, and Congregationalists $3,174 — but this represented a loss in buying power of almost 13 percent since 1940. The income of the lower-paid clergy in the smaller denominations did not even approximate those figures. In some denominations,

95. Bridston and Culver, *Pre-Seminary Education,* pp. 14, 20, 38, 225, 240; Moberg, *Church as a Social Institution,* p. 484.

96. Ralph A. Felton, *New Ministers* (Nashville: Interboard Committee, 1949), p. 5; Rockefeller Archive Center, Rockefeller Brothers Fund, Series 3, Box 247, Fund for Theological Education, #1, pp. 3, 5.

97. Salisbury, *Religion in American Culture,* pp. 210-11; Murray H. Leiffer, *The Methodist Ministry in 1952* (Evanston: Garrett Biblical Institute, 1952), p. 7; Wuthnow, *Restructuring,* p. 160.

98. Wuthnow, *Restructuring,* p. 29; Justin Wroe Nixon, "Parity for Pastors," *Christian Century* 69 (Feb. 6, 1952): 154.

rent-free parsonages and travel and housing allowances helped make up the difference, but the average salary of $5,158 in 1963 was far below the averages for most other professionals, as well as for salespeople and public school teachers. Throughout the 1960s, clergy income barely increased over the cost of living.[99]

By the end of the sixties, observers noticed an "increasing anxiety about the professional status of the ministry." Some sociologists wondered whether the large number of uneducated ministers made it possible to conceive of the ministry as a profession. Theologian Van Harvey complained that the churches required "no particular expertise" and seemed content with "a warm heart and a warm hand, a calling, and a spirit of dedication." The church did not "take its own ministry seriously as a profession." But even many educated clergy remained uncomfortable with the idea that they were "professionals." "Many ministers," wrote theologian James Glasse, were "repelled by the idea of professionalism," which to them suggested criteria of success foreign to the Christian message. It seemed to honor "technical" proficiency rather than "human concern." And as Gustafson pointed out, ministers did not function in the same way as physicians and lawyers. Physicians did not have to influence a community in order to exercise effective leadership; lawyers did not have to persuade their clients that the law was just and good. In comparison with the clergy, the doctors and lawyers had submissive clients, for whom they were "independent experts." But ministers were the leaders of a community, and their authority rested on communal acceptance, not on "particular expertise."[100]

The professional ideal continued to have defenders. In his *Profession: Minister* (1968), Glasse pointed out that the seminary-trained clergy had a specialized education, mastered particular techniques of practice, and worked with a sense of ethical responsibility to the people they served. These were the familiar marks of a professional class. Ministers also assumed specialized tasks, even when they served in a local church. Both the legal system and other professionals viewed them as members of a profession, and the ap-

99. "Clergy Salaries Are Still Dropping," *Christian Century* 70 (Sept. 23, 1953): 1070; "Worthy of Hire," *Christian Century* 82 (Jan. 6, 1965): 6-7; James Hudnut-Beumler, *In Pursuit of the Almighty Dollar: American Protestants, Churches, and Money, 1750-2000* (Chapel Hill: University of North Carolina Press, 2006).

100. Bridston and Culver, *Pre-Seminary Education*, p. 100; Warren Hagstrom, "The Protestant Clergy as a Profession: Status and Prospects," *Berkeley Journal of Sociology* 31 (1957): 57-58; Van A. Harvey, "On Separating Hopes from Illusions: Reflections on the Future of the Ministry," *Motive* 26 (1965): 4-6. Glasse, *Profession: Minister*, p. 29; Parker, *American Protestantism*, p. 94; Underwood, ed., *Church, University, Social Policy*, pp. 421, 432; Martin, *To Fulfill This Ministry*, p. 14.

propriate response of the church should be to recognize and enhance their professional qualifications.[101]

The unrest of the era challenged the authority of every profession, but the situation was more complex than the perception of crisis would suggest. The Princeton theologian Seward Hiltner ridiculed the "guerilla-warfare criticisms of the ministry" and claimed that pastors in "virtually all our churches" were "more able, better educated, more sensitive to the actual situations of need, and better informed" than ever before. A nationwide study of occupational prestige in 1963 showed that ministers still ranked almost as high as their predecessors in 1947. In the eyes of the public, they still earned respect and admiration, and other professionals still thought highly of the ministry. The clergy of the Protestant mainline lost their singular elevation in the religious culture: Catholics — and, increasingly, "evangelicals" — began to assume a public role that had been denied them in 1940. But a shift in the balance of public authority within clerical ranks did not constitute a crisis for the profession.[102]

Theology

Partly because of the optimism generated by the ecumenical impulse, partly because of the pessimism resulting from the feeling of crisis, the period between 1950 and 1970 brought renewed attention to the theological grounding for ministry. In 1958 Seward Hiltner contended that ministerial duties were not as fragmented and haphazard as they seemed. They could be subsumed under three perspectives — communicating the gospel, organizing the fellowship, and shepherding persons — that coalesced, in varying degrees, in every appropriate act of ministry, and the study of their relationships would clarify the theology implicit in the practices. But most theologians interested in clarifying the ministerial office turned to more familiar sources.[103]

Some of the discussion emerged out of conversations about the "theology of the laity" in Europe after the Second World War. Ferment in Germany, the Netherlands, and Britain bubbled up into the ecumenical assemblies, especially

101. Glasse, *Profession: Minister*, pp. 35, 119.

102. Seward Hiltner, *Ferment in the Ministry* (Nashville: Abingdon Press, 1969), pp. 8, 15; Hodge, Siegel, and Rossi, "Occupational Prestige," p. 290; Reba M. Bucklaw and Vernon J. Parenton, "Occupational Aspects of Social Work," *Social Forces* (1962): 39-43; Carlton M. Winslow and Edward C. McDonough, "The Architect Looks at Himself," *Journal of the American Institute of Architects* (1961): 32-35.

103. Seward Hiltner, *Preface to Pastoral Theology* (Nashville: Abingdon Press, 1958), pp. 55-61, 176-78.

into the World Council of Churches, which devoted a large part of its 1954 gathering in Evanston, Illinois, to the role of the laity in the modern church. Four years later, the Dutch theologian Hendrik Kraemer published *A Theology of the Laity*, in which he argued that the New Testament churches made no sharp distinction between laity and clergy and that the church's "ministry" belonged to "the whole Church."[104]

In sketching a view of ministry for Presbyterians, the theologian Robert Johnson tried to move beyond "clericalism." He noted that in the New Testament "priesthood" referred to the priestly work of Jesus and the priestly function of the entire church, not to a separate order of ordained priests. Christian ministry was "the ministry of the entire body" in response to God's "gracious self-emptying in Jesus Christ." The ordained clergy had responsibilities for Word and Sacrament, but it was not their calling to serve as spiritual examples or special representatives of God. They were to help the laity carry the ministry of the church into the world, no more and no less.[105]

The theology of the laity made inroads into the Protestant seminaries, but it created its own set of problems. The head of the Association of Theological Schools, Charles Taylor, wondered if "the emphasis on the ministry of the laity, one of the most important truths recovered by the Protestantism of our time, obscured the urgency of an ordained ministry." It was also difficult to know precisely what the ministry of the laity meant. For some, it pointed toward prophetic social action and evangelistic witness by the church in the world. For others, it suggested participation of the laity in the church's liturgy. Skeptics pointed out that the laity seemed of a divided mind about assuming the ministry of the church. Hiltner pointed out that the "ministry of the laity" was almost nonexistent without the leadership of ordained ministers.[106]

Traditional conceptions of ministry had their defenders. The Episcopal theologian W. Norman Pittenger, for instance, proposed in 1957, for purposes of ecumenical discussion, that "the priesthood of the ordained minister" — along with the threefold order of bishop, presbyter, and deacon — remained essential for "the fullness of the Church's life." A theologian at the high-church General Theological Seminary in New York, Pittenger had no reservations about designating the priest as a "representative" figure, set apart from the general priesthood of the church in order to offer its "sacrifice of praise and thanksgiving." While every Christian participated, by baptism, in the church's

104. Hendrik Kraemer, *A Theology of the Laity* (London: Lutterworth Press, 1958), p. 153.

105. Johnson, ed., *Church and Its Changing Ministry*, pp. 20, 26, 28, 31.

106. Charles L. Taylor, "Why Not the Ministry," *The Interseminarian* 1 (1962): 13; Hiltner, *Ferment in the Ministry*, p. 33.

priesthood, the ordained priest alone acted "sacramentally" in bringing to expression the "inner and spiritual reality of Christ's ongoing life in the world." A line of apostolic succession passed through the bishops, and ordination by the bishop set the priest apart from the laity even as he stood with and for them.[107]

Robert Paul, a historian and theologian at the Congregationalists' Hartford Seminary in Connecticut, thought that Kraemer's theology unduly minimized the ordained minister while Pittenger's exaggerated the centrality of the bishop. Paul also found fault with H. Richard Niebuhr's delineation of the "pastoral director," though he considered it "the only serious attempt in America to reconstruct an adequate view of the Church and the Ministry in our generation." He thought that Niebuhr had failed to recognize that the primary concern of the minister was "the proclamation of God's redeeming love in Jesus Christ." Ministry had to be Christocentric.[108]

Agreeing with Niebuhr that the work of the ordained minister was to "direct the total activity of the Church so that it fulfills its corporate mission," Paul insisted that the church needed someone who would exemplify "what true ministry is." As the "servant of Jesus Christ," the minister prepared the Church for its service by "re-presenting" Christ to the community of faith so that it could "re-present Christ to the world." No minister could ever escape sinfulness and frailty, but every minister could represent a model of service that pointed toward the pattern visible in Jesus.[109]

Like Paul, the Presbyterian James Smart shared the neo-orthodox accent on Christology as the foundation for ministry. In accord with the theology of the laity, Smart drew no sharp line between ordained ministry and the ministry of the whole church, authorized by baptism. But he found the singular norm for all Christian ministry in "the person and ministry" of Jesus, and he thought that the action of Jesus in setting aside apostles as bearers and heralds of his "life" entailed a need for his church to set aside special leaders. The important matter for Smart was that ministers find their self-understanding in the ministry of Christ by leading the church in prophetic care for the poor, hungry, and helpless; exercising a priestly leadership through preaching, worship, and teaching; and directing a congregation in the manner of the lowly king who refused to rule from compulsion.[110]

Ministry now required a justification that had once seemed unnecessary. The critique of American institutions in the 1960s — and the attacks on traditional

107. W. Norman Pittenger, *The Church, the Ministry, and Reunion* (Greenwich: Seabury, 1957), pp. 16, 92, 104.

108. Robert S. Paul, *Ministry* (Grand Rapids: Eerdmans, 1965), pp. 17, 40.

109. Paul, *Ministry*, pp. 41, 43, 80, 95, 125.

110. Smart, *Rebirth of Ministry*, pp. 11, 34, 58, 62.

conceptions of ministry — demanded a rethinking of assumptions. The professional ideal, for instance, fell under criticism, not so much from populists — though the populist impulse remained vigorous in small-town America — but rather from mainline theologians and social critics. The two decades between 1945 and 1965 had produced widespread support for a professional view of ministry, with seminaries growing, specialization expanding, and clergy finding new ways to cooperate with psychologists, social workers, and educators. The educated critics of the professional ideal had no intention of abandoning seminary education. They took it for granted. But they wanted iconoclastic prophets more than smoothly refined professionals in the pulpits, and at a time when other professions came under attack as monopolistic instruments of self-interest, it was no surprise that the image of the ministerial "professional" also drew fire.

After the rise of McCarthyism, both black and white clerical reformers came under attack from the political right, and during the 1960s the mainline clergy suffered the scorn of the cultural left. And the clergy themselves proved to be adept at unsparing self-criticism. Convinced that God was at work in the movements for civil rights and peace, many of the liberal clergy also believed that God stood in transcendent judgment on a complacent church and ministry. By 1970, the rhetoric of crisis echoed in many a clerical gathering, and worries about the decline of the profession surfaced once again. But the sixties demonstrated, in fact, the continued influence of the clergy in American cultural battles. They were the target of criticism because their critics thought they made a difference, as indeed they did.

CHAPTER 9

Priesthood: From Certainty to Complexity

1930-1970

In 1930 it was a commonplace in Catholic circles that "no office held by mortal man exceeds in dignity or sublimity that of the priesthood." The office possessed a power "equal to the power of Jesus Christ; for in this role, the priest speaks with the voice and authority of Christ himself." The priest was *alter Christus* — another Christ — who dispensed the mysteries of God and exercised the ministry of the church. One American bishop claimed — and many others surely agreed — that "the history of the Catholic Church is essentially the history of the priesthood."[1]

Four decades later, the distinguished Catholic historian John Tracy Ellis announced that a whirlwind of change had dislodged American priests "from their familiar and comfortable moorings." After the calm of the early 1950s, they had lived through "a revolution as profound as anything that the Church has experienced since the Protestant Reformation." An "unprecedented havoc" had battered the priesthood. By 1970, Catholic scholars were warning of a "crisis." They wrote of "the vanishing clergyman" and the "disappearing priesthood," and they imagined the possibility that the priestly vocation in America could someday almost cease to exist.[2]

---

1. Scott Appleby, "Present to the People of God: The Transformation of the Roman Catholic Parish Priesthood," in *Transforming Parish Ministry: The Changing Roles of Catholic Clergy, Laity, and Women Religious*, ed. Jay P. Dolan (New York: Crossroad, 1990), p. 8; Jay P. Dolan, "American Catholics in a Changing Society: Parish and Ministry, 1930 to the Present," in *Transforming Parish Ministry*, p. 291.

2. John Tracy Ellis, "Preface," in *The Catholic Priest in the United States: Historical Investigations*, ed. John Tracy Ellis (Collegeville, Minn.: Saint John's University Press, 1971), p. xii; Joseph

This revolution has no single explanation. It reflected the movement of Catholics out of ethnic ghettos, the economic advance of Catholic laity, and the changing educational experience of laity, sisters, and priests. It also reflected innovations in Catholic theology, new patterns of lay involvement, and conflicted responses to the Second Vatican Council. The habits of authority within the church and the resistance to change among some in the hierarchy deepened the unrest, as did decisions in Rome about such delicate issues as priestly celibacy and birth control. And the social turmoil of the late 1960s, when conflicts over race and war overflowed into the streets, prompted a critique of American institutions, including the church, that altered relationships within the church and caused some priests to question, in a veritable shibboleth of the period, the "relevance" of their calling. To understand the shock of these events, one must begin with the world of the Catholic priest in a simpler era.

Ministry in the Parish, 1930-1960

"Life for a Catholic without a priest," wrote the *Catholic Mirror* in 1947, would be "tragic," for the priest alone had "the power to bring God from Heaven to earth within our reach." For the three decades after 1930, the priest was the dominant figure in Catholic culture. Historian Jay Dolan has argued that these years formed the "golden age" of the priesthood in America: The priest "was put on a pedestal by the lofty theology of the office and kept there by the culture of clericalism." The theology of the office located the priest as the mediator between God and the people — "a kind of channel through whom supernatural life flows to the laity." The culture of clericalism rested on the assumption that the priest, elevated above the laity, was omni-competent and authoritative.[3]

In 1930, most Catholics were working-class people, and most of them stood in awe of priests, followed their directives, and depended on them as authorities in matters both religious and mundane. Priests were the arbiters of morality and the experts in a supernatural realm filled with threat and promise. They

---

Fichter, "Catholic Church Professionals," in *Annals of the American Academy of Political and Social Science* 387, ed. James M. Gustafson (Philadelphia: AAPSS, 1970), p. 77; Robert E. McNally, "The Disappearing Priesthood," *America* 114 (1966): 877; Ivan Illich, "The Vanishing Clergyman," *The Critic* 25 (1967): 18-27.

3. Kenneth Wilson Underwood, *Protestant and Catholic: Religious and Social Interaction in an Industrial Community* (Boston: Beacon Press, 1957), p. 78; Jay P. Dolan, "Patterns of Leadership in the Congregation," in *American Congregations,* ed. James W. Lewis and James P. Wind, 2 vols. (Chicago: University of Chicago Press, 1994), p. 248; Joseph H. Fichter, *Social Relations in the Urban Parish* (Chicago: University of Chicago Press, 1954), p. 125.

were educated, set apart by dress and manner, and able to dispense the means of grace that could open the eternal realm of heaven. They had their neighborhood critics, but priests were special. Pious Catholic families dreamed of sending a son into the priesthood.

In some neighborhoods, church members consulted the priest on all matters of importance, whether it was to baptize their children, work out family problems, or sell their house. After Father Vincent Gallagher went to Blessed Virgin Mary Parish in Philadelphia, some families regularly gave him their paychecks so that he could pay their bills and supervise their savings. Upper-class Catholics could be more standoffish, but they too respected the priest's religious authority. "All I do is try to follow the rules the priest gives," reported one layman in Massachusetts in 1947. "The good Catholic layman," added an officer in the Knights of Columbus, "expects to be held in line by the priests."[4]

On the surface, the priesthood seemed during the three decades after 1930 impervious to change. Underneath the appearance of unchanging continuity, however, priests were constantly adapting and adjusting. The move to the suburbs made a difference. Between 1945 and 1956, as many as two and a half million Catholics — out of a Catholic population of about twenty million in 1940 — moved to the suburbs. There they learned to be at home in culturally diverse neighborhoods, absorbed the middle-class ethos of individual advancement and material comfort, and imposed new expectations on their priests. Priests found that suburban laity viewed them not merely as religious authorities but also as administrators, parochial school supervisors, recreational directors, and "bargain basement" counselors.[5]

Most Catholics still lived in the countryside, the small town, and the city, and ministry could look — and feel — different in each setting. By the mid-sixties, the average big-city parish was about seven times larger than the small-town church. A normal city parish had three or four priests, and some had one or two more additional priests who lived in the rectory while working mainly outside the parish church. Each of the urban parish priests had responsibility for three times as many parishioners as the priests in the small towns. Many a

4. Philip J. Murnion, *The Catholic Priest and the Changing Structure of Catholic Ministry, New York, 1920-1970* (New York: Arno Press), p. 112; Appleby, "Present to the People of God," p. 12; Charles R. Morris, *American Catholics: The Saints and Sinners Who Built America's Most Powerful Church* (New York: Random House, 1997), p. 173; Underwood, *Protestant and Catholic*, pp. 91, 104.

5. Joseph P. Chinnici, O.F.M., "The Catholic Community at Prayer," *Habits of Devotion: Catholic Religious Practice in Twentieth-Century America*, ed. James M. O'Toole (Ithaca: Cornell University Press, 2004), p. 70; Dolan, "American Catholics," p. 284; Andrew M. Greeley, *The Church and the Suburbs* (New York: Sheed and Ward, 1959), p. 72.

priest preferred the smaller towns, where it was possible to form deeper relationships with members. In the countryside, nearly half the rural churches in the 1930s had no resident pastor; they depended on circuit riders whose main duties were sacramental. Thirty years later many still shared their priest with other congregations.[6]

The suburban trend did not mean the end of the ethnic "national" parish. Chicago in the mid-1960s had 138 ethnic parishes — almost half the city's total of 279 parishes — in which the membership was predominantly Polish, German, Italian, Lithuanian, Bohemian, Slovak, Greek, French, Croatian, Slovenian, Hungarian, Mexican, African American, Dutch, Belgian, Lebanese, or Chinese. But Catholics were no longer forming new national parishes, and throughout the nation, only about 10 percent of the parishes were national by official designation. Most parishes resembled the suburban congregations that brought together people from different ethnic backgrounds. Ethnicity still counted, but for the priest it presented now another kind of challenge: he had to nurture communities in which people had less in common.[7]

According to Hollywood moviemakers, the priest could do the job. The film industry suddenly discovered that the priest was an admirable and likable fellow. The infatuation began with Spencer Tracy's depiction of Father Flanagan in *Boys Town* (1938), took a whimsical turn with Bing Crosby's "piano-pounding, golf-playing" Father O'Malley in *Going My Way* (1944), and valorized the reforming cleric with Karl Malden's Father Barry in *On the Waterfront* (1954). Some Catholic critics feared that the movie priests, especially the Crosby character, made the priesthood too mundane and ignored its sacramental essence, but moviegoers liked the celluloid priests. For the first time, large numbers of Protestants encountered the priest as a "nice guy."[8]

In real life, priests were facing some of the same problems as Protestant ministers. "Whatever the canonical and hortatory injunctions may say," wrote Andrew Greeley, "the American pastor usually thinks of himself as primarily an administrator." The pastor had to "run an efficient and active parish," looking after buildings, bills, debts, classrooms, parking lots, fundraising, purchasing, and scheduling. Priests felt pulled into a constant flow of administrative duties: "priests are swamped," wrote Leo Ward in 1959. When Ward looked closely at one typical parish, he found seventeen groups and societies, each busily scheduling activities that often had little relation to "spiritual life and apostolic for-

---

6. Fichter, *Social Relations*, p. 123; Joseph H. Fichter, *Priest and People* (New York: Sheed and Ward, 1965), p. 159; Appleby, "Present to the People of God," p. 35.

7. Edward Wakin and Father Joseph F. Scheuer, *The De-Romanization of the American Catholic Church* (New York: Macmillan), pp. 104, 106.

8. Greeley, *Church and the Suburbs*, p. 71.

mation." The priest was responsible for every one of them. Priests felt that they spent much of their time on "tasks for which they are least prepared and in which they take least satisfaction — the big-city priests in directing lay groups and the small-town priests in parish financial problems."[9]

Whatever the administrative burdens, the apex of parish life and the chief symbol of community was still the moment when the priest stood before the altar and celebrated the mass. Every morning — and several times on Sundays, both in the morning and in the evening — priests faced the altar and recited the ritual as the laity followed along in missals or silently prayed the rosary in a stillness broken only by Latin words and the occasional sound of bells. About half the laity regularly attended. Saturdays often brought additional requiem masses on behalf of grieving families.[10]

Priests still painstakingly learned every word and gesture of the rite, performing it with choreographed precision, every Latin syllable set, every bow measured according to a scale of three degrees, every kneeling predetermined, and every particle of the Host protected from desecration. Only the thumb and first finger could be used to grasp the consecrated bread, and the priest had to keep them joined throughout the rest of the service, lifting the paten and chalice with the third and fourth fingers. The priest learned five distinct bows and had to know precisely when to make each of twenty-five signs of the cross or blessings. He had to pay attention to the exact number of inches separating his hands when he extended them in prayer. Every priest was to celebrate the rite in the same way. The assumption was that the priest's own personality was to be "subsumed in the ritual action."[11]

By the 1930s, more priests were encouraging laity to use missal books that translated the words into English. A few parishes experimented with "dialogue masses," in which the laity collectively read aloud short portions of the ritual. They also received communion more frequently. For most of the laity, even those who attended the mass every week, communion had been infrequent. Appealing to a 1905 encyclical by Pius X, reformers called for change, and by the 1920s they were making converts. The International Eucharistic Congress in

---

9. David O. Moberg, *The Church as a Social Institution: The Sociology of American Religion* (Grand Rapids: Baker Book House, 1984), p. 131; Leo O. Ward, *The Living Parish* (Notre Dame: Fides Publishers, 1959), pp. 21-24, 25; Fichter, *Priest and People*, pp. 159-60.

10. Dolan, "American Catholics," p. 285; Joseph H. Fichter, *Southern Parish Volume I: Dynamics of a City Church* (Chicago: University of Chicago Press, 1951), p. 167; Thomas F. Casey, *Pastoral Manual for New Priests* (Milwaukee: Bruce, 1961), p. 24.

11. Murnion, *Catholic Priest*, p. 68; Garry Wills, *Bare Ruined Choirs: Doubt, Prophecy, and Radical Religion* (Garden City: Doubleday, 1972), p. 65; Casey, *Pastoral Manual*, p. 51; Thomas P. Rausch, S.J., *Priesthood Today: An Appraisal* (New York: Paulist Press, 1992), p. 4.

Chicago in 1926, attended by several hundred thousand people, publicized the cause, and during the 1930s the numbers rose. One priest recorded nine thousand communions the first year that he promoted the change, 14,400 the second, and 22,000 the third. After 1953, Catholics no longer had to do without water for twelve hours before receiving communion, and after 1957 they abstained from food for only three hours rather than twelve — a change that slightly increased the level of participation.[12]

Among the more enthusiastic advocates of frequent communion were the company of priests and bishops drawn to liturgical renewal. The renewal began in Europe but found its way to America especially through the labors of the Benedictine monks at St. John's Abbey in Minnesota. Father Virgil Michel began to edit there in 1926 the journal *Orate Fratres* (later *Worship*) that helped over time to redefine the liturgy as a collective action that schooled a community for an apostolate in the world. Michel joined with other theologians in describing the church as the Mystical Body of Christ whose members discovered their unity through the liturgy, an image promoted by Pius XII that shifted the emphasis away from the prevailing depiction of the church as the "perfect society" governed by a fixed hierarchical order.[13]

In 1947 the pope endorsed the revival of liturgical studies and called for greater participation by the laity. By then, liturgical reformers were asking for a change from Latin to English in the liturgy, and by the 1950s, an occasional priest sometimes sought permission to face the congregation rather than the altar during the mass. After 1955 priests encouraged the use of the new *People's Hymnal*. The desire for change struck many insiders as eccentric, but by 1959 the liturgical movement was "spreading with some speed to more and more parishes."[14]

The older forms of devotion still maintained their hold, both for priests and for the laity. In addition to the daily mass, priests still felt obligated each day to recite the scriptures, prayers, readings, and hymns of the Daily Office. The ideal was to space these readings throughout the eight canonical hours of the day, but the priest could "anticipate" sections, reciting some early and combining others, so some priests squeezed in readings on the subway or walking from one place to

12. Chinnici, "Catholic Community at Prayer," pp. 25, 33-34, 40; Fichter, *Social Relations*, p. 135; Margaret M. McGuinness, "Let Us Go to the Altar: American Catholics and the Eucharist, 1926-1976," in *Habits of Devotion*, pp. 194, 212-14.

13. Dom Virgil Michel, *The Liturgy of the Church* (New York: Macmillan, 1937), pp. 20, 28, 53; Paul B. Marx, *Virgil Michel and the Liturgical Movement* (Collegeville, Minn.: The Liturgical Press, 1957), pp. 176-210, 298-336.

14. Andrew Greeley, *The Hesitant Pilgrim: American Catholicism After the Council* (1st ed., 1966; Garden City: Doubleday, 1969), p. 28; Ward, *Living Parish*, p. 141; McGuinness, "Let Us Go to the Altar," p. 117; Greeley, *Church and the Suburbs*, p. 171.

another. In addition, they were expected to offer prayers of thanksgiving after the mass, to pray alone, and to recite the rosary — more than two hours of prayer and meditation every day. By the end of the 1950s, more priests were privately acknowledging that the pressures of the parish made the Daily Office and meditation too difficult to maintain, confessing that they had abbreviated or abandoned the practices even though they still felt them as a duty.[15]

The priests spent much of their time leading popular lay devotions, especially the evening novenas that lifted up the virtues of a particular saint or honored some facet of the life of Mary and sought her favor. The Benediction of the Blessed Sacrament — which included the reverent display of the Host — occurred almost as frequently as the mass. The men's Holy Name Society, the women's Legion of Mary, and a number of sodalities for the faithful of all ages still gathered for extra-liturgical worship, and the Forty-Hours Devotion, with its processions, music, and continuous vigil, continued to draw participants. Parishioners sought priestly blessings for candles, medals, rosary beads, and scapulars (two small badges of cloth or plastic worn under a shirt or dress), and the priests determined the number of indulgences gained from their use. Catholics still flocked to the "blessing of throats," a ritual for preserving health.[16]

The adoration of God in Christ occurred within a communion of saints with Mary at its head, each saint honored for acts of sacrifice, devotion, and patronage — "St. Christopher for travel, St. Jude for lost causes, and St. Anthony for lost objects," three among a multitude who offered benefits and exemplified virtues. Priests led the faithful in prayers of intercession, imploring the saints to approach Christ on behalf of needs and desires both mundane and eternal, from health and work to relief for souls in purgatory. But this constituted only one part of the world of devotion that occupied the priest. Weekend retreats attracted crowds, and the parish mission remained a fixture of parochial life, with visiting preachers urging the faithful to amend their lives and do penance.[17]

During the 1950s, however, Catholic piety slowly shifted away from individualistic acts of petition and devotion. As early as 1951, Joseph Fichter, studying a Southern urban parish, found that people had stopped coming to the Sunday evening adoration of the Blessed Sacrament. By 1959, Catholics noticed

---

15. Casey, *Pastoral Manual,* p. 13; Murnion, *Catholic Priest,* pp. 75, 55, 339.

16. Dolan, "American Catholics," p. 13; Murnion, *Catholic Priest,* pp. 75, 77, 339; Thomas Boslooper, "At the End of the Marian Year," *Christian Century* 71 (Dec. 15, 1954): 1514-16; Chinnici, "Catholic Community at Prayer," pp. 61, 63; Casey, *Pastoral Manual,* p. 11; Fichter, *Southern Parish,* p. 80; Marcian J. Mathis, O.F.M., and Nicholas W. Meyer, O.F.M., *The Pastoral Companion: A Handbook of Canon Law* (Chicago: Franciscan Herald Press, 1961), pp. 71-78.

17. Morris, *American Catholic,* p. 174; Murnion, *Catholic Priest,* p. 372; Dolan, "American Catholics," p. 287.

declining interest in the traditional devotions and a decrease in the member-ship of parish devotional societies. Novenas remained popular through the 1950s, but the introduction of evening masses cut into attendance. The devo-tions still demanded priestly attention, but not as much as they once had.[18]

Even in the sacrament of penance, priests encountered — and often pro-moted — change. For years, they had urged frequent confession, and in the larger urban parishes, penance required long hours. At St. Augustine's in Mil-waukee in 1944, about 1,300 members, more than half the parish, confessed at least monthly, and 15 percent confessed weekly. At nearby St. John's parish, with 3,000 parishioners, priests heard 1,800 confessions a month. In 1950, priests at one Southern urban parish heard 17,986 confessions. On average, each active parishioner there confessed a little more than three times a year. Some parishes had lower rates; in one Southern parish, less than 3 percent of the members confessed weekly, a third confessed once a year and another third twice. But some parish priests spent at least a day a week in the confessional.[19]

By the late fifties, one could hear stirrings of discontent. Some priests com-plained that confession was too often a mechanical exercise in which penitents repeated the same list of sins and mumbled through routine prayers. Each con-fession took about two minutes, though some could last longer. It was not un-usual for priests to hear forty-five confessions in an hour. Most priests learned to ask only necessary questions, to require only reasonable acts of penance (usually prayers or recitations of the rosary), and to encourage each penitent. Some wanted more depth, and some laity shared the unease. A lay gathering in Detroit in 1962 expressed the hope that penance might become "a means of spiritualizing the layman" rather than the "enumeration of sins and the provi-sion of absolution."[20]

By the end of the 1950s, laity seemed also less content with the preaching. Forty percent of them ranked it as excellent; the majority gave a lower grade. "Wouldn't it be wonderful," one lay woman told a researcher, "to hear a good sermon on anything!" A survey in the mid-1960s found that only 20 percent gave the sermons an "excellent" ranking. Criticisms came especially from the best educated, who complained about "jejune sermons," and some priests themselves scorned the "pious platitudes" and the "lamentable" absence of theological content. Almost half of them conceded in one survey that their ser-

18. McGuinness, "Let Us Go to the Altar," p. 219; Fichter, *Southern Parish*, p. 71; Paula M. Kane, "Marian Devotion Since 1940: Continuity or Casualty?" in *Habits of Devotion*, pp. 97, 118.

19. Fichter, *Southern Parish*, p. 54; James O'Toole, "In the Court of Conscience: American Catholics and Confession, 1900-1975," in *Habits of Devotion*, pp. 134, 139.

20. Fichter, *Southern Parish*, p. 47; O'Toole, "Court of Conscience," pp. 153, 166-67; Mathis and Meyer, *Pastoral Companion*, pp. 79-150.

mons were not "well prepared." Daniel Patrick Moynihan, later a U.S. senator from New York, declared that "protest" was in order: "The time has come to walk out" on "puerile" sermons.[21]

The church had stars of the pulpit. The most charismatic was Bishop Fulton J. Sheen, who sparkled for two decades as a radio personality before beginning in the 1950s a television series called *Life Is Worth Living*. A spellbinding speaker, he became a fixture on Tuesday nights, drawing a radio and television audience of up to thirty million. The radio sermons and his television talks elevated him to celebrity status. His anti-communism and ultra-patriotism added to his appeal. It was an extraordinary moment in the mainstreaming of the priesthood when a cassocked, melodramatic Thomist monsignor could outdraw the popular comedian Milton Berle on television. But the seminaries sought less to create celebrities than to train priests to give competent homilies. In 1958, seminary instructors created the Catholic Homiletic Society to promote better sermons.[22]

Even such familiar routines as the home visit underwent change. In the 1940s, priests tried to visit each family at least once a year. Most conducted a yearly census — some called it the "block collection" — in which they visited every home, assessed its spiritual health, and sought the pledge of annual giving. In the larger parishes, however, they found such visiting difficult, and as parishes grew some priests found it impossible. In 1958, fully 70 percent of the pastors reported in one survey that they could no longer visit all the families of the parish. Members no longer clustered in neighborhoods of a few crowded blocks; they spread out over the city and the suburbs. The old habits of visitation could not endure.[23]

The demand from the laity for face-to-face interaction remained high. Priests reported that they counseled with anywhere from six to fifteen people on the days when they remained in the rectory for visitors. But the style of counseling was slowly changing. Like Protestants during the 1950s, priests shared an interest in new methods, and the seminaries responded with more

21. Ward, *Living Parish*, p. xiii; Andrew M. Greeley, *Priests: A Calling in Crisis* (Chicago: University of Chicago Press, 2004), p. 92; Fichter, *Priest and People*, pp. 28, 194; Thomas DuBay, *The Seminary Rule: An Explanation of the Purposes Behind It and How Best to Carry It Out* (Westminster, Md.: Newman Press, 1954), pp. 72-73; Fichter, *Southern Parish*, p. 203. Moynihan quote in John Tracy Ellis, *Essays in Seminary Education* (Notre Dame: Fides Publishers, 1967), p. 225.

22. Thomas C. Reeves, *America's Bishop: The Life and Times of Fulton J. Sheen* (San Francisco: Encounter Books, 2001), pp. 78-82, 223-50, 256; Joseph M. White, *The Diocesan Seminary in the United States: A History from the 1780s to the Present* (Notre Dame: University of Notre Dame Press, 1989), p. 385.

23. Morris, *American Catholic*, p. 181; Ward, *Living Parish*, p. xii; Fichter, *Priest and People*, p. 164.

courses. During the 1960s, some priests tried the same non-directive counseling that appealed to the Protestant mainline clergy.[24]

A "catechetical revolution" altered the way they taught children. In the thirties, Catholic educational reformers began to call for a "pedagogy of participation." They wanted priests and nuns to move away from the age-old methods of memorization and drill. In 1944, Rome instructed the seminaries to strengthen "catechetics" and teach educational and psychological theory. Catechetical practice did not change overnight; in 1950, children in some churches still memorized answers to repeat back to the bishop on the day of confirmation. But for the next ten years, reformers in religious education told anyone who would listen that they could improve catechesis if they turned away from drilling and incorporated more scripture, more exposure to the liturgy, and more attention to the child's experience. The obedient answer was not enough.[25]

Parents wanted more than catechesis. Greeley found that "activities dealing with children and their problems were the most popular in the parish," and he wondered if some suburban parishioners were beginning to value the local church mainly for "child-centered" instruction and recreation. Did they see the parish as a "glorified day nursery and the priests and nuns as highly trained baby sitters"? They certainly liked Cub Scouts, parochial schools, and athletic programs. One priest marveled at the importance that parishioners attached to recreational and athletic activities that seemed remotely distant from "the general supernatural functions of the Church."[26]

Catholics were changing in ways that altered the aura of priestly ministry. In 1946, two-thirds of American Catholics were in the lower economic classes, 25 percent were middle class, and 9 percent were upper class. In the next ten years, they found a secure place in the middle class: by 1958, 19 percent of Catholics held managerial or professional positions, only 2 percent below the Protestant number. While fewer than half of all Protestants in the labor force earned $5,000 a year, more than half of all Catholics earned that much or more. By the mid-1960s, 29 percent of younger Catholics — compared to 28 percent of their Protestant counterparts — occupied a place in the upper-middle or upper class. Prosperity brought autonomy and mobility. Middle-class Catholics no longer needed priests to help them manage their money.[27]

24. Murnion, *Catholic Priest*, pp. 118-20; Ward, *Living Parish*, p. xii.

25. Chinnici, "Catholic Community at Prayer," pp. 46, 50; White, *Diocesan Seminary*, p. 285; Fichter, *Southern Parish*, p. 92; Morris, *American Catholic*, p. 175.

26. Morris, *American Catholic*, pp. 66-67; Debra Campbell, "The Struggle to Serve: From the Lay Apostolate to the Ministry Explosion," in *Transforming Parish Ministry*, p. 248; Fichter, *Social Relations*, p. 132.

27. Wakin and Scheuer, *De-Romanization*, p. 204; Greeley, *Hesitant Pilgrim*, p. 155; Roger

The priesthood benefited from the economic ascent. In 1930, only 30 percent of seminarians had fathers in white-collar occupations — professional, managerial, or sales — but by 1960 the number rose to more than 60 percent. In 1930, 70 percent of the fathers of seminarians were service or unskilled workers or craftsmen; by 1960, the figure fell to 29 percent. Sixty percent of seminarians now came from families with above-average income. This meant, as one priest pointed out, that they were more accustomed to family discussion and more exposed to cultural trends than their grandfathers. They were also less likely to be content with what they viewed as unreasonable authority.[28]

The economic advance meant that Catholics could finish high school, move on to college, and pursue graduate education. In the thirties and forties, they lagged behind Protestants; early in the century, only half as many Catholics (12 percent) as Protestants (25 percent) attended college. But among Catholics born in 1933 or later, 28 percent attended college, compared with 29 percent of Protestants. (The G.I. Bill assisted both groups.) By 1960, younger Catholics were, on average, better educated than Protestants of their age level. They were also "more likely to go to graduate school and more likely to choose academic careers than white Protestants." A world of educational opportunity that their parents and grandparents had not enjoyed opened up to them.[29]

Higher education seemed to deepen commitment to the church — more graduates than non-graduates attended weekly mass — but it also meant that the priesthood was now one among many possible occupations. The church had to compete against other professions for recruits much in the same way the Protestant ministry had been forced to compete half a century earlier. And priests were no longer always the best-educated persons in the parish. An educated laity was less deferential, more inclined to hold priests to higher standards. They no longer gave the priesthood "automatic adulation and respect." There was "less obedience," wrote John Tracy Ellis; the priest's work was "more complicated."[30]

Finke and Rodney Stark, *The Churching of America 1776-1990: Winners and Losers in our Religious Economy* (New Brunswick: Rutgers University Press, 1992), p. 262.

28. W. Seward Salisbury, *Religion in American Culture: A Sociological Interpretation* (Homewood, Ill.: Dorsey Press, 1964), p. 209; Fichter, *Priest and People,* p. ix; Greeley, *Hesitant Pilgrim,* pp. 111-12.

29. Greeley, *Hesitant Pilgrim,* p. 155; Joseph Fichter, *Religion as an Occupation: A Study in the Sociology of the Professions* (South Bend: University of Notre Dame Press, 1961), p. 65; Greeley, *Confessions,* p. 207.

30. Fichter, *Social Relations,* p. 50; Greeley, *Church and the Suburbs,* p. 55; Eugene M. Kennedy, *Comfort My People: The Pastoral Presence of the Church* (New York: Sheed and Ward, 1968), p. 8; Ellis, "Preface," in *Catholic Priest,* p. 92.

Part of the complexity came from an emerging vision of lay ministry. The education of the laity for witness in the world became a priestly project as early as 1935, when priests, encouraged by Pius XI, helped form "Catholic Action" groups as part of a "lay apostolate" alongside the apostolate of the clergy. Catholic Action took various forms: Father Reynold Hillenbrand, who presided over the seminary in Mundelein, became known throughout the church for teaching seminarians to develop lay leaders for witness in the workplace, and others followed his lead. They promoted the Cana Movement to strengthen families, the Christian Family Movement to draw couples together over local issues, Friendship Houses that sought racial reconciliation, labor schools, Young Catholic Workers, and other projects that called upon the laity to do the work of the church. In the past, the priest had been the sole agent of ministry; by the 1950s, the push for a lay apostolate seemed to entail a "different way of priesthood."[31]

In the early fifties, proponents of the lay apostolate sought more initiative and autonomy. By 1962, Donald Thorman could write in *The Emerging Layman* that the laity constituted the church, that they held the responsibility for its ministries, and that too many of the clergy had rebuffed their rightful apostolate. The following year, the editor of the lay journal *Commonweal*, Daniel Callahan, claimed in *The Mind of the Catholic Layman* that priests who tried to rule their parish "with a rod of iron" and hold on to "the decisive power" were losing educated laity, and that bishops could no longer maintain "control" of the lay apostolate. *Commonweal* frequently printed essays on "lay-clerical tensions."[32]

Most Catholic laypeople were, in fact, fond of their priests. They thought "more highly of the priests," wrote one researcher, "than the priests think of themselves." They called on the priests for services, expressed high esteem, and showed a willingness to cooperate. While they might criticize the sermons, they reported "cordial" feelings about the priests. In one 1964 survey, only 7 percent said that they would like to have their present pastor removed. But lay-clerical relations were changing. During the early 1960s, the church edged away from the practice of appointing irremovable priests, replacing it with a tendency to assign priests for six-year terms. The change gave more authority to the laity. In the parishes, lay committees now more often dealt with finances, maintained the parish census, and repaired the buildings. In some parishes in the 1960s, laypeople

31. Campbell, "Struggle to Serve," pp. 222, 233; Chinnici, "Catholic Community at Prayer," p. 67; Appleby, "Present to the People of God," p. 13.

32. Donald J. Thorman, *The Emerging Layman: The Rise of the Catholic Layman in America* (Garden City: Doubleday, 1962), pp. 31, 34, 38; Daniel Callahan, *The Mind of the Catholic Layman* (New York: Charles Scribner's Sons, 1963), pp. 115, 121, 129; James O'Gara, "Lay-Clerical Tensions," *Commonweal* 76 (July 6, 1962): 373.

dropped the title "Father" and referred to priests by their first names. "The laity," wrote Fichter in 1968, "is now the 'new' element in the American church."[33]

Hierarchy and Profession, 1930-1970

Within the clerical culture of the golden age, everyone knew that not all priests were equal. The gap between the pastor and the curate remained wide. Almost every curate — or assistant priest — longed to become the pastor of a parish, but some never made it. Priests could serve as curates for as long as thirty-five years before they became pastors. In the larger dioceses, curates sometimes had to wait until they were fifty or older. In those dioceses, less than a third of the priests occupied the pastor's seat. Promotions rested mainly on seniority, though merit and achievement could sometimes make a difference.[34]

In the meantime, the bishops admonished curates to obey the pastor, follow his orders, and implement his policies. Pastors could set the daily tasks of the curates, decide how late they could stay out at night, determine which parishioners they could see, decide whether they could have a car, and impose rules about dress and behavior. The curates were expected to obey even the pastor who was "unreasonable, harsh, or vindictive." The best policy, advised one handbook, was "to keep quiet, and to bend with the wind."[35]

In most dioceses, the difference in power between the pastor and the curate could be seen in the salary structure. In Philadelphia, pastors received $1,200 a year and curates $500 well into the 1940s. In others the differential was not quite so pronounced. In New York, the average curate in the 1920s made around $650 a year, while the pastor made closer to $1,000. Forty years later, New York curates earned $1,800 a year during their first fifteen years of service; pastors earned from $2,700 to $3,120. In addition, all had room and board, the services of a housekeeper, and fees and donations from parishioners. The pastor alone, however, held the parish as a "benefice." He was entitled to all the income derived from the ordinary offerings, and after paying the assistants and caring for the expenses, he could pocket the surplus, though he also had to pay dues to the archdiocese. The legal title to the parish belonged to a corporation

33. Fichter, *Priest and People*, pp. 60, 198; Ward, *Living Parish*, pp. 22-30; Murnion, *Catholic Priest*, p. 326; Joseph H. Fichter, *America's Forgotten Priests — What They Are Saying* (New York: Harper and Row, 1968), p. 13; Interview with Katarina M. Schuth, Saint Paul Seminary School of Divinity, University of St. Thomas.

34. Fichter, *Priest and People*, pp. 174, 175.

35. Murnion, *Catholic Priest*, p. 113; Salisbury, *Religion in American Culture*, p. 235; Greeley, *Hesitant Pilgrim*, pp. 110-28; Greeley, *Confessions*, p. 183; Casey, *Pastoral Manual*, p. 17.

headed by the bishop, but for all practical purposes, the pastor "effectively owned" it.[36]

Just as the curate was to obey the pastor, so also the pastor was to obey the bishop. The golden age of the priest was also the era of the princely bishop. The battles between bishops and advocates of priests' rights had ceased after the First World War; by the 1930s, the topic elicited little discussion or interest. In *The Concept of the Diocesan Priesthood* (1951), the editor of the *American Ecclesiastical Review*, Joseph C. Fenton, expressed a consensus: "the diocesan priest does the work of Christ in His Church only when he gives a charitable and ungrudgingly loyal obedience to his bishop." The pastor was simply a member of a community organized to "aid the bishop in carrying out his obligations." The bishop was the ex-officio president of every parish governing board, and he appointed the members. He controlled parish budgets, appointed new pastors, and could transfer all curates and most pastors at will. In addition, he chaired the board of every diocesan institution, from hospitals and orphanages to universities. "His authority," wrote one observer, "is unchallengeable; his power bestrides the diocese."[37]

Bishops varied in style, temperament, and piety, but the celebrity bishops of the era lived as monarchs, and they skillfully used money, masonry, and spectacle to raise the status of the American Catholic church. On being appointed as the archbishop of Philadelphia, Dennis Cardinal Dougherty entered the city in a motorcade of seventy-five cars, fifty brass bands, and the cheers of 150,000 Catholics. He lived in a house with sixteen rooms, a six-car garage, a pool, and a stable. He determined what his priests wore, how they traveled, how much they could earn, what they could say publicly, and in some rare instances what their legal names should be. When he forbade Philadelphia Catholics in 1934 to attend the movies, they reduced the attendance in the theaters by around 40 percent. William Cardinal O'Connell, who ruled the archdiocese of Boston from 1907 to 1944, exemplified the excesses of the princely episcopacy: he lived in a world of grand estates and customized cars, intimidating his priests and enriching his relatives.[38]

36. Morris, *American Catholic*, p. 179; Murnion, *Catholic Priest*, pp. 43, 145, 342; Dolan, "American Catholics," pp. 291-92.

37. Joseph C. Fenton, *The Concept of the Diocesan Priesthood* (Milwaukee: Bruce, 1951), pp. 6, 7, 12, 47-60, 62; Robert Trisco, "Bishops and Their Priests in the United States," in *Catholic Priest*, p. 270; Fichter, *Social Relations*, p. 184; Wakin and Scheuer, *De-Romanization*, pp. 121, 125; John H. Donovan, "The Social Structure of the Parish," in *Sociology of the Parish*, ed. C. J. Nuesse and Thomas J. Harte (Milwaukee: Bruce, 1950), pp. 88-93.

38. Morris, *American Catholic*, pp. 64, 120-22, 171, 179, 190; Edward Kantowicz, "Cardinal Mundelein of Chicago and the Shaping of Twentieth Century American Catholicism," *Journal of American History* 68 (1981): 52-68.

The era's most powerful bishop — Francis Cardinal Spellman — intimidated even politicians. As archbishop of New York from 1939 through 1967, Spellman oversaw the largest non-governmental building program in the state, and he made the church the biggest private real-estate holder in New York City. He dispensed political patronage by helping to select judges, officeholders, and even school board members. Pope Pius XII depended on him for much of the Vatican's revenue, and his political reach extended from Italy to Guatemala. A vehement cold warrior, he served as the military vicar of Catholic army and navy chaplains and became one of the most visible advocates for the war in Vietnam. He governed even the smallest details of priestly existence, from dress to shaving to haircuts. His Manhattan chancery was known as "the Powerhouse."[39]

Few bishops copied the ostentation of Dougherty, emulated the ambition of O'Connell, or attained the political influence of Spellman. Some gained a reputation of a different kind: "He was a genius, he was honest, and he was a saint," noted one observer about Chicago's Albert Cardinal Meyer. "Besides that he wasn't spectacular." Some exercised their power on behalf of the powerless even when it brought opposition from the powerful. During the labor strife of the 1930s, Archbishop John T. Nichols in Cincinnati assigned priests to help the workers unionize, instruct them in collective bargaining, and teach them the social principles of the church. Archbishop Edward Mooney of Detroit defied the city's power elite by standing with striking autoworkers. In St. Louis, Archbishop Joseph Ritter required Catholic schools in 1947 to admit African American students despite opposition from white parents. In the 1950s, Archbishop Joseph Francis Rummel in New Orleans enraged demagogic politicians when he ended racial segregation in Catholic schools and churches. These bishops could assist people on the margins because the church accorded them monarchical authority.[40]

Of course, the bishops never had absolute power, as each of them owed loyalty to the pope. Cardinal Gibbons had hoped for an authoritative council of American bishops, but Rome insisted on a direct line of authority to each bishop. In 1917, the bishops formed a centralized organization known as the National Catholic War Council, which two years later became the National Catholic Welfare Conference, a voluntary association designed to coordinate the initiatives of the church. The Vatican, however, circumscribed the conference's powers: it had no authority over diocesan bishops, who reported directly to

39. John Cooney, *The American Pope: The Life and Times of Francis Cardinal Spellman* (New York: Times Books, 1984), pp. xv, 56, 100-101, 108, 170, 173, 243, 296, 302.

40. Greeley, *Confessions*, p. 176; O'Brien, "American Priest and Social Action," p. 445; Morris, *American Catholic*, pp. 210, 241.

Rome. Within each diocese, the bishop continued to have the last word, subject only to Roman oversight.

Despite this continuity of hierarchical authority, the American episcopate in the 1950s showed signs of slow but steady change. In 1947, Richard Cardinal Cushing of Boston proudly proclaimed that no Catholic bishop in the United States was the son of a college graduate. By 1958, 5 percent of the bishops came from homes with college-educated fathers. Almost all of them were native-born Americans. Increasing numbers came from the middle class: 27 percent had fathers who owned their own businesses, and another 11 percent were the sons of business executives. Early in the century, most bishops had attended European seminaries; by 1950, most were graduates of schools in the United States, although post-seminary schooling in Rome could be a boost toward an episcopal appointment. Bishops were also becoming more educated. By 1958, 77 percent had not only seminary training but also an advanced degree.[41]

Seminary training in 1930 still served as an introduction to this world of hierarchical authority. Many priests began in the ninth grade by attending a minor seminary. For six years they studied normal high school and college subjects, including Latin, in an atmosphere of order, discipline, and religious devotion. By 1959 the church had forty-two diocesan minor seminaries and about 125 administered by the orders. For most priests, however, formation began in the major seminary, which required two to three years of philosophy and four of theology, normally taught in Latin. Both bishops and religious orders wanted their own seminaries, so they sprang up everywhere — at least 209 by 1938, about 388 by 1950. The aim was still "formation."[42]

Seminarians followed a routine governed by rules designed to promote "a life of perfection and holiness." The seminary rule informed the student "at any given moment of the day" exactly what God wanted him to do. Among the highest virtues, therefore, was "docility toward the rule," a "ready and humble acceptance and submission" to its dictates, which governed dress, devotions, recreation, relationships, and study. "If the rule calls for recreation at 3:30 in the afternoon," wrote Thomas Dubay, "the seminarian is advancing in holiness by playing basketball or baseball." Students attended the mass daily, prayed frequently, said the rosary, observed long periods of silence, and meditated before going to bed. They rose early and observed a strict uniformity of dress in black

---

41. Fichter, *Religion as an Occupation*, p. 64; John D. Donovan, "The American Catholic Hierarchy: A Social Profile," *The American Catholic Sociological Review* 19 (1958): 100, 105, 108-09; Wakin and Scheuer, *De-Romanization*, p. 119.

42. Murnion, *Catholic Priest*, p. 10; Fichter, *Religion as an Occupation*, p. 27; Gerald S. Slogan, "Seminaries in America," *Commonweal* 73 (Oct. 7, 1960): 37; Robert S. Ellwood, *1950: Crossroads of American Religious Life* (Louisville: Westminster John Knox, 2000), p. 131.

cassocks and clerical collars. In their final year of study, they recited the Daily Office.[43]

The regimen assumed a paramilitary cast. It taught the student to subordinate individual desires and goals to the common good. Cardinal O'Connell once explained that "there is no such thing as the personality of a bishop or the personality of a parish priest. Personal qualities are subject to change. These are transient things on which depends nothing of the certainty of the Catholic faith." The authority came from the office, not the person and not the education. Students therefore learned to conform their views and yearnings to the common vision of the church. They heard frequent warnings against "particular friendships" — individual comradeship that might disrupt the sense of common formation or threaten the integrity of the community.[44]

"You train them," said one faculty member, "for hearing confessions, saying mass, and preaching to the people." In the classroom, students heard Latin lectures on moral and dogmatic theology, scripture, canon law, church history, music, and the rubrics for mass, the sacraments, and the Daily Office. The aim was to learn authoritative answers. In St. Joseph's Seminary in the Dunwoodie section of Yonkers, for instance, the students absorbed mainly Thomistic thought in scholastic manuals from which they memorized answers in Latin. There was little class discussion or personal investigation. Faculty members expected little reading outside the textbooks. Students at Dunwoodie in 1930 wrote no papers and had access to the library only four hours a week.[45]

By the 1950s, Catholic critics were voicing disappointment with the quality of seminary education. Ellis kept pointing out that the proliferation of schools meant too many small and weak institutions. Other critics complained about the low admission standards, the tolerance for mediocre performance, inattention to such pastoral skills as counseling and preaching, and the isolation of students from the outside world. Most schools continued to ban secular magazines and radio broadcasts. "We were," recalled Andrew Greeley, "cut off completely from the world whose salvation was to be entrusted to us in a few years. No newspapers, no radios, and heaven help us no television." As a student at St. Mary of the Lake Seminary in Mundelein he and some of his classmates

43. DuBay, *Seminary Rule*, pp. 7, 19, 20, 132; Murnion, *Catholic Priest*, p. 22; Appleby, "Present to the People of God," p. 19.

44. Appleby, "Present to the People of God," p. 9.

45. Murnion, *Catholic Priest*, pp. 27, 42-44, 187, 358; Gannon, "Before and After Modernism," p. 351.

46. Ellis, *Seminary Education*, p. 203; White, *Diocesan Seminary*, p. 400; Appleby, "Present to the People of God," p. 19; Greeley, *Confessions*, p. 127.

offended the rector by "committing the unspeakable crime of sneaking *Time* into the Sacred Orders building."[46]

The French refugee theologian Jacques Maritain said in the 1940s that he found the intellectual level of many American seminary graduates "appalling." By 1955, Catholic clergy were willing to talk about the problem openly. In that year, John Tracy Ellis delivered an address in St. Louis on "American Catholics and the Intellectual Life." He argued that Catholics in the United States seemed to lack a tradition of inquiry, that they sent few teachers to the best universities, and that the clergy found it difficult to "reach the intellectual elite." At least some of the subsequent debate focused on the seeming indifference of American priests to the world of thought.[47]

Despite the pessimism, the Catholic laity were poised to move into the academic and intellectual mainstream, and changes in the seminaries were altering the intellectual horizons of priests. Even in the 1940s, students and faculty in some schools organized extracurricular seminars on social ethics, liturgy, and racial issues. Within a decade, some seminaries were keeping their libraries open, encouraging discussion in seminars, and sponsoring guest lecturers. Students gained more freedom to leave the seminary grounds, to stay up later at night, and to substitute study time for baseball. Some schools conceded that few seminarians knew Latin well enough to absorb lectures. In 1962, about 39 percent of seminaries still used Latin as the language of instruction, 18 percent used some Latin, and about 43 percent used almost none.[48]

The schools began to seek accreditation for their academic programs. The college departments of some seminaries had joined regional accreditation associations even in the 1930s, but the "theologates," the programs that provided the final four years of theological training, showed little interest until the 1950s. In 1961, no more than eight schools of theology had sought and attained an accredited status. But three years later, thirty-four schools in the Midwest created an association to help with accreditation issues, and schools on the coasts followed their example. By the mid-1960s, they were ready to join the American Association of Theological Schools. By 1968, fifteen had begun the process of review that would make them full members.[49]

Viewing such changes from Rome, the Prefect of the Sacred Congregation of Seminaries criticized the desire for "up to date" methods of priestly training. He contended that the "true foundations" of seminary formation should be the

---

47. John T. McGreavy, *Catholicism and American Freedom: A History* (New York: W. W. Norton, 2003), p. 203; John Tracy Ellis, "American Catholics and the Intellectual Life," *Thought* 30 (1955): 368, 372.

48. Murnion, *Catholic Priest*, pp. 177, 207, 354; White, *Diocesan Seminary*, p. 378.

49. White, *Diocesan Seminary*, pp. 394, 402, 421, 422.

cultivation of humility, obedience, and separation from the world. But the Catholic seminaries, which had been primarily places of spiritual formation, were gradually also becoming "academic and professional" institutions subscribing to "educational standards outside of church control." The church was creating a new kind of Catholic seminary.[50]

The question of seminary training bore upon the larger topic of the professional status of the priesthood. In 1952, Pope Pius XII encouraged the Sister Formation Movement, a push toward special training that would allow sisters to obtain "knowledge and skills necessary for becoming better qualified professionally" as teachers and nurses. If sisters were to have professional expertise, then why not also priests? The pope spoke of the priesthood, after all, as "the profession of all professions."[51]

The Jesuit sociologist Joseph Fichter argued in 1961 that priests could be professionals in their "subsidiary roles" — as teachers or administrators, for example — but that the image of "professional" did not quite capture the essence of priesthood. He worried about potential conflicts between "the traditional structure of diocese and order" and men whose "professional competence" conferred more autonomy and authority than the parish priest had been accustomed to demand. And was not the priesthood a vocation defined by fidelity to Christ and faithfulness to the church rather than by the provision of services for clients? Fichter pointed out that priests, unlike most other professionals, had little choice about where to work and limited options for mobility. Yet he also noticed the parallels between priests and other professionals, and he intimated that a more professional priesthood might well require "adaptation" from the church.[52]

Within a few years, the priest-educator Eugene Kennedy claimed that the culture was moving even the diocesan priest "toward a more professional position in society whether he likes it or not." Some priests felt uncomfortable with "the very word 'professional,'" associating it with distance, impersonality, and a service function, but Kennedy drew attention to its positive connotations: he wanted priests to seek continuing education, to hold themselves to high standards as preachers, liturgists, and counselors, to read the journals on priestly work, and to cultivate an ethic of "responsibility for the welfare of others." He wanted the seminaries to supervise students in work with "flesh and blood

50. White, *Diocesan Seminary,* pp. 290, 388.

51. Appleby, "Present to the People of God," p. 66; Edgar W. Mills, "The Sacred in Ministry Studies," in *The Sacred in a Secular Age: Toward Revision in the Scientific Study of Religion* (Berkeley: University of California Press, 1985), p. 172; Fichter, *Religion as an Occupation,* p. 107.

52. Fichter, *Religion as an Occupation,* pp. 164-65, 220, 233; Fichter, *America's Forgotten Priests,* p. 208.

people," not merely lecture at them in the classroom. He represented the Catholic educators who wanted to enhance the professional standing of the priest, whether by training every priest in "some kind of specialization" or by raising the bar of expectations for learning and competence.[53]

The age-old division of secular and regular priests proved to be amenable to a "professional" conception of the priesthood because it provided an institutional setting for specialization. By the mid-twentieth century, the church had some 125 religious orders for men in the United States, some with thousands of members, others with twenty-five or fewer. In 1940, a third of American priests belonged to a religious order. The orders provided the "trained professionals" who staffed the Catholic schools, colleges, hospitals, and social welfare agencies, and some of the orders defined themselves through specialized ministries.[54]

By 1958, for example, the largest order, the Society of Jesus, educated about a third of the students in Catholic colleges, operating twenty-eight schools with more than 110,000 students. When a 1932 internal Jesuit study complained of mediocre faculties and a lack of scholarly achievement, the order began to send the brightest Jesuit seminarians to earn doctorates at the top American universities, and after twenty years the Jesuit schools began moving into the academic mainstream. The Dominicans, heirs to a long tradition of learning, also produced more than their share of college and high school teachers, and the Holy Cross Fathers, with similar inclinations, made the University of Notre Dame a flagship school of the Catholic system.[55]

The larger orders cultivated specialties. The Maryknoll Fathers organized themselves around foreign missions. The Paulists became specialists in mass communication; their Paulist Press was the publishing giant of the American church, printing almost eighteen million pamphlets, magazines, and books a year while operating mail-order bookshops and the Catholic Library Service. The Franciscans, second in size only to the Jesuits, were more diverse, but they gained a reputation for youth work. The Salesians produced missionaries, organized boys' clubs, and led camping programs, while the Columban Fathers focused on foreign missions, and the Benedictines, who organized their lives around the disciplines of prayer, became known for their knowledge of the liturgy. The pattern resembled the structures of the modern professions.[56]

The orders had always eyed bishops warily, and their independence continued to generate conflict. They competed with the bishops in recruiting new

53. Kennedy, *Comfort My People*, pp. 61, 62-64, 101, 205.

54. Wakin and Scheuer, *De-Romanization*, p. 151; O'Brien, "American Priest and Social Action," p. 405; Fichter, "Catholic Church Professionals," pp. 77-85.

55. Morris, *American Catholic*, pp. 270-71; Wakin and Scheuer, *De-Romanization*, p. 128.

56. Wakin and Scheuer, *De-Romanization*, pp. 141, 148.

priests, and they sometimes contended with them over fundraising and control of finances. Some bishops refused to let the orders recruit within their dioceses, and a few forbade them to publish advertisements in diocesan newspapers. Relations between diocesan and regular priests were also not always harmonious. "We Religious might as well face up to the fact," conceded the head of one order, "that some of our habits irritate the diocesan clergy; for example, our inclination to talk as if we were the only ones in the state of perfection."[57]

Priesthood lent itself to a myriad of specialties. Priests served as principals of schools and presidents of colleges. The Chancery office — the central headquarters of a diocese — required chancellors and deans with administrative skills, examiners, and directors. Some priests conducted retreats and missions, some served as military chaplains, and others did publishing work. By the end of the 1950s, Catholics printed more than 550 newspapers and magazines with a circulation of 28 million. Some priests became experts in urban ministries, others worked in Catholic charities, and still others devoted themselves to the Catholic Youth Organization. Catholics operated nursing schools, hospitals, homes for the aged, and orphanages, and almost all of them required priestly oversight. Beginning in the fifties, some larger parishes instituted their own forms of specialized ministry, with some priests assuming heavy duties as premarital counselors, others as general counselors, and still others as specialists in religious education.[58]

Fichter had been right when he pointed out the potential for tension between the authority attained through specialized mastery of a delimited field and the traditional authority exercised within a hierarchical religious community. He was also right when he observed that the church would have to learn new ways of adapting itself to the professional ideal and incorporating its strengths into the work of ministry. It was no accident that when priests began to resign in the early 1960s, the main losses came among the best-educated priests in the "specialized ministries."[59]

Catholic Theology and Vatican II, 1950-65

Some impatient laity saw the priests as resistant to change, but priests — and bishops — were more eager for change than most laypeople could have realized.

57. John P. Marschall, "Diocesan and Religious Clergy: The History of a Relationship, 1789-1969," in *Catholic Priest*, pp. 386, 404, 412.

58. Wakin and Scheuer, *De-Romanization*, p. 180; Appleby, "Present to the People of God," p. 17; Fichter, *Religion as an Occupation*, p. 146; Murnion, *Catholic Priest*, p. 328.

59. Fichter, "Catholic Church Professionals," p. 77.

They displayed their eagerness in their excitement about the Second Vatican Council. In 1950 Pius XII, in the encyclical *Humani Generis,* had demanded obedience to papal authority, the acceptance of Thomist theology, and an end to speculation by Catholic theologians about evolutionary change in nature and history, including the history of the church. Bishop Fulton Sheen's *The Priest Is Not His Own* articulated the theology of priesthood that had prevailed during the 1950s: The priest was the mediator between God and humanity, a sacral figure who was in the world but not of it. Because of his ordination, the priest bore a special status that submerged his own personality in the personality of Christ. He was *alter Christus,* and he presided at the mass because he possessed a sacred power not given to the laity. Sheen was repeating traditional certainties. When Pius XII died in 1958, the cardinals chose Angelo Roncalli to replace him. As Pope John XXIII, he invited the bishops and theologians of the world to meet in Rome in 1962 for *aggiornamento,* the updating of the church. The council did not repudiate the theology that Sheen was representing, but it located it within a new context that altered its meaning.[60]

Vatican II was a three-year struggle between progressives and traditionalists, and the council's documents reflect the crosscurrents, but they confirmed changes already underway. Most of the Americans who went — bishops and theologians — stood with the progressives. In America, priests followed the proceedings by reading the "Letters from Vatican City" by the Redemptorist Father Francis X. Murphy, an American teaching at the Alphosian Academy in Rome. Written under the pseudonym "Xavier Rynne" and published in the *New Yorker,* Murphy's letters created a sensation. Seminarians at Dunwoodie were not supposed to read the *New Yorker.* They read it anyway.[61]

Without abandoning older images, the council envisioned the church chiefly as the people of God — an image that accented collegiality, unity of purpose among bishops and priests, and the entwining of the "hierarchical priesthood" and "the common priesthood of the faithful." It generated a vision of the church as engaged with the world, committed to service, and willing to minister within pluralistic societies without seeking a special status from the state. It affirmed alterations in the liturgy, encouraged innovation in the seminaries, and threw open the door of ecumenical cooperation with other Christians and other religions, emphasizing that Protestants and the Orthodox shared with

60. Pope Pius XII, *Humanae Generis,* in *The Papal Encyclicals,* ed. Claudia Carlen, 5 vols. (Raleigh: McGrath, 1981), vol. 4, pp. 177, 180; Fulton J. Sheen, *The Priest Is Not His Own* (New York: McGraw Hill, 1963), pp. 23, 39, 43, 47, 86.

61. Xavier Rynne, *Letters from Vatican City* (Garden City: Doubleday, 1964), p. 11; Murnion, *Catholic Priest,* p. 252.

Catholics a life "in the Holy Spirit." Almost everything it did had implications for the way priests would carry out their ministries.[62]

Describing the bishops as the successors of the apostles, the council affirmed their collegial relation with each other and with the pope. This had the potential of strengthening their hand in their relations with the Roman Curia (the offices of the Vatican) and with their priests. From their perspective, it was helpful when the council said that bishops shared, as a collective body, "the infallibility promised to the Church." The council described them as the "shepherds of the Church" and asserted that "those who heard them, heard Christ," and "those who rejected them, rejected Christ." The priests over whom they held authority were their "helpers," sharing the office of ministry "in a lesser degree," and priests were to "respect" in the bishops "the authority of Christ." Rome had once discouraged standing conferences of bishops; the council now encouraged them.[63]

At the same time, the council described the bishop and the priests as "co-workers," and it said that bishops should work closely with their priests "in the government of the diocese." It urged bishops to hear and respect the views of their priests and even to establish "senates" of priests to help carry out their governing task. In place of the master-servant images of an earlier age, the council spoke of a familial relationship between priests and bishops. And it emphasized that the "eminent" duty of the bishop was "the preaching of the gospel," a duty that bishops shared with their priests. The documents led priests to expect a different kind of relationship with their bishops.[64]

The council both celebrated and broadened the work of the priest. While it declared that the priest and the laity participated in "the one priesthood of Christ," it still insisted that priests differed "in essence and not only in degree" and that the ordained priest was to "mold and rule" the "priestly people." He "shared" the authority of the bishop. As always, his chief duties were "to offer Sacrifice and to forgive sins," and the sacramental functions stood out, but the council also stressed the priest's "sacred duty of preaching the gospel," his proficiency in the "Sacred Liturgy," his responsibility as an educator, his nurturing of a community, and his "special obligation to the poor and the weak."[65]

Yet this was not the omni-competent priest of the early twentieth century. The council reminded the laity to abandon any idea that priests were "always

---

62. "Dogmatic Constitution on the Church," in *The Documents of Vatican II*, ed. Walter M. Abbott (New York: Herder, 1966), pp. 27, 34.

63. "Dogmatic Constitution on the Church," pp. 39-40, 42, 48-49; "Decree on the Ministry and Life of Priests," in *Documents of Vatican II*, pp. 533-35.

64. "Decree on the Life and Ministry of Priests," pp. 548-49.

65. "Dogmatic Constitution on the Church," p. 27; "Decree on the Ministry and Life of Priests," pp. 533-46.

such experts, that to every problem which arises, however complicated," they could always provide "a concrete solution." The council's decisions produced abrupt symbolic reversals that reduced the distance between priests and laity. In accord with the Constitution on the Sacred Liturgy, American priests began in 1964 to celebrate most of the mass in English rather than Latin and to face the congregation. The laity could now stand to receive communion, and within a few years they, like the priest, could touch the wafer and drink from the chalice. Lay readers now stood alongside the priests before the congregation at worship. The liturgical changes were popular; after two years of living with them, 93 percent of American Catholics gave their approval. Most priests — especially younger ones — were pleased with the council, though some thought it should have said more about the status of the priesthood in the modern world and the distinctive ministry of the priests within religious orders.[66]

The changes symbolized by the new mass were breathtaking. The Latin mass and the Eucharist consecrated by a priest with his back turned to the congregation had been celebrations of a transcendent God whose presence was mediated by the institutional church and the sacerdotal priest. The council made the mass a celebration also of divine immanence, with the altar a table and the presbyter speaking in the vernacular to a community who together broke bread and drank the wine of sacrifice. The change meant that the sacerdotal high priest reenacting the sacrifice of Christ was now also the host of a communal meal shared by fellow apostles who were reenacting that sacrifice in their daily lives of service, justice, and self-sacrifice.[67]

The council gave extraordinary attention to the laity. It defined the lay apostolate as "a participation in the saving mission of the Church," and affirmed that all of the baptized shared in the priesthood of Christ. It urged priests to "acknowledge and promote the dignity of the laity" and scrupulously honor their "freedom," listening to them willingly, considering their wishes, and recognizing their "experience and competence." No one was certain precisely what this would mean for the work of the parish. Ellis remarked, as the council was beginning, that the rise of the laity required priests to "relax some of their power and authority," but this was venturing into the unknown.[68]

---

66. Appleby, "Present to the People of God," p. 54; Chinnici, "Catholic Community at Prayer," pp. 11, 26; Wills, *Bare Ruined Choirs*, p. 65; Fichter, "Catholic Church Professionals," p. 79; Thomas P. Rausch, S.J., "Priesthood in the Context of Apostolic Religious Life," in *The Theology of Priesthood*, ed. Donald J. Goergen and Ann Garrido (Collegeville: Liturgical Press, 2000), pp. 113-15.

67. Scott Appleby of the University of Notre Dame helped me see and express the significance of this change.

68. "Dogmatic Constitution on the Church," p. 59; "Decree on the Ministry and Life of

The council's statements on ecumenicity had a similar kind of ambiguity. Up to the 1940s, the church forbade Catholics to appear in joint undertakings with Protestants and Jews for fear that they might imply "indifferentism," or belief in the equal validity of all religions. It was a mortal sin for a Catholic to worship in a Protestant church. "The Protestants have no religion," remarked a priest in Holyoke. In 1950 Rome gave permission for certain limited meetings, but not for discussion of faith or morals. But by 1958 Catholic ecumenists in America were eager for conversation, and by 1962 a Catholic bishop could rejoice that "dialogue has replaced religious debate." Vatican II encouraged the dialogue. It still said that membership in the Catholic Church was "necessary for salvation," though it also affirmed, in accord with Catholic tradition, that salvation was possible for others who did not have full knowledge of the church's message. It acknowledged the gifts and graces of the Spirit in other churches. Most American priests welcomed the openness to dialogue.[69]

Before the council ended, Protestant, Orthodox, and Catholic theologians were engaging in regular conversations, a bishop had preached in a Protestant church and encouraged Catholics to attend a Billy Graham crusade, an archdiocese had joined an interdenominational state Council of Churches, and about seventy-five dioceses had sponsored meetings and clergy gatherings across confessional lines. Catholic priests began to teach in Protestant seminaries, and social activists from both traditions met one another on the picket lines. But for some the prospect of dialogue could be unsettling, and a Catholic traditionalist movement pulled away from the conversation. Monsignor Fenton severely criticized the leading ecumenist Gustave Weigel, and Catholic University barred Weigel from speaking.[70]

The council reflected and encouraged change in Catholic theology. Catholic moral theologians had already begun to move away from an accent on law toward an emphasis on the primacy of charity. The tendency to quantify progress toward salvation — to count merits and add up the benefits of indulgences — faded into the background. Theologians were more critical of the age-old

---

Priests," pp. 552-53; John Tracy Ellis, "The Catholic Layman in America Today," *Commonweal* 76 (June 22, 1962): 319-22; Appleby, "Present to the People of God," p. 53.

69. McGreevy, *Catholicism and American Freedom,* p. 204; O'Toole, "Court of Conscience," p. 147; Underwood, *Protestant and Catholic,* p. 150; "For Collaboration and Proselyting," *Christian Century* 67 (Mar. 15, 1950): 323; "Protestant-Catholic Tensions," *Commonweal* 68 (June 27, 1958): 315-16; Wakin and Scheuer, *De-Romanization,* p. 274; "Dogmatic Constitution on the Church," p. 467.

70. Wakin and Scheuer, *De-Romanization,* p. 276; Michael Novak, "American Catholicism After The Council," *Commonweal* 40 (1965): 50-58; Charles D. Kean, "Controversy Within Catholicism," *Christian Century* 80 (Mar. 20, 1963): 358.

distinction between mortal and venial sins that had governed the atmosphere of the confessional. They were more open to themes of personhood and human dignity. Some were less inclined to talk about the church's "Deposit of Faith" — transmitted unchanged not only in substance but also in forms of expression — and more apt to explore history and experience as sources for interpreting Catholic doctrine. Debates over these ideas would intensify the rift between progressives and traditionalists.[71]

Vatican II changed the way many Catholics thought about priests. For a considerable number, the sacral view of priesthood, with its focus on the status conferred by ordination and the sacramental power of the priest, gradually gave way to the conception of the priest as the pastoral leader of a community, defined more by what he did than by his sacramental status. Three-quarters of the Catholic laity liked the changes. But the council became the subject of conflicting interpretations. Traditionalists lifted up one set of themes, progressives another. The council promised change. Some resisted while others found the pace far too slow. Some would blame it for the difficulties in the church; others would blame the resistance to it. One reason for its far-reaching influence on the priesthood was that it coincided with a period of dramatic change in the engagement of American priests with the dilemmas of race and war.[72]

The Priesthood and Social Issues, 1930-1970

In 1922, Father John Ryan wrote in *The State and the Church* that governments were obliged to protect the true Catholic faith and to show it "special favor." This traditional teaching caused anti-Catholic critics in America to question the church's devotion to religious liberty and democracy. In the midst of Protestant and Catholic battles over church and state, birth control, and attitudes toward repressive governments in Europe and South America, the fear that Catholics sought political power to suppress freedom of religion remained intense in Protestant America. Even in the early 1950s, however, large numbers of younger priests disliked the idea of a "confessional state," and they found their champion in a Jesuit professor of theology at Woodstock College in Maryland. John Courtney Murray battled traditionalists for more than a decade

71. O'Toole, "Court of Conscience," p. 178; Murnion, *Catholic Priest*, p. 262; Appleby, "Present to the People of God," p. 56.

72. Paul Philibert, O.P., "Issues for a Theology of Priesthood: A Status Report," in *Theology of Priesthood*, pp. 1-3.

while working out the views he presented to the public in 1960 in *We Hold These Truths.*[73]

No American Catholic theologian of the era had more influence than Murray. Silenced for a time by the Vatican, he reemerged at the time of council, and his carefully argued position that the church and state should be independent of each other and autonomous in their own spheres prevailed. Murray drew on a theology of natural law to argue that governments had no authority "to resolve the dispute between conflicting truths, all of which claim the final validity of transcendence." "Parliaments," he wrote, "are not to play the theologian." In its "Declaration on Religious Liberty," which he largely drafted, the council adopted his argument. Traditionalists deplored his position — Catholic University barred him from speaking — but for most priests of the era his writings reaffirmed a respect for American democratic traditions that they had always held.[74]

Even in 1930, Catholic clergy were long accustomed to the social battles of a democratic society. Their forms of social action hinted at the diversity within the church. For many, the greatest challenge was to overcome vice and protect individual morality. A Jesuit theologian, Daniel Lord, drafted the 1929 Hollywood Movie Production Code, and the Catholic bishops joined in support of it. Six years later the bishops formed the Legion of Decency, which determined the movies that Catholics could see, and urged Catholics to take a decency pledge. The pledge was one expression of a preoccupation with sexual morality that covered everything from indecent literature to birth control.[75]

For many other priests, however, the more serious challenge was economic justice. In 1931, the year in which Pius XI issued the encyclical *Quadragesimo Anno* criticizing untrammeled economic individualism, the American bishops condemned "the concentration of inconceivable wealth in the hands of a comparatively small group." For a few priests in 1933 — and for more in later years — the formation of Dorothy Day's Catholic Worker movement exemplified the virtues of self-sacrificial action on behalf of the poor.[76]

73. John A. Ryan and Francis J. Boland, *Catholic Principles of Politics* (1st ed., 1940; New York: Macmillan, 1943), p. 295. (This was a revised version of *The State and the Church.*) See "The Widening Gulf," *The Christian Century* 71 (Apr. 7, 1954): 421-23; Underwood, *Protestant and Catholic*, p. 352.

74. John Courtney Murray, "The Catholic Experience in America," *Commonweal* 60 (Aug. 6, 1954): 437; John Courtney Murray, "Religious Freedom," in *Documents of Vatican II*, pp. 672-74; "Declaration on Religious Freedom," in *Documents of Vatican II*, p. 681; Donald E. Pelotte, S.S.S., *John Courtney Murray: Theologians in Conflict* (New York: Paulist Press, 1975), pp. 27-59, 74-106.

75. McGreevy, *Catholicism and American Freedom*, p. 156.

76. Murnion, *Catholic Priest*, p. 177; McGreevy, *Catholicism and American Freedom*, p. 151; Morris, *American Catholic*, p. 142.

During the 1930s, priests in almost every large industrial center attached themselves to labor unions. Bishops assigned priests to labor schools that spread Catholic social teachings among the workers. Priests helped organize unions, served on regional labor boards, and took part in workplace negotiations. In Philadelphia in the 1950s, ship owners and longshoremen agreed that Father Dennis Comey would be the sole arbitrator for waterfront disputes. In New York, the labor activism of Father John Corridan inspired the movie *On the Waterfront,* and Father Phil Carey helped create the public employee unions. Monsignor George Higgins at the National Catholic Welfare Conference ran industrial-relations conferences and organized meetings of union and management leaders. In an era when half the membership of labor unions was Catholic, priests were regular participants on arbitration boards dealing with labor issues.[77]

The labor priests were not without opposition within the church. In Holyoke, the conservative bishop in the late 1940s discouraged any priests from taking "public stands on labor's rights in the city." When one curate spoke out on behalf of the labor movement, the bishop transferred him. But for many of the bishops in the large cities, the labor priests represented the church's call for economic justice. For others, they also represented a voice against communism within the labor movement.[78]

In the three decades after 1930, no political cause generated more energy among parish priests than the crusade against communism. On occasion, the opposition could take extremist forms. The most widely known parish priest in America in the 1930s was Father Charles Coughlin of Royal Oak, Michigan, who began a career as a radio preacher sympathetic to Franklin Roosevelt's New Deal. After the CBS network dropped his program because of his animus against big business, he created his own network, and by 1932 his broadcast drew a larger audience than any radio program in the country. In 1936, he dropped Roosevelt and took up the anti-communist cause, to which he gave an anti-Semitic slant that led him to praise the Nazi regime in Germany. By 1942, his diatribes against Jews — and his influence on anti-Jewish "Christian Front" groups — prompted the church to silence his broadcasts, and he returned to his parish.[79]

77. Ronald W. Schatz, "American Labor and the Catholic Church, 1919-1950," in *Modern American Catholicism,* ed. Edward R. Kantowicz (New York: Garland, 1988), pp. 248-60; Aaron I. Abell, *American Catholics and Social Action: A Search for Social Justice, 1865-1950* (Garden City: Doubleday, 1960), pp. 235-85; John F. Cronin, *Catholic Social Action* (Milwaukee: Bruce, 1948), pp. 75-137; O'Brien, "American Priest and Social Action," pp. 443, 445.

78. Underwood, *Protestant and Catholic,* p. 262.

79. Charles J. Tull, *Father Coughlin and the New Deal* (Syracuse: Syracuse University Press, 1965), pp. 20, 173-200, 235-37; Ronald H. Carpenter, *Father Charles E. Coughlin: Surrogate Spokesperson for the Disaffected* (Westport: Greenwood Press, 1998), pp. 13, 53, 59, 115.

Coughlin was an anomaly. Politically most priests, like most Catholics of the era, were Democrats. One estimate in 1936 was that three-fourths of the priests and most of the bishops favored Roosevelt. But in the immigrant Catholic communities — especially after the Soviet takeover of Eastern Europe — opposition to communism became a hallmark of Catholic faith. *Catholic Action,* the journal of the National Catholic Welfare Conference (NCWC), called in 1943 for a "prayer crusade" for victory that included prayers for the conversion of Russia. After 1946, pastors encouraged Block Rosaries, outdoor gatherings in the neighborhoods to "recite the beads" in prayers for safety from atomic bomb attacks and an end to the spread of communism. Marian piety took on an anti-communist tenor. Priests in Holyoke told the sociologist Kenneth Underwood that Protestant ministers there failed to recognize the demonic nature of communism.[80]

When Joseph McCarthy inaugurated his campaign against communism in America, he drew support from Catholic bishops. Francis Cardinal Spellman in New York gave him unstinting encouragement, and Spellman's rival, Fulton Sheen, also applauded his aims. Catholics formed no monolithic block in favor of McCarthy, but a majority of the clergy approved his crusade. Bishop Bernard J. Sheil in Chicago warned that McCarthy was a danger to American liberties, but no other member of the hierarchy criticized McCarthy's methods. Father John Cronin and the staff at the NCWC thought that his tactics hurt rather than helped the cause, and the largest of the orders — the Jesuits — suffered some agonizing internal struggles. But the conservative clergy who favored McCarthy were the ones who received the most attention.[81]

For the most part, the cause of anti-communism promoted consensus among Catholics and a unity of purpose among clergy and laity. But as McCarthy's demagogic excesses became visible — and as the Cold War settled into a distant stalemate — priests and bishops turned their attention to a cause that proved more divisive. In the civil rights movement, a good many priests opposed the racial mores of their own parishes. Equally important, some of them opposed their bishops. The conjunction of the Vatican Council and the civil rights movement intensified the call for a reordering of Catholic culture and the priesthood.[82]

80. Morris, *American Catholic,* pp. 145, 148-49, 151, 229; Ellwood, *1950,* pp. 36-37; Chinnici, "Catholic Community at Prayer," pp. 54, 57; Kane, "Marian Devotion Since 1940," p. 102; Underwood, *Protestant and Catholic,* p. 330.

81. Donald F. Crosby, S.J., *God, Church, and Flag: Senator Joseph R. McCarthy and the Catholic Church* (Chapel Hill: University of North Carolina Press, 19780, pp. 14-15, 56, 62, 83, 155, 158, 183; Cooney, *American Pope,* p. 222; Vincent P. DeSantis, "American Catholics and McCarthyism," *Catholic Historical Review* 51 (1965): 4-29; Wakin and Scheuer, *De-Romanization,* p. 208.

82. John T. McGreevy, "Racial Justice and the People of God: The Second Vatican Council, the Civil Rights Movement, and American Catholics," *Religion and American Culture* 4 (1994): 224.

Since the 1930s, the priesthood had furnished recruits in the struggle against racial segregation, but they always swam upstream. The twenty-three black priests who served the church in 1941 — a number that grew to 115 by 1966 — conducted their own individual battles on behalf of racial equity, even though their small numbers limited their scope. The Jesuit John LaFarge, author of *Interracial Justice* (1937), denounced discrimination when few other white Americans even gave it a thought, and several bolder priests thought that even LaFarge was too cautious. Prior to the Supreme Court's 1954 decision against segregated schools, Catholic bishops in five Southern states had already taken a stand for racial integration in schools and parishes. After the Court's decision, most of the clergy supported it. In 1958, the bishops called for an end to "oppressive conditions."[83]

By 1963 Catholic priests were marching in the streets, often alongside Protestant clergy. They were, as *Commonweal* observed, "rejecting respectability" for the sake of a higher good. When some bishops forbade the demonstrations, some priests, in a shocking departure from accepted decorum, condemned their bishops. After Father William DuBay complained to the Vatican about the racial attitudes of Francis Cardinal McIntyre in Los Angeles, the cardinal compelled him to kneel before two hundred diocesan priests and kiss his ring in apology and submission. (DuBay began a campaign to unionize priests, but he soon left the priesthood.) But when Martin Luther King Jr. called for clergy to march in Selma in 1965, hundreds of priests and nuns from sixty dioceses journeyed to Alabama, many of them without securing permission from their bishop. An Alabama bishop derided the marchers as "eager beavers."[84]

Some of the bishops marched — some even accepted arrest — but the movement caused conflict between clergy and their parishioners: 44 percent of Catholics disapproved of the priests and nuns who marched in Selma. In Chicago, angry white Catholics mocked, cursed, and even attacked priests and nuns marching for black civil rights. Laity in California resisted sermons on fair housing. But the priests — 77 percent of them, 80 percent of the younger ones

---

83. Wakin and Scheuer, *De-Romanization*, p. 234; David W. Southern, *John LaFarge and the Limits of Catholic Interracialism 1911-1963* (Baton Rouge: Louisiana State University Press, 1996), pp. xix, 83-104; "Ban on Segregation," *Commonweal* 60 (Apr. 30, 1954): 85; Henry G. Ruark, "Catholics Challenge Segregation," *Christian Century* 70 (Sept. 30, 1953): 1106-7; "The Bishops on Race," *Commonweal* 69 (Nov. 28, 1958): 219.

84. Harvey Cox, "Dialogue Among Pickets," *Commonweal* 79 (Nov. 22, 1963): 245-46; "Rejecting Respectability," *Commonweal* (Nov. 22, 1963): 547; "The Voice of the Churches," *Commonweal* 80 (May 15, 1964): 226-28; Msgr. Francis J. Weber, *His Eminence of Los Angeles: James Francis Cardinal McIntyre*, 2 vols. (Mission Hills, Calif.: Saint Francis Historical Society, 1997), vol. 2, pp. 442-443, 448, 458.

— supported the civil rights movement, and they often made a difference in their parishes. One study indicated that the best predictor of change in lay Catholic attitudes toward civil rights was the stand taken by the parish priest. But for some priests, the church seemed too cautious and change seemed too slow. After Selma, one priest remarked that the National Catholic Welfare Conference was not only "irrelevant" but also "totally ignorant of racial matters." The civil rights crusade helped alter age-old habits of authority among both laity and priests.[85]

The conflict over Vietnam widened the fractures. The Catholic tradition had produced critics of military tactics in America even during World War II. The ethicist Father John Ford had produced a searching critique of American and British obliteration bombing and described the bombing of Hiroshima and Nagasaki as "the greatest and most extensive single atrocity of all this period." But the earlier war had not produced — at least in America — critics like Father Daniel Berrigan, S.J., and Father Philip Berrigan, S.S.J. The Berrigan brothers undertook actions of civil disobedience that kept them on the front pages. Thousands gathered in St. Ignatius Church during the trials that sent them to prison for destroying selective service files. As late as 1967, 69 percent of older priests approved of U.S. policy, but only 50 percent of the younger ones agreed. Cardinal Spellman praised the "soldiers of Jesus Christ" who were showing in Vietnam "the best traits of human courage and endurance in the annals of history." But four Jesuit priests conducted silent protests in front of his New York residence.[86]

Catholics had always promoted acts of charity, so it was no innovation when priests during the 1950s oversaw programs to feed the hungry, set up over nine hundred parish credit unions, distributed clothing and furniture, and sponsored free health clinics and legal aid offices. It was also not unprecedented when dioceses across the country after Vatican II established legislative offices near state capitols to lobby for housing for the poor and adequate welfare benefits. What was new in the late sixties were the growing numbers of priests — 74 percent of all curates, for instance — who insisted that priests should speak out on controversial social problems, and the considerable minority — 39 percent

85. Wakin and Scheuer, *De-Romanization*, pp. 242, 247, 248; Fichter, *America's Forgotten Priests*, p. 188; Greeley, *Hesitant Pilgrim*, p. 30.

86. Joseph G. Morgan, "A Change of Course: American Catholics, Anticommunism, and the Vietnam War," *U. S. Catholic Historian* 22 (2004): 117-30; William Van Etten Casey, S.J., and Philip Nobile, eds., *The Berrigans* (New York: Praeger, 1971), pp. 7-9; Morris, *American Catholic*, pp. 227-28; Anthony Towne, "Reflections on Two Trials," *Christian Century* 84 (Dec. 4, 1968): 1535-40; Fichter, *America's Forgotten Priests*, p. 190; "Cardinal Spellman's Holy War," *Christian Century* 84 (Jan. 11, 1967): 36.

of all priests — who said that the priest had the right to act in conscience on social issues even against the wishes of the bishop.[87]

Two issues internal to the church deeply exacerbated the tensions. The first was priestly celibacy. In 1954 Pius XII proclaimed in *Sacra Virginitas* — the first encyclical devoted entirely to the topic — that the insistence on a celibate priesthood ensured both freedom for ministry and purity for service at the altar. Seminarians were taught that celibacy was "to be preserved at all costs." One priest remembered whimsically the admonition of a retreat master: "Always," he said, "keep the vesting table between you and a woman." But by 1966 priests were giving the matter increasing scrutiny. An article in the *Saturday Evening Post* — "I Am a Priest, I Want to Marry," by a young priest named James Kavanaugh — ignited a flurry of discussion, which continued the following year with the publication of his *A Modern Priest Looks at His Outdated Church*. The debates intensified when Pope Paul VI issued in 1967 yet another encyclical mandating a celibate priesthood and the bishops published an episcopal letter reaffirming it. The authoritarian tone of the letter offended many and did little to still the debate. Activist priests formed organizations on both sides of the issue.[88]

By 1968 priests all over the country were discussing celibacy. The younger priests had the most interest; 62 percent of the diocesan curates wanted the church to allow priests to marry either before or after their ordination, even though more than half of them agreed that celibate priests were more effective. A handful held press conferences to publicize their unhappiness with the tradition. Some scholars argued that the discontent with celibacy was a decisive reason for the exodus of priests. One noted that more than two-thirds of the departed priests soon married. The counterargument was that priests resigned because they were dissatisfied with their ministry. But the prospect of celibacy prompted almost a third of the students in major seminaries to decide finally against the priesthood. The laity split right down the middle.[89]

The second internal issue was the dilemma of birth control. In the 1930s most Protestant churches finally accepted contraception, but Pius XI, in *Casti Connubii*, reasserted the claim that artificial birth control was "intrinsically against nature." In the 1950s the practice stood in the list of mortal sins. But

87. Ward, *Living Parish*, p. 174; McGreevy, *Catholicism and American Freedom*, p. 269; Fichter, *America's Forgotten Priests*, pp. 183-84.

88. Pope Pius XII, *Sacra Virginitatis*, in *Papal Encyclicals*, vol.4, pp. 241, 242, 243, 245: Kennedy, *Comfort My People*, pp. 12-13; Father James Kavanaugh, *A Modern Priest Looks at His Outdated Church* (New York: Trident, 1967), p. vii; Fichter, "Catholic Church Professionals," p. 80.

89. Fichter, *America's Forgotten Priests*, pp. 163, 170, 172, 190; "Celibacy in Springtime," *Christian Century* 86 (May 14, 1969): 668; Fichter, "Catholic Church Professionals," p. 84; Fichter, *Religion as an Occupation*, p. 190.

some priests were saying as early as the 1930s that contraception was "the hardest problem in the confessional," and by the 1940s one-third of married Catholics conceded that they used contraception. By the 1960s the figure was as high as 70 percent, and some theologians, convinced that the birth control pill altered the status of the question, urged a change in Catholic teaching. Pope Paul VI agreed to allow reconsideration, but when his commission recommended change, he issued in 1968 the encyclical *Humanae Vitae* in which he reasserted the prohibition. The reaction bitterly divided the clergy.[90]

The theologians disagreed about it. Charles Curran at Catholic University emphasized that the encyclical left room for dissent, but the Jesuit John Ford at the seminary in Weston, Massachusetts, believed that any change would call into question the teaching office of the church. The church promptly disciplined Curran, but one survey found that more than 80 percent of the clergy refused to enforce the prohibition in the confessional and that almost the same number believed that the papal teaching was invalid. Seventy percent of the bishops said that contraception was morally wrong, but a minority even of the bishops had reservations. Among priests under thirty-five, only 13 percent agreed with the pope.[91]

The encyclical was a disaster for the American church. Many felt that the process producing the papal decision was flawed and that the decision was itself wrong. More than any other earlier event, the debate over *Humanae Vitae* undermined the standing of bishops as moral guides, shattered the morale of the clergy, and helped produce a precipitous decline in confessions, as vast numbers of laity simply stayed away, refusing to deceive the priest but also refusing to abandon the use of contraception. At the same time, many priests refused to make an issue of it in the confessional. The effect was so polarizing that numerous bishops and priests ceased to offer public guidance on sexual ethics. Catholic historians speak of a virtual conspiracy of silence in the three decades after the encyclical. Caught in the middle between the laity and the bishops, the parish priests felt trapped.[92]

90. Pope Pius XI, *Casti Connubii*, in *Papal Encyclicals*, vol. 3, p. 399; Pope Paul VI, *Humanae Vitae*, in *Papal Encyclicals*, vol. 5, pp. 223-32; Wakin and Scheuer, *De-Romanization*, p. 50.

91. "Catholic Concerns," *Christian Century* 85 (Aug. 14, 1968): 1010; John C. Ford and Germain Grisez, "Contraception and the Infallibility of the Ordinary Magisterium," *Theological Studies* 39 (1978): 312; Greeley, *Confessions*, p. 295; Andrew M. Greeley, et al., *The Catholic Priest in the United States: Sociological Investigations* (Washington, D.C.: United States Catholic Conference, 1972), pp. 103, 114.

92. Leslie Woodcock Tentler, *Catholics and Contraception: An American History* (Ithaca: Cornell University Press, 2004), pp. 262-79.

A Different Church

In 1967 the Roman Catholic Church in America had 59,892 priests, but within five years the number declined by almost 3,000. The reduction came partly from resignations. It had once been a scandal, whispered only in "sorrowful and shocked tones," when a priest resigned his position. Since the early 1960s it had become easier to leave. In 1968, 64 percent of American priests wanted the church to permit an honorable voluntary resignation. In the next two years, more than 2,500 resigned. It was even more troubling that the number of Catholic seminarians fell, during the 1960s, from 39,896 to 28,819. In one five-year period, the number of men preparing for the diocesan priesthood declined by 27 percent. The religious orders underwent an even more severe loss; they had 35 percent fewer seminarians in 1970 than they did five years earlier. Many priests said they had little enthusiasm for recruiting.[93]

The downturn had parallels in the exodus of sisters from the women's orders. In 1966, 181,421 women religious worked and prayed within more than 287 orders; they constituted more than 70 percent of the full-time workers in the church. Three years later, 14,254 of them were gone without being replaced. The loss foreshadowed a mass departure of the people on whom the priests were most dependent for the staffing of schools and hospitals and for ministerial duties in the parish. Sisters had also recruited boys for the priesthood and served as reliable associates, and sometimes even mentors, for younger priests. The change had profound repercussions for the work of priests.[94]

The religious life of Catholic laity was also undergoing a transition. Interest in the older Catholic Action programs faded in the sixties, as did participation in the popular devotions. Catholic laity showed less inclination to attend novenas, public rosaries, and services featuring the Stations of the Cross. Critics within the church questioned the attention given to appeals to the saints, and since devotions connected to the saints had always had ethnic overtones, the multiethnic parish lacked the same attachment to patron saints once linked to national backgrounds. By 1965 observers noted that neither visits to the Blessed Sacrament nor parish missions and retreats had quite the appeal they once had.

93. Appleby, "Present to the People of God," pp. 71-72; Fichter, *Religion as an Occupation,* p. 197; Fichter, *America's Forgotten Priests,* pp. 154-204; John A. O'Brien, "Why Priests Marry," *Christian Century* 87 (Apr. 8, 1970): 418; Murnion, *Catholic Priest,* p. 174; Fichter, "Catholic Church Professionals," p. 79.

94. Fichter, "Catholic Church Professionals," p. 78; Helen Rose F. Ebaugh, *Women in the Vanishing Cloister* (New Brunswick: Rutgers University Press, 1993), pp. 6, 67, 70-71; Wakin and Scheuer, *De-Romanization,* p. 161.

More and more laypeople felt free to stay away from church services altogether. The decline in Sunday attendance between 1963 and 1974 was as high as 20 percentage points.[95]

Catholics shied away from the confessional in large numbers. In one growing Milwaukee parish, monthly penitents dropped from 450 to 150 in the four years after 1965; in another, equally flourishing, they fell from 450 to 100; in still another, the drop was from 1,200 to 300 — even though the membership increased. It was not that Catholics now refused to reveal their flaws to their priests. They rather sought other ways of doing it. Already by 1965 many priests reported that they spent most of their time counseling. They gave it more time than administration, or parochial schools, or attending the sick, or teaching or preaching, or liturgical leadership. They still gained satisfaction from the confessional — perhaps even more since the lines were not so long — but the counseling session presented a different mode of "genuine listening."[96]

Relationships between priests and parishioners were changing in other ways. The church experimented widely in the years after Vatican II with parish councils of leaders elected from the laity. The goal was to involve the laity in the operation of the parish. The change came slowly, and many pastors resisted. "My pastor has such a distrust of laypeople," said one curate, "that I cannot even invite them into the rectory to do the work of the parish." Three-fourths of the curates wanted their pastors to move more quickly to assign real responsibility to lay leaders. But Eugene Kennedy was probably right when he said that priests were being drawn — whether eagerly or reluctantly — into a "communal, highly personal life of sharing" with their people.[97]

The 1960s saw the renewal of the nineteenth-century effort of priests to share power with bishops. The Vatican Council produced an "explosive" flurry of organizing that set up priests' senates intended to give priests a voice in diocesan policy or the appointment of bishops. The senates were only one example of an activism that produced associations of clergy, personnel boards, and regional networks of priests. In 1968 activists formed the National Federation of Priests' Councils to coordinate the effort and to negotiate with the bishops over rights, policies, and procedures. Some of the priests' councils called for radical change, including optional celibacy and the election of bishops. Others were

95. Chinnici, "Catholic Community at Prayer," pp. 75, 82; Wakin and Scheuer, *De-Romanization*, pp. 268-69; Greeley, *Confessions*, p. 333.

96. O'Toole, "Court of Conscience," p. 169; Fichter, *Priest and People*, pp. 185, 186; Fichter, *America's Forgotten Priests*, p. 87; Kennedy, *Comfort My People*, p. 94.

97. Fichter, "Catholic Church Professionals," p. 80; Fichter, *America's Forgotten Priests*, pp. 37, 45; Kennedy, *Comfort My People*, p. 15.

more interested in due process, continuing education, spiritual formation, and issues of social justice.[98]

Much of the early organizing was adversarial, and bishops resisted. They renamed the senates as "councils" and held on to authority, maintaining an especially wary distance from the NFPC. By the end of the decade, priests widely expressed disillusionment with the whole effort. They believed that decision-making power still lay in the bishop's chancery, and many showed no interest in joining an association. Fewer than 30 percent of the priests reported that their diocese even had a priests' council.[99]

"The priest of today," wrote Eugene Kennedy in 1968, "is growing into a new role." The growth could be wrenching. "The Church we are now in," said one priest, "is a different church from the one we anticipated in seminary." Many Catholic laity now gave selective assent to the church's teaching — some called it "cafeteria Catholicism" — and no one quite knew what would happen to the old structure of authority. It seemed that "extremes in both traditionalism and modernism" had arisen among the clergy. Some priests despaired: "Everything," one said, "is under question." One poll found almost half of them "dissatisfied." But some found the ferment "exciting" and "promising." In one of the largest surveys ever undertaken, the National Opinion Research Center found that most priests were happy, that they had good relationships with their parishioners, and that they did not regret their decision to enter the priesthood. The crisis was not over — the 1970s would bring further disarray — but the Catholic clergy were adapting themselves to ministry in a more complex church and world.[100]

98. Marschall, "Diocesan and Religious Clergy," p. 408; Appleby, "Present to the People of God," p. 76; James H. Stewart, "When Priests Began to Bargain," *Review of Religious Research* 20 (1979): 177.

99. Appleby, "Present to the People of God," p. 74; Kennedy, *Comfort My People*, p. 11.

100. Kennedy, *Comfort My People*, p. 43; Fichter, *America'a Forgotten Priests*, pp. 34-35, 141; Appleby, "Present to the People of God," p. 73; Greeley, *Hesitant Pilgrim*, p. 11; Greeley, *Confessions*, p. 294.

CHAPTER 10

A Divided Vocation

1970-2005

In the 1970s a large team of researchers undertook yet one more study of the clergy. Surveying more than five thousand laity and seminary-educated ministers, they found, like earlier scholars, a substantial amount of "anxiety and frustration" and "fear of ineffectiveness." They also found that priests and ministers were testing divergent styles of ministry. While some undertook a recovery of tradition, others turned outward to contemporary society in a quest for relevant involvement. Believing that the church suffered from an individualistic piety, many welcomed the vision of the minister as a "change agent" committed to social reform. Others, convinced that the activism of the sixties had led to a spiritual exhaustion, sought ways to deepen "the inner life of people" through disciplines of "spirituality." Consensus was elusive. "Ministers," wrote the director of the project, "will apparently have to live with a higher degree of tension and ambiguity as the normal way of life."[1]

The story of the clergy in the three decades after 1970 displays that tension and ambiguity. The period saw mainline losses but evangelical gains, a decline of Catholic vocations but the growth of Catholic ministries, advance and yet difficulty for women in ministry, and increased attention to clerical integrity in the face of widely publicized scandals. The professional ideal gained mounting assent and yet drew intensified questioning. And the ministry appeared to suffer from polarization over political, theological, and cultural matters even though most priests and ministers sought a middle

---

1. David S. Schuller, Merton P. Strommen, and Milo L. Brekke, eds., *Ministry in America* (San Francisco: Harper and Row, 1980), pp. 4, 6, 8.

ground. Like the nation, the ministry was divided, but the vast majority of the clergy expended their energies not on the hot topics of cultural and theological division but on the time-honored duties of shaping local Christian communities in familiar ways.

The Reversal

In the mid-1960s, the mainline Protestant clergy began to notice more and more empty pews. In the three decades after 1970, the seven largest mainline denominations lost two to three million members, suffered severe budget reductions, cut back on building projects, sent fewer missionaries abroad, and restricted their publishing activity. They reported membership losses every year. In some quarters, the temptation was irresistible to cast blame on the mainline clergy; it was said that the social activists, albeit a small minority, bore responsibility, or that the liberal theology of many mainline ministers failed to attract and hold new members, or that the long experiment with seminary education had produced leaders out of touch with the grass roots.[2]

In 1972 a researcher for the National Council of Churches, Dean Kelly, argued in a widely read scholarly manifesto that "strict" churches with rigorous demands had grown while more tolerant and culturally accommodated denominations had declined. He did not blame the ministers or fault the activists or the liberals, but his book implied that mainline clergy were not doing their job. Within a few years, the *Christian Century* noticed a "loss of morale."[3]

The congregations shrank for many reasons, but the losses had little to do with social activism, liberal theology, or the shortcomings of mainline clergy. The primary impetus was that mainline families had fewer children than did families in most of the conservative churches. Other trends intensified this "demographic imperative." Fewer conservatives switched to mainline churches, and the mainline denominations also had greater difficulty retaining the allegiance of their children. A shift in cultural values during the 1960s affected college-educated young people more than others, and mainline families sent

2. See the various explanations listed in David A. Roozen and Jackson W. Carroll, "Recent Trends in Church Membership and Participation," in *Understanding Church Growth and Decline, 1950-1978*, ed. Dean R. Hoge and David A. Roozen (New York: The Pilgrim Press, 1979), p. 26; Roger Finke and Rodney Stark, *The Churching of America 1776-1990: Winners and Losers in Our Religious Economy* (New Brunswick: Rutgers University Press, 1992), p. 247.

3. Dean W. Kelley, *Why Conservative Churches Are Growing* (1st ed., 1972; Macon: Mercer University Press, 1986), pp. 9-10; "A Wish for '79," *Christian Century* 96 (Jan. 3-10, 1979): 3-4.

more children to college. The clergy had little control over most of the forces that were emptying the mainline pews.[4]

By one count, mainline Protestant denominations in 2001 provided a home for about 37 percent of the nation's clergy. They debated about how they might best give expression, as a minority voice, to their vision of the gospel. Some argued for a "public" stance, bringing their traditions of social witness, tolerance of ambiguity, and civic involvement into debates over social policy and priorities. Others wanted to pull away from policy arenas and concentrate their energies on creating faithful and loving communities that could testify by their example against the violence and consumerism of the larger culture.[5]

While mainline Protestants suffered membership losses, the Catholic Church gained members but lost priests. Between 1966 and 1984, 15,000 men entered the diocesan priesthood, but more than 22,000 priests resigned, retired, or died. Losses in the religious orders were even more catastrophic. And the most portentous omen of all was the decline in the number of seminarians. In 1966, almost nine thousand studied in the "theologate," the final four years of seminary training. Thirty years later, the number was lower by two-thirds. In 2001, the total number of priests was 45,191, a reduction of more than 12,000 since 1985. In 1950, the Catholic Church had one priest for every 652 Catholics; in 2004, it had one priest for every 1,478. Never before had the American church suffered losses of this magnitude.[6]

---

4. Ruth A. Doyle and Sheila M. Kelly, "Comparison in Trends of Ten Denominations," *Understanding Church Growth*, pp. 155, 157; Michael Hout, Andrew Greeley, and Melissa Wilde, "Birth Dearth: Demographics of Mainline Decline," *Christian Century* 122 (Oct. 4, 2005): 24-27; Michael Hout, Andrew Greeley, and Melissa Wilde, "The Demographic Imperative in Religious Change in the United States," *American Journal of Sociology* 107 (2001): 468-500; Wade Clark Roof and William McKinney, *American Mainline Religion: Its Changing Shape and Future* (New Brunswick: Rutgers University Press, 1987), p. 160; Dean R. Hoge, "A Test of Theories of Denominational Growth and Decline," *Understanding Church Growth*, p. 17.

5. Mark Chaves, *Congregations in America* (Cambridge: Harvard University Press, 2004), p. 235; Jackson W. Carroll, *God's Potters: Pastoral Leadership and the Shaping of Congregations* (Grand Rapids: Eerdmans, 2006), pp. 59-60; Martin E. Marty, *The Public Church: Mainline, Evangelical, Catholic* (New York: Crossroad, 1981), pp. 94-110; 123-37, 138-68; Stanley Hauerwas and William Willimon, *Resident Aliens: Life in the Christian Colony* (Nashville: Abingdon Press, 1989), p. 121. Larry A. Witham, *Who Shall Lead Them? The Future of the Ministry in America* (New York: Oxford University Press, 2005), p. 11, gives a smaller percentage of mainline clergy, but he accepts without correction the reports of the *Yearbook*, which in some instances are seriously inaccurate.

6. Richard Schoenherr and Lawrence Young, *Full Pews and Empty Altars: Demographics of the Priest Shortage in United States Catholic Dioceses* (Madison: University of Wisconsin Press, 1993), pp. 4-29; Richard A. Schoenherr, *Goodbye Father: The Celibate Male Priesthood and the Future of the Catholic Church*, ed. David Yamane (New York: Oxford University Press, 2002),

Why did they leave? Why did others not take their place? Explanations abounded, though they sometimes conflicted. The cultural upheaval of the early 1970s influenced some. Disillusion with the slow pace of reform after Vatican II led others out of the priesthood. Some left simply because they no longer found satisfaction in the work, and once the taboo of resignation faded, it was easier for the dissatisfied to depart. Demographics made a difference: smaller families meant fewer candidates for the priesthood. And the cultural assimilation of German and Irish Americans, who had once sent their sons into the priesthood in disproportionate numbers, offered them a wider choice of inviting occupational possibilities.[7]

The movement of Catholics into the main currents of the middle class meant that a separated subculture no longer operated to encourage vocations, and the resignations of sisters from the religious orders reduced a community that had encouraged boys to follow in the footsteps of their priests. The sisters had once identified promising schoolboys, suggested priesthood to them, and constantly praised the priesthood in their school classrooms. They had also provided friendship and assistance to the priests. Their declining numbers profoundly affected priestly life. Ideals of freedom and fulfillment that filtered through the culture during the 1970s, moreover, made priests less tolerant of arbitrary authority, and changing lay attitudes toward priests, prompted by the same cultural mood, made some priests feel that they no longer had lay affection and respect.[8]

And then there was the question of celibacy. Catholic scholars agreed that some priests left because they wanted to marry, and that even more potential candidates for the priesthood declined to enter the vocation for the same reason. No one knew for certain the extent to which feelings about celibacy drove the downturn. A slight majority of priests in 1970 preferred that celibacy be optional, and the number sharing this preference increased in the next three decades despite the publication of a *Letter on Priestly Celibacy* by Pope Paul VI in

---

p. 15; Dean R. Hoge and Jacqueline E. Wenger, *Evolving Visions of the Priesthood: Changes from Vatican II to the Turn of the New Century* (Collegeville, Minn.: Liturgical Press, 2003), pp. 14-15; Dean R. Hoge and Aniedi Okuere, *International Priests in America: Challenges and Opportunities* (Collegeville, Minn.: Liturgical Press, 2006), p. 6.

7. Andrew M. Greeley, *Priests: A Calling in Crisis* (Chicago: University of Chicago Press, 2004), pp. 9, 60-72; Charles R. Morris, *American Catholic: The Saints and Sinners Who Built America's Most Powerful Church* (New York: Random House, 1997), p. 317.

8. Hoge and Wenger, *Evolving Visions*, p. 122; Edgar W. Mills, "The Sacred in Ministry Studies," in *The Sacred in Secular Life* (Berkeley: University of California Press, 1985), p. 171; Andrew M. Greeley, et al., *The Catholic Priest in the United States: Sociological Investigations* (Washington: D.C.: United States Catholic Conference, 1972), p. 253.

1971 reaffirming the celibate life as an "incomparable sign of total dedication to the love of Christ."[9]

Most diocesan priests agreed that the absence of family responsibilities enabled them to devote more energy to the work of the priesthood. The *Los Angeles Times* survey in 1993 found that only 16 percent of priests said they would certainly or probably marry if they had the option. But celibacy still ranked high in the explanations of many who left. In any case, the great majority remained in the priesthood, and by 1998 Catholic priests still ministered in more than 6 percent of the nation's congregations. Catholics formed around 29 percent of the population, and about 5 percent of American parish clergy were Catholic.[10]

By global standards, the decline produced no shortage of priests. The United States still had a more favorable ratio of priests to laity than Asia, Africa, or Latin America. But Catholics in America had become accustomed to ratios that made possible the active parish life of the mid-twentieth century, and during the 1980s they began to worry that the downturn in vocations had produced a shortage that harmed both parishes and other Catholic institutions.[11]

The church attempted to fill the gaps by turning to immigrant priests. By 2005, one in six priests in America came from Europe, Africa, South America, or Asia. Between 1950 and 1980, the Irish still sent more priests to America than any other nation, but a collapse in the number of vocations in Ireland during the 1980s meant that Americans began to draw most heavily on Latin America, with large numbers also coming from Vietnam, India, the Philippines, Poland, Nigeria, and the Iberian peninsula. The influx was no panacea. Nearly 4,000 American parishes had Hispanic majorities among the faithful, but the church had only 2,900 Hispanic priests, and in English-speaking parishes the cultural and linguistic differences between priests and parishioners could present challenges. The policy generated sharp debate within the church.[12]

The declining numbers had a paradoxical effect. They left some parishes without full-time priests, increased the workload of the ones who remained,

9. Greeley, *Catholic Priest*, pp. 22, 237; Scott Appleby, "Present to the People of God: The Transformation of the Roman Catholic Parish Priesthood," in *Transforming Parish Ministry*, ed. Jay Dolan (New York: Crossroad, 1990), pp. 82-83.

10. Greeley, *Priests*, p. 62; Dean R. Hoge, *The Future of Catholic Leadership: Responses to the Priest Shortage* (Kansas City: Sheed and Ward, 1987); Chaves, *Congregations*, p. 235; Carroll, *God's Potters*, pp. 59-60.

11. Hoge and Okure, *International Priests*, pp. 24-35.

12. *The Study of the Impact of Fewer Priests on the Pastoral Ministry* (Washington, D.C.: National Conference of Catholic Bishops, 2000), p. 33; Witham, *Who Shall Lead Them?* pp. 77, 110, 221; Hoge and Okuru, *International Priests*, pp. 36-68, 151, 153.

and dissolved some of the systems of support. Fewer priests could live with four or five others in the rectory. In two-thirds of the nation's parishes, a single priest lived and worked alone. But shortages gave far more priests a chance to assume pastorates rather than spending so much of their lives as assistants. As a result, surveys at the turn of the new century found high levels of morale alongside the worries about declining numbers.[13]

The Eastern Orthodox continued to represent a minority voice among American clergy, but the conservatism of the religious culture after the 1970s made Orthodox membership — and Orthodox priesthood — an attractive choice for a growing segment of Christians. About a half million Orthodox Christians had migrated to America in the late nineteenth century, and they had promptly erected separate Russian, Greek, Serbian, Arab, Albanian, and Romanian churches, each theoretically linked to mother churches in the homelands but practically independent and lay controlled.

Orthodox clerics had found themselves bound to the authority of lay trustees who hired and supervised the priests, and they had to adapt to a shortage of qualified priests, the presence of non-canonical priests, and the absence of a resident bishop. Political divisions in Europe swept over the Orthodox churches in America, which sometimes hired and fired clergy in accord with their views about monarchy and republicanism or their attitudes toward the 1917 Bolshevik Revolution. Ethnic traditions died hard.[14]

By the 1940s, the Orthodox began to create an American incarnation of their traditions. Graduates of Holy Cross Orthodox School of Theology (1937) in Brookline, Massachusetts, and St. Vladimir's Orthodox Theological Seminary (1938) in New York carried the liturgical theology of Father Alexander Schmemann into their parishes and inaugurated a fuller cycle of liturgical services, encouraged frequent communion at the Eucharist, and added more spoken prayers and English-language services. At the same time, the Orthodox liturgy conveyed a feeling of unbroken continuity with tradition.[15]

In the 1950s the Eastern Orthodox clergy started to explore new forms of participation in American life. They joined ecumenical organizations, and they assumed a public presence. In 1957 Archbishop Michael Constantinides, the head of the Greek Orthodox Archdiocese, became the first Orthodox bishop to

---

13. Morris, *American Catholic*, p. 377; Greeley, *Priests*, pp. 48-59.

14. Thomas F. Fitzgerald, *The Orthodox Church* (Westport: Greenwood, 1995), pp. 23, 25, 32, 37; John H. Erickson, *Orthodox Christians in America* (New York: Oxford University Press, 1999), pp. 53-91.

15. Erickson, *Orthodox Christians*, pp. 108-10; Paul Meyendorff, "Liturgical Life in the Parish: Present and Future Realities," in *The Orthodox Parish in America*, ed. Anton C. Vrame (Brookline: Holy Cross Orthodox Press, 2003), pp. 143-53.

take part in a presidential inauguration. When Archbishop Iakovos Coucouzes stood alongside Martin Luther King Jr. at the march in Selma and newspapers published the picture from coast to coast, the image depicted an Orthodoxy at home in America and engaged in its most pressing struggle.[16]

The growing acculturation of the Orthodox churches produced tensions about the language of worship and the performance of the clergy. At the Greek Orthodox Clergy-Laity Congress in 1990, one committee reported that lay-people were dissatisfied with both the liturgy and the quality of preaching in their congregations: "just when presbyters have become more sophisticated and sensitive in their pastoral ministry, the laity have raised their level of expectations." But by then the Eastern traditions were attracting converts — some of whom became priests — and building an ecumenical "pan-Orthodox" sensibility among Orthodox clergy once divided by ethnicity and language.[17]

While the Orthodox were adapting to the culture, mainline Protestant churches were losing members, and Catholics were losing priests, conservative Protestant denominations gained in both ministers and members. By 1976 — after Jimmy Carter's presidential campaign reintroduced the media to the revivalist theme of "rebirth" — 34 percent of Americans claimed to be born again. *Newsweek* declared 1976 the "year of the evangelical" — a time-honored term that came to refer to Christians who claimed an experience of rebirth, favored literal interpretations of the Bible, and felt a duty to evangelize. Evangelical denominations drew both public attention and new members. Their growth continued long-term trends, but mainline losses made evangelical gains more visible.[18]

Even patterns of immigration after 1965 increased conservative numbers. Many Hispanic immigrants felt the appeal of Pentecostal churches, and Korean Americans, who arrived in large numbers during the 1970s, formed churches led by pastors who usually taught an evangelical or fundamentalist form of the gospel and who enjoyed the benefits of a culture that valued deference to authority. Combining biblical literalism with a message that often included promises of "health, prosperity, and salvation," Korean pastors led 3,500 congregations by the beginning of the new millennium.[19]

The trend meant that clergy in the conservative churches continued, as

16. Erickson, *Orthodox Christians*, pp. 110-12.

17. Thomas Fitzgerald, "The Development of the Orthodox Parish in the United States," in *Orthodox Parish in America*, pp. 25, 28; Erickson, *Orthodox Christians*, pp. 122-23.

18. Roof and McKinney, *American Mainline Religion*, p. 23; Kelley, *Why Conservative Churches*, pp. 21-22, 25. By 1970, the Church of the Nazarene was growing by 3 percent a year, the Seventh-day Adventists by 3.8 percent, and the Assemblies of God by 9.2 percent annually.

19. Witham, *Who Shall Lead Them?* pp. 114-19.

they had throughout the twentieth century, to outnumber the more liberal and moderate clergy, who clustered in the mainline denominations. By 2001 conservative Protestant denominations housed about 45 percent of the parish clergy, with an additional 13 percent, mostly conservative in theology, within the historic black denominations. The mainline churches also had a strong conservative voice, especially in the South and Southwest. This conservatism was not new, but conservatives now had a visibility in the culture that they had lacked half a century earlier.[20]

They attracted public attention by mastering the popular media. Changes in federal regulation of television — along with new technologies — enabled the televangelists, conservative in theology and often Pentecostal in piety, to build broadcasting empires that elevated a select few into spheres of religious celebrity. Expenditures for religious television rose from $50 million in 1970 to $600 million in 1980, and the electronic preachers drew an audience of seven to ten million viewers. Some went beyond mere syndication to create cable networks, and these stars of the airways replaced conventional preaching with an entertainment format that emulated the style of popular network programming.[21]

Evangelicals — especially their fundamentalist wing — proved to be equally adept at packaging their ideas in books that reached a mass audience. A graduate of Dallas Theological Seminary, Hal Lindsey, set the trend when he published an apocalyptic forecast of the end of the world, *The Late Great Planet Earth* (1970), that sold over 20 million copies. Evangelical ministers produced bestselling science-fiction thrillers, marriage and sex manuals, apocalyptic manifestos, and devotional tracts. Between 1994 and 2005, the *Left Behind* novels of Tim LaHaye and Jerry Jenkins — a fictional depiction of premillennial dispensationalism — sold some sixty million copies in print, video, and cassette forms. The books of Bishop T. D. Jakes, the African American pastor of a Dallas megachurch who preached a version of Pentecostalism promising prosperity and well-being, had such widespread appeal that he could draw crowds of 150,000 people to some of his rallies.[22]

20. Carroll, *God's Potters*, pp. 59-60; Chaves, *Congregations*, pp. 222-35.

21. Roof and McKinney, *American Mainline Religion*, p. 24; Erling Jorstad, *Popular Religion in America: The Evangelical Voice* (Westport: Greenwood, 1993), p. 31; Robert Wuthnow, *The Restructuring of American Religion: Society and Faith Since World War II* (Princeton: Princeton University Press, 1988), p. 194.

22. Jorstad, *Popular Religion*, p. 145; Kevin Phillips, *American Theocracy: The Peril and Politics of Radical Religion, Oil, and Borrowed Money in the 21st Century* (New York: Viking, 2006), p. xv; Sridhar Pappu, "The Preacher," *The Atlantic* 297 (March 2006): 92-103.

Polarization?

Conservative clergy drew even more attention after they took up political campaigning. Angered by Supreme Court rulings on school prayer and Bible reading and distressed by the sexual revolution, feminism, legal abortion, and the gay liberation movement, the independent Baptist minister Jerry Falwell organized "I Love America" rallies in 1976 and a "Moral Majority" organization in 1979 that sparked the reentry of clerical conservatives into electoral politics. Once critical of direct political action by liberal clergy, they changed their minds by 1980, when eighteen thousand activists, many of them ministers, converged on Dallas for a National Affairs Briefing intended to launch a conservative Christian political movement. By the end of the decade, the conservatives were more politically engaged than the liberals.[23]

Political engagement could be as modest as urging members to vote or as adventurous as endorsing candidates. In the Southern Baptist Convention, for instance, 20 percent of the ministers joined a conservative interest group by 1996, and 93 percent reported at least one political activity. The Republican Party worked hard to mobilize conservative clerical support, and they had some success. By the mid-1990s only 12 percent of Southern Baptist ministers leaned toward the Democrats. Conservatives focused on alcohol use, gambling, the regulation of sexuality, family issues, pornography, abortion, and evolutionary biology and sex education in the schools. By the 1980s, some included support for Israel — which figured heavily in apocalyptic end-time scenarios — and the strengthening of the U.S. military.[24]

Clergy in the mainline churches were more likely to expend their political energies on such issues as hunger and poverty, civil rights, gender equality, and the environment. By 1998, 80 percent of the ministers in the Episcopal Church and the Evangelical Lutheran Church had given attention to social justice issues, and more than 70 percent stood on the liberal side of the political spectrum, favoring governmental actions that promised to alleviate poverty, expand social welfare, help minorities, protect the environment, and limit military expansion. Strong theological convictions correlated with decisive political

23. Paul A. Djupe and Christopher P. Gilbert, *The Prophetic Pulpit: Clergy, Churches, and Communities in American Politics* (Lanham, Md.: Rowman and Littlefield, 2003), p. 96.

24. James L. Guth, "Reflections on the Status of Research on Clergy in Politics," in *Christian Clergy in American Politics* (Baltimore: Johns Hopkins University Press, 2001), p. 40; James L. Guth, "The Mobilization of a Religious Elite: Political Activism Among Southern Baptist Clergy in 1996," in *Christian Clergy*, pp. 141, 147; James L. Guth, John C. Green, Corwin E. Schmidt, Lyman A. Kellstedt, Margaret M. Poloma, *The Bully Pulpit: The Politics of Protestant Clergy* (Lawrence: University Press of Kansas, 1997), pp. 15-16.

stances: most theologically liberal clergy preferred the Democrats, and most conservatives leaned toward the Republicans.[25]

The political stance of the more outspoken leaders differed sharply. On the one side, United Church of Christ minister William Sloane Coffin headed a national organization to eliminate nuclear weapons; Presbyterian John Fife helped organize a sanctuary movement to protect refugees from brutal South American regimes; Episcopalian Paul Gorman led a campaign to save the environment; and Baptist Jesse Jackson ran for president as a liberal Democrat. On the other side, LaHaye launched the American Council for Traditional Values to register conservative voters; California Baptist Robert Grant founded Christian Voice and lobbied for a constitutional amendment protecting school prayer; and Marion G. "Pat" Robertson, a Southern Baptist with a Pentecostal theology, ran for president as a conservative Republican. Television news programs gave an impression of the clergy as polar opposites.[26]

By 1987 it was easy to conclude that Protestants were "rearranging" themselves along ideological lines. Differences about ethics, politics, and theology now seemed to loom larger than historic denominational commitments, and there was ample evidence of "culture wars" among the laity and a "two-party system" among the clergy. Surveys of clerical reading discovered little overlap even in the reading habits of conservative and mainline ministers. In listing their favorite ten authors, clergy in the two groups shared an interest only in three. For the most part, they lived in "distinct intellectual and cultural worlds."[27]

Nowhere did the divide appear wider than in the Southern Baptist Convention, in which fundamentalist clergy launched in 1979 a campaign to oust the denomination's moderates from the seminaries, boards, and publishing agencies. Once in control, they demanded adherence to biblical inerrancy, opposition to the ordination of women, and lay obedience to pastoral authority in the interpretation of scripture. At their 1991 convention, where delegates waved fifteen thousand American flags as they cheered Republican President George H. W. Bush, the Southern Baptists also declared themselves in support of a conservative political program. Some Southern Baptist moderates formed parallel institutions.[28]

25. Guth et al., *Bully Pulpit*, pp. 99, 112, 119; Djupe and Gilbert, *Prophetic Pulpit*, pp. 49, 108; Chaves, *Congregations*, pp. 94-121.

26. Matthew C. Moen, *The Transformation of the Christian Right* (Tuscaloosa: University of Alabama Press, 1992), pp. 15-32.

27. James Davison Hunter, *Culture Wars: The Struggle to Define America* (New York: Basic Books, 1991); Guth et al., *Bully Pulpit*, pp. 30, 51; Carroll, *God's Potters*, p. 109; Jackson W. Carroll, "Pastors' Picks: What Preachers Are Reading," *Christian Century* 120 (August 23, 2003): 32. The three authors were Eugene Peterson, Philip Yancey, and C. S. Lewis.

28. Roof and McKinney, *American Mainline Religion*, p. 223; Wuthnow, *Restructuring*,

In the mainline denominations, activist clergy on both sides of the divide began in the 1980s to multiply "special purpose groups" — caucuses, associations, fellowships — that advocated opposing positions on theology, the ordination of women, minority rights, and the admission of practicing gay and lesbian candidates to the ministry. The organizing began with groups that supported the cause of women and African Americans, but conservative pastors in the mainline churches also found special purpose organizing an effective means to advance their ideas. By 2000 twenty-one mainline advocacy groups calling for a "return to orthodoxy" had united in an interdenominational Association for Church Renewal.[29]

In the Catholic Church, a division between "traditionalist" and "progressive" priests mirrored the Protestant conflict. By the mid-1970s, the Vatican was reasserting traditional orthodoxies. Pope John Paul II, who assumed the papacy in 1978, appointed conservative bishops, and by the time he died, some Catholic insiders were writing of a "shrinking band of liberals." Traditionalism found a warm reception among a new generation of young priests ordained after 1980. In 1994 one poll found that 40 percent of priests under thirty-five thought of themselves as conservatives, as opposed to 20 percent of older priests. The younger men were still a minority, but they appeared to foreshadow a more conservative priesthood.[30]

The younger traditionalists were more likely than the previous generation to emphasize the submission and obedience of priests to their bishops and of laity to their priests. They tended more to affirm clerical celibacy, to oppose the ordination of women, and to reassert traditional teachings about divorce, birth control, premarital sex, and homosexuality. They were less likely to tolerate any alteration of the rubrics of the mass or to disregard liturgical regulations. They preferred traditional priestly attire. The Roman collar, the cassock, and the biretta sometimes became symbols of party sympathies.[31]

Many of the younger priests wanted to restore practices that had fallen

---

p. 215; Guth et al., *Bully Pulpit*, pp. 30, 51; Witham, *Who Shall Lead Them?* pp. 81-99; Nancy T. Ammerman, *Baptist Battles: Social Change and Religious Conflict in the Southern Baptist Convention* (New Brunswick: Rutgers University Press, 1990), pp. 40-156.

29. Wuthnow, *Restructuring*, pp. 100-132; Carroll, *God's Potters*, pp. 46-48.

30. Joseph P. Chinnici, "The Catholic Community at Prayer, 1926-1976," in *Habits of Devotion: Catholic Religious Practice in Twentieth Century America* (Ithaca: Cornell University Press, 2004), p. 17; Morris, *American Catholic*, p. 344; Hoge and Wenger, *Evolving Visions*, p. 47; Thomas Kunkel, *Enormous Prayers: A Journey into the Priesthood* (Boulder: Westview Press, 1998), p. 41.

31. Hoge and Wenger, *Evolving Visions*, pp. 47-48, 89; Morris, *American Catholic*, p. 385; Greeley, *Priests*, pp. 77-79; Greeley, *Catholic Priest*, p. 142.

into disuse since Vatican II. Some worked to reinstate novenas, the Benediction of the Blessed Sacrament, and meatless Fridays. They wanted to be addressed as "Father," and instead of defining themselves as "servant-leaders" — as many had done in the previous generation — they preferred a more hierarchical and rite-centered image of their ministry. Much of the change had its origin in the policies of John Paul II, but cultural dynamics were also at work. As one younger traditionalist put it, "the instability of the '60s and '70s did lead my generation to seek out the stability of the more traditional forms."[32]

Among Protestants, the conservative surge made theological differences increasingly visible. As many as 88 percent of the ministers in the Assemblies of God and 60 percent in the Southern Baptist Convention insisted on biblical inerrancy, while only 6 percent of the ministers in the Disciples of Christ and 5 percent in the Presbyterian Church (USA) agreed. As many as 74 percent in the Evangelical Covenant Church affirmed that belief in Jesus was the sole means of salvation, but in the United Methodist Church the number was closer to 40 percent. In the Assemblies of God, 95 percent of the clergy believed in the existence of a personal Devil, but among Disciples only 15 percent shared that belief. Eighty to 90 percent of the ministers in conservative denominations expected a "rapture" of the church in the final days and a physical return of Christ to set up a millennial kingdom; in the mainline denominations, less than 20 percent had such an expectation. Protestants were as theologically divided as they had ever been.[33]

Catholics disagreed with each other about a different set of issues. In 1972 most priests taught that Catholicism was "the one true Church," but by the 1980s a third of the younger clergy had doubts. (By 2000 the Vatican felt it necessary to reaffirm the teaching.) Traditionalists refused to compromise on birth control — a few of them even argued that the proscription was an infallible teaching — but by 2002 only 27 percent of the clergy believed that artificial birth control was always wrong, and the majority was no longer prepared to exclude all possibility of justifiable divorce. On all these issues — and others — younger priests in the 1990s were more conservative than older ones, but they faced silent resistance from the laity, who downplayed or ignored much official

32. Chinnici, "Catholic Community at Prayer," p. 17; Hoge and Wenger, *Evolving Visions*, pp. 87, 116.

33. Guth et al., *Bully Pulpit*, pp. 44, 47, 50; Wuthnow, *Restructuring*, pp. 45, 51; Djupe and Gilbert, *Prophetic Pulpit*, p. 24; Dean R. Hoge and John E. Dyble, "The Influence of Assimilation on American Protestant Ministers' Beliefs, 1928-1978," *Journal for the Scientific Study of Religion* 20 (1981): 64-77; Theodore Caplow et al., *All Faithful People: Change and Continuity in Middletown's Religion* (Minneapolis: University of Minnesota Press, 1983), pp. 286-87.

teaching about birth control, sexual ethics, papal infallibility, and the sole validity of the Catholic Church.[34]

The varying attitudes toward "modernity" that energized the doctrinal disagreements also expressed themselves in the continuing disputes about the ordination of women, especially in churches that understood themselves sacramentally or held to biblical inerrancy. After the National Organization of Women formed an ecumenical task force in 1967, the battle for ordination assumed, even more than it had in earlier struggles, the features of a campaign for gender equality. The energy came less from denominational offices and seminaries than from the initiatives of women themselves, who flowed into the seminaries, increasing their enrollment from 5 percent in 1972 to 22 percent in 1988, and formed grassroots movements that pushed for change.[35]

Episcopal women broke the barriers, for example, only after they convinced retired bishops to ordain eleven candidates in an extra-canonical ordination service in 1974. Similar unauthorized ordinations occurred in the Christian Reformed Church, the Reformed Church in America, and the Southern Baptist Convention. The women's groups argued that both the Bible and the ancient traditions of the church provided support for their cause, but the opposition claimed, in the words of one conservative, that "having a woman as pastor generally indicates a liberalism which denies the authority of scripture."[36]

In 1996 half the American denominations ordained women, but the other half stiffened their resistance, and even in the mainline churches opposition did not entirely fade away. Episcopalians adopted a "conscience clause" that allowed bishops to say no. In 1992, conservatives in the Christian Reformed Church reversed a committee decision to allow congregations to ordain women. The fundamentalist takeover of the Southern Baptist Convention led by 2000 to a doctrinal assertion that men alone were to be ordained. Pentecostal churches backed away from their earlier openness to women as preachers. And in the 1994 apostolic letter *Ordinatio Sacerdotalis*, the Catholic Church "definitively" announced

34. Greeley, *Catholic Priest*, pp. 115, 120; Witham, *Who Shall Lead Them?* p. 202; Morris, *American Catholic*, p. 293; Greeley, *Priests*, pp. 75, 77; John C. Ford and Germain Grisez, "Contraception and the Infallibility of the Ordinary Magisterium," *Theological Studies* 39 (1978): 259-312; Paul A. Djupe, "Cardinal O'Connor and His Constituents: Differential Beliefs and Public Evaluations," in *Christian Clergy*, p. 191.

35. Mark Chaves, *Ordaining Women: Culture and Conflict in Religious Organizations* (Cambridge: Harvard University Press, 1997), p. 91; Wuthnow, *Restructuring*, p. 230; Mark Chaves and James Cavendish, "Recent Changes in Women's Ordination Conflicts: The Effects of a Social Movement on Interorganizational Controversy," *Journal for the Scientific Study of Religion* 36 (1997): 576.

36. Chaves and Cavendish, "Recent Changes," p. 580; Wuthnow, *Restructuring*, p. 230; Ammerman, *Baptist Battles*, p. 94.

that it had "no authority whatever" to ordain women to the priesthood, though in 2001 about half of the American Catholic priests supported their ordination.[37]

In the historic African American churches, only the three large Methodist denominations went on record as favoring the ordination of women, and even in those churches women had to push against inertia. After an initial encounter, reported one African Methodist Episcopal woman pastor, it was "ten years before I dared to tell another person in authority that God had called me to preach the gospel." As early as 1973, African American women made up 5 percent of the women enrolled in seminaries, but many of them had to go into chaplaincies — military or college — or form their own independent congregations. The ambivalence in the churches expressed itself when one of the largest denominations, the Church of God in Christ, ruled in 1973 that women could teach and even lead a church but could not be ordained. By the end of the 1990s, 5 percent of the pastors in the largest African American denominations were women, though as many as five thousand more women preached in independent and storefront churches.[38]

According to the 2000 census, 14 percent of all American clergy were women. It took them longer than men to find a pulpit, they were more likely to work part time, they remained underrepresented in senior positions, most served in small congregations, and they still earned less than men, though by 2005 the gap was narrowing. The largest number served in the mainline United Methodist Church (3,003 in 1994) and the evangelical Salvation Army (3,220 in 1986). But even in churches that refused to ordain them, women taught and preached, usually with some alteration of their official titles. The drive launched by the Catholic Women's Ordination Conference in 1975 produced no change in policy, but by 2001 fully 81 percent of Catholic lay ministers were women, and they constituted 80 percent of the ministers in paid positions. Resistance to women's ordination had little to do with the activity of ministry. It was about opposition to modern innovation.[39]

37. Mark Chaves, "Ordaining Women: The Diffusion of an Organizational Innovation," *American Journal of Sociology* 101 (1996): 840-73; Chaves and Cavendism, "Recent Changes," p. 581; Charles H. Barfoot and Gerald T. Sheppard, "Prophetic vs. Priestly Religion: The Changing Role of Women Clergy in Classical Pentecostal Churches," *Review of Religious Research* 22 (1980): 2-16; Morris, *American Catholic*, p. 334; Greeley, *Priests*, p. 316.

38. Cleophus J. La Rue, ed., *This Is My Story: Testimonies and Sermons of Black Women in Ministry* (Louisville: Westminster John Knox, 2005), p. 37; Vashti M. McKenzie, *Not Without a Struggle* (Cleveland: United Church Press, 1996), pp. xvi-xvii; Anthony B. Pinn, *The Black Church in the Post-Civil Rights Era* (Maryknoll, N.Y.: Orbis, 2002), p. 129. See also Delores Causion Carpenter, *A Time for Honor: A Portrait of African American Clergywomen* (St. Louis: Chalice, 2001).

39. Witham, *Who Shall Lead Them?* p. 16; Barbara Brown Zikmind, Adair T. Lummis, Patri-

In the mainline churches, the most polarizing topic after 1990 was the ordination of non-celibate gay and lesbian candidates for ministry. When an Episcopal bishop ordained a gay man in that year, other bishops brought charges against him for breaking his vows, but the bishops were divided. When the Diocese of New Hampshire elected a gay bishop in 2003, the denomination verged on the edge of schism. In the Presbyterian Church (USA), the 1991 refusal of ordination to a candidate in a lesbian relationship began a debate that led in 1996 to a "fidelity and chastity" amendment to the church's official resolutions. It required ministers to live in faithful heterosexual marriage or chastity in singleness. But it did not end the conflict. The United Methodist Church voted in 2004 to uphold a ban on non-celibate homosexual clergy, but the denomination remained divided. By 2005 the United Church of Christ, the Unitarian-Universalists, and the Metropolitan Community Church accepted gay and lesbian ordination. In a 1997 survey of five thousand ministers in fifteen denominations — mainline and conservative — about 5 percent of the clergy identified themselves as gay or lesbian. No other issue bore such potential for breaking apart the mainline churches.[40]

The Catholic Church, assuming that every priest would abstain from sexual activity, had never asked candidates for the priesthood to declare their sexual orientation. By 1982, however, critics were complaining of a "homosexual network" in the priesthood, and within five years Catholic theologians and sociologists were debating about the extent of a "homosexual subculture" in Catholic seminaries and dioceses. In a 2002 *Los Angeles Times* poll, 16 percent of the Catholic clergy said that they were gay or inclined in that direction. By then only half the American priests shared the Vatican's view of homosexuality as a "disorder." Almost all of them, however, thought that priests should maintain the vow of celibacy.[41]

Divisions over the emotional issues gave the appearance of polarization,

cia Mei Yin Chang, *Clergy Women: An Uphill Calling* (Louisville: Westminster John Knox Press, 1998), pp. 4, 70; Patricia M. Y. Chang, "In Search of a Pulpit: Six Differences in the Transition from Seminary to the First Parish," *Journal for the Scientific Study of Religion* 36 (1997): 614; Paula D. Nesbitt, "Clergy Feminization: Controlled Labor or Transformational Change," *Journal for the Scientific Study of Religion* 36 (1997): 588-97; Carroll, *God's Potters,* pp. 66-70; Edward C. Lehman Jr., *Women's Path into Ministry: Six Major Studies* (Durham: Pulpit and Pew, 2002), pp. 4-37; Jackson Carroll, Barbara Hargrove, and Adair Lummis, *Women of the Cloth: A New Opportunity for the Churches* (San Francisco: Harper and Row, 1983), pp. 129-31; Mark Chaves, *Ordaining Women,* pp. 21-25; Hoge and Wenger, *Evolving Visions,* p. 127.

40. Witham, *Who Shall Lead Them?* pp. 159-75; Zikmund, et al., *Clergy Women,* p. 39.

41. Witham, *Who Shall Lead Them?* p. 167; Dean R. Hoge, *The First Five Years of Priesthood* (Collegeville, Minn.: Liturgical Press, 2002), pp. 3, 31; Greeley, *Priests,* pp. 38, 76; Donald B. Cozzens, *The Changing Face of the Priesthood* (Collegeville, Minn.: Liturgical Press, 2000), pp. 97-110.

but despite the headlines, most priests and ministers stood closer to the political and theological center than to either wing of the ideological divide. In the political sphere, the pastors of 58 percent of American congregations held back even from encouraging people to vote. On several questions of social justice, as many as a third to a half of the conservatives — depending on denomination — agreed with the more liberal clergy, while large minorities of ministers in the mainline churches shared at least some of the goals of the conservative moral reform agenda.[42]

The black clergy exemplified the complexity. In the 1970s black voters said that their ministers influenced their political views more than anyone else, and in the 1980s fully 92 percent of African American clergy thought that they should express their views on social and political questions. Candidates for office in the larger cities, especially Democrats, usually felt obliged to visit some of the larger churches. A few black clergy ran successfully for office themselves. But in 1998 only about a third of black congregations exposed their members to candidates, handed out voter guides, or encouraged registration to vote. And black clergy did not stand uniformly on the liberal end of the spectrum. Large numbers took conservative positions on family issues, abortion, gay ordination, and personal morality, and a few pastors built megachurches around a gospel of prosperity that viewed the Christian gospel as an aid to the amassing of wealth.[43]

The campaign to elevate black pride and ethnic self-awareness that followed the civil rights movement created ripples of change among African American clergy. By the 1980s 64 percent of them took those themes into account in their preaching and teaching. And the theology of black liberation — increasingly visible in the seminaries after 1970 — penetrated into the everyday work of urban black clergy. By the late 1980s, 35 percent of them said that the liberation theologians had influenced their practice of ministry. But the concern for black liberation did not signal the racial polarization that some had predicted. More than half the black clergy said that their ministry was different because they served black congregations, but most of them — 63 percent in one poll — also said that the black and white churches shared essentially the same mission.[44]

Catholic priests also confused observers who thought in simple dichotomies. As many as 77 percent of them said that they were involved in social and moral issues, and in 1979 the bishops issued a document on "Political Responsi-

42. Chaves, *Congregations,* pp. 66, 85, 99, 108, 119; Djupe and Gilbert, *Prophetic Pulpit,* p. 49.

43. C. Eric Lincoln and Lawrence H. Mamiya, *The Black Church in the African American Experience* (Durham: Duke University Press, 1990), pp. 213, 214-15; Mary R. Sawyer, "Theocratic, Prophetic, and Ecumenical: Political Roles of African American Clergy," in *Christian Clergy,* p. 78; Chaves, *Congregations,* pp. 112, 117.

44. Lincoln and Mamiya, *Black Church,* pp. 169, 181.

bility" that called for pastors and congregations to act on a wide range of topics. In "A Challenge to Peace" (1983), the bishops defied American nuclear policy, and in their "Pastoral Letter on Catholic Social Teaching and the U.S. Economy" (1984) they criticized unbridled capitalism and called for greater efforts to aid the poor. On most issues they stood close to the mainline Protestants, but their sense of dismay about abortion aligned them often with conservative Protestants as well. Simple "liberal" or "conservative" stereotypes failed to capture the complexity.[45]

Ministry and the Professional Ideal

Priests and ministers continued after 1970 to debate the professional status of the ministry. Andrew Greeley made the case in 1972 that the Catholic priesthood was a profession because it required "expertise, autonomy, responsibility, and commitment for serving people," even though it was a unique kind of profession. But Greeley recalled the bishop who vehemently disagreed: "I became a priest," he said, "to serve Jesus Christ, not to be a professional." Greeley concluded that one could not talk about "professionalizing" the clergy without being accused of "desacralizing the role." Still, by 2001, 67 percent of priests said that the priesthood should become "more professional," meaning both credentialed and competent in defined areas.[46]

Episcopal priest Urban Holmes ignited once more the debate among Protestants when he argued in 1971 that the "professional model" diminished the symbolic role of the priest as a "mystagogue" who led people "into the mystery that surrounds our life." Without denying that the minister required special education and learning, he argued that the cleric had to be, above all, the image-making storyteller whose very presence evoked unconscious associations and projections and whose identity as an "enchanter" broke through the boundaries of ordinary consciousness.[47]

The debate had at least two dimensions. Partly it was a question of the degree to which the ministry fit a standard sociological definition of a profession. Some argued that priests and ministers, unlike professionals, served churches

45. Hoge and Wenger, *Evolving Visions*, p. 49; "Choices for the '80s," *Christian Century* 96 (Nov. 28, 1979): 1179; Laura R. Olson and Sue E. S. Crawford, "Clergy in Politics: Political Choices and Consequences," in *Christian Clergy*, p. 11.

46. Greeley, *Catholic Priest*, p. 771; Greeley, *Confessions*, p. 134; Hoge and Wenger, *Evolving Visions*, p. 49.

47. Urban T. Holmes III, *The Priest in Community: Exploring the Roots of Ministry* (New York: Seabury Press, 1978), pp. 67, 90, 127, 182.

rather than society, that they lacked much of a sense of collegiality across denominational lines, and that parishioners were not "clients" in the same way as
patients and litigants. They observed that the state licensed other professions
but not ministers, that many preachers had no specialized education, and that
ministerial duties were not as sharply defined as those of other professions.[48]

Partly the question was one of theology. Theological critics of the professional image argued that it neglected an appropriate sense of vocation and calling and a correct view of ordination. Some argued that the ministry was not a
"helping profession" but rather a form of discipleship to Jesus that stood in tension with a society that enshrined professional values. While ministers helped
people with individual needs, the "essence" of their work was to "bring people
into the community of worship and mutual support." Others claimed that the
concern about professionalism reflected a "clerical paradigm" that diminished
the ministry of the whole church, clerical and lay. "Any ministry that finds its
authority in contemporary notions of professionalism," concluded one minister, "is on perilous ground indeed."[49]

Populist themes reemerged in new forms, finding expression even among
some sociologists, who argued that seminary training distanced clergy from the
laity and that the denominations with a more professional clergy had suffered a
falling "market share" in the denominational competition. In many of the new
(and growing) charismatic congregations, the criterion for leadership was not
"the list of degrees behind one's name." They asked a different set of questions:
Did the pastor have "a passionate commitment to God," "a vision for transforming people," and "a Spirit-filled life"? The founder of one of the largest
Pentecostal networks, Chuck Smith of Calvary Chapel in California, contended
that "God does not call those who are qualified, but qualifies those who are
called."[50]

The professional ideal still had articulate defenders. Some emphasized its
ethical dimension. In thinking of pastoral ministry as a profession, one wrote,

48. Thomas M. Gannon, S.J., "Priest/Minister: Profession or Non-profession," *Review of
Religious Research* 12 (1971): 66-67; Ivan Vallier, "Religious Specialists: Sociological Study," in *International Encyclopedia of the Social Sciences*, ed. David Sills, 12 vols. (New York: Crowell, Col-
lier, and Macmillan, 1968), p. 453; see the discussion in Jackson W. Carroll, "The Professional
Model of Ministry: Is It Worth Saving?" *Theological Education* 21 (1985): 7-48.

49. Hauerwas and Willimon, *Resident Aliens*, p. 121; William H. Willimon, *Pastor: The Theology and Practice of Ordained Ministry* (Nashville: Abingdon Press, 2002), p. 14; Edward Farley,
Theologia (Philadelphia: Fortress Press, 1983), pp. 87-88; Neuhaus, *Freedom for Ministry*, pp. 64, 65.

50. Finke and Starke, *Churching of America*, pp. 83-84, 154-59; Donald E. Miller, *Emergent
Patterns of Congregational Life and Leadership in the Developing World* (Durham: Pulpit and
Pew, 2003), p. 20; Witham, *Who Shall Lead Them?* p. 139.

we not only ask the minister to "master a body of knowledge and use it in a dis-ciplined way," but we also expect standards of honesty, confidentiality, and re-sponsibility. Others added that the churches needed "reflective practitioners" who could draw on theology, tradition, and the arts and sciences in order to in-terpret the contexts in which they ministered. Some contended that the profes-sional image was a reminder that ministers functioned within larger communi-ties that set standards of both competence and conduct. They argued that clergy had authority to the extent that they displayed "both spirituality and ex-pertise, not one without the other."[51]

Despite the divisions over whether ministry should be considered a profes-sion, the clergy tended in ever-growing numbers to seek out opportunities for special training. One result was that seminary enrollments continued to in-crease. By 1993 the Association of Theological Schools listed 189 accredited in-stitutions, with thirty more awaiting affiliation. The conservative churches led in the race to educate ministerial students. Already in the 1970s all but two of the ten largest seminaries operated under evangelical leadership. Among the ac-credited seminaries in 1993, the seventy-two evangelical schools had 32,544 stu-dents, the ninety-five mainline institutions had 27,075, and the fifty-three Cath-olic seminaries had 7,384.[52]

The differing theological orientations of the schools led them to educate students in different ways. In studying an evangelical and a mainline seminary, researchers found a distinctive ethos in each. The evangelical school honored correct doctrine, lively informal worship, no-holds-barred argument, and a personal relationship to Christ. The mainline seminary valued critical knowl-edge of the Christian tradition, correct attitudes toward diversity, more formal patterns of worship, and a conviction that discipleship to Jesus required service on behalf of justice for the poor and vulnerable. In accord with the 1993 *Pro-gram of Priestly Formation*, Catholic schools, drawing on the encyclical *Pastores dabo vobis* (I Will Give You Shepherds) by Pope John Paul II, showed a renewed interest in forming "the spiritual life of priests." Catholic bishops called on seminarians to celebrate the Eucharist daily, observe the Liturgy of the Hours, and practice frequent confession of sin.[53]

51. Gaylord Noyce, "The Pastor Is (Also) a Professional," *Christian Century* 105 (Nov. 2, 1988): 975; Paul Camenish, "Are Pastors Professionals?" *Christian Ministry* 16 (1985): 12-13; Carroll, *As One with Authority*, p. 54; Carroll, "Professional Model of Ministry," pp. 31, 35.

52. Jackson W. Carroll, Barbara G. Wheeler, Daniel O. Aleshire, and Penny Long Marler, *Being There: Culture and Formation in Two Theological Schools* (New York: Oxford University Press, 1997), pp. 9, 10; Wuthnow, *Restructuring*, p. 192.

53. Carroll et al., *Being There*, pp. 218, 238, 265; Robert J. Wister, "The Program of Priestly For-mation: National Conference of Catholic Bishops," *Ministerial Formation* 70 (July 1995): 35-38.

Critics said that the seminaries suffered from many of the same problems that had beset them in the 1930s. They accepted 87 percent of their applicants, and the range of academic abilities was therefore wider among their students than in more selective professional schools. One seminary president argued that the ease of admission diminished the authority of the profession, and it was a matter of concern that seminaries still attracted only about 3 percent of the students who stood near the top of their college classes. Others argued that too many of the schools still had less than demanding academic standards and little willingness to dismiss underperforming students. A sociologist who spent a year in a mainline seminary argued that its egalitarianism and its image of the minister as a "friend" rather than an expert contributed to the "deprofessionalization" of the ministry by stripping it of its "authority and basis in expertise."[54]

On the other hand, however, some critics complained that the schools were *too* academic and gave insufficient attention to the practical work of ministry. Graduates sometimes grumbled that seminaries did not teach them how to deal with people, handle conflict, or perform the routine tasks of ministry. Their worry was that the seminaries were too attentive to the intricacies of theology and more interested in teaching students to read texts than to run churches.[55]

In response to such criticisms, seminaries launched new initiatives. Among the most important was the increased attention to programs in "supervised ministry," or "contextual education," or "on-site training" that gave students an opportunity to do hands-on ministry under the supervision of hospital chaplains, social welfare ministers, and parish clergy. An expansion of the earlier experiments in "field work" and clinical pastoral education, these programs attempted to establish a pedagogy of activity and reflection. After instituting such programs, and after moderating the military-style discipline of earlier seminary training, the Catholic schools drew far higher approval ratings from graduates in 2001 than they had thirty years earlier.[56]

54. Barbara G. Wheeler, "Fit for Ministry?: A New Profile of Seminarians," *Christian Century* 118 (Apr. 11, 2001): 17; Barbara G. Wheeler, "Critical Junctures: Theological Education Confronts Its Futures," *Religion in the Nineties: The Annals of the American Academy of Political and Social Sciences,* ed. Wade Clark Roof, 527 (1993): 95; Chaves, *Congregations,* p. 39; Gregory Jones and Susan Pendleton Jones, "Pivotal Leadership," *Christian Century* (Sept. 12-19, 2001): 24-28; Sherryl Kleinman, *Equals Before God: Seminarians as Humanistic Professionals* (Chicago: University of Chicago Press, 1984), pp. 1-23; Greeley, *Catholic Priest,* p. 45; George Barna, *Today's Pastors* (Ventura: Regal Books, 1993), p. 140. See the defense of the image of the minister as "friend" in Edward C. Zaragoza, *No Longer Servants But Friends: A Theology of the Ordained Ministry* (Nashville: Abingdon, 1999).

55. Hoge and Wenger, *Evolving Visions,* p. 23; Greeley, *Catholic Priest,* pp. 45, 52; Barna, *Today's Pastors,* pp. 125, 140.

56. Conrad Cherry, *Hurrying Toward Zion: Universities, Divinity Schools, and Protestantism*

The ministry remained, however, a vocation more than a profession, even though it had a professional component. Uppermost in the motivation of most priests and ministers was the sense of divine calling. For some, this came as a gradual deepening of conviction, but for more than 70 percent of ministers it also included a particular experience of God's call. By 1970, more and more of those who felt the call also felt a pull toward seminary preparation, but the numbers varied by denomination, race, and class. In the 1980s, only 45 percent of Southern Baptist pastors had graduated from a seminary. African American clergy still had less access than whites to seminary education. More than 41 percent of them had only a high-school education or less, 15 percent graduated from college only, and 29 percent had both college and seminary training.[57]

By the beginning of the twenty-first century, the largest study of American congregations found that 89 percent of the local churches had a minister with at least a college degree, but only 45 percent had ministers with both college and seminary or higher graduate preparation. According to the Pulpit and Pew survey in 2001, 49 percent of Protestant and Catholic clergy reported that they had earned a master's degree — the degree normally granted by the seminaries — although 11 percent also reported an earned doctorate, which was probably an indication of the continuing popularity of the Doctor of Ministry degree.[58]

Seminary education was beginning to attract denominations that once had avoided it. In the fast-growing holiness and Pentecostal "Spirit-centered" churches, about 40 percent of the clergy had a seminary education, though in one of the largest Pentecostal denominations, the Assemblies of God, the number was closer to 19 percent. The historic black denominations increasingly encouraged clergy to complete seminary training.[59]

At the same time, even the mainline churches had to depend more and more on lay ministers to serve their smaller congregations. In the United Methodist Church, "local pastors" without a seminary education still served 25 percent of the congregations, and in some regions of the South and Midwest half the total number of United Methodist pastors lacked a seminary degree.

(Bloomington: Indiana University Press, 1995), pp. 126-55; Hoge and Wenger, *Evolving Visions*, p. 25.

57. Zikmund et al., *Clergy Women*, p. 96; Finke and Stark, *Churching of America*, p. 197; Roger Finke, "The Quiet Transformation: Changes in the Size and Leadership of Southern Baptist Churches," *Review of Religious Research* 36 (1994): 13; Wuthnow, *Restructuring*, p. 194; Lincoln and Mamiya, *Black Church*, pp. 99, 129.

58. Chaves, *Congregations*, p. 235; Carroll, *God's Potters*, p. 274; Barna, *Today's Pastors*, p. 35; Guth et al., *Bully Pulpit*, p. 53.

59. Zikmund et al., *Clergy Women*, p. 100; Guth et al., *Bully Pulpit*, p. 53; Lincoln and Mamiya, *Black Church*, p. 129.

Twenty-five percent of the ministers in the Evangelical Lutheran Church and 30 percent of Episcopalians serving in the smaller and more remote parishes had no seminary training.[60]

Nonetheless, no previous generation of ministers since the American Revolution contained such a large percentage of college and seminary graduates, and their education was more demanding — and more attuned to ministry in local congregations — than it had been in 1934. The expansion of clinical pastoral education, institutes for lifelong learning, and religious publishing aimed at clerical readers also bespoke a continuing commitment to an educated ministry. But the populist impulse remained strong, and preachers without theological training sometimes attained a greater public presence than the seminary graduates.

Ministry

Priests and ministers continued to work after 1970 in a familiar assortment of institutions, from high schools and colleges to hospitals, counseling centers, prisons, the military, seminaries, and social welfare agencies. But most of them served as pastors in local congregations, and they continued to perform duties that harkened back to the earliest days of the church. When asked to describe their most satisfying tasks, Catholic priests spoke of administering the sacraments, presiding over the liturgy, preaching, and working with people. Given a similar question, Protestants said that they liked most to preach, lead worship, teach, and counsel. In their everyday routines, the clergy remained within well-worn paths. Most expended little energy on the polarizing topics that divided American culture.[61]

In 1994 two sociologists, Gary Kuhne and Joe Donaldson, spent a week closely observing each of five Protestant ministers. They found that the ministers worked fifty-one hours a week and that they averaged forty-one discrete activities every day. The schedule was fast-paced. Almost half their activities lasted five minutes or less; only 6 percent lasted more than an hour. They spent 46 percent of their time in scheduled events, from counseling sessions to committee meetings, funerals, weddings, and worship services. Deskwork required 23 percent of their time — about twelve hours a week, five of which went into sermon preparation. They spent 12 percent of their time in their

60. Patricia M. Y. Chang, *Assessing the Clergy Supply in the 21st Century* (Durham: Pulpit and Pew, 2004), p. 8; Djupe and Gilbert, *Prophetic Pulpit*, p. 22.

61. Hoge and Wenger, *Evolving Visions*, pp. 25-26; Carroll, *God's Potters*, p. 115.

cars, taking five trips a day. They had thirteen scheduled and unscheduled daily meetings; the scheduled meetings took about forty-nine minutes each, the unscheduled about seven. They averaged eight phone conversations, each lasting four minutes. They devoted several minutes to prayer and meditation. On average, they had thirty-one contacts with other people, alternating between the casual and the crucial and tragic, which meant that they had to shift their moods and responses quickly. Their work was marked by "brevity, fragmentation, and variety."[62]

When pastors filled out surveys, they confirmed this depiction. Some saw themselves as spending more time preparing their sermons — ten hours a week was the median time in one study — but they reported a workweek rich in variety. "You don't know the meaning of variety," remarked one, "until you've been a pastor." Conservative ministers spent a few more hours a week than the mainline clergy in teaching and a few less in administration and organization. Catholic priests spent four to five more hours a week than Protestants in ritual activity and two to four fewer hours in preparing sermons. They also devoted more time to prayer and meditation. But Catholics and Protestants spent about the same amount of time on all the other tasks.[63]

Compared to the clergy who filled out Samuel Blizzard's surveys in the 1950s, Protestant ministers in the 1990s worked fewer hours a week, spent a little more time on their sermons, devoted a couple of hours more each week to counseling, and gave less time to administration. They did less visiting and spent fewer hours in denominational and ecumenical gatherings. Catholic priests also differed slightly from their predecessors. Priests in 1970 had found their most fulfilling ministry in visiting the sick, helping the poor, and working with small groups, though presiding over the liturgy was also a source of satisfaction. For priests in 2001, sacramental and liturgical leadership provided the deepest joy, though priests also liked to work with people.[64]

Mainline Protestants embraced the ministry of the laity with enthusiasm. For some of them, the most important statement on the nature of the pastorate was the 1982 ecumenical document "Baptism, Eucharist, and Ministry," produced by the Commission on Faith and Order of the World Council of

62. Gary William Kuhne and Joe F. Donaldson, "Balancing Ministry and Management: An Exploratory Study of Pastoral Work Activities," *Review of Religious Research* 37 (1995): 148-52, 149, 151.

63. Barna, *Today's Pastors*, pp. 129, 130; Sandra Brunette-Hill and Roger Finke, "A Time for Every Purpose Under Heaven: Updating and Extending Blizzard's Survey of Clergy Time Allocation," *Review of Religious Research* 41 (1999): 55.

64. Brunette Hill and Finke, "A Time for Every Purpose," p. 54; Greeley, *Catholic Priest*, p. 201; Hoge and Wenger, *Evolving Visions*, pp. 25-26.

Churches. It identified widespread agreement that Christian ministry was the work of "the whole people of God."[65]

The document acknowledged that the churches needed persons who were "publicly and continually" responsible for reminding it of its witness, and it defined the ordained minister's chief duty as the building of the body of Christ by preaching, teaching, and celebrating the sacraments, but it insisted that these tasks had as their goal the "mission" and "caring ministry" of the whole church. The theologians tried to affirm the "priesthood of the baptized" without diminishing the "authority of ordained ministers."[66]

"Baptism, Eucharist, and Ministry" expressed the hopes of leaders in the mainline denominations, but many evangelicals spoke also of "equipping the laity to minister." Sixty percent of the pastors in Protestant congregations made it a priority to train the laity. But it remained difficult for Protestant congregations to realize the ideal. Most laity in the 1970s still viewed themselves "primarily as spectators" rather than as persons "mutually called to share a ministry with others." Twenty years later, one pollster summarized a nationwide survey: the idea that "lay members are called to minister" had not yet, he said, replaced the image of the pastor as the "chief performer in all areas of ministry."[67]

Catholics, meanwhile, were of two minds about the ministry of the laity. In writing the story of the twentieth-century priesthood, historian R. Scott Appleby described the two decades after 1970 as the period of the priestly "orchestra leader" who empowered or enabled the lay ministry of the whole church. The Vatican in 1972 opened up certain liturgical functions to lay Catholics, and eventually the distinction between clergy and laity became slightly blurred even in the celebration of the mass, since lay Eucharistic ministers could join the priests in the sanctuary space. Some theologians fully embraced the ministry of the laity. T. F. O'Meara's *Theology of Ministry* (1983) for instance, insisted that "Christian ministry" was a "public activity of a baptized follower of Jesus Christ."[68]

---

65. "Baptism, Eucharist, and Ministry," *Creeds of the Churches*, ed. John Leith (3rd ed.; Atlanta: John Knox Press, 1982), p. 631.

66. "Baptism, Eucharist, and Ministry," pp. 638-39.

67. Kuhne and Donaldson, "Balancing Ministry," p. 158; Barna, *Today's Pastors*, pp. 18, 103, 131; Carroll, *As One with Authority*, p. 89; David S. Schuller, et al., *Readiness for Ministry* (Vandalia: Association of Theological Schools, 1975), p. 10.

68. Appleby, "Present to the People of God," pp. 91, 101, 103; Debra Campbell, "The Struggle to Serve: From the Lay Apostolate to the Ministry Explosion," in *Transforming Parish Ministry*, pp. 203, 270; Hoge and Wenger, *Evolving Visions*, p. 11; Thomas F. O'Meara, *Theology of Ministry* (New York: Paulist Press, 1983), p. 142.

But the traditionalist resurgence in Catholicism reemphasized the unique character of the priesthood and the essential difference between laity and priest. Some priests and bishops felt wary about the increasing scope of lay leadership. Catholics, along with the Orthodox, expressed reservations about the absence of attention in "Baptism, Eucharist, and Ministry" to "sacramental ordination in the apostolic succession." By 2001, 73 percent of American Catholic priests affirmed the goal of empowering lay ministers, but the younger traditionalist priests were less favorable.[69]

Yet it was in the Catholic Church that lay ministry often became the most visible form of ministerial presence. With the shrinkage in the numbers of priests, parishes depended on full-time lay ministers who did everything that priests did except say mass and hear confessions. In 1967, the Vatican restored the "permanent diaconate" as an office — with its own ordination — open to single and married laymen. Within thirty-five years, 12,851 permanent deacons were at work in Catholic parishes. But an even greater expansion brought "lay ecclesial ministers" — 80 percent of whom were women — into the forefront of Catholic parish life. By the end of the 1990s, more than twenty thousand paid lay ministers helped hold Catholic congregations together. Negotiating the relationships between priests and lay ministers proved to be a challenge.[70]

In one large survey, 47 percent of the laity — 57 percent among conservative Protestants and 37 percent among Catholics — "strongly agreed" that their pastor was a good match for the parish, and the laity seemed to know what they wanted. They talked about religious authenticity, gifted preaching, skillful leadership of worship, and warmth and good "people skills." They valued ministers who would visit and could offer sound counsel. Protestants also still tended to want young males with a family.[71]

Theologians struggled to articulate a vision of ministry that drew its strength from the Christian tradition rather than reflecting merely the desires of the laity. Part of that quest for theological deepening came from ecumenical dialogues. Lutheran and Catholic theologians in the early 1970s reached tentative agreements about ordination, the apostolic succession, and Eucharistic ministry. They also agreed that ministry was the work of every baptized Christian but that

---

69. Witham, *Who Shall Lead Them?* p. 21; Hoge and Wenger, *Evolving Visions,* p. 51.

70. Morris, *American Catholic,* p. 389; Peter Stravinskas, ed., *Our Sunday Visitor's Catholic Encyclopedia* (Huntington: Our Sunday Visitor, 1991), 285-86; Hoge and Wenger, *Evolving Visions,* p. 14.

71. Greeley, *Priests,* p. 93; Barna, *Today's Pastors,* p. 51; Dean Hoge, Jackson W. Carroll, and Francis K. Sheets, *Patterns of Parish Leadership: Cost and Effectiveness in Four Denominations* (Kansas City: Sheed and Ward, 1988), p. 118; Carroll, *God's Potters,* pp. 84-87, 118-19; Adair T. Lummis, *What Do Lay People Want in Pastors?* (Durham: Pulpit and Pew, 2003), pp. 7-13, 16.

the church needed the "particular form of service" traditionally rendered by priests and ministers.[72]

Other theologians sought to clarify images of ministry, some new and some traditional. In 1972 the Catholic Henri J. M. Nouwen described ministers as "wounded healers," people acutely aware of their "professional loneliness" in a culture that accorded them a "diminished" hearing. He suggested that the sense of vulnerability might enable them to invite the sharing of pain in redemptive ways. The image proved singularly attractive for a decade, but eventually women theologians, especially African Americans, questioned whether its accent on pain and fragility offered much help to the people for whom they were writing, and other theologians wondered aloud whether Nouwen's image encouraged an unhelpful self-preoccupation.[73]

In the 1980s some were ready to recover older images, even the image of the minister as a "shepherd," which had been frequently ridiculed twenty years earlier as irrelevant to an urban technological society. Some saw it as a reminder that pastoral work continued "Christ's own ministry," with its paradoxical unity of "dignity and service." Others liked the image because it recalled that ministers cared "for the people on the periphery." Methodist William Willimon summarized some of the motivation behind the turn to traditional images when he noted that ministers were "no longer keeping house in an essentially hospitable and receptive culture."[74]

Some of the most serious theological reflection came from Catholics attempting to define ministry in an era when one could find "no single Roman Catholic theology of the ministerial priesthood." Avery Dulles — a theologian

72. Paul C. Empie and T. Austin Murphy, eds., *Eucharist and Ministry: Lutherans and Catholics in Dialogue IV* (Minneapolis: Augsburg, 1979), pp. 22, 32; Richard P. O'Brien, *Ministry: A Theological, Pastoral Handbook* (San Francisco: Harper and Row, 1987), p. 9. Catholics made slight alterations in their understanding of ordination. In 1972, Pope Paul VI ruled that the older "minor orders" — porter, lector, exorcist, and acolyte — that had once marked stages toward the priesthood could now become "ministries" open to the laity. The "clerical state" would begin with the diaconate that preceded full ordination to the priesthood. See Odile M. Liebard, ed., *Clergy and Laity* (Wilmington: McGrath, 1978), pp. 346-49.

73. Henri J. M. Nouwen, *The Wounded Healer: Ministry in Contemporary Society* (Garden City: Doubleday, 1972), pp. 87, 94; Kathleen Grider, Gloria A. Johnson, and Kristen J. Leslie, "Three Decades of Women Writing for Our Lives," *Feminist and Womanist Pastoral Theology*, ed. Bonnie J. Miller-McLemore and Brita L. Gill-Austern (Nashville: Abingdon, 1999), p. 31; L. Gregory Jones and Kevin R. Armstrong, *Resurrecting Excellence: Shaping Faithful Christian Ministry* (Grand Rapids: Eerdmans, 2006), pp. 91-92.

74. Thomas C. Oden, *Pastoral Theology: Essentials of Ministry* (San Francisco: Harper and Row, 1983), pp. 53, 59; John Killinger, *The Tender Shepherd* (Nashville: Abingdon, 1985), p. 14. See the discussion of "images of ministry" in Willimon, *Pastor*, pp. 55-74, and Donald E. Messer, *Contemporary Images of Christian Ministry* (Nashville: Abingdon, 1989).

and cardinal of the church — acknowledged in 1974 that at least five "models" of the priesthood had currency in the church. Was the priest the possessor of a special power conveyed by ordination? Was he a sacral figure able to dispense sacramental grace? Was he the leader who integrated and coordinated the ministries of the community? Was he the preacher who proclaimed the gospel? Or was he perhaps the servant who sought justice for the poor and the marginal?[75]

Two competing tendencies marked Catholic reflection on the priesthood. The first featured communal leadership; the second emphasized sacral order. In one of the most ambitious accounts of the era, *Ministry to Word and Sacrament* (1976), Bernard J. Cooke gave priority to priestly ministry as the formation of community. Cooke argued that the priest represented and symbolized the Christ who was already present within the community and that his main task was to make Christ sacramentally visible in ways that fostered the ministries of others. He joined other theologians who emphasized the priest's leadership within a community of ordained, religious, and lay ministers. In *A Theology for Ministry* (1983), George Tavard chose, however, to accent a sacral view of the priest as one who fulfilled the end of his ordination by attending "exclusively" to sacramental activity.[76]

A few theologians worried especially about the priests in the religious orders, who felt that Vatican II defined the priesthood in ways that slighted their distinctive ministries. They argued for the need to rethink the role of the orders, drawing from the past in order to recover the image of a priesthood marked by mobility, evangelization, and a quest for social justice within a variety of settings. The "prophetic" point of view of the orders, they argued, was a necessary counterpart to the more sacral orientation of the secular priest.[77]

Some worried that it was the image of the "manager" — the operator of an efficient organization — that continued, in practice, to guide and define the minister in the larger churches. To sociologist Theodore Caplow, the pastors in

75. Daniel Donovan, *What Are They Saying About the Ministerial Priesthood?* (New York: Paulist Press, 1992), p. 138; Avery Dulles, *Models of the Church* (1st ed., 1974; Garden City: Image Books, 1983), pp. 163, 165, 166, 175; Avery Dulles, "Models for Ministerial Priesthood," *Origins* 20 (1990): 287-88.

76. Bernard J. Cooke, *Ministry to Word and Sacrament: History and Theology* (Philadelphia: Fortress Press, 1976), pp. 35, 203; O'Meara, *Theology of Ministry,* p. 210; E. J. Kilmartin, "Bishop and Presbyter as Representatives of the Church and Christ," in *Women Priests: A Catholic Commentary on the Vatican Declaration,* ed. Leonard J. Swidler and Arlene Swidler (New York: Paulist Press, 1977), pp. 295-302; George Tavard, *A Theology for Ministry* (Wilmington: Michael Glazier, 1983), pp. 51, 157; see the discussion in Donovan, *What Are They Saying,* pp. 105-38.

77. Thomas P. Rausch, "Priesthood in the Context of Apostolic Religious Life," in *Theology of Priesthood,* pp. 107-15; John W. O'Malley, "Priesthood, Ministry, and the Religious Life: Some Historical and Historiographical Considerations," *Theological Studies* 49 (1988): 233-37, 256.

the large city churches seemed like "corporate executives" who orchestrated a multitude of diverse activities. For priests and ministers burdened by administrative chores, the difficult task was to find a way to make administration a form of serious Christian ministry.[78]

By the 1980s many ministers believed that they had discovered new ways of carrying out administrative duties. In accord with trends in American corporate leadership generally, the preferred style was democratic rather than directive, with ministers sharing power and leadership with the laity. The great majority of ministers — one survey found 95 percent — said that they preferred to encourage the laity to make communal decisions, though most said that they were prepared to act alone if necessary. Some evidence suggested that women ministers were slightly more inclined than men to encourage participatory decision-making, but the trend was widespread among both women and men.[79]

In conservative churches, a top-down leadership style still had its defenders. The members of the fundamentalist "Southside" church studied by sociologist Nancy Ammerman understood themselves as belonging to "Pastor Thompson's church." "The pastor," argued W. A. Criswell, "is the ruler of the church," and fundamentalists often viewed the calls for servant leadership and lay ministry as nothing more than "anti-Pastor sentiment." In 1988, the Southern Baptist Convention warned that the doctrine of the priesthood of all believers was being used as a tool to "undermine pastoral authority." The convention's admonition to the laity was simple: "obey the pastor." Most Southern Baptist laity were of another mind: 81 percent of them refused to say that the pastor should have the final authority.[80]

On Sunday mornings, at least, the preacher even in the mainline Protestant churches was in fact still the dominant figure. The demise of the Sunday evening services meant that preachers spent less time on sermon preparation than the clergy of the 1930s, but the sermon remained the center of Protestant worship. Most sermons were about thirty minutes long; conservative ministers fre-

78. Joseph Hough and John Cobb, *Christian Identity and Theological Education* (Atlanta: Scholars Press, 1985), p. 16; Brunette-Hill and Finke, "A Time for Every Purpose," p. 54; Caplow, *All Faithful People*, p. 246.

79. Zikmund, et al., *Clergy Women*, pp. 44, 56; Carroll, *God's Potters*, pp. 132-33; Patricial M. Y. Chang, "Female Clergy in the Contemporary Protestant Church: A Current Assessment," *Journal for the Scientific Study of Religion* 36 (1997): 563-73.

80. Witham, *Who Shall Lead Them?* p. 86; Carroll, *God's Potters*, p. 132; Nancy T. Ammerman, *Bible Believers: Fundamentalists in the Modern World* (New Brunswick: Rutgers University Press, 1987), p. 123. For examples in other denominations, see Jay E. Adams, *Pastoral Leadership: Shepherding God's Flock* (Grand Rapids: Baker Book House, 1975), pp. 9, 13; Hardy W. Steinberg, "The Pastor and His Lord," in *And He Gave Pastors: Pastoral Theology in Action*, ed. Thomas F. Zimmerman (Springfield: Gospel Publishing House, 1979), p. 3.

quently preached longer, mainline ministers and seminary graduates more briefly. By the 1990s, most Protestant ministers — around 68 percent of the senior pastors — preached twice on Sunday mornings.[81]

Inspired by the insistence at the Second Vatican Council on the primacy of preaching, some Catholic theologians made determined efforts to convince priests that their "first task" was to preach, and they issued fresh calls to the seminaries to encourage more creativity in homilies. In surveys of the laity, however, only about 18 percent assigned the highest grade to the sermons. Catholic laity were more critical of the preaching than of any other priestly activity.[82]

Changing attitudes toward worship also posed, as always, delicate questions. For Protestants, the options multiplied. Was the pastor to encourage traditional hymns, "praise choruses," gospel music, "contemporary gospel," or even rock music? Most went with tradition, but the 60 percent who also used the newer songs claimed that their attendance increased. Many mainline clergy remained committed to liturgical renewal: such service books as *The Worshipbook* (1972) of the Presbyterians, the *Lutheran Book of Worship* (1978), and the United Church of Christ's *Book of Worship* (1986) recovered traditional practices. Liturgical differences could generate strong emotion; some spoke of "worship wars."[83]

Catholics also experimented with new forms of worship, ranging from folk masses with guitars to speaking in tongues within charismatic congregations. Weekly attendance at mass fell to 50 percent of Catholics in the 1980s and 28 percent by 2002, but Catholics now typically received communion at every mass. In 1980 priests were rarely leading the popular Marian devotions of an earlier day or displaying the Body of Christ in the benediction ritual; nor were younger Catholics observing the Stations of the Cross or public rosary. By the 1990s, Catholic worship sometimes proceeded without priests, with lay ministers distributing bread and wine that a priest had consecrated earlier.[84]

Changing trends in sacramental practice altered the workday of priests. The long lines of penitents at confession disappeared during the 1970s. By the mid-1980s more than 60 percent of Catholics rarely or never went to confession. The

81. Barna, *Today's Pastors,* pp. 35, 93; Brunette-Hill and Finke, "A Time for Every Purpose," p. 57.

82. Greeley, *Priests,* pp. 92-93; Andrew Greeley, "Rating the Clergy," *America* 184 (2001): 6-10.

83. Barna, *Today's Pastors,* p. 94; Lincoln and Mamiya, *Black Church,* p. 362; James F. White, *Protestant Worship: Traditions in Transition* (Louisville: Westminster John Knox, 1989), pp. 55, 77.

84. Margaret M. McGuinness, "Let Us Go to the Altar: American Catholics and the Eucharist," in *Habits of Devotion,* p. 22; Carroll, *God's Potters,* p. 39; Paula M. Kane, "Marian Devotion Since 1940: Continuity or Casualty?" in *Habits of Devotion,* p. 122; Jay Dolan, "American Catholics in a Changing Society: Parish and Ministry 1930 to the Present," in *Transforming Parish Ministry,* pp. 304-5; Greeley, *Catholic Priest,* p. 71.

church broadened the options: confession could occur in the traditional manner, or it could be a face-to-face meeting with the priest — more like counseling than the older ritual — but 65 percent of the priests reported that they were hearing only twenty or fewer confessions a week rather than hundreds. The younger traditionalists of the 1990s made a concerted effort to restore older practices.[85]

Clergy spent less time with children than they once had. Catechizing no longer occupied much of the Protestant minister's time. Most pastors placed the quality of programs for children and youth among their top priorities, but in most congregations senior ministers spent less than an hour a week with children, though youth ministers maintained programs with adolescents. Children's choirs — and brief sermons to children on Sunday morning — remained popular, but Catholic priests gave more time to children than Protestant ministers, mainly because many of them remained responsible for parochial schools. Catholics and Protestants alike spent most of their working time with middle-aged or older adults.[86]

Most ministers spent most of their time within the boundaries of their congregations. A 1970 study of Catholic priests in San Francisco illustrated a truth that applied to most parish ministers in every tradition: two-thirds said that they approved of involvement in extra-parochial ministries, but two-thirds also said that they lacked the time. In 2004, as in 1934, most ministers reported little community involvement, though clergy in poorer neighborhoods were more involved than suburban pastors, and liberals or moderates more than conservatives. African American pastors were no more likely than white ministers to devote time to their communities. More than half of American congregations practiced some form of social service — a third of them helped feed the hungry — but such ministries did not top the list of clerical preoccupations. One survey found that only 11 percent considered them a priority.[87]

By 2001, both Protestant ministers and Catholic priests — as many as 74 percent in one survey — said that their greatest difficulty and challenge was reaching people with the gospel. In part, the difficulty reflected problems with attendance at church. Forty percent of Americans told pollsters that they attended a church or synagogue during the previous ten days, but by 1997 actual counts suggested that, on any given week, only about 25 percent attended religious services. Some polls also found an increase in the number of Americans who claimed no church affiliation. If such counts were representative of a gen-

85. O' Toole, "Court of Conscience," pp. 131, 171, 183.
86. Brunette-Hill and Finke, "A Time to Every Purpose," p. 55; Carroll, *God's Potters*, p. 117.
87. Appleby, "Present to the People of God," p. 86; Chaves, *Congregations*, pp. 50, 52; Barna, *Today's Pastors*, p. 105.

eral trend, they indicated a decrease from earlier patterns of attendance and highlighted the challenge of ministry in a more secular age.[88]

The Status of the Profession

At the turn of the century, the image of the clergy absorbed some wounding blows. In the 1980s, several popular televangelists became involved in sexual and other scandals that drew heavy press coverage. Other television preachers later drew criticism for crimes and lapses of judgment that ranged from fraud to inappropriate appeals for money and outrageous comments that invited public shock and ridicule. Reports of clerical misconduct caused several denominations to institute new procedures for disciplining wayward clergy. In one survey in the 1980s, 12 percent of the clergy in four denominations admitted to a breach of clerical vows — ranging from sexual affairs to other ethical indiscretions — that later troubled them.[89]

Most tragic were the revelations of the sexual abuse of children and adolescents by Catholic priests. In 1985, the Catholic bishops meeting at St. John's Abbey heard a dire warning about the problem, but the truth was worse than anyone imagined. By 2002 over two hundred priests had been accused of disgraceful behavior, and some of the most prominent bishops faced charges of having covered up the misdoings. Some of the accusations proved to be false, but others led to the discovery that some priests had abused scores of children and adolescents, mainly boys, for years.[90]

As revelations continued to hit the newspapers — and some dioceses faced the possibility of bankruptcy as a result of lawsuits filed by victims — the bishops met in the summer of 2002 and set up new investigative and disciplinary procedures. But nothing could still the outrage. Victims made charges against perhaps 3 percent of the priests in all fourteen regions of the Catholic Church in the U.S. One careful study found that the charges were apparently justified for less than 2 percent of American priests, but morale fell as the grievous misbehavior of a few cast suspicion on everyone.[91]

88. Carroll, *God's Potters*, p. 266; Chaves, *Congregations*, p. 3; C. Kirk Hadaway and Penny Lane Marler, "Did you Really Go to Church This Week? Behind the Poll Data," *Christian Century* 115 (May 6, 1998): 472-75; Mark Chaves and James C. Cavendish, "More Evidence on U.S. Catholic Church Attendance," *Journal for the Scientific Study of Religion* 33 (1994): 376-81.

89. Witham, *Who Shall Lead Them?* p. 169.

90. Greeley, *Priests*, p. 111; John T. McGreevy, *Catholicism and American Freedom: A History* (New York: W. W. Norton, 2003), p. 289.

91. Philip Jenkins, *Pedophiles and Priests: Anatomy of a Contemporary Crisis* (New York:

The sexual abuse scandals created the most serious crisis in the history of the American priesthood. For many laity and priests — and for some bishops — they cast a retrospective light of suspicion and doubt on what had once been certitudes about clerical formation, mandatory celibacy for secular priests, and the procedures of decision making in the church. Never before had American Catholic laity — and many priests — felt such disillusionment with the priesthood and dismay about the response of the bishops. The scandals left the church and its clergy shaken and divided.

The vast majority of priests and most Protestant ministers continued to labor with integrity and fidelity in the nation's congregations. A few of them were the pastors of the so-called megachurches, with anywhere from two thousand to twenty thousand members. Catholics had long been accustomed to parishes of three to four thousand, and a few Catholic parishes by the 1990s had as many as twenty thousand members. The revision of canon law in 1983 confirmed that parish membership need no longer be restricted to a specific territory, and members could come from all over the city. But the attention went to the Protestant megachurches — around 1,200 of them by 2005 — which drew members with "high-voltage preaching," the use of technology, popular music, and services for each "market niche." By the end of the century, some of the largest — Calvary Chapel and the Vineyard in California, for example, or Willow Creek Community Church in Illinois — had partnered with other congregations and become virtual small denominations.[92]

Most of the clergy served a smaller congregation — much smaller. The average American congregation in 1998 had 171 regular participants. Seventy-one percent of the local churches consisted of fewer than one hundred regularly participating adults, and the median congregation had only seventy-five. Most congregations were still rural; more than 70 percent of Protestant churches and possibly more than half of Catholic parishes were in the countryside and small towns, and they often lacked priests and ministers. Only 10 percent of the clergy served churches with more than 350 members, but fully half of American churchgoers belonged to those larger congregations; 50 percent of the clergy, serving small congregations, preached to about 10 percent of the laity.[93]

The pastors of these congregations were becoming older. During the 1980s seminaries began to note an influx of second-career students, who within two decades sometimes outnumbered the younger college graduates. By 2001 the

Oxford University Press, 1996), pp. 8, 81, 83; Witham, *Who Shall Lead Them?* p. 172; Kunkel, *Enormous Prayers*, p. 57.

92. Jorstad, *Popular Religion*, p. 194; Carroll, *God's Potters*, p. 63; John Blake, "Big on Worship," *Atlanta Journal-Constitution*, Feb. 15, 2006, p. A1.

93. Chaves, *Congregations*, pp. 18-19; Witham, *Who Shall Lead Them?* p. 17.

churches were worrying about "the graying of the ministry" and puzzling about why the profession was not attracting young people. In the mainline denominations, 46 percent of the clergy entered the ministry after working in another career, and the same was true of two-thirds of the pastors in the conservative churches and 78 percent in historic black denominations. Younger students continued to enter the seminaries, but many of them had no intention of becoming parish ministers.[94]

Ministers continued to work for relatively low salaries. From 1980 to 2001, mean clergy income remained relatively flat in relation to other professionals, averaging less than a third of the salaries of physicians and only half that of lawyers. Clergy with a graduate-level education earned more than others; their salaries managed to outpace inflation, and in 1999 the mean income was $40,000. Salaries depended on the size of the church: in 2001 the smallest churches paid from $14,200 to $34,500, while the larger ones paid from $24,719 to $67,326. Protestants received more than Catholics (by almost 40 percent), men more than women, and whites more than blacks. The highest-paid Protestant clergy in 2001 received six times the salary of the lower-paid ministers.[95]

It was in the local congregations that one needed to look in order to gauge the place of the clergy in the culture. "It is not the Vatican or the chancery that are important to the laity," wrote one Catholic priest. "It is the performance of the local clergy." They led small communities in which their authority rested on the same kinds of face-to-face relationships that had characterized the church throughout the nation's history. In those communities, they sat with the grieving, visited the sick, counseled the young, and encouraged the elderly. They helped people express and nurture religious faith, learn to work together, and talk about morality and meaning.[96]

Some still worked to transform the larger community. In 1974 the Reverend Johnnie Ray Youngblood moved into the pulpit of the Saint Paul Community Baptist Church in East New York. This African American church had eighty-four worshipers who gathered in a building that eventually had to be protected by a chain-link fence with razor wire, but by 1989 close to five thousand worshiped there, and St. Paul was a partner with fifty-two other churches and one synagogue in an organization that succeeded, through hard political work in

94. Carroll, *God's Potters*, pp. 74-75; Erickson, *Orthodox Christians in America*, p. 122.

95. Matthew J. Price, "Fear of Falling: Male Clergy in Economic Crisis," *Christian Century* 118 (Aug. 15-22, 2001): 18-21; Carroll, *God's Potters*, pp. 88-94; Becky R. McMillan and Matthew J. Price, *How Much Should We Pay the Clergy: Salaries in the 21st Century* (Durham: Pulpit and Pew, 2003), p. 4; Zikmund, et al., *Clergy Women*, p. 72; Barna, *Today's Pastors*, p. 37; Hoge, et al., *Patterns of Parish Leadership*, p. 45.

96. Greeley, *Priests*, p. 94; Carroll, *As One with Authority*, p. 62.

the local precincts, in building two thousand low-cost housing units, nurturing numerous self-help projects within the community, organizing community policing, and teaching residents of the neighborhoods how to join together to battle crooked merchants and indifferent politicians.[97]

But Youngblood was a pastor, not a politician, and he preached, taught, counseled, baptized, and distributed the bread and wine. He taught the men of his congregation to organize themselves into a society of Gideonites who would extend ministry to the community. He convinced a member who had been addicted to drugs to lead a group for recovering addicts. He supported a member who bought a small summer cottage to serve as a camp that offered children a refuge from the violent streets. He offered skillful marriage counseling, gathered the men of the church for weekly discussions on topics that helped them make sense of their lives, and set up programs for children. "If you minister to the poor," he said, "you help them deal with the system that keeps them in poverty, you deal with their shackles and chains from the inside out."[98]

Few priests and ministers sought to transform their communities in the manner of Johnnie Ray Youngblood, but for the most part, priests and ministers found the work of ministry satisfying and rewarding. Survey research between 1980 and 2001 presented a mixed picture. Some denominational polls found the clergy frustrated, troubled, and unsure of their authority. But the most extensive surveys, cutting across denominational boundaries, found the clergy satisfied with their priesthood or ministry, committed to it, and happy. As many as 88 percent of Catholic priests and 91 percent of Protestant ministers — mainline and conservative — felt "very satisfied" with their current job. All of them, to be sure, reported difficulties, but most of them said that they would choose priesthood or ministry again if they were starting over. Like the Presbyterian author and pastor Eugene Peterson, they were drawn by "the intense relational and personal quality of this life." For "those who are called to it," he told an interviewer, "the pastoral life is really a good life. Not an easy life, but one full of resonances with everything else that's going on in creation and in history."[99]

97. Samuel G. Freedman, *Upon This Rock: The Miracles of a Black Church* (New York: HarperCollins, 1993), pp. 2, 308-36.

98. Freedman, *Upon This Rock,* pp. 37, 127, 242, 269.

99. Jackson W. Carroll, *As One Without Authority: Reflective Leadership in Ministry* (Louisville: Westminster John Knox, 1991), pp. 23-24; Carroll, *God's Potters,* pp. 31, 161-62, 165-87; Witham, *Who Shall Lead Them?* pp. 10-11, 98, 102; Greeley, *Priests,* pp. 50, 88; Barna, *Today's Pastors,* pp. 57, 59; Zikmund et al., *Clergy Women,* p. 47; Caplow, *All Faithful People,* p. 251; Rausch, *Priesthood Today,* p. 5; David Wood, "The Best Life," *Christian Century* 119 (March 13-20, 2002): 18-19.

Epilogue

At the turn of the millennium, priests and ministers oversaw the fortunes of more than 300,000 local churches, which week after week drew more participants than any other American voluntary or cultural organization. Millions of Americans turned to them for counseling, teaching, moral guidance, and help in times of trouble. Thousands of other clergy served in religious orders, counseling centers, hospitals, prisons, children's homes, colleges, universities, denominational offices, ecumenical institutions, think tanks, publishing houses, and seminaries. Priests and ministers have continued to exert significant influence on national institutions, local cultures, and individual lives.

A historical account accentuates the repetitive features of the clerical life: the unrelenting demands of preaching, baptizing, serving the bread and wine (or grape juice), teaching, administering, organizing, raising money, helping the poor, instructing children, visiting, marrying and burying, and counseling with heartbroken parents and bewildered adolescents and people seeking one or another kind of salvation. From the seventeenth century to the present, the nation's clergy have performed those tasks even as cultural change and social transformation have altered the ways they have approached them.

The story has had some momentous turning points. The diversity of the colonial settlers meant that no one clerical group would ever enjoy a national monopoly. The eighteenth-century revivals popularized informal and colloquial styles of communication from the pulpit. The disestablishment of the state churches during the Revolutionary era severed the tie between the clergy and the magistrates and cast clerics into competition within a religious marketplace. The clash between populists and professionals in the early republic created permanent fault lines. The freeing of the slaves created a clerical leadership class in the black community, while the urban pastors and immigrant priests of the late nineteenth century transformed local congregations into social centers with manifold functions that turned clergy into busy administrators.

The proliferation and prestige of other professions after the late nineteenth century affected the way clergy thought about themselves and laity thought about clergy, and the division between liberals and conservatives in the early twentieth century dug a deep chasm that still forms boundary lines. The entry of Catholics into the American mainstream during the 1950s began to alter the priesthood even before the first bishop set foot in the Second Vatican Council. And the transitions of the 1960s — the civil rights movement, the women's movement, changing relations among Protestants and Catholics, the declining membership in the mainline Protestant churches, and the increasing visibility of the evangelical surge — created a new environment for ministry. The subsequent influx of women into the ministry was unprecedented.

Some of the changes have narrowed gaps once deemed unbridgeable. Half a century ago it seemed that Protestant and Catholic clergy, for example, had little in common apart from a determination to represent the wisdom of the Christian tradition to the church and the society, and they interpreted that wisdom in strikingly different ways. Gradually the similarities became more pronounced. They struggled with the same questions about appropriate ministry, clerical education, cultural influence, and the relation of vocation and professional standing. Catholics now emphasize preaching more than they once did; mainstream Protestants emphasize liturgy more than they once did; and Catholics and Protestants share more common ethical concerns than they did in the past.

The forms of authority that defined the colonial pastor — official, personal, and rational — have continued to intersect with each other in varying ways throughout the later history. In the colonial churches, clergy bore authority by virtue of their office and education, though not without equal concern for the divine calling and the capacity to minister effectively. After the Revolution, the populist surge elevated personal charisma above authority of office and rational authority, while the spread of seminary education during the same period accorded more weight to competence and learning. Many twenty-first-century pastors believe, with good reason, that their authority has once again become more personal and less official: their authority depends more on who they are and what they do than on the office they occupy.

Catholics and Protestants still assign a different weight to the ordination that confers the office, but even Catholic priests have noted that their authority does not rest on their office to the same degree as it did, for example, in the

346

1930s, when Cardinal O'Connell could say that there was "no such thing" as the "personality of a parish priest." The older mass, in which the priest stood with his back to the congregation and repeated the words of the church in a language none of the laity understood, symbolized a period in which the personhood of the priest was submerged in the office. When the priest turned around and faced the congregation, speaking in English, his personhood was in public view, symbolically, in a new way. One priest, who had earlier been a Lutheran pastor, commented on clerical authority in 1992: It is never, he observed, "secured against the threat of loss." It has to be "demonstrated" again and again. To some extent this has always been true, but it is truer today than it was in the past.[1]

The authority attached to the clergy as "professionals" has been a matter of contention from the early nineteenth century to the present. Priests and ministers have never been certain whether they constitute a profession, at least in the modern sense of the term, and the debates about professionalism have taken two forms. The first has featured the challenge of the populists, whose convictions still touch something deep in American religious culture. The second has been about the appropriate self-understanding of the educated priest and minister, with one side viewing the professional ideal as a problematic temptation and the other seeing it as a promising gift. In this debate, however, neither side would abandon clerical education or the desirability of competence, accountability, and ethical probity, nor would either dismiss the importance of spiritual depth, faithfulness, and vocational commitment. They have more in common than the arguments might suggest.

And what about the seeming decline of the profession? More than a few scholarly accounts of ministry have affirmed or implied the narrative of decline. It has become common to say that in the twenty-first century the clergy exercise leadership over a smaller number of domains than they did in previous centuries. They no longer help write the laws of the state, as they did in seventeenth-century New England. They no longer constitute, as they did until the late eighteenth century, the intellectual class of the culture. They seldom lead, as they had in antebellum America, the largest humanitarian and philanthropic institutions, or edit the culture's leading journals. They rarely become the presidents and trustees, as they once had, of the elite colleges and universities. They have lost exclusive "jurisdiction over personal problems" as a result of

1. Scott Appleby, "Present to the People of God: The Transformation of the Roman Catholic Parish Priesthood," in *Transforming Parish Ministry: The Changing Roles of Catholic Clergy, Laity, and Women Religious,* ed. Jay P. Dolan (New York: Crossroad, 1990), p. 9; John Richard Neuhaus, *Freedom for Ministry* (Grand Rapids: Eerdmans, 1992), pp. 66-67. See also Martin E. Marty, "The Clergy," in *The Professions in American History,* ed. Nathan O. Hatch (Notre Dame: University of Notre Dame Press, 1988), pp. 73-91.

competition from psychiatrists and social workers. Clergy typically receive lower salaries than most other professionals. And with 25 percent of Americans now graduating from a college or university, ministers are, in most communities, no longer the most highly educated persons. In more than one cultural realm, the ministry has indeed lost authority. And if this is what decline means, the argument is convincing.[2]

It is important, however, not to exaggerate the authority of clergy in earlier centuries. In colonial America they enjoyed immense respect, but outside New England they were almost always in short supply — American youth did not flock to the ministry — and observers sometimes complained about mediocrity. In the early nineteenth century most were uneducated, and by the end of the century Protestants were already complaining about a loss of status, while Catholics were struggling with ethnic division in an immigrant priesthood. The sociological studies of the 1930s concluded that the ministry was a troubled profession. The ministry in the twenty-first century has some serious problems, but so did the ministry in earlier centuries.

One might also counter unqualified assertions of decline by contending that, even in the light of conventional American criteria of success, the clergy have continued to prosper. At the turn of the millennium they were writing best-selling books, producing popular television programs, and directing large-scale religious institutions. Some of them exercised power in both state and national politics. Clerical celebrities could reach as many people through one televised sermon as an eighteenth-century preacher reached in a lifetime. Because of television, some were as well known on other continents as they were in America. The scholarship produced by clergy in colleges, universities, and seminaries outranked, in sophistication and quantity, the productivity of all but the select few among the clergy of the past. Under clerical leadership, the churches have collected more money than any other voluntary American charitable institution.

Yet it seems more compelling to ask precisely how most clergy have envisioned their vocation over the years. The vast majority have not set out to write laws, publish books, edit journals, serve as presidents and trustees, organize social welfare efforts, or practice psychotherapy. Most clergy, from the seventeenth century to the present, have understood themselves as the leaders of local congregations that attempt to practice the Christian life. This has been the central activity and the animating ambition, and it is difficult to see how the

2. Fred H. Goldner, Thomas P. Ference, and R. Richard Putti, "Priests and Laity: A Profession in Transition," *The Sociological Review*, monograph 20 (1973): 119-37; Andrew Abbott, *The System of Professions: An Essay on the Division of Expert Labor* (Chicago: The University of Chicago Press, 1988), p. 308; see Jackson W. Carroll, *God's Potters: Pastoral Leadership and the Shaping of Congregations* (Grand Rapids: Eerdmans, 2006), p. 34.

clergy have declined in either their commitment to this task or their faithfulness and effectiveness within it.

Viewed from within the paradox of Christian faith, the question about decline becomes even more difficult to adjudicate. If every achievement reflects the presence of God and yet stands under God's judgment, if the gospel affirms human cultures and yet questions every inordinate loyalty to them, and if the churches, as cultural formations, also live and worship in the tension between immanence and transcendence, then any theological assessment of the clergy — as of Christian life generally — must always retain an element of ambiguity. One never knows for sure when one has succeeded or failed; it is always possible that the most self-confident assertions of success represent a deeper failure, or that seeming failure succeeds at a level invisible to the observer. Such judgments move us beyond the limits of historical scholarship, but not every judgment needs to be bound by the canons of historical knowledge.

Index

Abbelen, Peter M., 186-87
Academy of Parish Clergy, 248
Accademia, The, 190
Administration of churches: in 19th century, 159, 160-61, 209, 212; in 20th century, 212, 220-21, 224-25, 239-40, 242, 278-79; style of, 338
African American clergy: and black theology, 326; and civil rights, 258-61; education of, 118, 154-55, 229-30, 245; in early 19th century, 117, 118, 127-28; in late 19th century, 148, 166; in 20th century, 217, 226-27, 229, 240, 245, 324-26, 340; as priests, 189; as social activists, 343-44; and women preachers, 127-28, 324
Age of clergy, 91-92, 229-30, 268, 343
American Association of Pastoral Counselors, 251
American Association of Theological Schools, 231-32, 246
American Revolution, 11, 100-102
Americanists, Catholic, 196-98
Anabaptists, 26-28, 126
Andover Seminary, 116, 170
Anglicans: views of ministry, 23, 51
Anti-Catholicism, 112, 157, 226, 255
Anti-clericalism. See Criticism of clergy

Anti-communism, 256-57, 302-3
Apostolic succession, 12, 14; Anglican views of, 23-24; Lutheran views of, 23; Reformed views of, 26; in 17th century, 51; in 18th century, 74; in 19th century, 111; in 20th century, 273
Associations of clergy, 56, 69-73
Attendance at church, 57, 78-79, 79n28, 113, 148-49, 340-41
Authority: defined, 2-3, 4-5, 9; in 16th century, 28-32, 33-35; in 17th century, 51-65; in 18th century, 69-88; in 19th century, 103-4, 113-38, 172-81, 190-95; in 20th century, 227-36, 267-77, 308-18, 341-44

Backus, Isaac, 82
Baird, Robert, 112, 114, 131
Baptism: in 16th century, 21, 27; in 17th century 40, 45; in 18th century, 68, 78; in 19th century, 153, 206; in 20th century, 227, 334, 344. See also Sacraments
Baptism, Eucharist, and Ministry, 333-34
Bedell, Gregory, 172
Beecher, Henry Ward: and evolution, 169; on manliness, 175; on politics, 109, 166; on preaching, 616; and scandal, 161

350

Beecher, Lyman: on church and state, 110; on educated clergy, 114, 126
Benevolent societies, 107-8, 141
Berger, Peter, 267
Berrigan, Daniel and Philip, 305
Bible schools, 232, 247
Bible: authority of, 12-13; historical criticism of, 169; as infallible, 167; Reformed view of, 25
Birth control, 306-7
Bishops: Anglican views of, 23-24; authority of, 137, 184, 288, 297; conflicts with religious orders, 294-95; Council of Trent and, 20; debates over, 51, 74, 100-101, 111; Episcopal view of, 111; Lutheran view of, 22; origins of, 13-14; power of, 190-95, 288-89; Reformed view of, 25-26; Vatican II and, 297
Black Power, 260
Blizzard, Samuel, 239, 333
Boisen, Anton T., 232
Breviary, 41, 200, 280-81, 291
Brooks, Phillips, 161
Brown, Antoinette, 122
Brown, William Adams, 171, *The Education of American Ministers,* 216; theology of, 219
Brownson, Orestes, 190
Bureaucracy, denominational, 160
Burtsell, Richard, 192-93
Bushnell, Horace, 126
Busyness of clergy, 242-43, 332-33

Cabot, Richard, 224, 233
Cahenslyism, 187
Call to the ministry, 2, 60, 82-83, 117, 172, 331
Callahan, Daniel, 286
Calvin, John, 24, 26
Cambridge Platform, 49, 55
Campus ministers, 251
Cannon, James R., Jr., 157
Canons, 17
Cartwright, Peter, 124-25, 126-27
Catechism: Catholic use of, 19-20, 46-47, 162, 207, 284; Protestant use of, 25, 26, 46-47, 90-91, 107, 162, 223

Catholic Action, 286
Celibacy, 20, 306, 314-15
Chaplaincy: institutional, 217, 252; military, 146-47, 237
Children: Catholics and, 47-48, 162-63, 207-8, 241, 284, 340; Protestants and, 25-26, 46-47, 90-91, 106-7, 162-63, 223, 340; in suburbs, 241, 284
Church and state: in 17th century, 48; in 18th century, 95-102, in early 19th century, 108-9, 110, 112; in 20th century, 238, 300. *See also* Political activity; Public duties
Civil rights movement, 258-61, 303-4
Civil War, 146-47
Clinical Pastoral Education, 232-33, 247-48
Colleges: clergy as graduates, 75-76, 115-16, 199; clergy as presidents, 75-76, 119, 178, 217; clergy as teachers, 75, 119, 252, 294
Commissaries, Anglican, 71
Conference, Methodist, 72
Confession: origins of, 17-18; in 17th century, 40, 45; in 19th century, 139, 140-41, 142, 204, 206; in 20th century, 282, 309, 340; Lutheran views of, 22-23; Reformed views of, 26
Conflict: among clergy, 59, 111, 137, 194-95, 294-95; of clergy and congregations, 61-63, 87-88; ethnic, 134-35, 185-90; theological, 220-21, 222, 265-66
Congregationalism, 51, 55
Congregations: devotional, 104-5, 140; as megachurches, 342; rural, 150; size of, 342; social, 158-60; urban, 164
Conservative theology, 167-72, 220-22
Consultation on Church Union, 248-49
Conwell, Russell, 166
Cooke, Bernard J., 337
Corrigan, Michael, 193
Cotton, John, 48
Coughlin, Charles, 302
Councils: Fourth Lateran, 17; Third Plenary, 190, 192, 194, 199; Trent, 20; Vatican II, 255, 295-300
Counseling: in 17th century, 45; in 18th